STOP!

This is the back of the book.
You wouldn't want to spoil a great ending!

This book is printed "manga-style," in the authentic Japanese right-to-left format. Since none of the artwork has been flipped or altered, readers get to experience the story just as the creator intended. You've been asking for it, so TOKYOPOP® delivered: authentic, hot-off-the-press, and far more fun!

DIRECTIONS

If this is your first time reading manga-style, here's a quick guide to help you understand how it works.

It's easy... just start in the top right panel and follow the numbers. Have fun, and look for more 100% authentic manga from TOKYOPOP®!

ART BY: **BENJAMIN ROMAN** STORY BY: **KEITH GIFFEN**

FH FAIRVIEW:HOSPITAL

X-RAY REPORT : NOTES
1 bag of Halloween candy, 2 razor blades found in apples, 1 that at the next car found lodged in the bottom of an apple, 1 nail you found in candy bar

IT'S LIKE TAKING CANDY FROM A DEAD GUY...

They say bad things come in threes, and the third round of trick o' treating is here amidst a close encounter of the disturbing kind.

"**I Luv Halloween is pure filth.**"
- Robert Sparling, fanboyplanet.com

"**Crass, tasteless, and brilliant.**"
- Newtype USA

 HORROR   **OT** OLDER TEEN AGE 16+

© Keith Giffen and Benjamin Roman

FOR MORE INFORMATION VISIT:

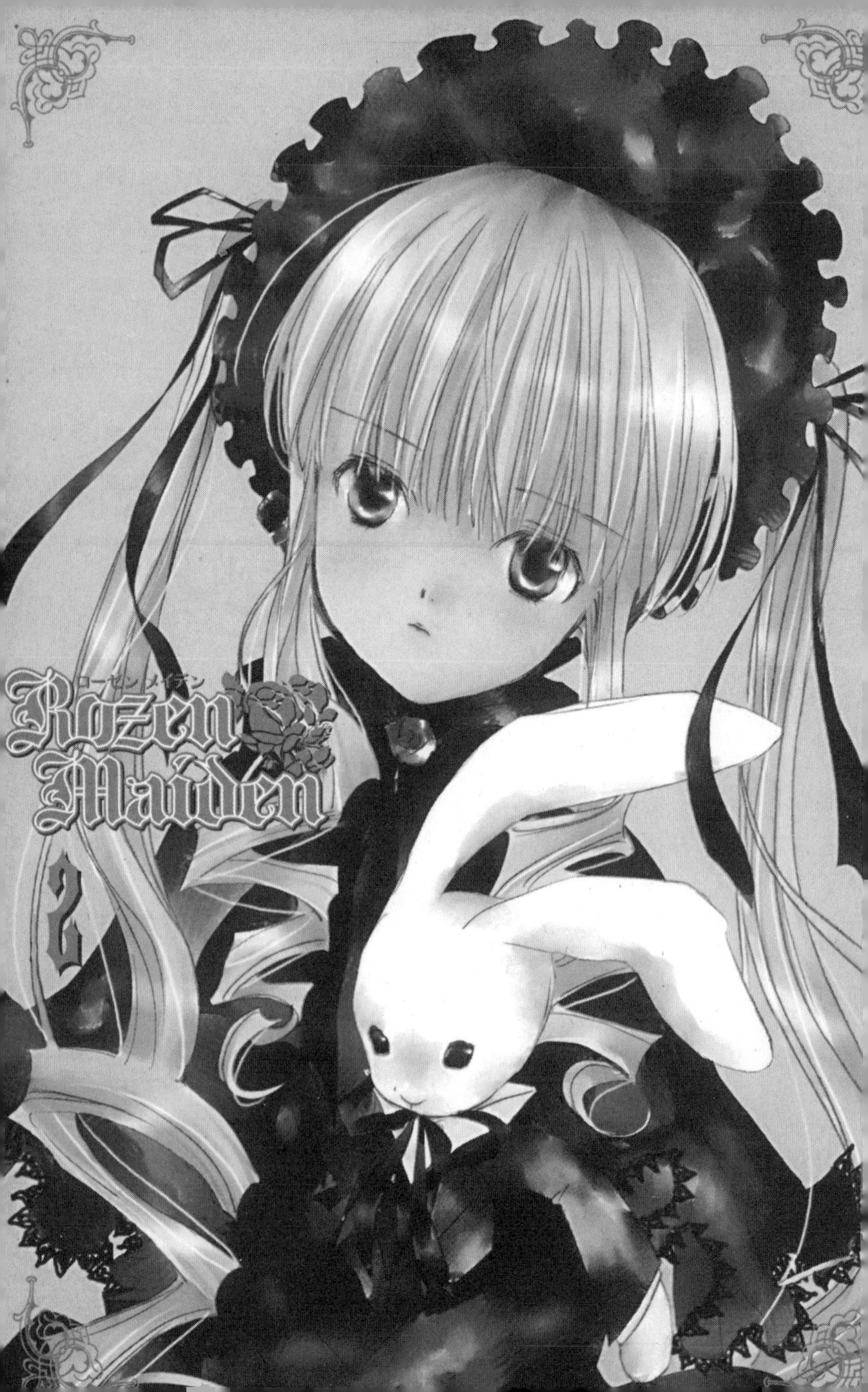
ローゼンメイデン
Rozen Maiden
2

Rozen Maiden Vol. 2
Created by Peach-Pit

Translation - Yuko Fukami
English Adaptation - Jerome Halligan
Retouch and Lettering - Jennifer Carbajal
Production Artist - Bowen Park
Cover Design - Al-Insan Lashley

Editor - Luis Reyes
Digital Imaging Manager - Chris Buford
Production Manager - Elisabeth Brizzi
Editor-in-Chief - Rob Tokar
VP of Production - Ron Klamert
Publisher - Mike Kiley
President and C.O.O. - John Parker
C.E.O. and Chief Creative Officer - Stuart Levy

A  Manga

TOKYOPOP Inc.
5900 Wilshire Blvd. Suite 2000
Los Angeles, CA 90036

E-mail: info@TOKYOPOP.com
Come visit us online at www.TOKYOPOP.com

T 251324

ISBN: 1-59816-313-2

First TOKYOPOP printing: September 2006
10 9 8 7 6 5 4 3 2 1
Printed in the USA

Rozen Maiden

PEACH-PIT

2

DISCARD

TOKYOPOP®

HAMBURG // LONDON // LOS ANGELES // TOKYO

The Story So Far...

Jun Sakurada is your typical "Hikikomori."
He refuses to go to school, and instead passes the
time by ordering crazy rip-off spiritual items over the
Internet and sending them back barely before the deadline of
the "cooling off period." His older sister, Nori, is concerned
about him and his new hobby, but
can't say anything to their parents about the situation
since both are away on business overseas.

One day, Jun receives an order form simply asking
him if he will "Wind or Not Wind." He circles "Wind"
and puts the card in his desk drawer as directed. The
next day, Nori discovers a large trunk outside the house,
and Jun realizes that the weird order form he had filled
out the previous day was for a beautiful doll. The doll is
so skillfully made that when Jun winds it up with a key,
the doll comes alive, slaps him, and begins to order him
around. The doll introduces herself as Shinku and claims
that she is the fifth doll in the Rozen Maiden series. She
tells Jun that he has to swear to protect her Rosa Mystica,
otherwise he will be killed by a stuffed bear that another
doll has sent to attack the two of them. Jun finally
swears and the bear is defeated.

The next day Jun and Shinku find an antique
mirror among all the various items Jun's parents have
bought while traveling around the world that Shinku
claims is an entrance to the N-Field. They are about
to enter when another Rozen Maiden doll appears and
tries to attack Shinku after taking responsibility for the
stuffed bear attack. Jun is able to help Shinku just in time,
though, and Suigintou runs away before Shinku can retali-
ate. Shinku tells her artificial spirit Hollier
to go after Suigintou and then goes limp.

Jun panics after not being able to wake Shinku
up and asks Nori for help. Nori is elated, because Jun
usually insults her whenever he's not ignoring her or
the rest of the world. Nori and Jun figure out how to
revive Shinku, but just as Jun starts to worry about her
reaction to a "living doll" his fears are alleviated when
Nori begins to excitedly serve Shinku whatever the doll
wants. Jun and Shinku embark on their journey into the
N-Field once more, but they find themselves in some odd
worlds while trying to find Shinku's spirit Hollier. One
world even comes close to explaining why Jun stopped
going to school, but before the reason becomes exposed
Jun and Shinku discover that they are not alone...

Character Guide

Jun Sakurada

Jun is a typical "Hikikomori." He refuses to go to school and spends most of his time in his room. To pass the time, his hobby is buying weird spiritual items over the Internet and then returning them right before the "cooling off period" ends. His older sister Nori worries about him, but he either ignores her or insults her. Jun is also upset with his parents, who are always out of the country on business. When Shinku appears on his doorstep, she turns his life into something more chaotic than he could have ever imagined.

Shinku

Shinku is a antique doll from the Rozen Maiden collection, created by a mysterious but very talented doll maker. After Jun wakes her up and she declares him to be an acceptable servant, she immediately begins to prepare for fights with the other Rozen Maidens to protect her Rosa Mystica. Shinku is very proud and often behaves like a queen by commanding others to do her bidding.

Nori Sakurada

A high school student as well as Jun's older sister, Nori takes care of the household while their parents are away. She serves Jun as best she can, but is concerned by his withdrawing from the rest of the world. Nori constantly tries to get her brother to leave his room and go back to school, but her attempts are usually insulted or ignored. Nori worries about others and is extremely good-natured, but she is also a little naïve.

Rozen Maiden

ローゼン メイデン

2

Contents

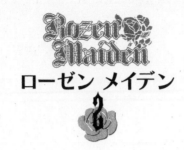

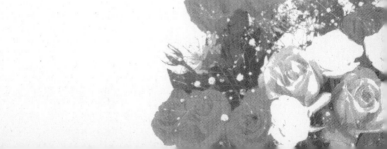

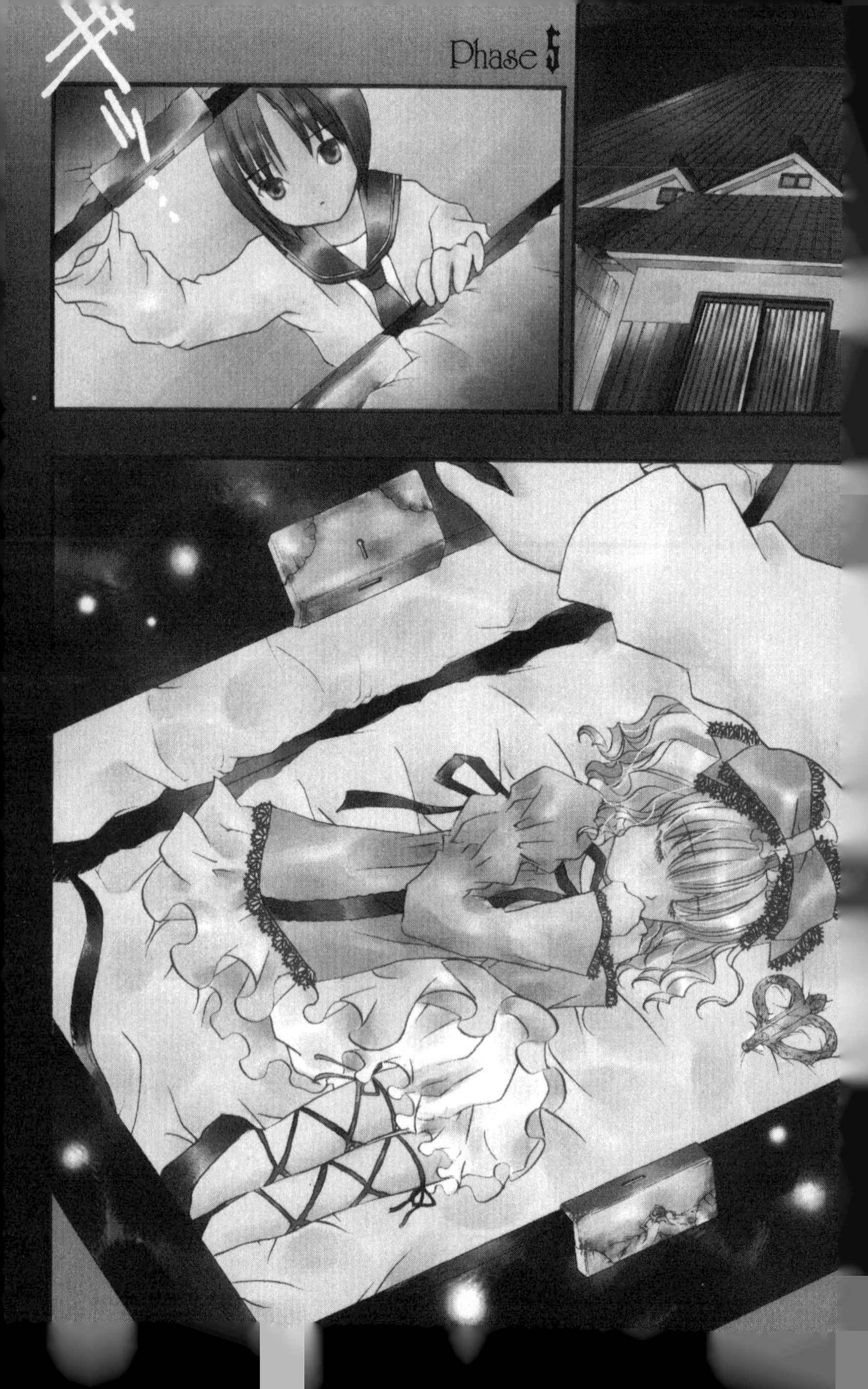
Phase 5
ギシ

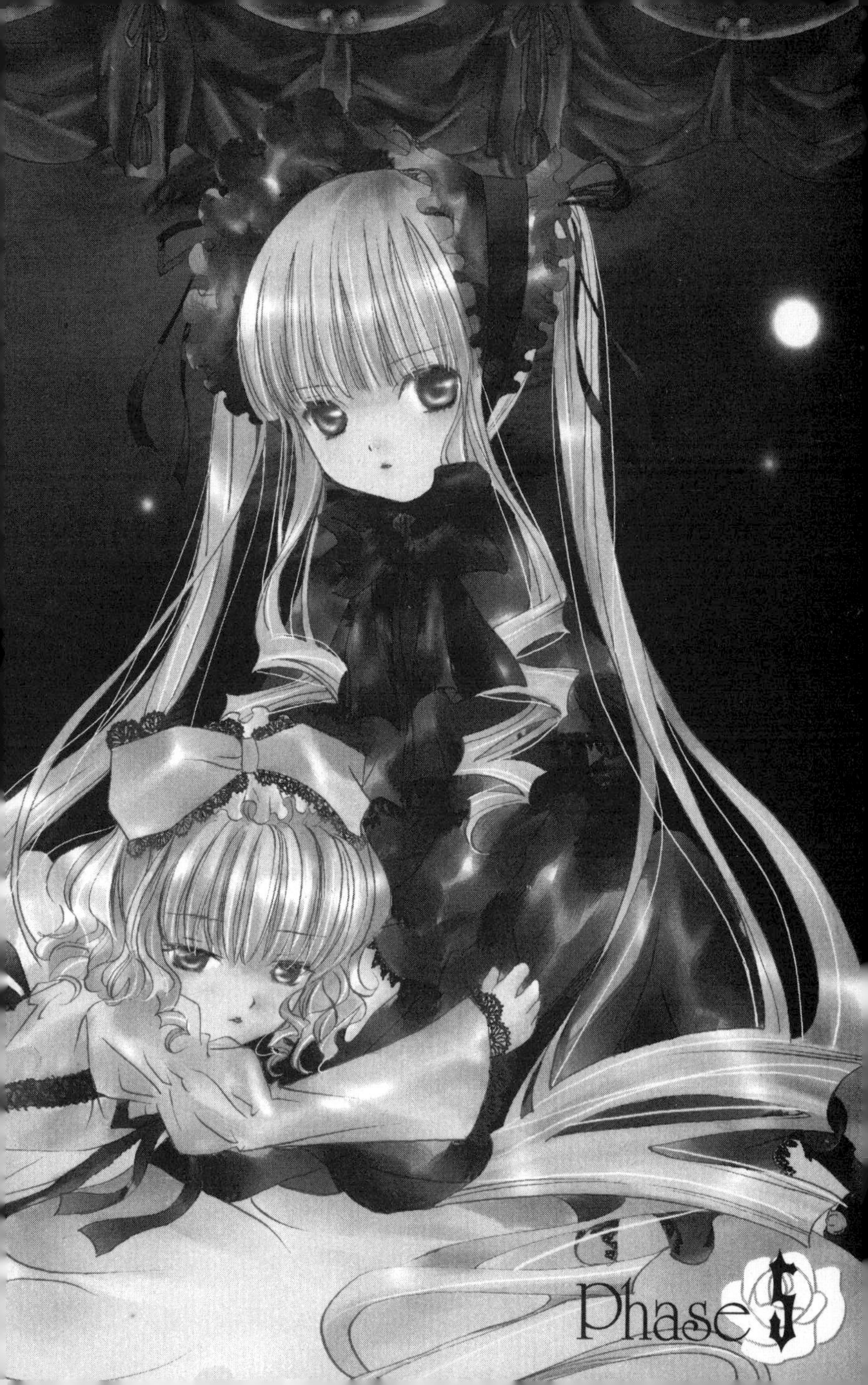
Phase 5

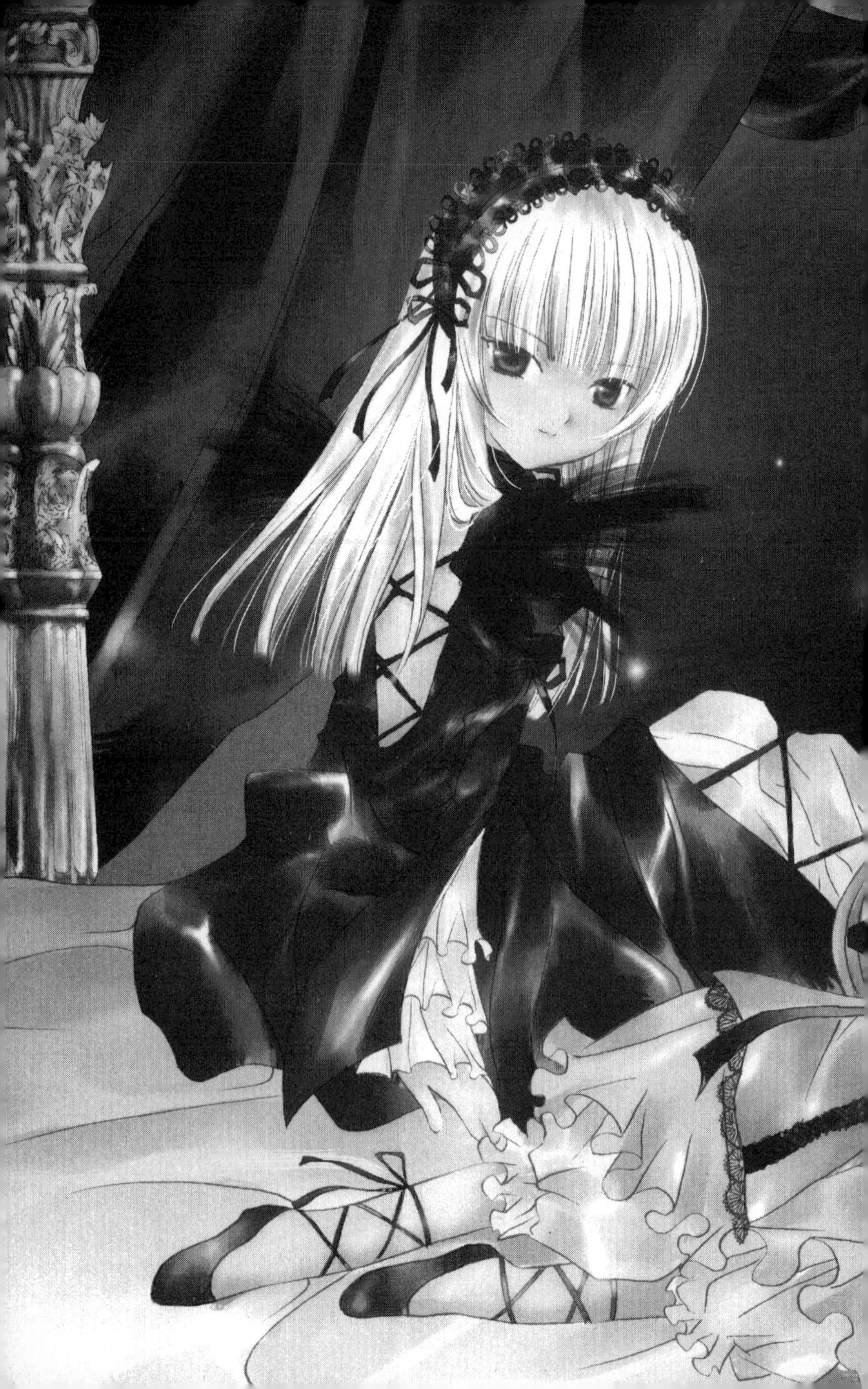

ローゼン メイデン

Rozen Maiden

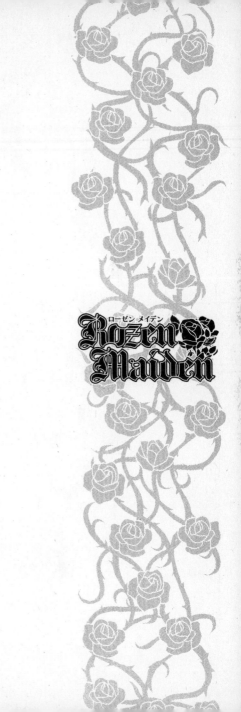

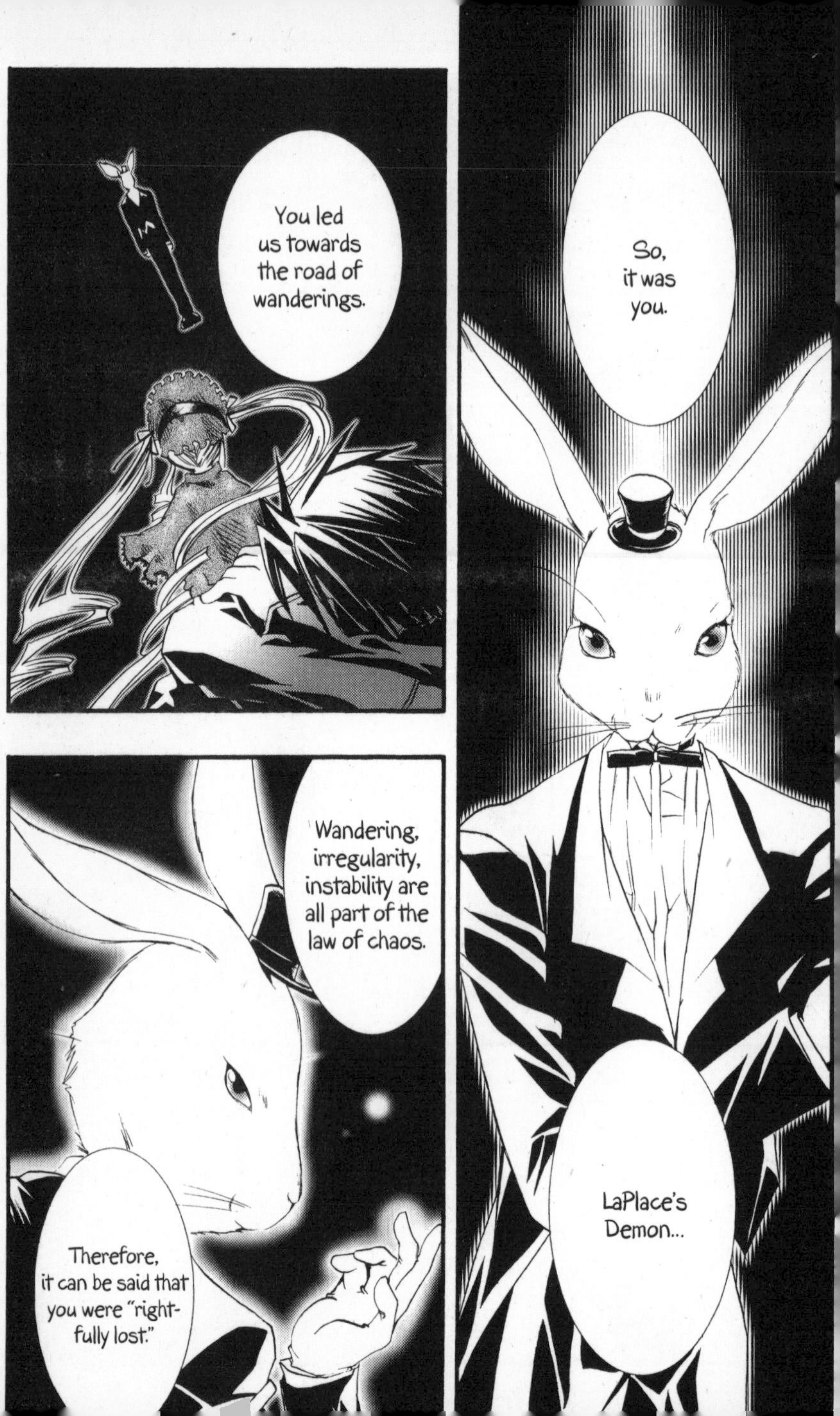
So, it was you.
LaPlace's Demon...
You led us towards the road of wanderings.
Wandering, irregularity, instability are all part of the law of chaos.
Therefore, it can be said that you were "right-fully lost."

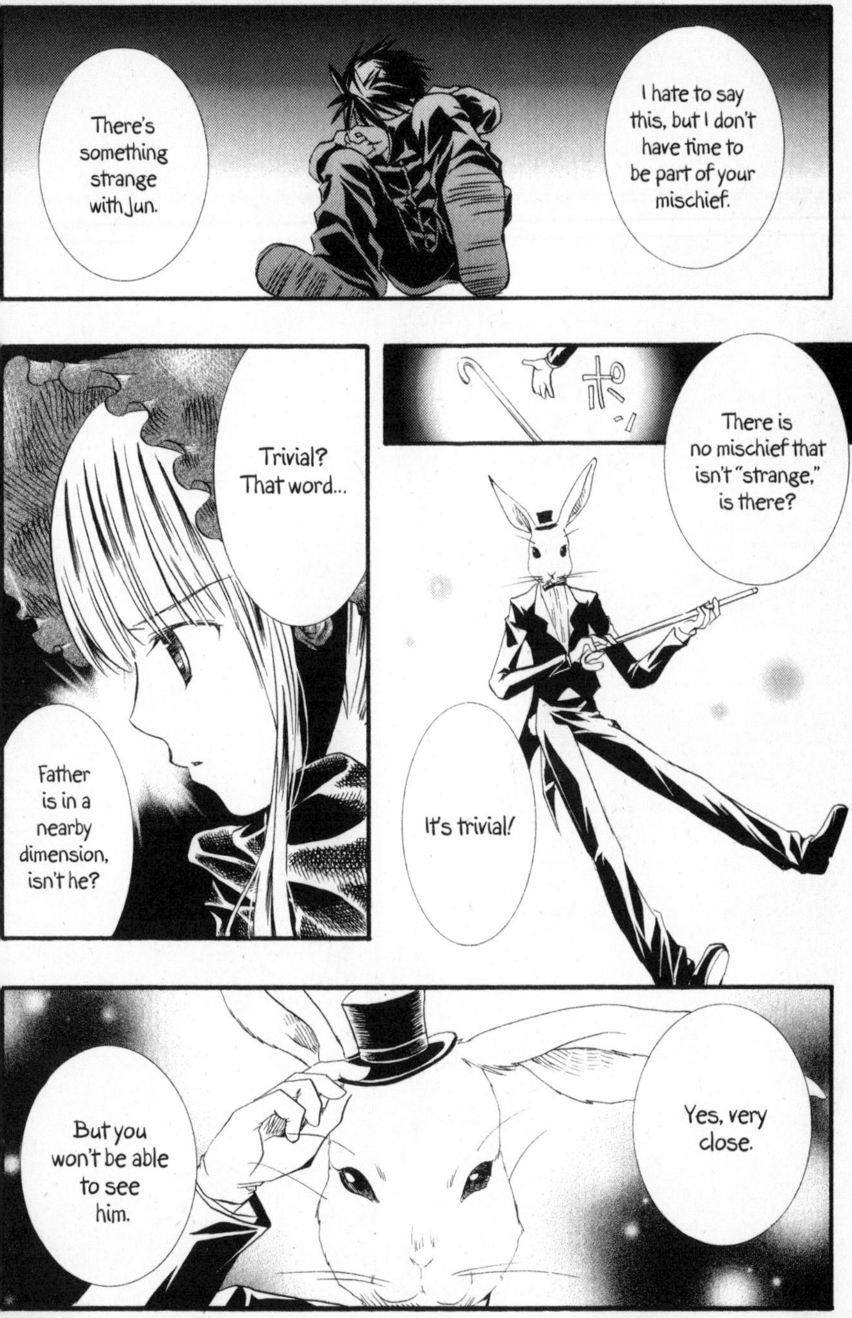
I hate to say this, but I don't have time to be part of your mischief.
There's something strange with Jun.
ポン
There is no mischief that isn't "strange," is there?
It's trivial!
Trivial? That word...
Father is in a nearby dimension, isn't he?
Yes, very close.
But you won't be able to see him.

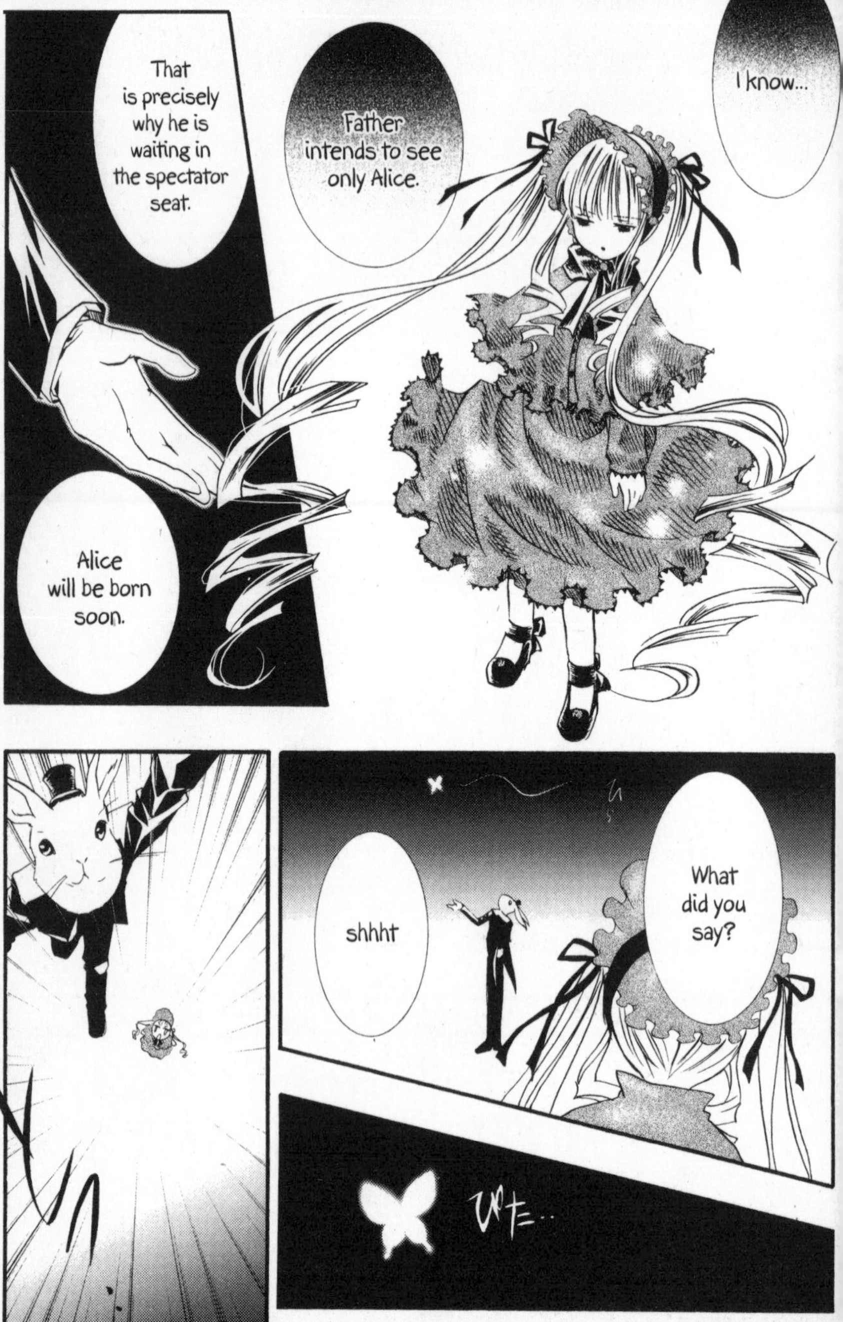
I know...
Father intends to see only Alice.
That is precisely why he is waiting in the spectator seat.
Alice will be born soon.
What did you say?
shhht

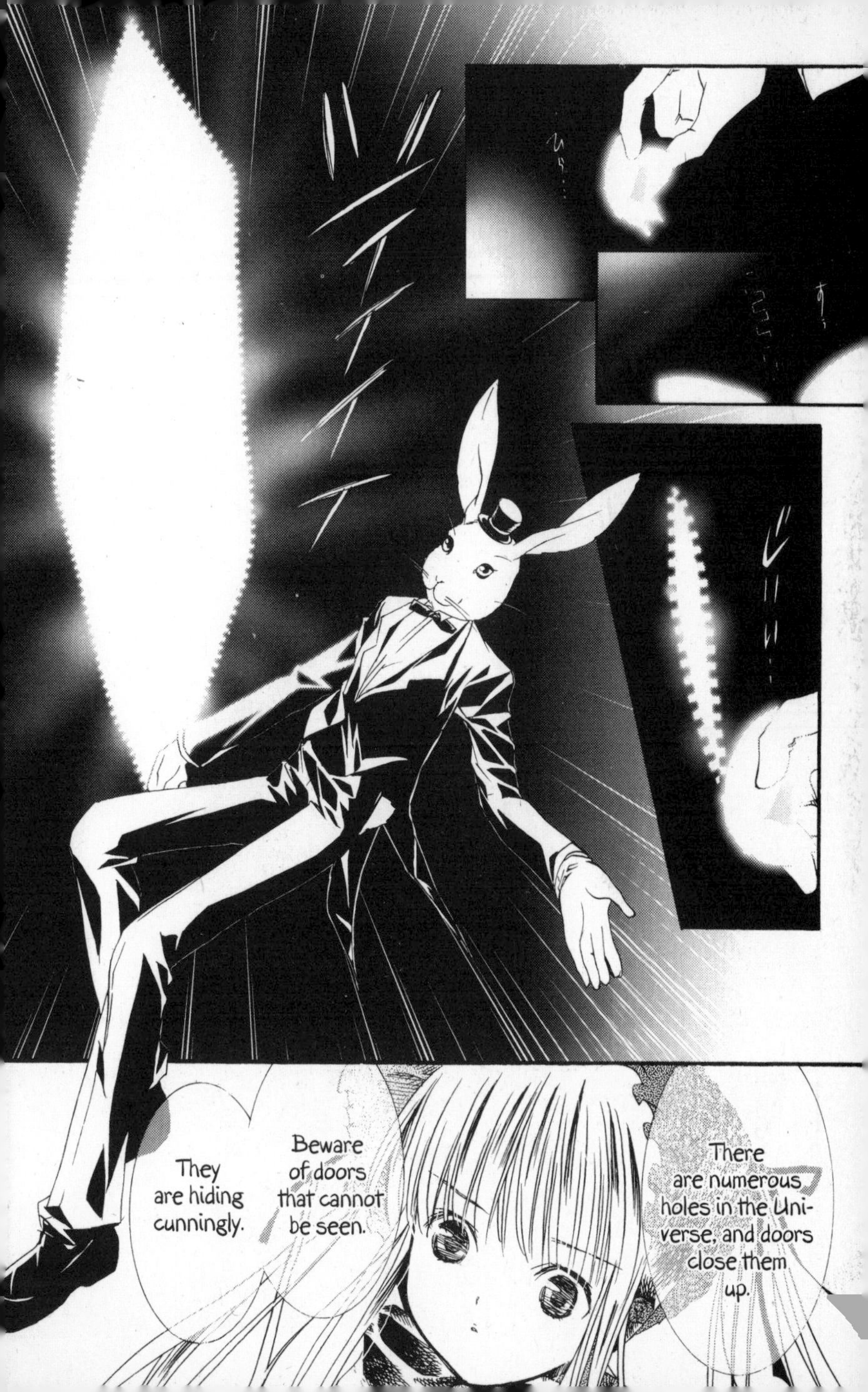
There are numerous holes in the Universe, and doors close them up.
Beware of doors that cannot be seen.
They are hiding cunningly.

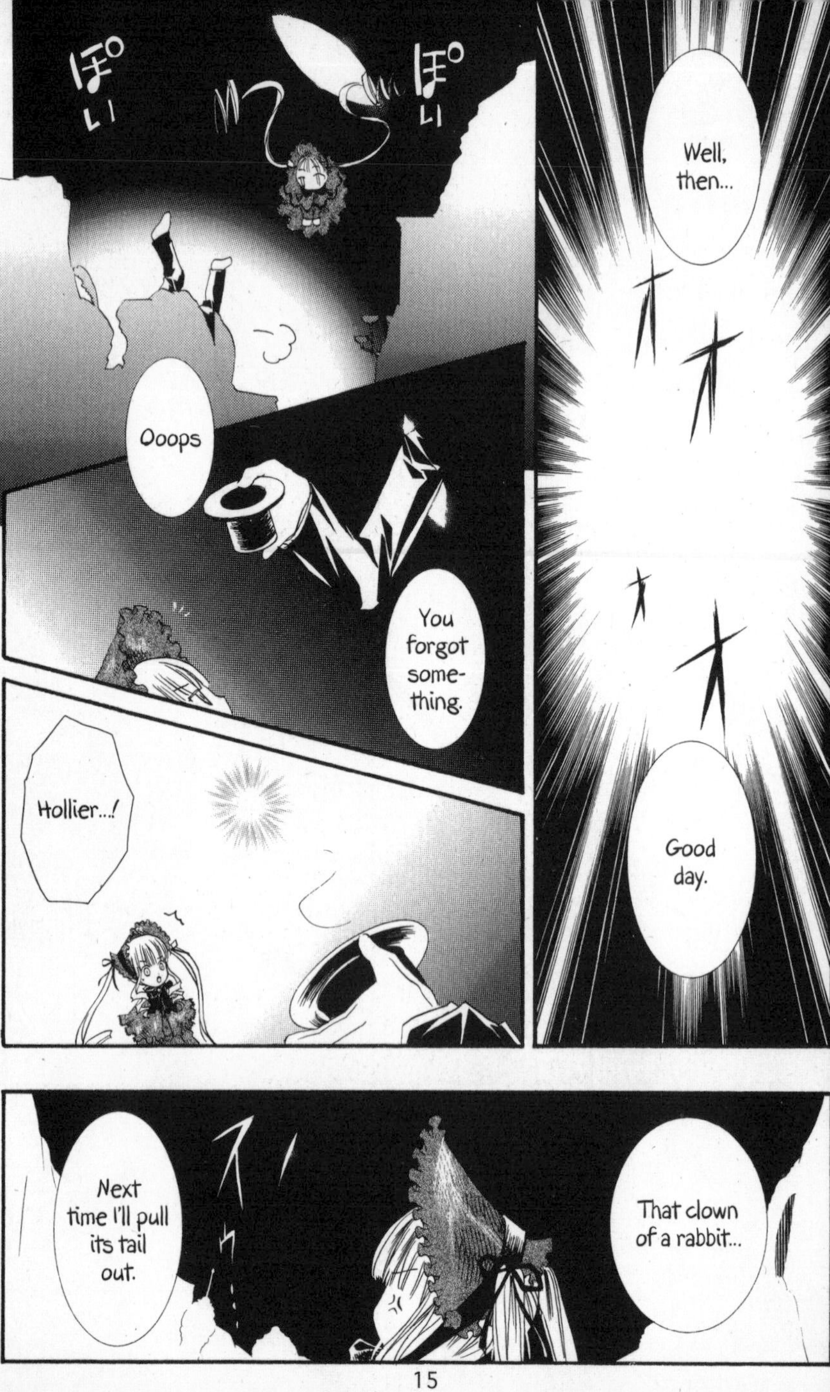
Well, then...
Good day.
ぽい
ぽい
Ooops
You forgot something.
Hollier...!
That clown of a rabbit...
Next time I'll pull its tail out.

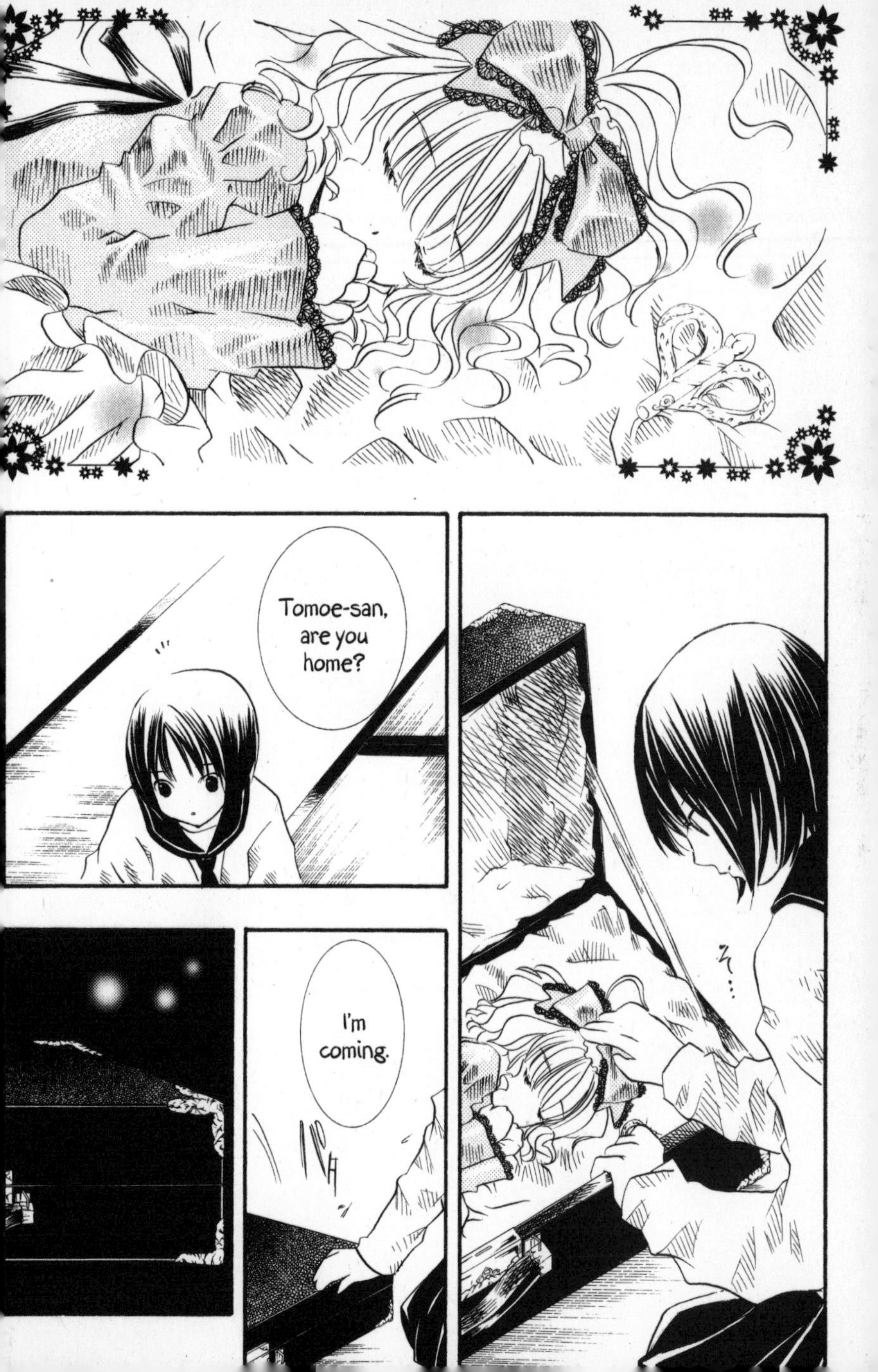
Tomoe-san, are you home?
I'm coming.

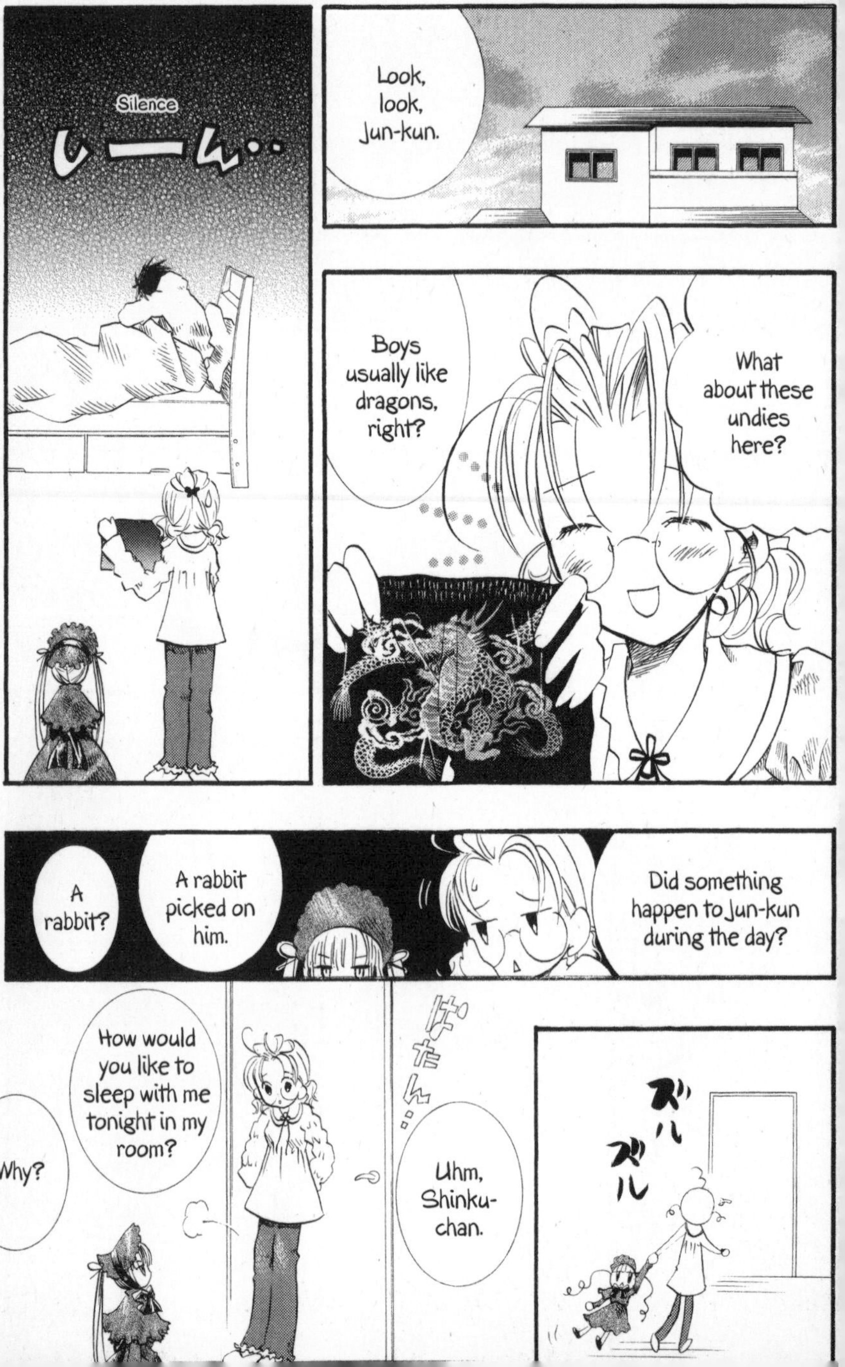
Look, look, Jun-kun.
What about these undies here?
Boys usually like dragons, right?
Silence
しーん‥
Did something happen to Jun-kun during the day?
A rabbit picked on him.
A rabbit?
ズルズル
ぱたん‥
Uhm, Shinku-chan.
How would you like to sleep with me tonight in my room?
Why?

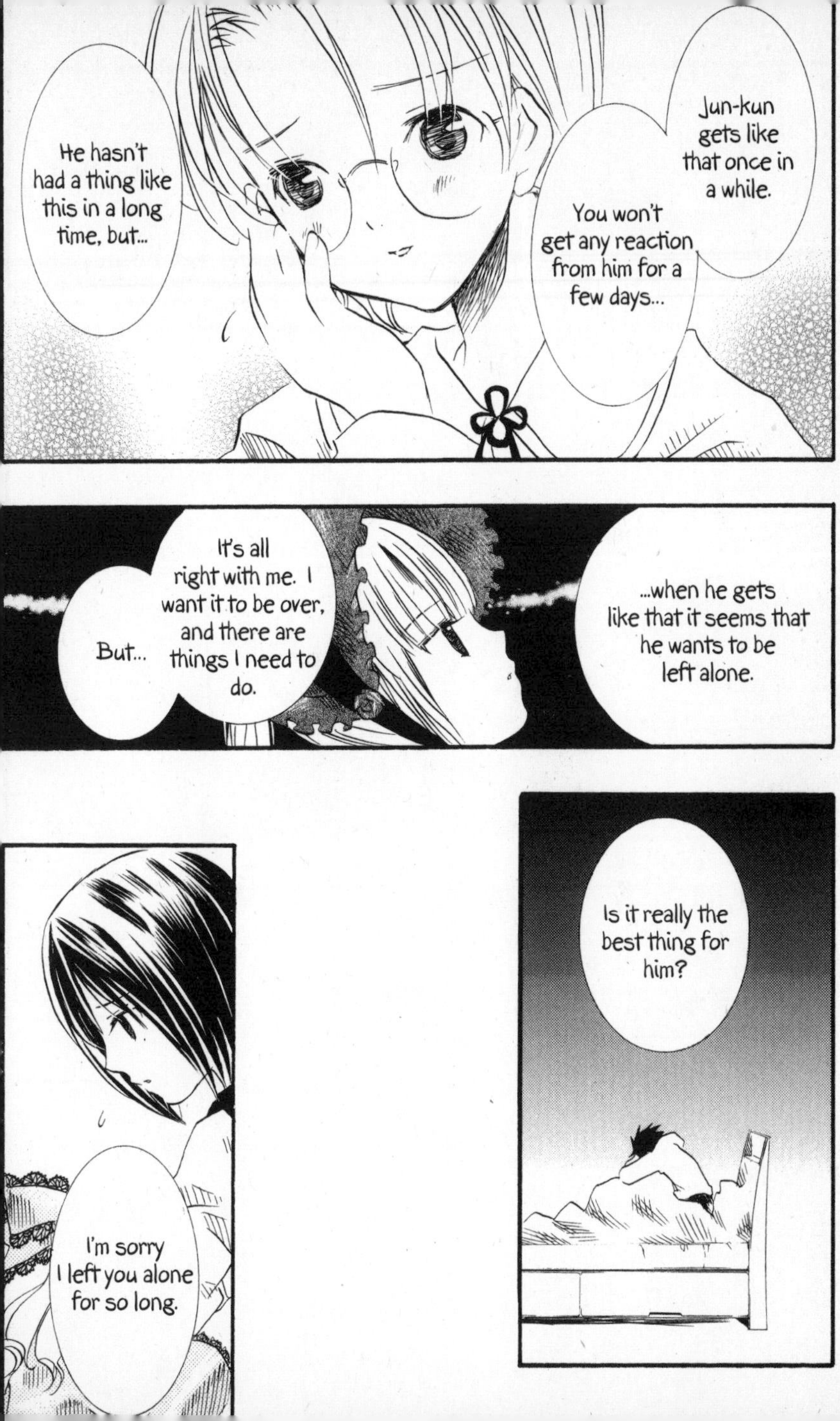
Jun-kun gets like that once in a while.
You won't get any reaction from him for a few days...
He hasn't had a thing like this in a long time, but...
...when he gets like that it seems that he wants to be left alone.
It's all right with me. I want it to be over, and there are things I need to do.
But...
Is it really the best thing for him?
I'm sorry I left you alone for so long.

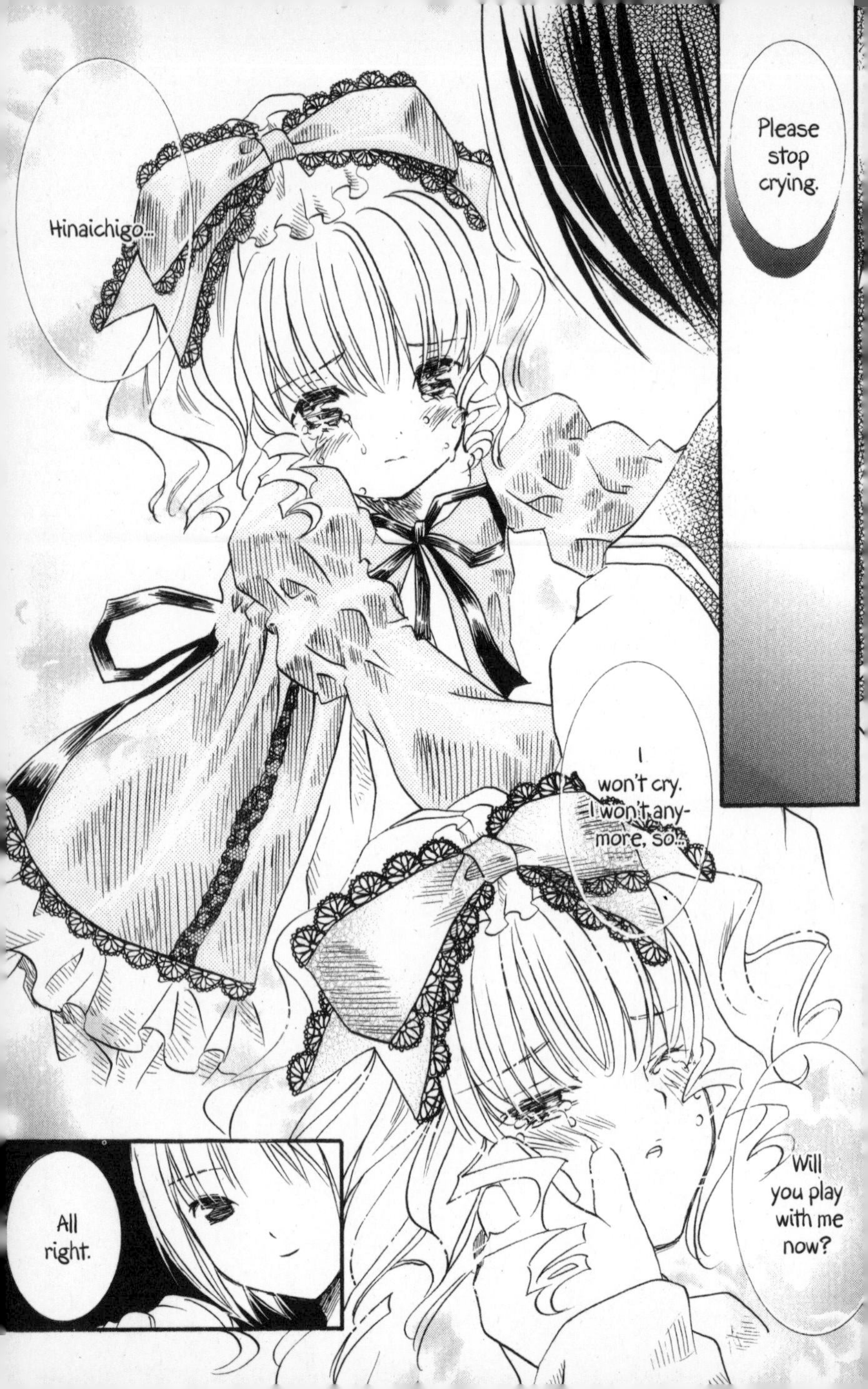
Please stop crying.
Hinaichigo...
I won't cry. I won't any-more, so...
Will you play with me now?
All right.

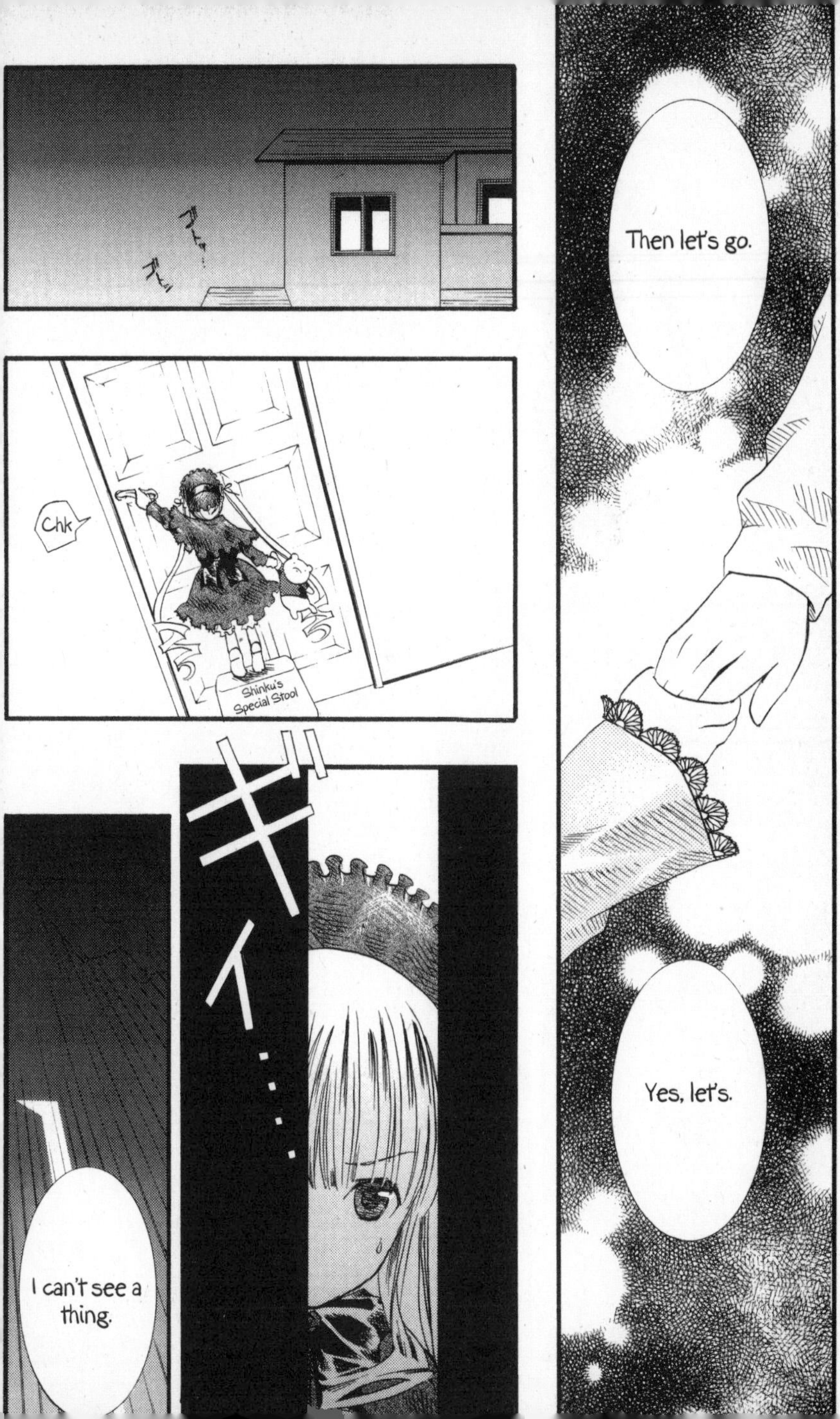
Then let's go.
Yes, let's.
Chk
Shinku's Special Stool
ギイ…
I can't see a thing.

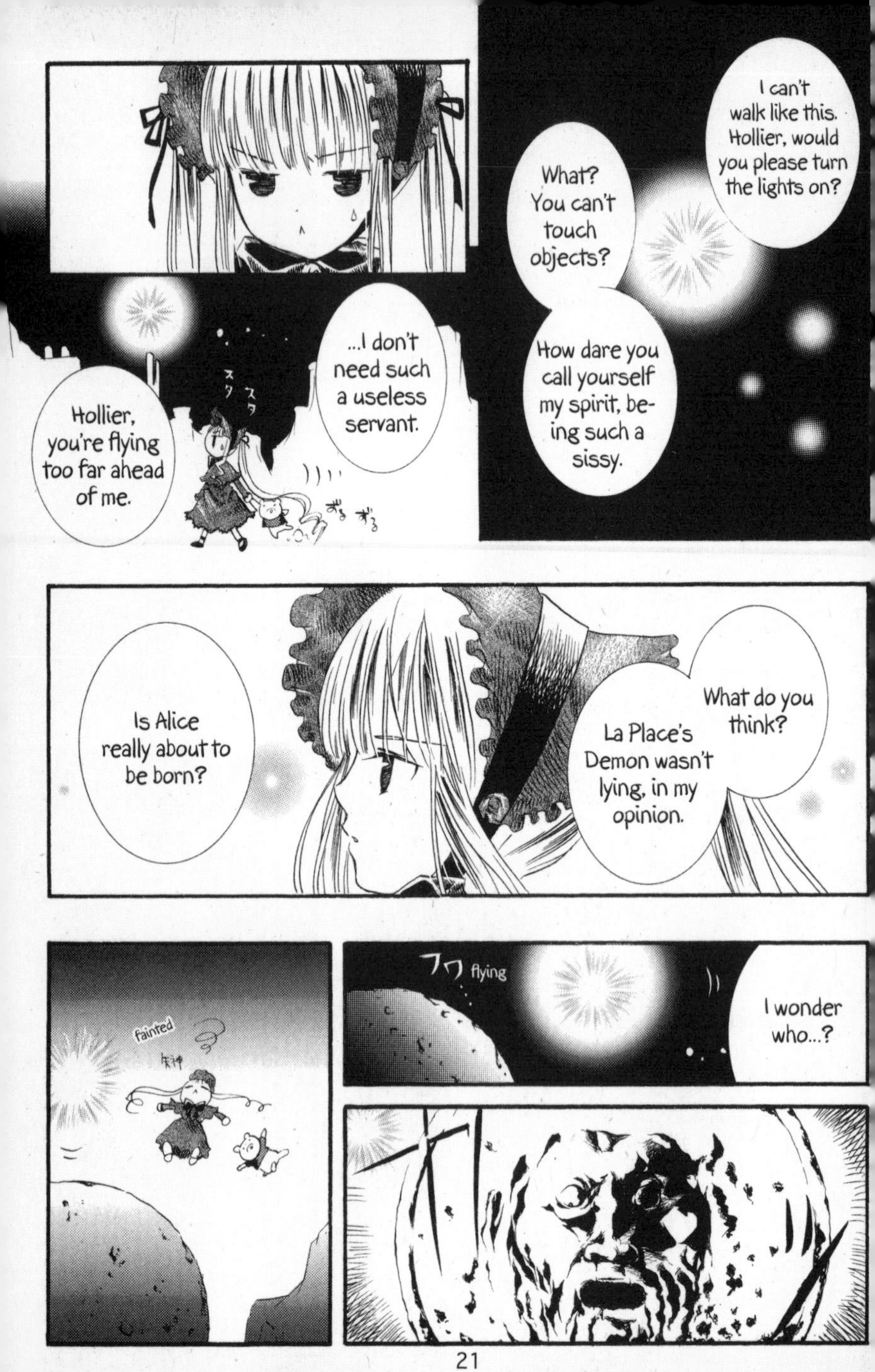
I can't walk like this. Hollier, would you please turn the lights on?
What? You can't touch objects?
How dare you call yourself my spirit, being such a sissy.
...I don't need such a useless servant.
Hollier, you're flying too far ahead of me.
What do you think?
La Place's Demon wasn't lying, in my opinion.
Is Alice really about to be born?
flying
I wonder who...?
fainted

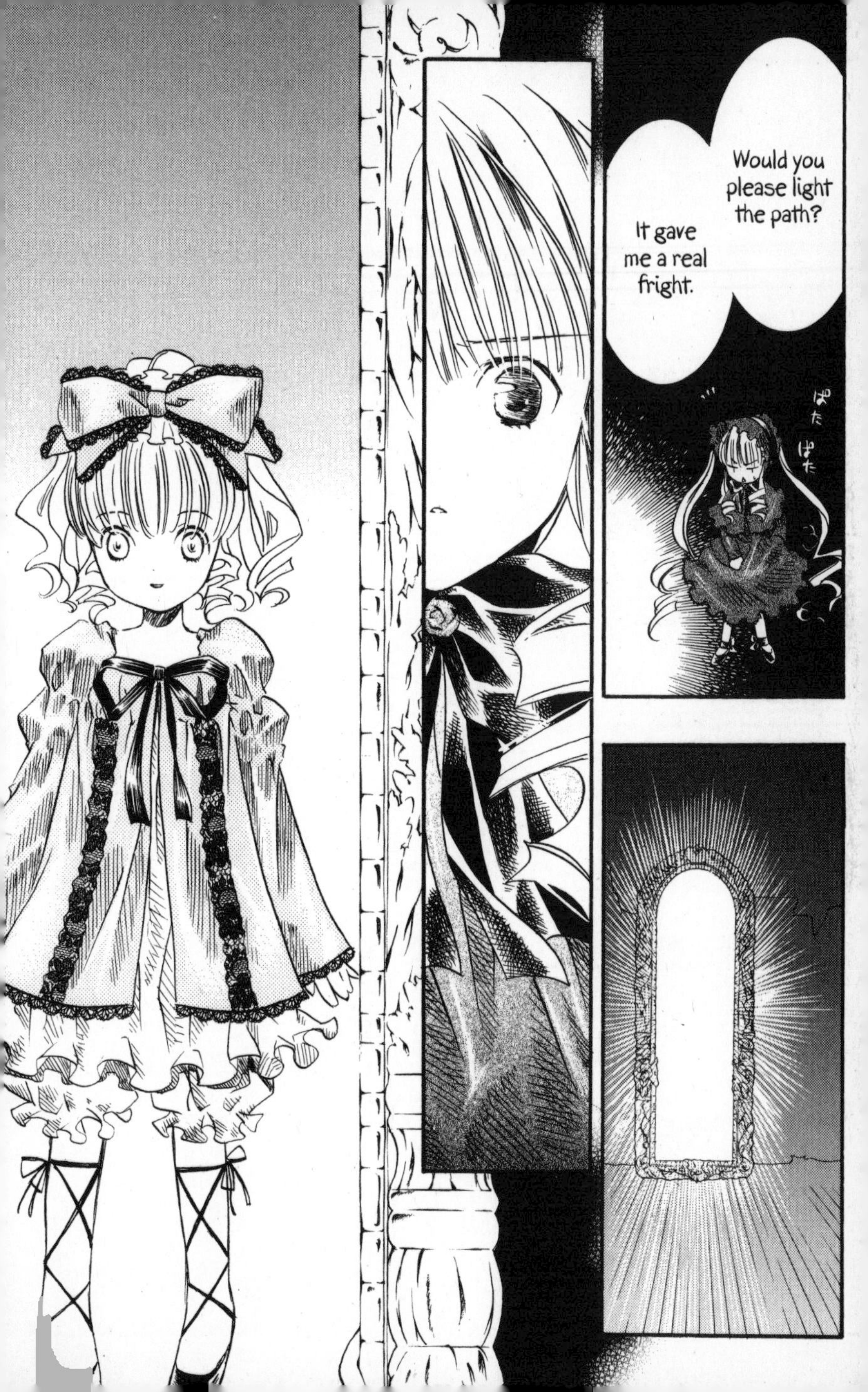
Would you please light the path?
It gave me a real fright.
ぱた ぱた

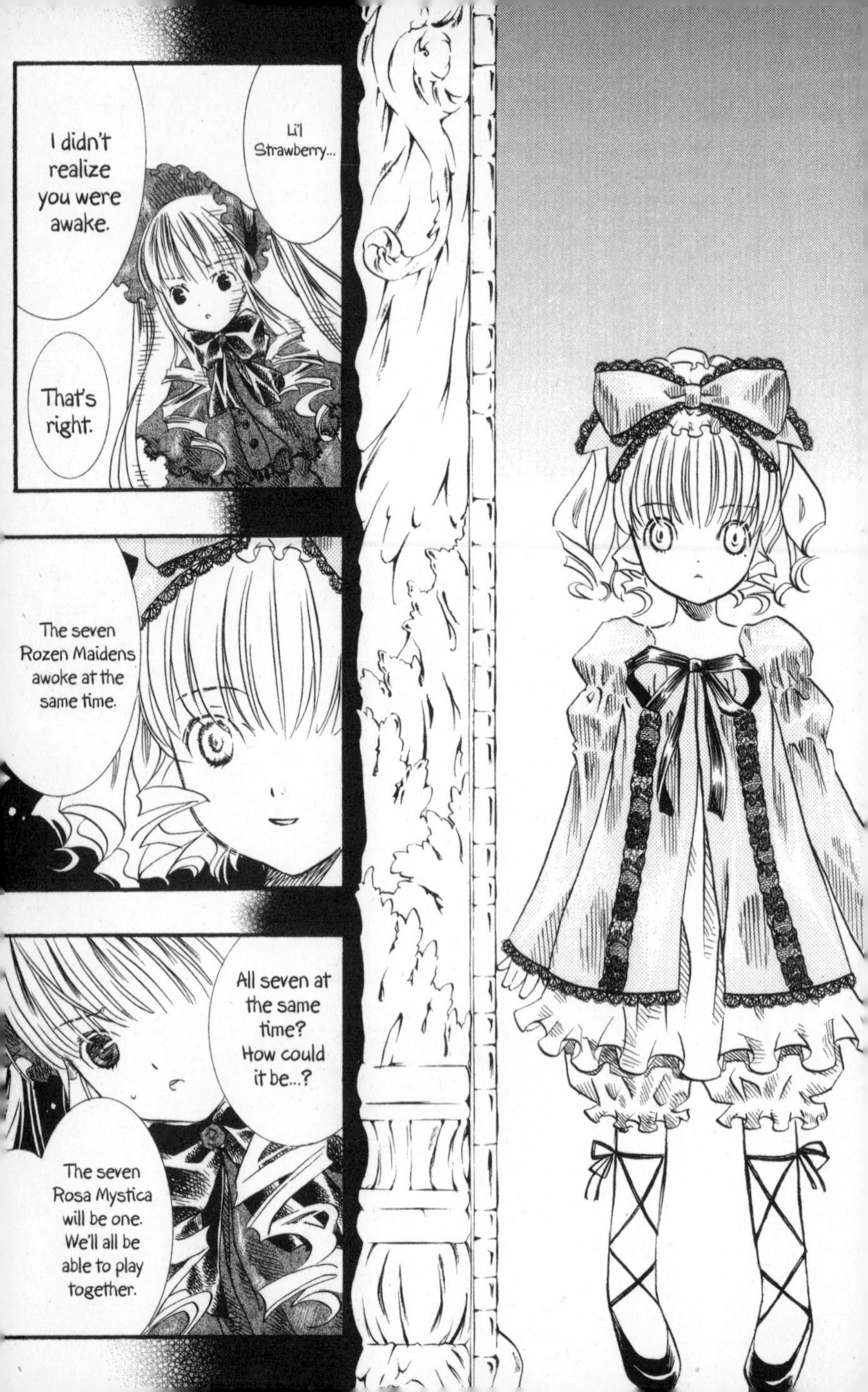

Li'l Strawberry...
I didn't realize you were awake.
That's right.
The seven Rozen Maidens awoke at the same time.
All seven at the same time? How could it be...?
The seven Rosa Mystica will be one. We'll all be able to play together.

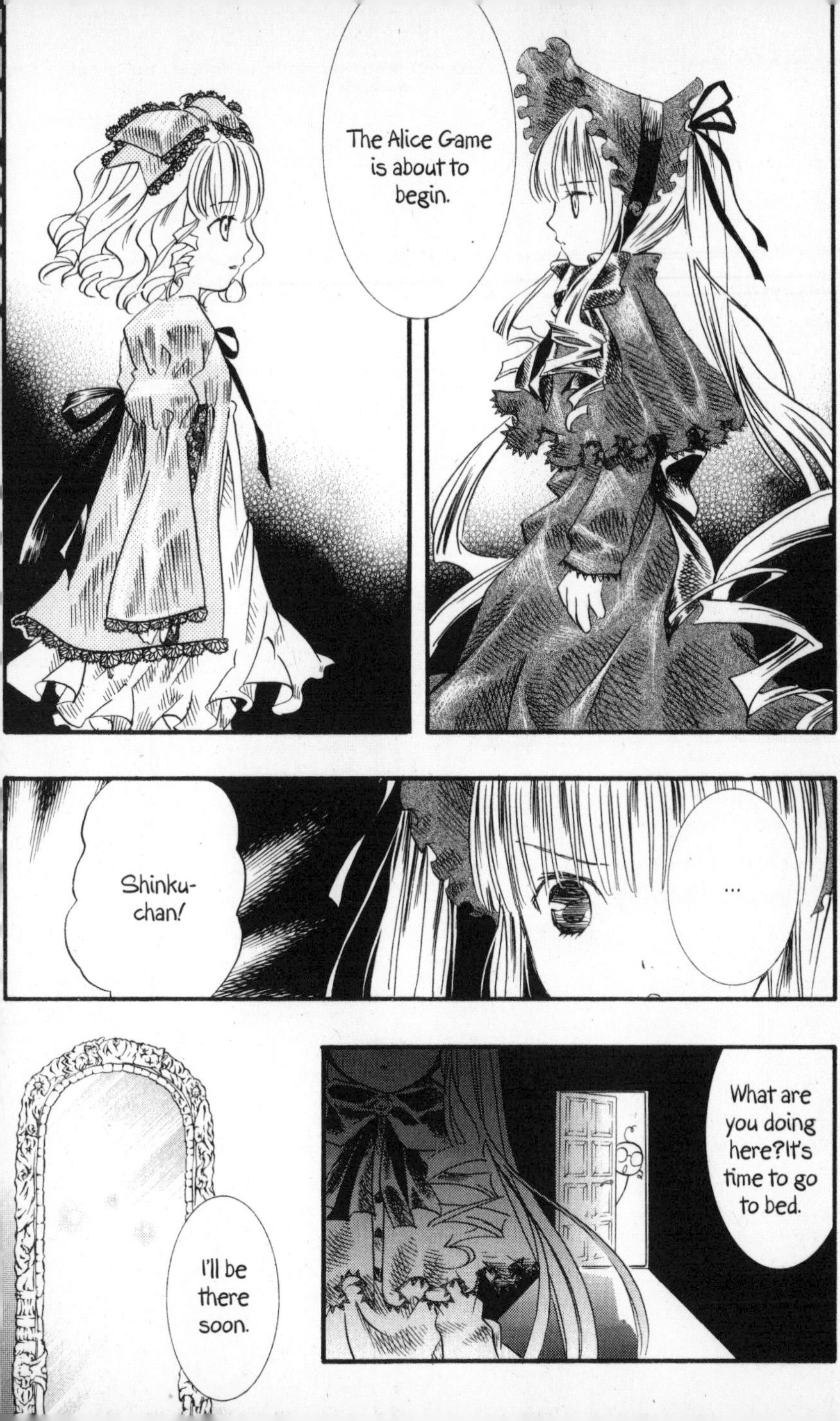
The Alice Game is about to begin.
...
Shinku-chan!
What are you doing here? It's time to go to bed.
I'll be there soon.

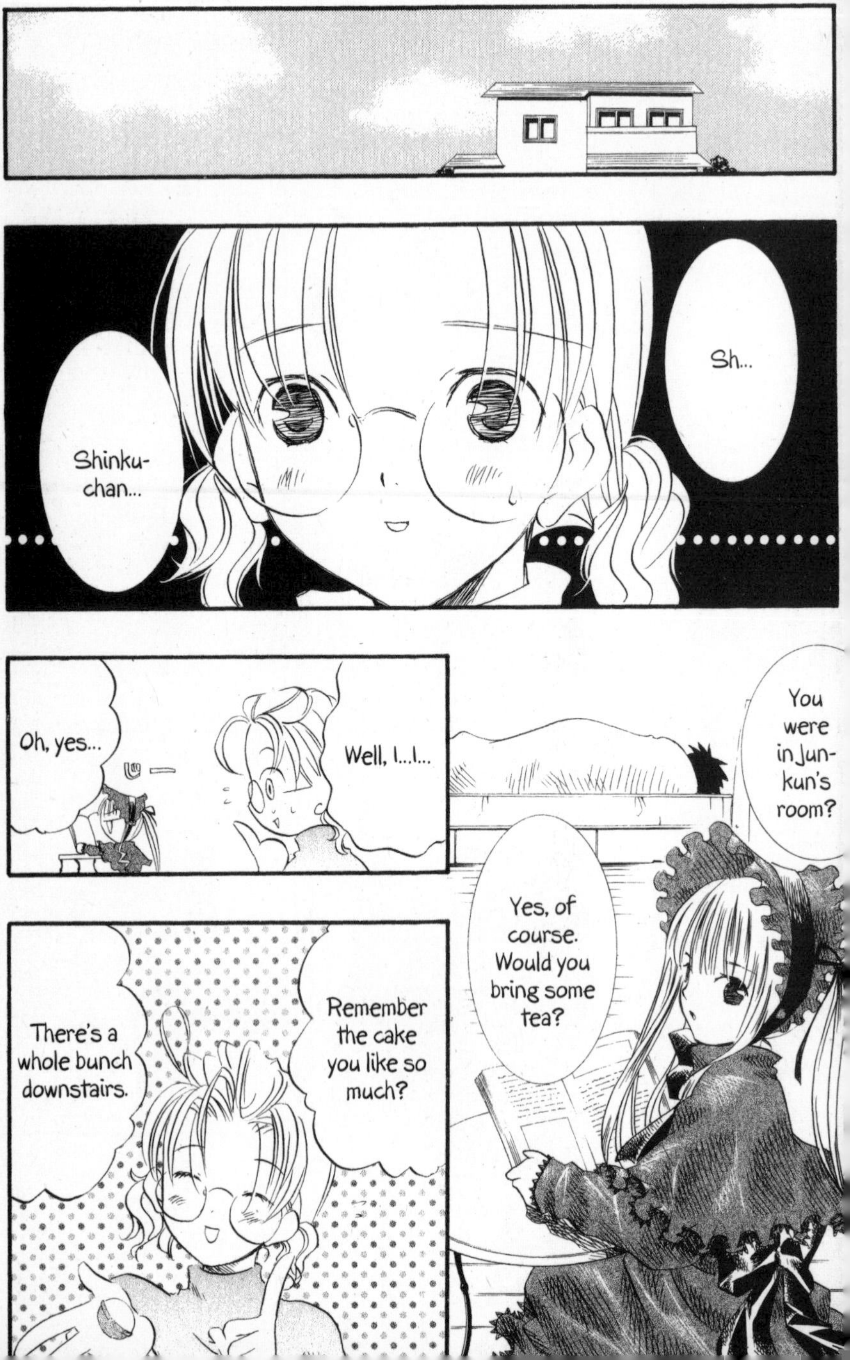
Sh...
Shinku-chan...
You were in Jun-kun's room?
Yes, of course. Would you bring some tea?
Well, I...I...
Oh, yes...
Remember the cake you like so much?
There's a whole bunch downstairs.

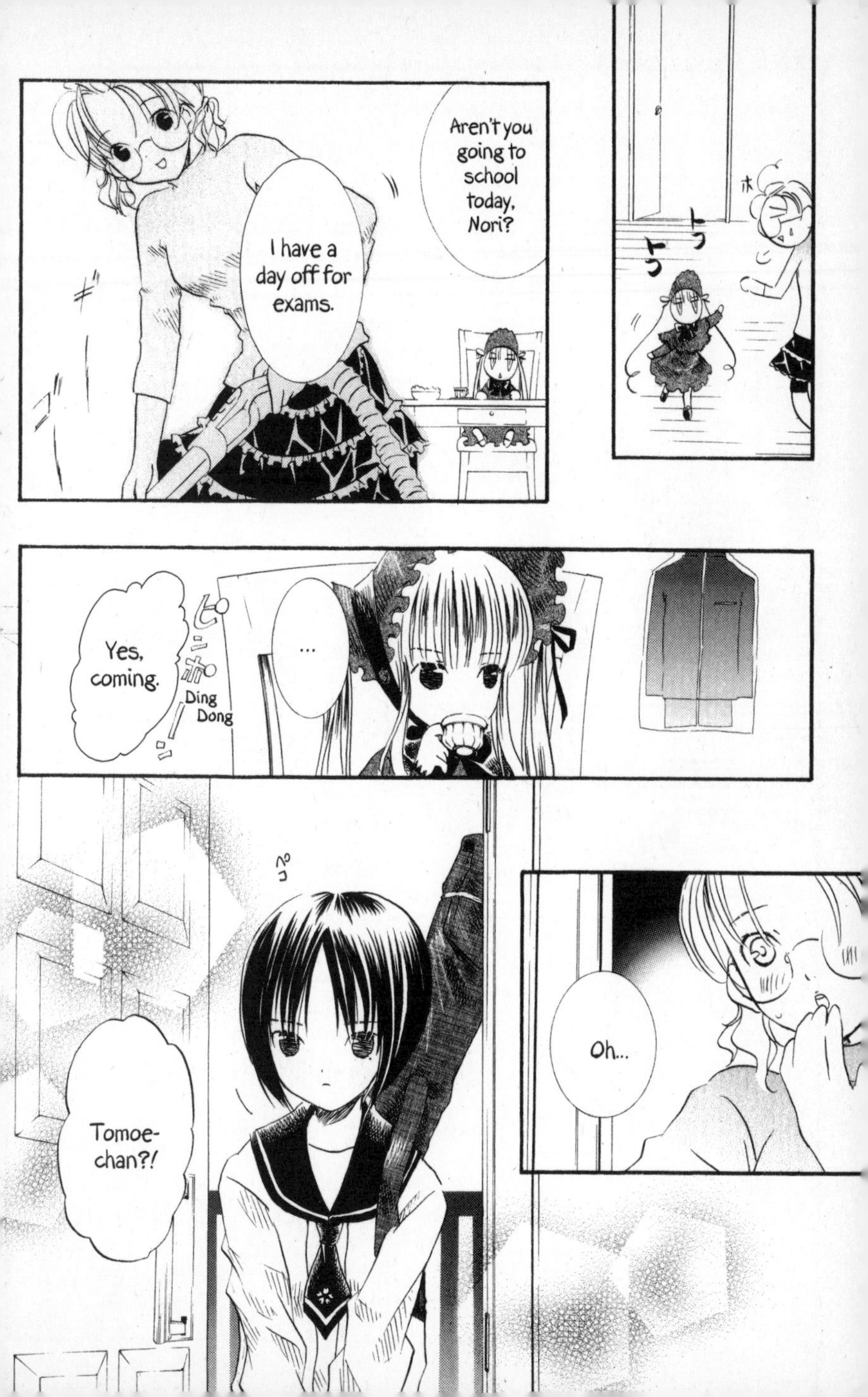
Aren't you going to school today, Nori?
I have a day off for exams.
...
Yes, coming.
Ding Dong
Oh...
Tomoe-chan?!

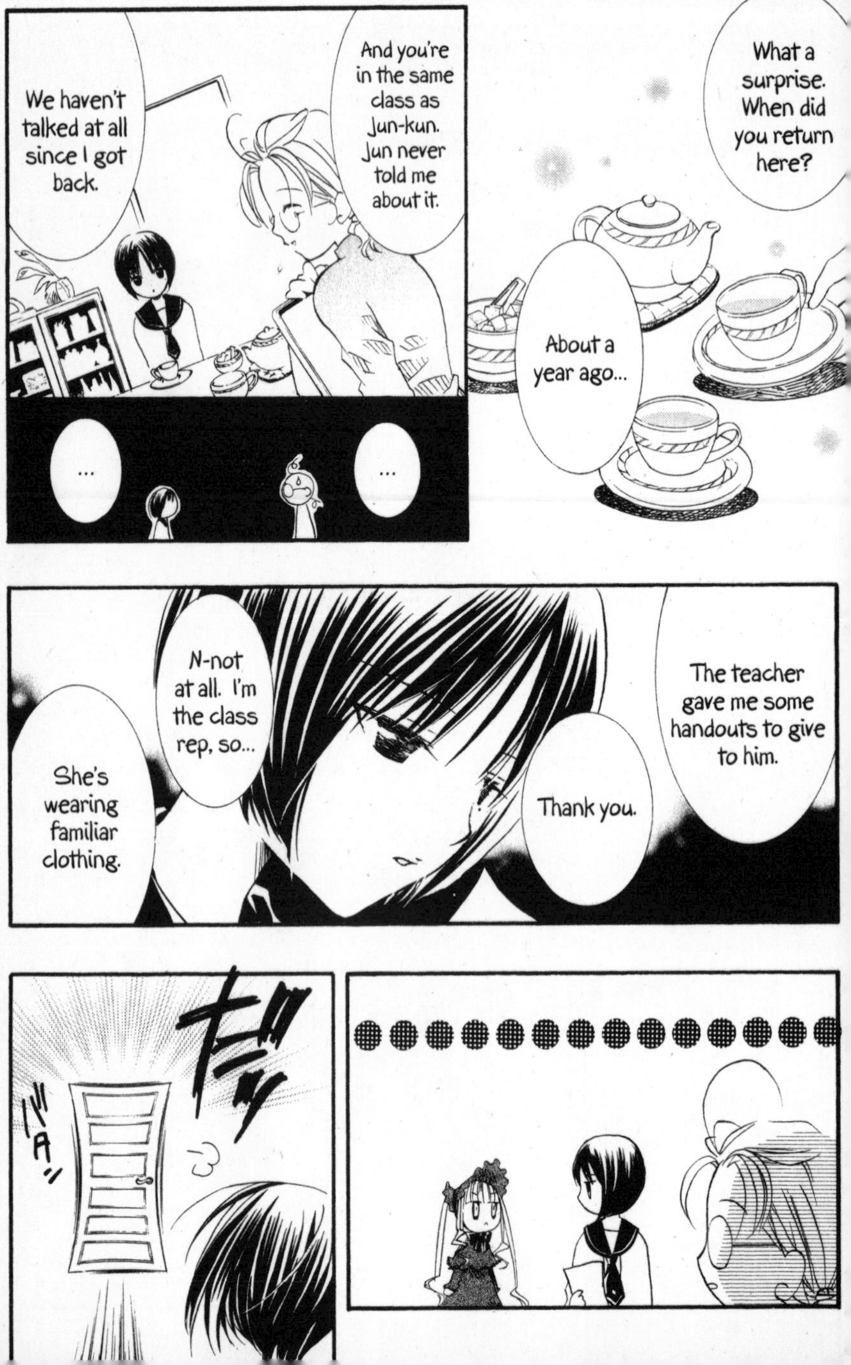
What a surprise. When did you return here?
About a year ago...
And you're in the same class as Jun-kun. Jun never told me about it.
We haven't talked at all since I got back.
...
...
The teacher gave me some handouts to give to him.
Thank you.
N-not at all. I'm the class rep, so...
She's wearing familiar clothing.
ダッ
バタン

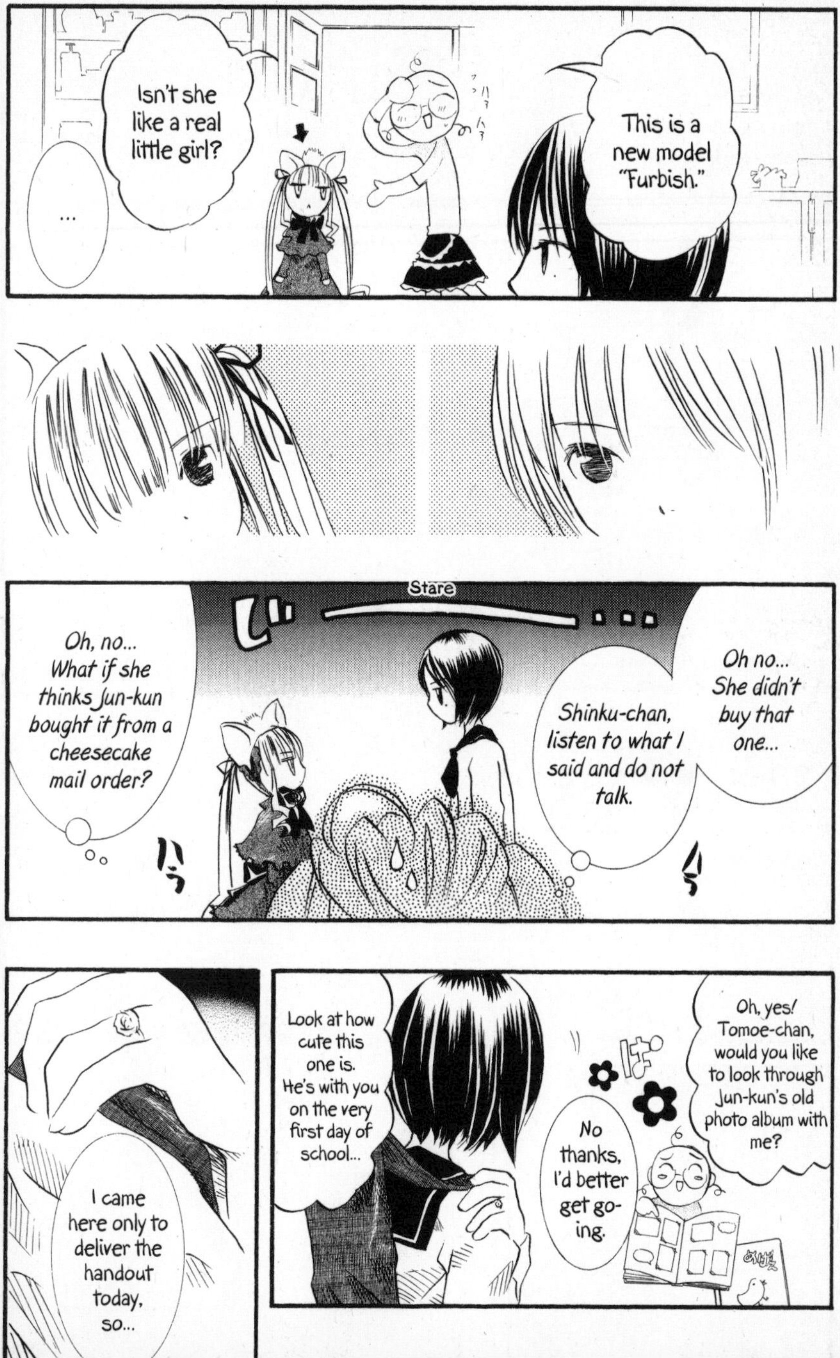
This is a new model "Furbish."
Isn't she like a real little girl?
...
Stare
Oh no... She didn't buy that one...
Shinku-chan, listen to what I said and do not talk.
Oh, no... What if she thinks Jun-kun bought it from a cheesecake mail order?
Oh, yes! Tomoe-chan, would you like to look through Jun-kun's old photo album with me?
No thanks, I'd better get go-ing.
Look at how cute this one is. He's with you on the very first day of school...
I came here only to deliver the handout today, so...

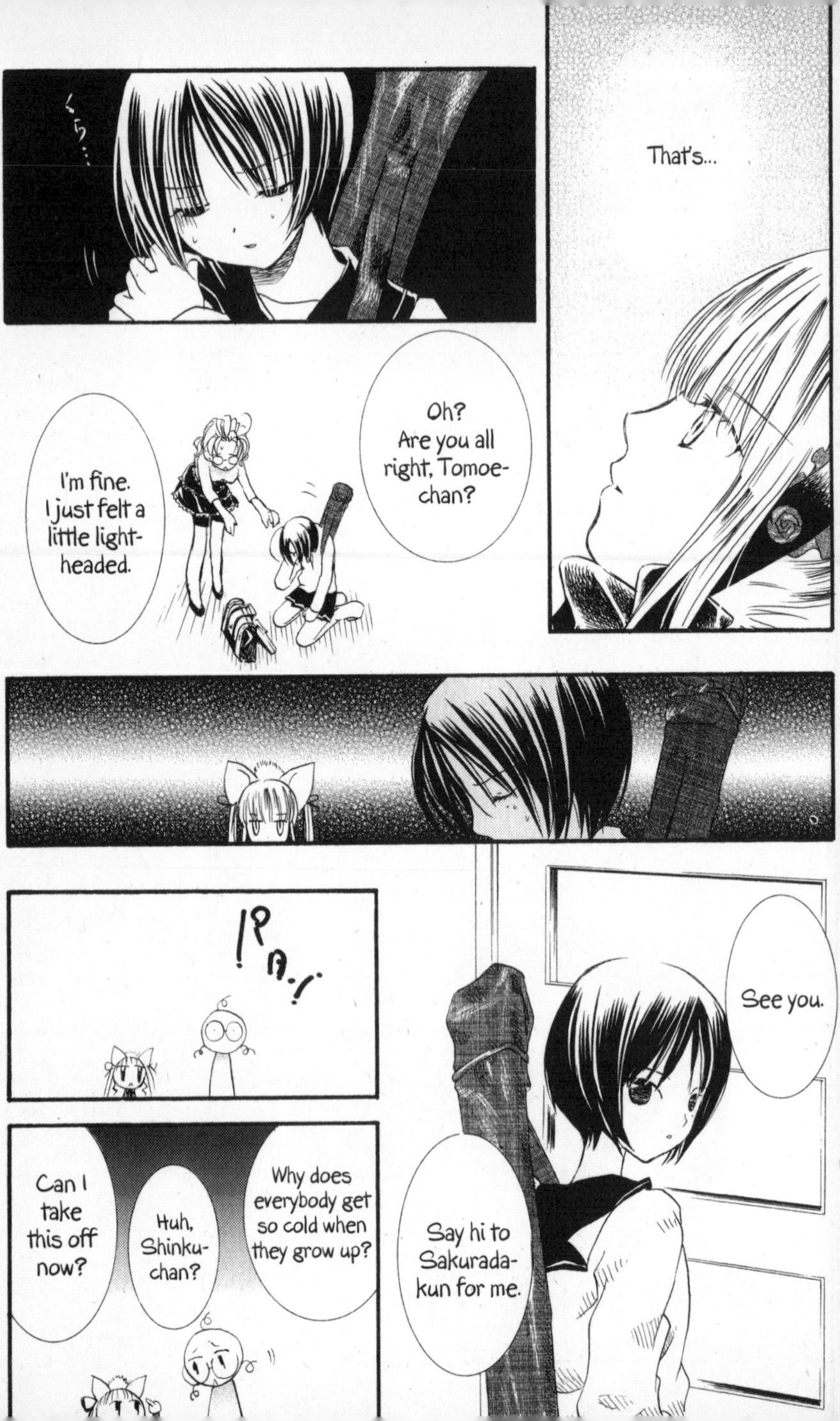
That's...
くら…
Oh? Are you all right, Tomoe-chan?
I'm fine. I just felt a little light-headed.
See you.
Say hi to Sakurada-kun for me.
Why does everybody get so cold when they grow up?
Huh, Shinku-chan?
Can I take this off now?

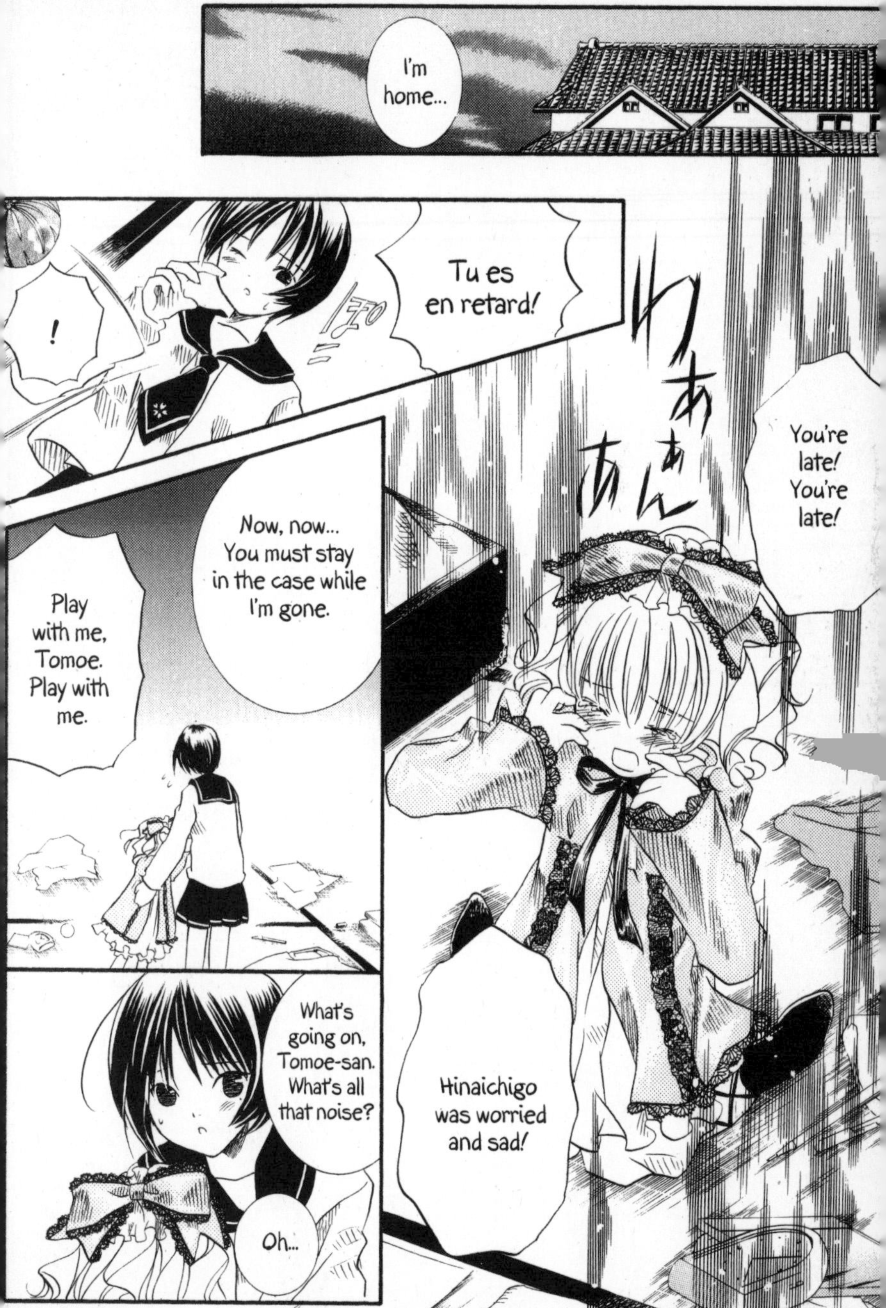
I'm home...
You're late! You're late!
Hinaichigo was worried and sad!
Tu es en retard!
!
Now, now... You must stay in the case while I'm gone.
Play with me, Tomoe. Play with me.
What's going on, Tomoe-san. What's all that noise?
Oh...

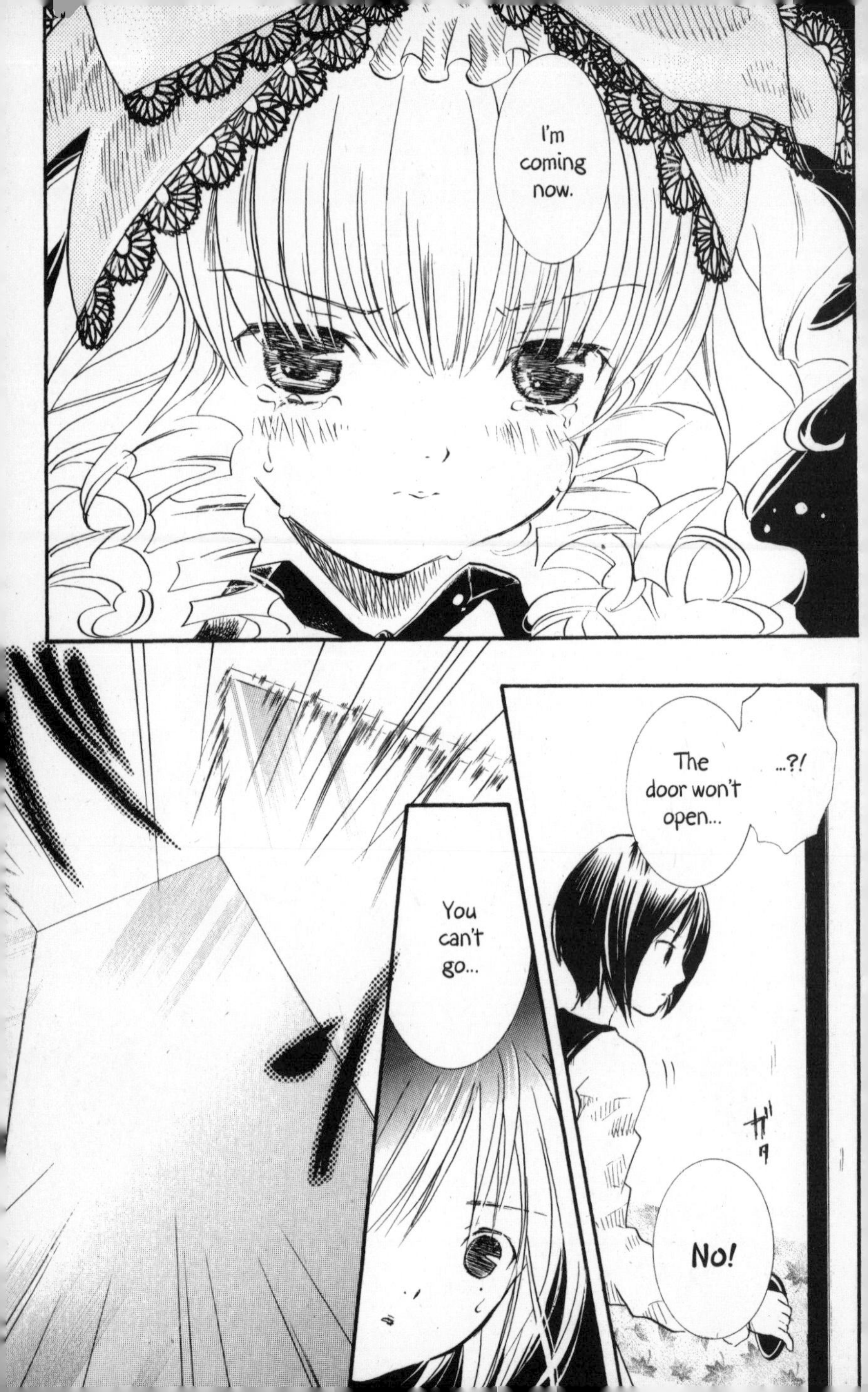
I'm coming now.
...?!
The door won't open...
No!
You can't go...

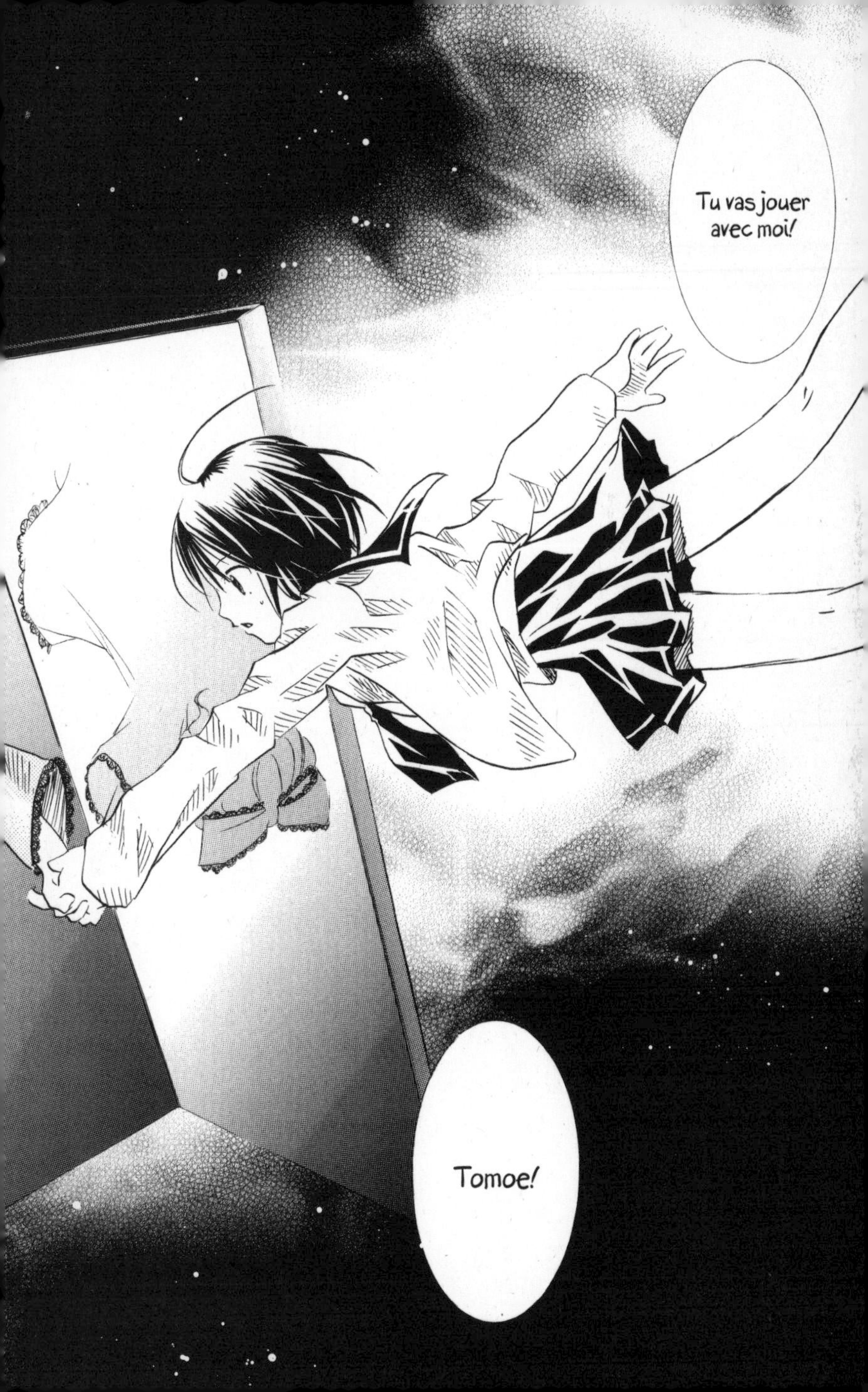
Tu vas jouer avec moi!
Tomoe!

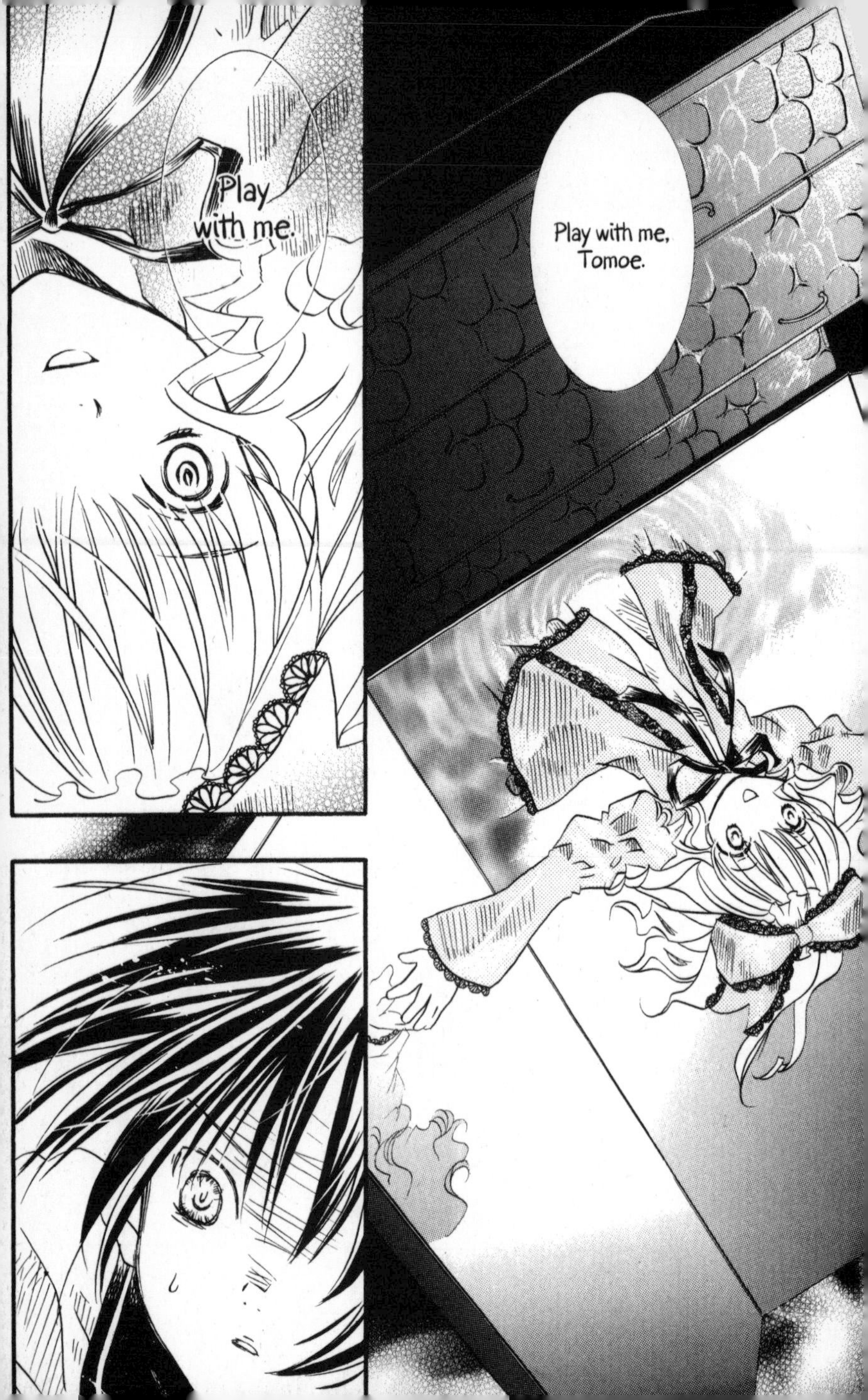
Play with me, Tomoe.
Play with me.

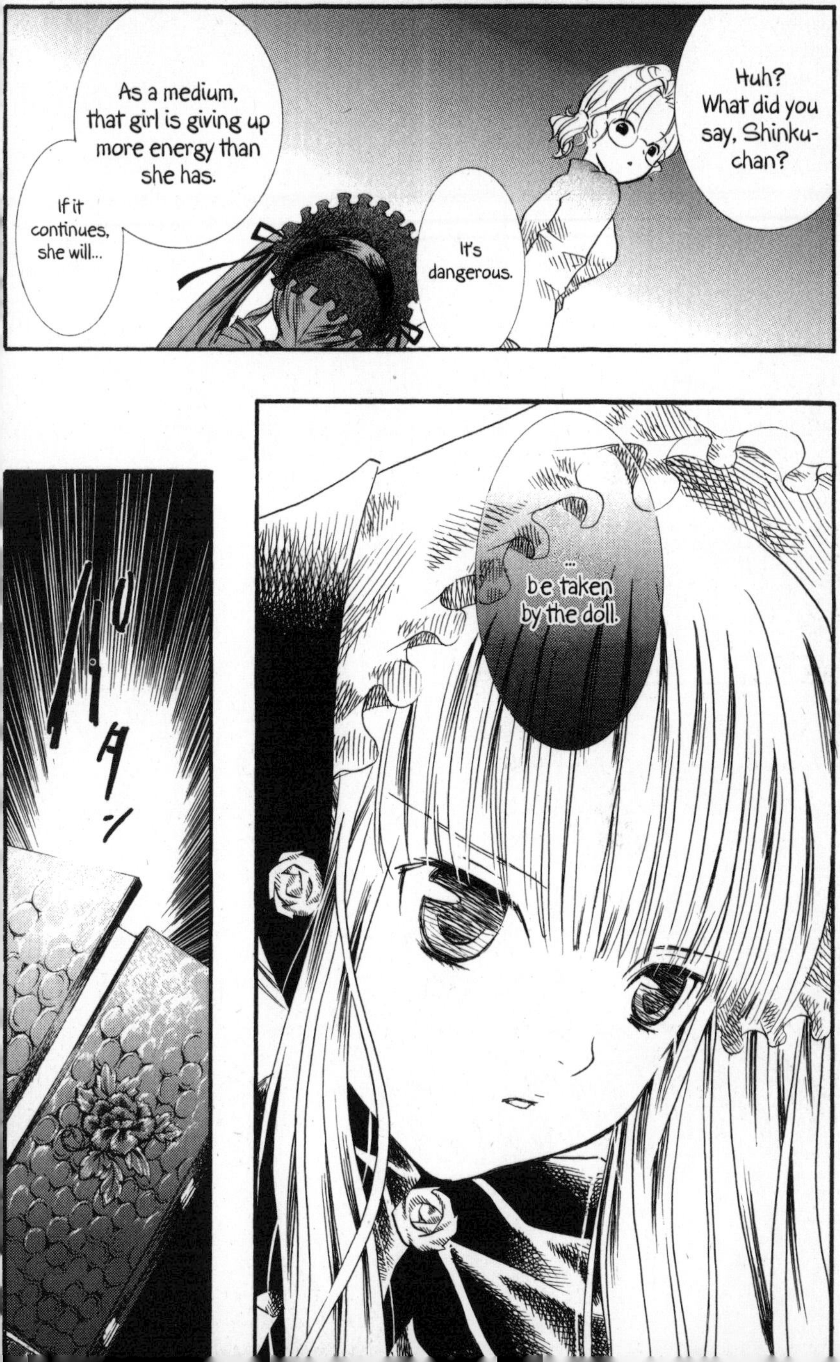
Huh? What did you say, Shinku-chan?
It's dangerous.
As a medium, that girl is giving up more energy than she has.
If it continues, she will...
... be taken by the doll.
バタン

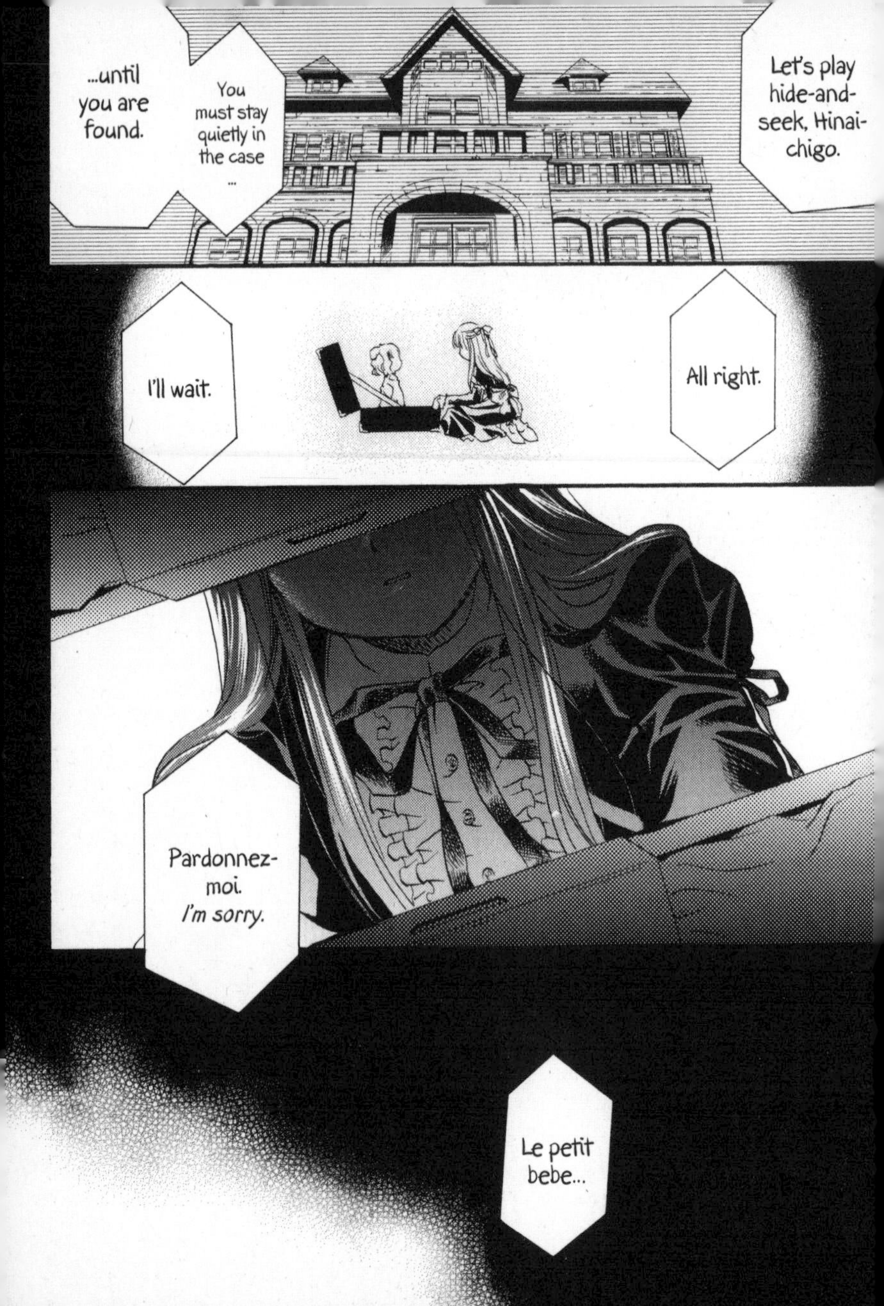
Let's play hide-and-seek, Hinaichigo.
You must stay quietly in the case ...
...until you are found.
All right.
I'll wait.
Pardonnez-moi. *I'm sorry.*
Le petit bebe...

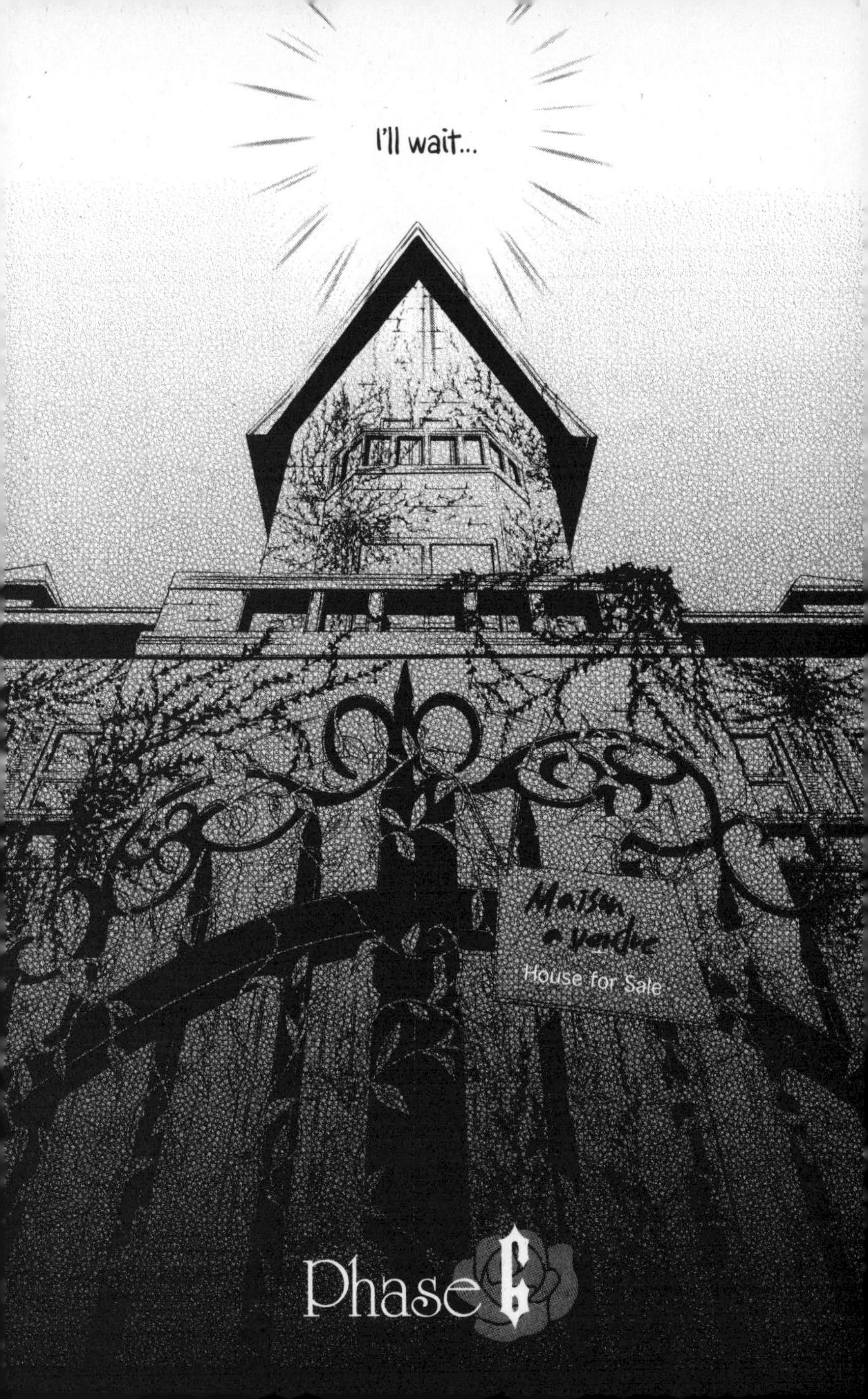
I'll wait...
House for Sale
Phase 6

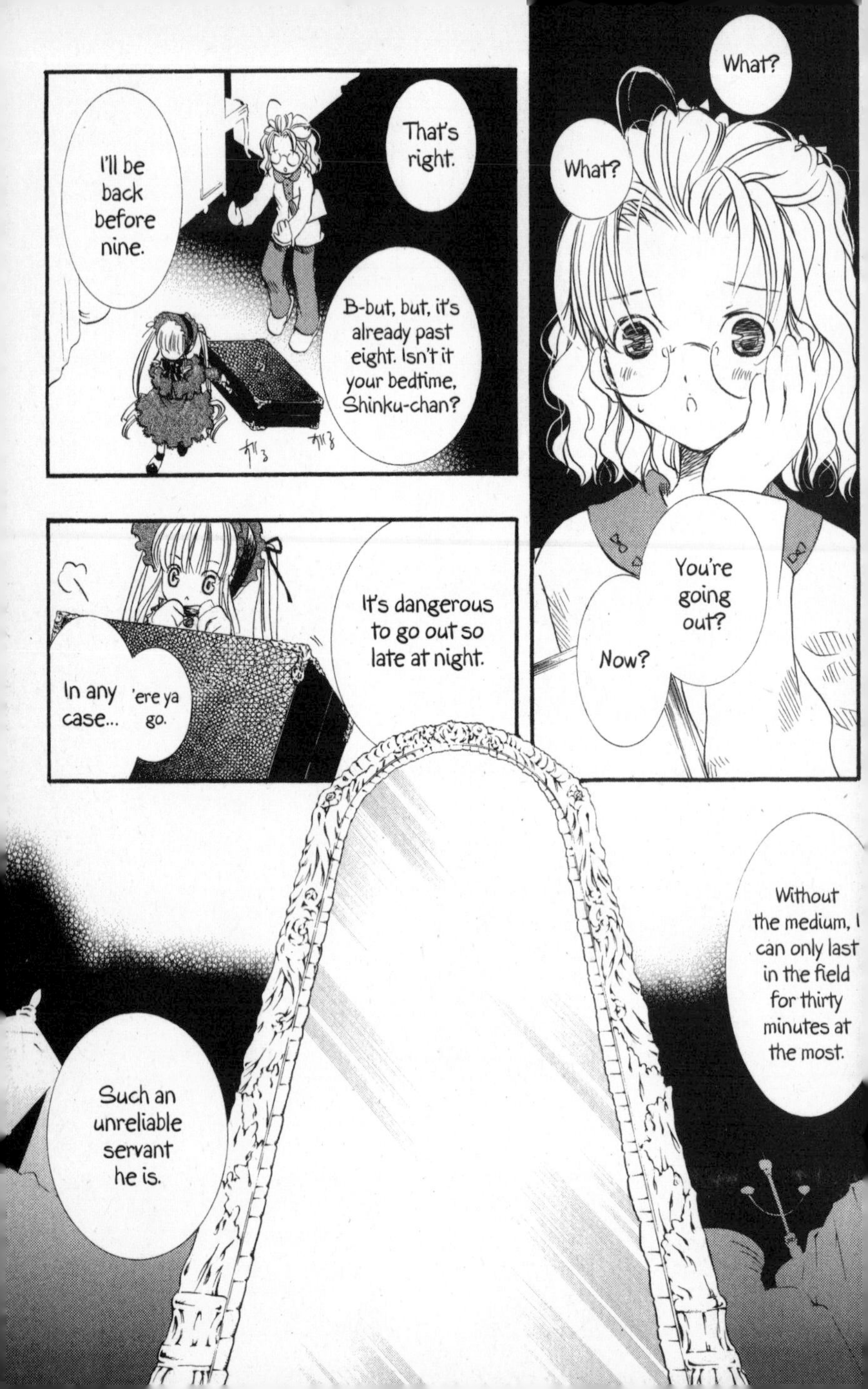
What?
What?
You're going out?
Now?
That's right.
I'll be back before nine.
B-but, but, it's already past eight. Isn't it your bedtime, Shinku-chan?
It's dangerous to go out so late at night.
In any case...
'ere ya go.
Without the medium, I can only last in the field for thirty minutes at the most.
Such an unreliable servant he is.

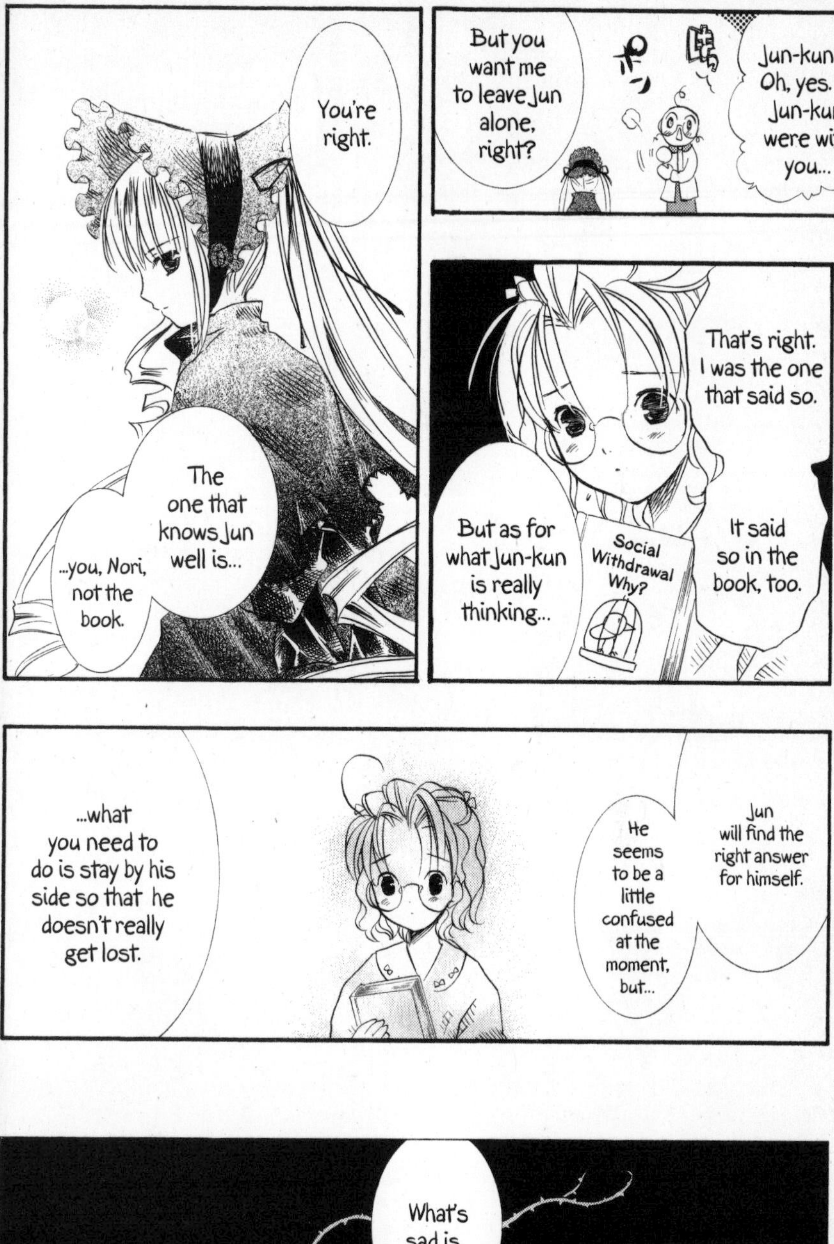
Jun-kun?! Oh, yes. If Jun-kun were with you...
But you want me to leave Jun alone, right?
That's right. I was the one that said so.
It said so in the book, too.
Social Withdrawal Why?
But as for what Jun-kun is really thinking...
You're right.
The one that knows Jun well is...
...you, Nori, not the book.
Jun will find the right answer for himself.
He seems to be a little confused at the moment, but...
...what you need to do is stay by his side so that he doesn't really get lost.
What's sad is...

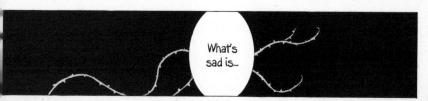

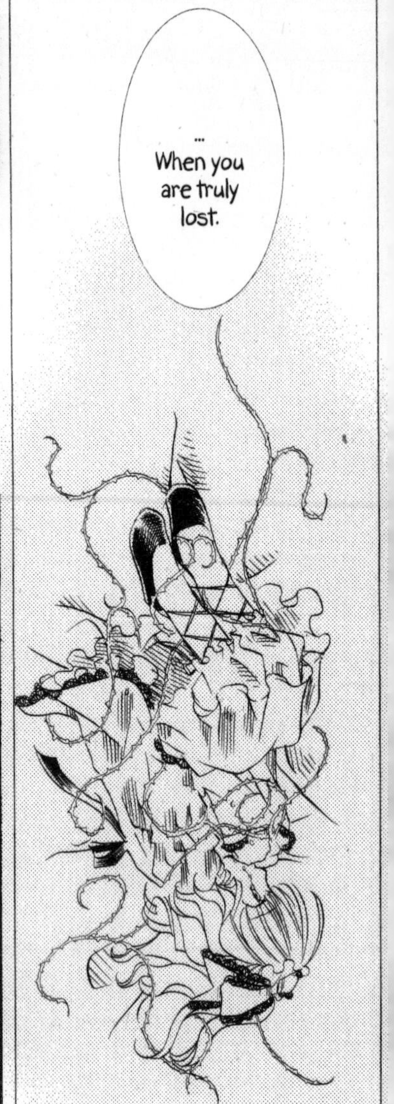

... When you are truly lost.

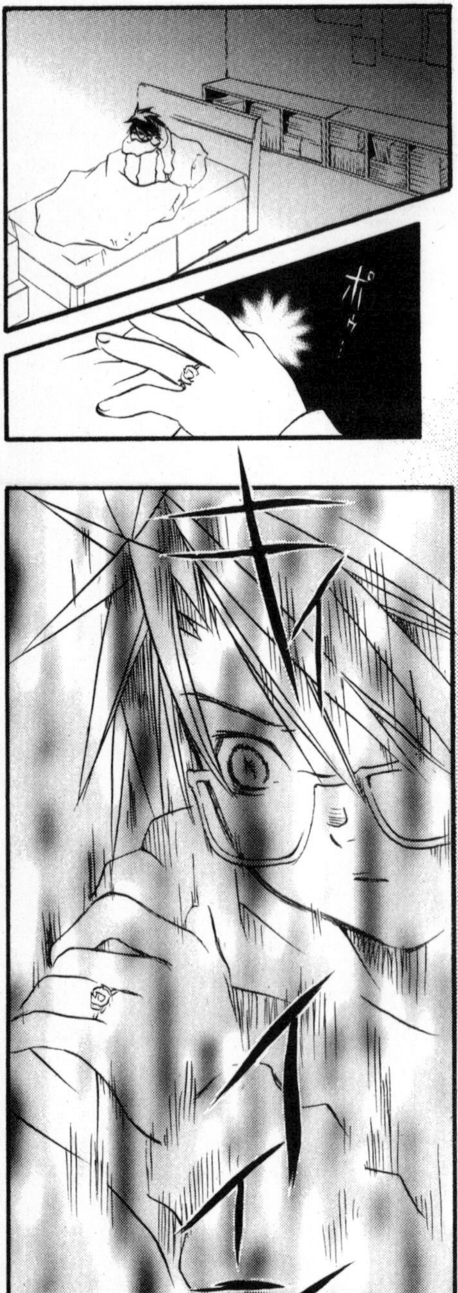

ポゥ…

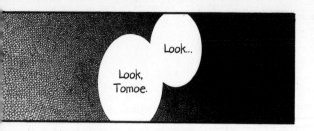

Look...

Look, Tomoe.

Look at all our friends here.

Where are we? Hiniachigo...

It's World Number 82633.

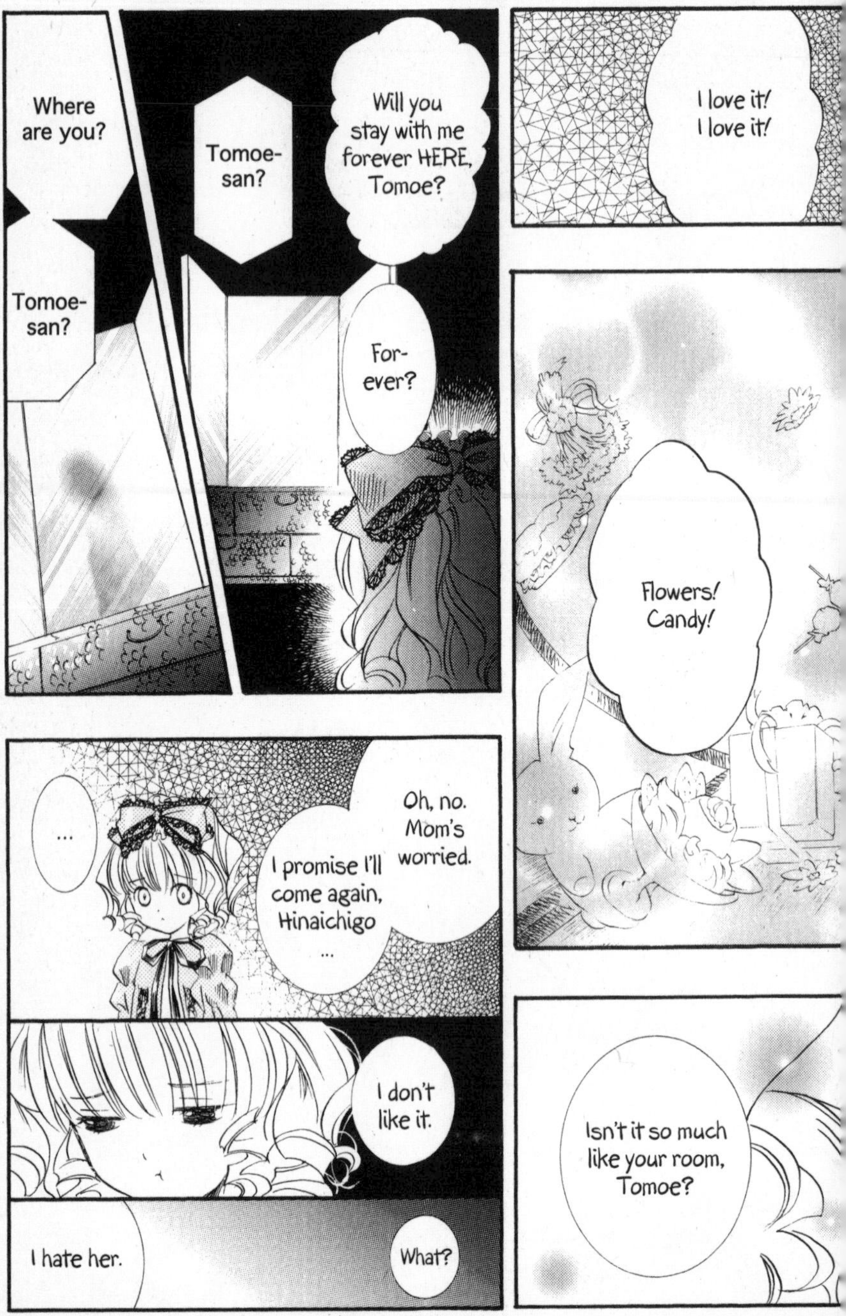
I love it!
I love it!
Flowers!
Candy!
Isn't it so much like your room, Tomoe?
Will you stay with me forever HERE, Tomoe?
For-
ever?
Tomoe-san?
Where are you?
Tomoe-san?
Oh, no. Mom's worried.
I promise I'll come again, Hinaichigo ...
...
I don't like it.
What?
I hate her.

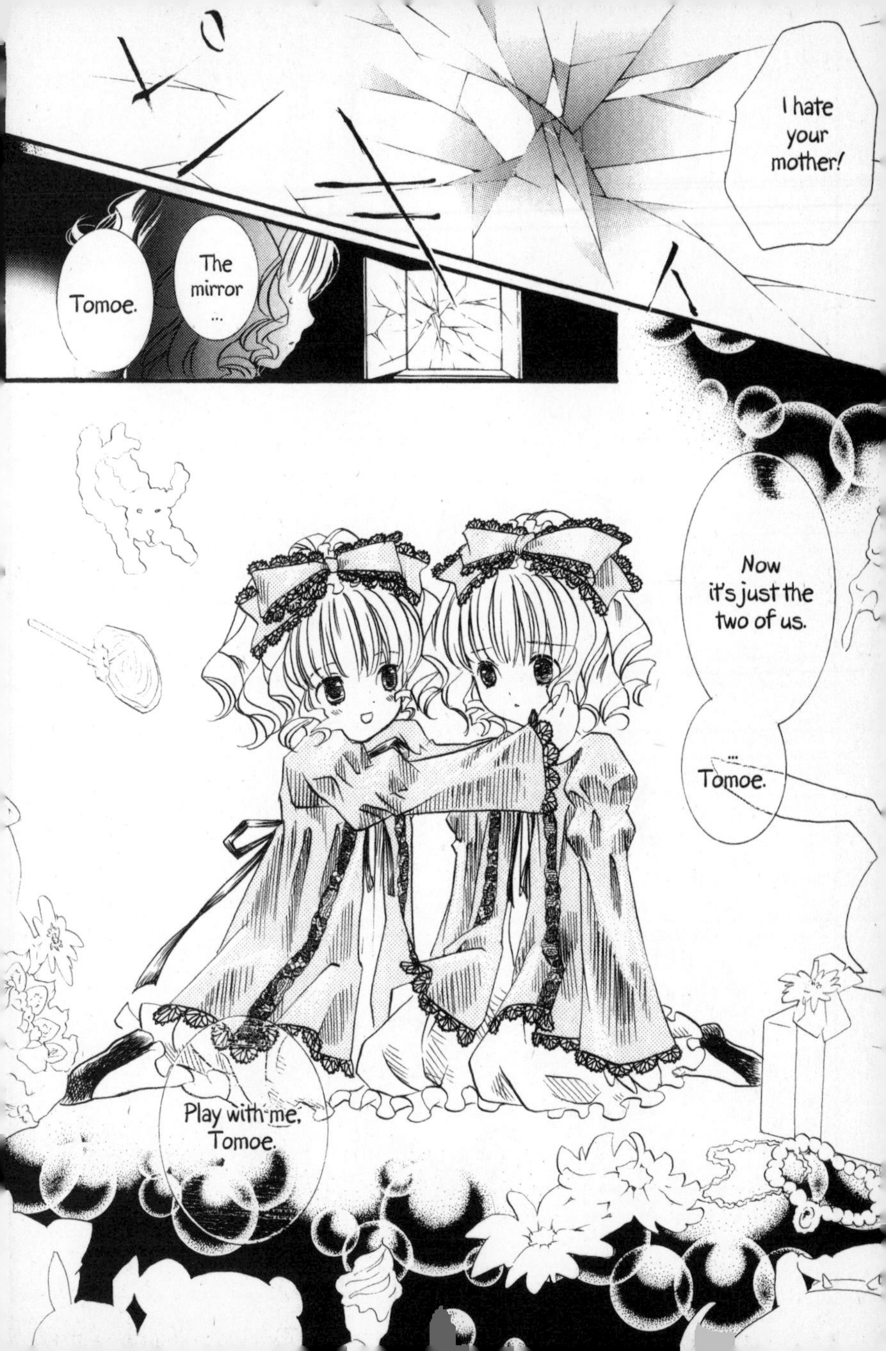
I hate your mother!
The mirror ...
Tomoe.
Now it's just the two of us.
... Tomoe.
Play with me, Tomoe.

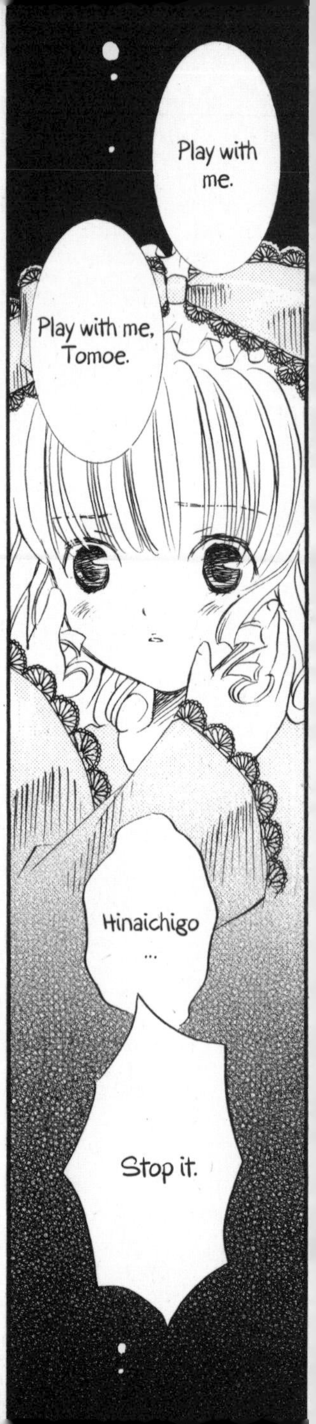
Play with me.
Play with me, Tomoe.
Hinaichigo ...
Stop it.

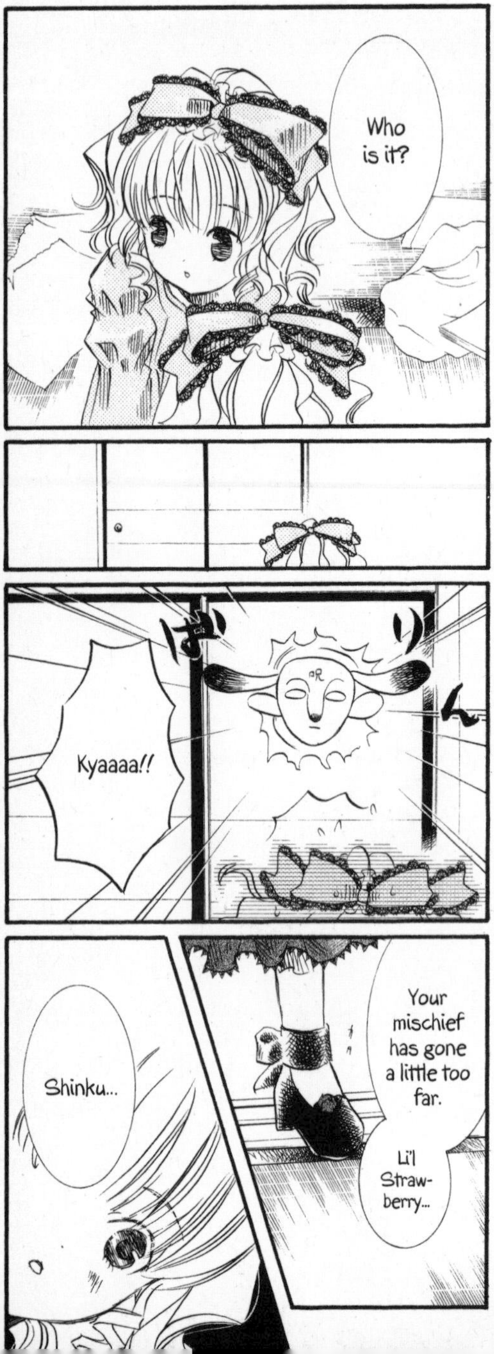
Who is it?
ぱりん
Kyaaaa!!
Your mischief has gone a little too far.
Li'l Straw-berry...
Shinku...

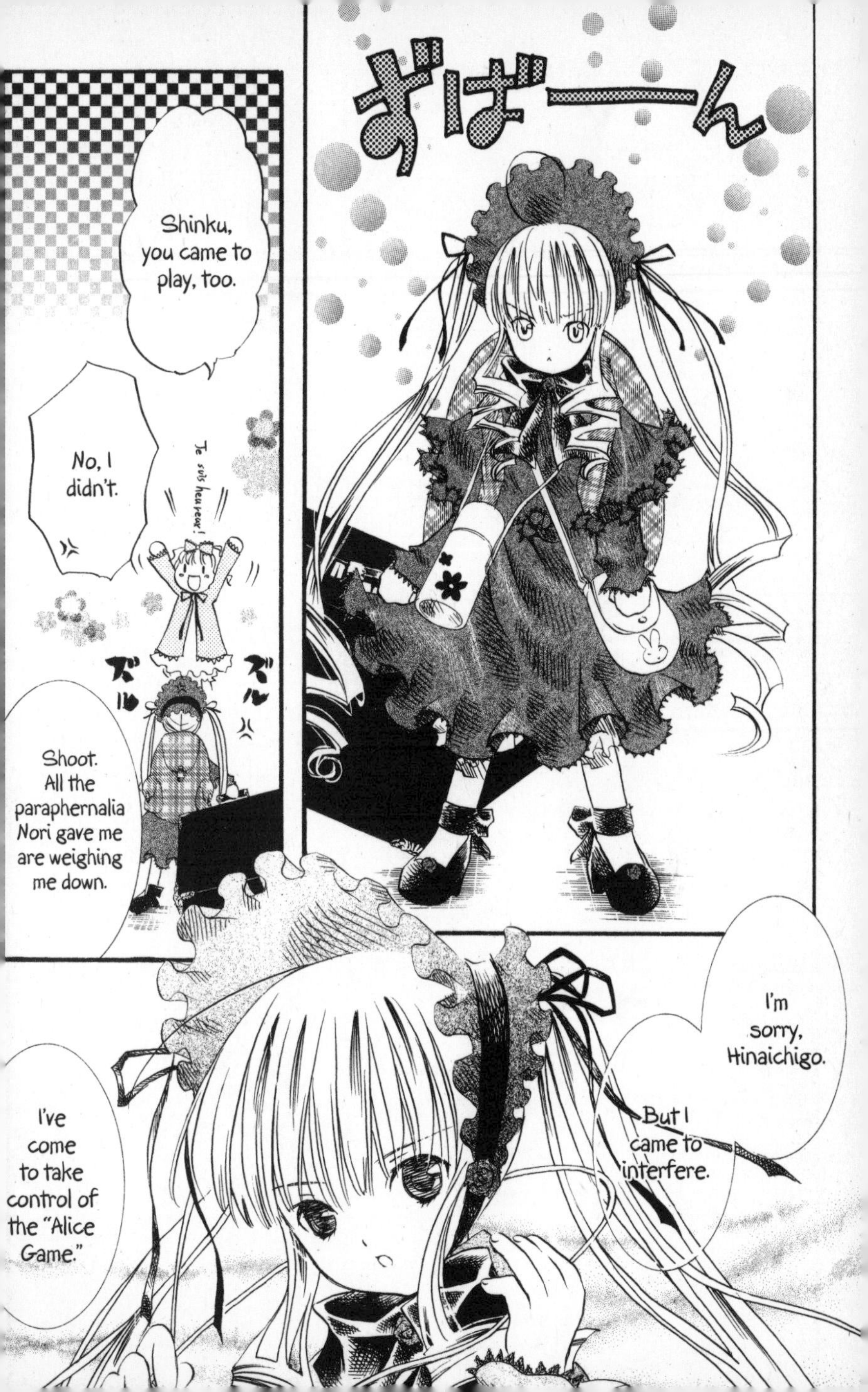
ずばーん
Shinku, you came to play, too.
No, I didn't.
Je suis heureux!
ズル ズル
Shoot. All the paraphernalia Nori gave me are weighing me down.
I'm sorry, Hinaichigo.
But I came to interfere.
I've come to take control of the "Alice Game."

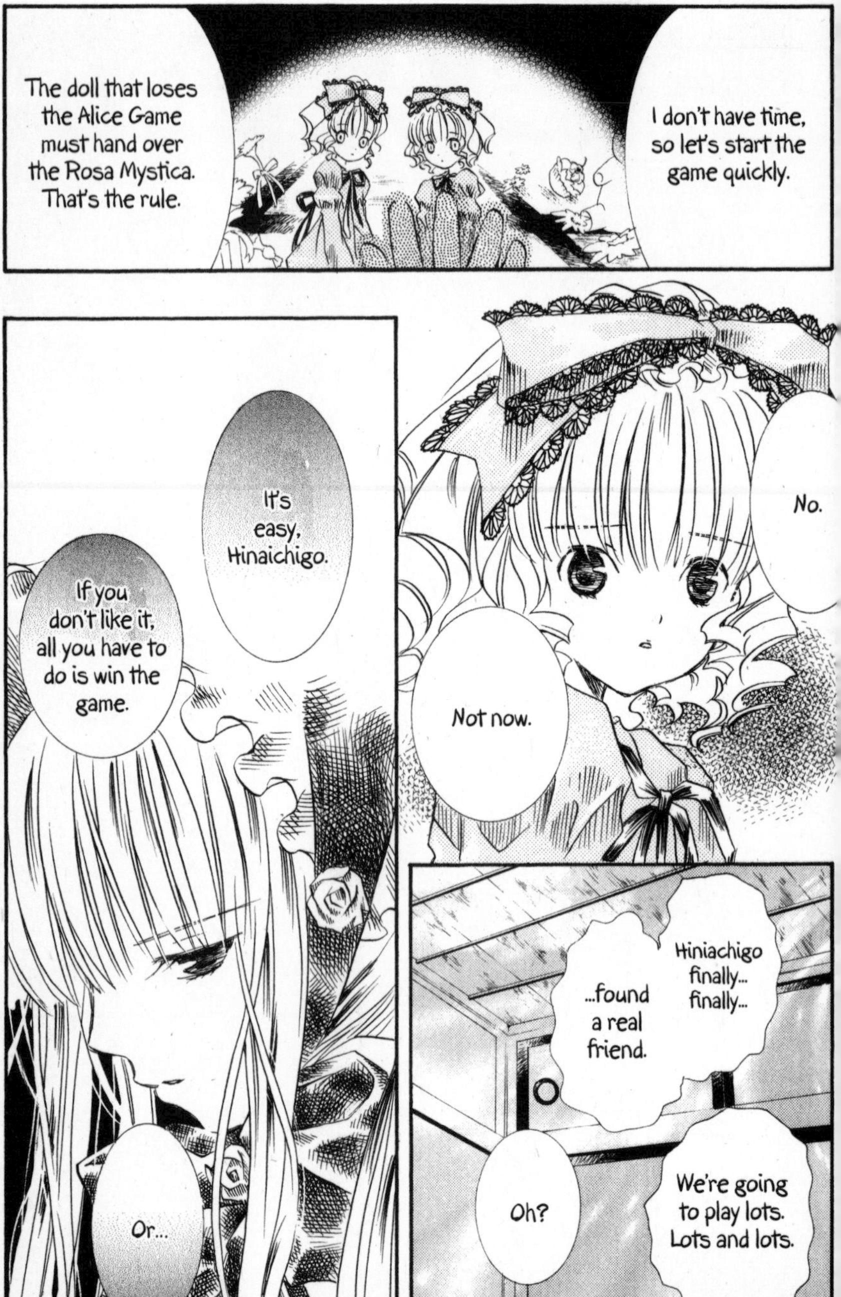
I don't have time, so let's start the game quickly.
The doll that loses the Alice Game must hand over the Rosa Mystica. That's the rule.
No.
Not now.
Hiniachigo finally... finally...
...found a real friend.
We're going to play lots. Lots and lots.
Oh?
It's easy, Hinaichigo.
If you don't like it, all you have to do is win the game.
Or...

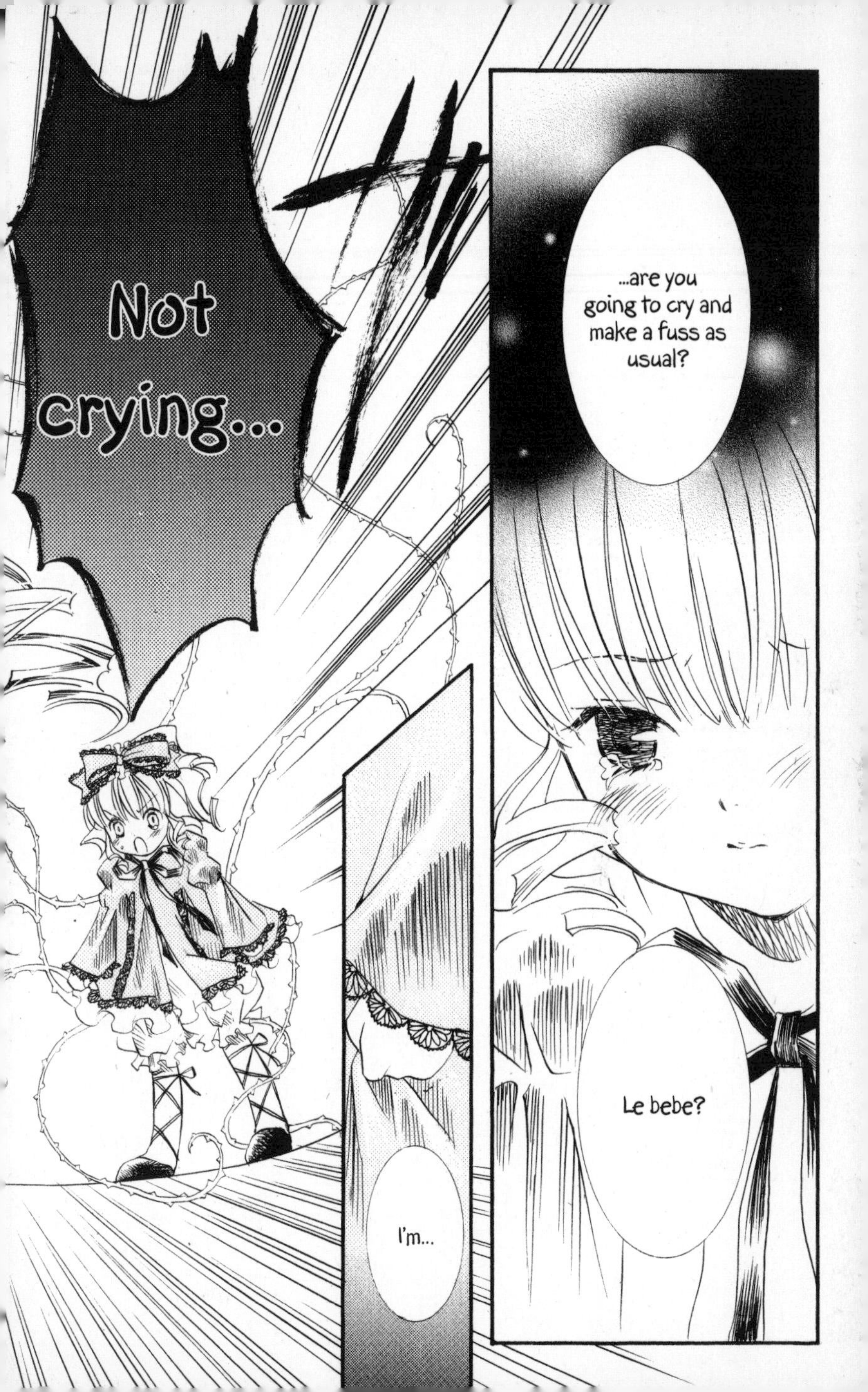
...are you going to cry and make a fuss as usual?
Le bebe?
I'm...
Not crying...

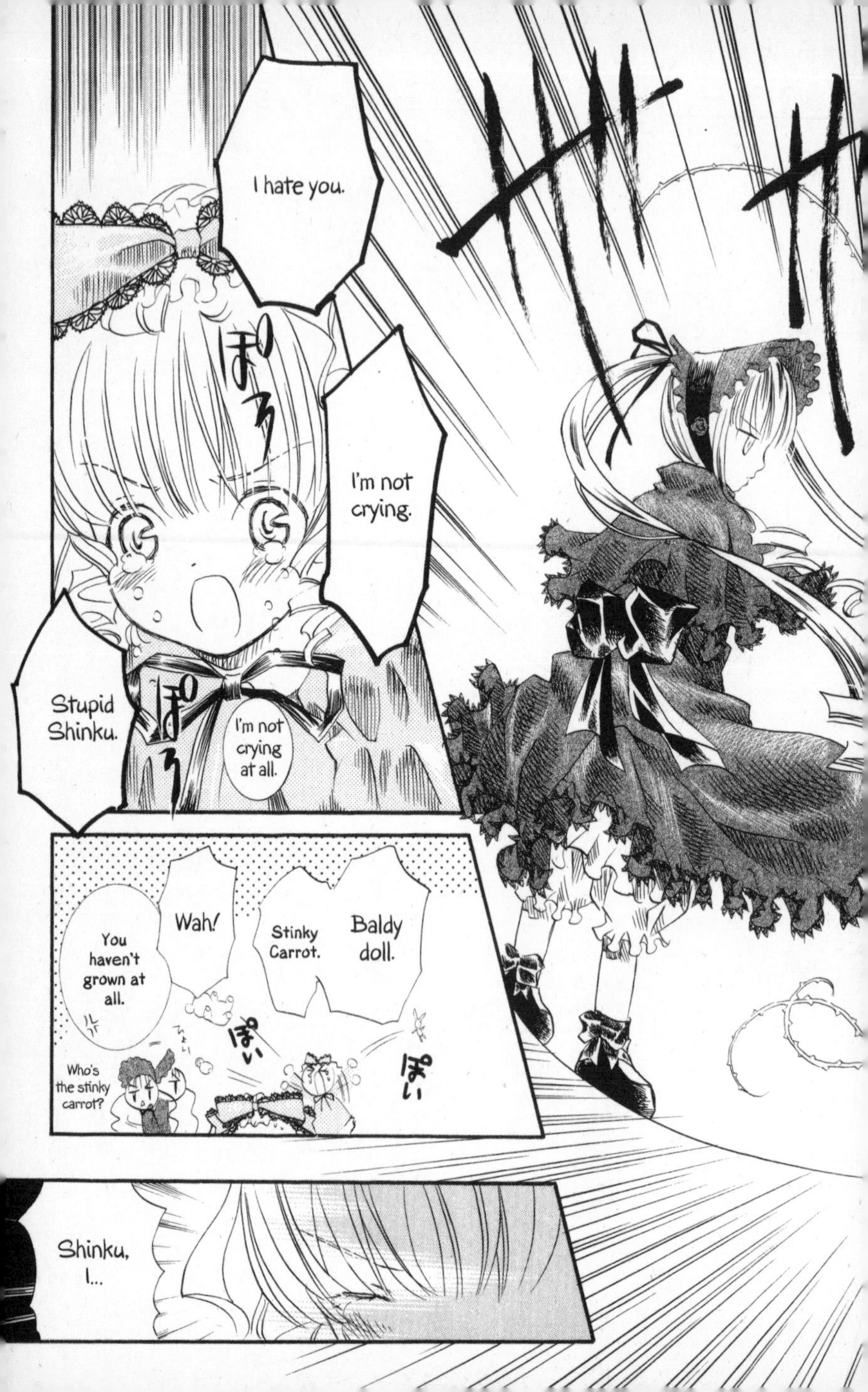

I hate you.
ぽろ
I'm not crying.
ぽろ
Stupid Shinku.
I'm not crying at all.
Baldy doll.
Stinky Carrot.
Wah!
You haven't grown at all.
ぽい
ぽい
Who's the stinky carrot?
Shinku, I...

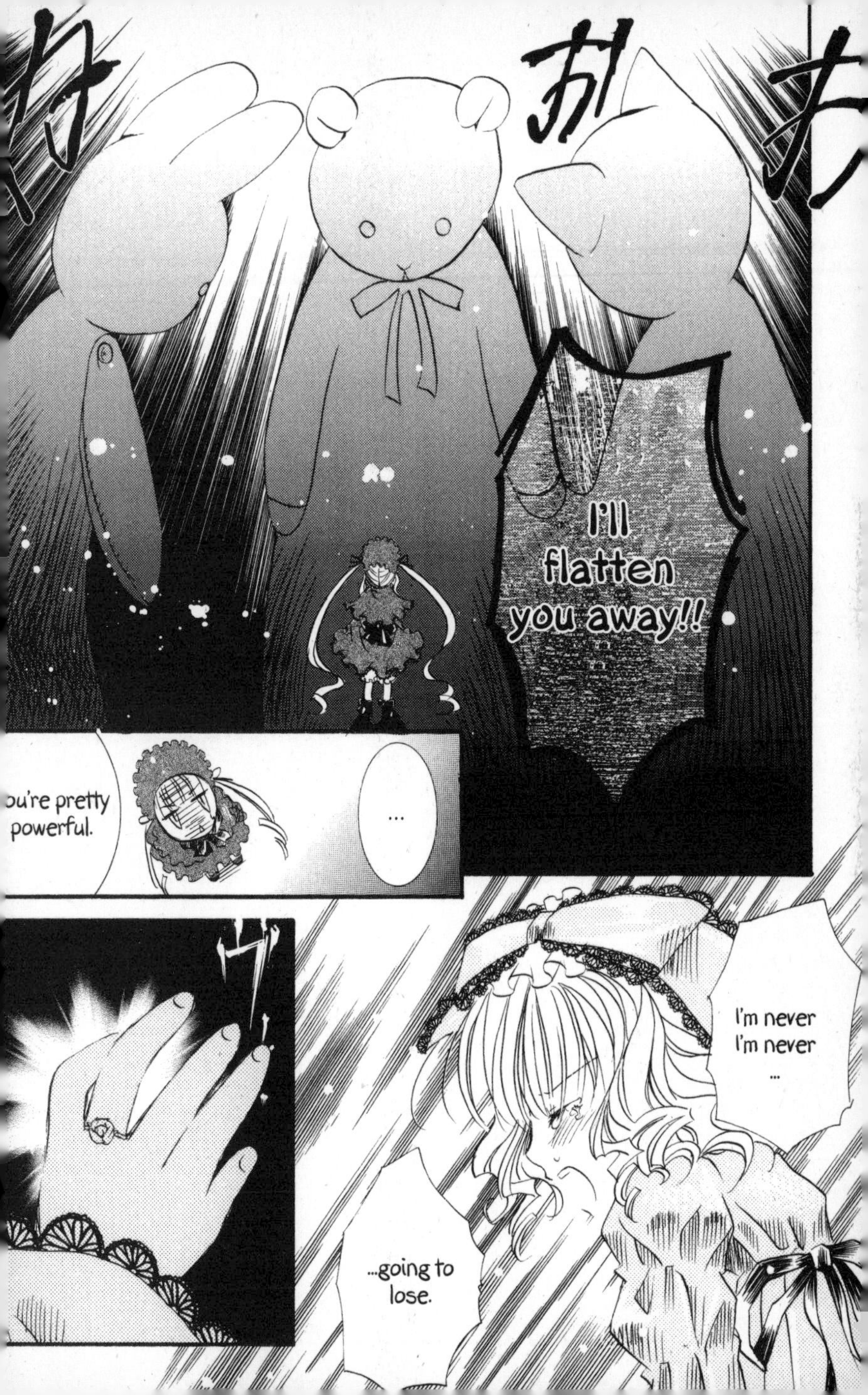
I'll flatten you away!!
...
ou're pretty powerful.
I'm never I'm never ...
...going to lose.

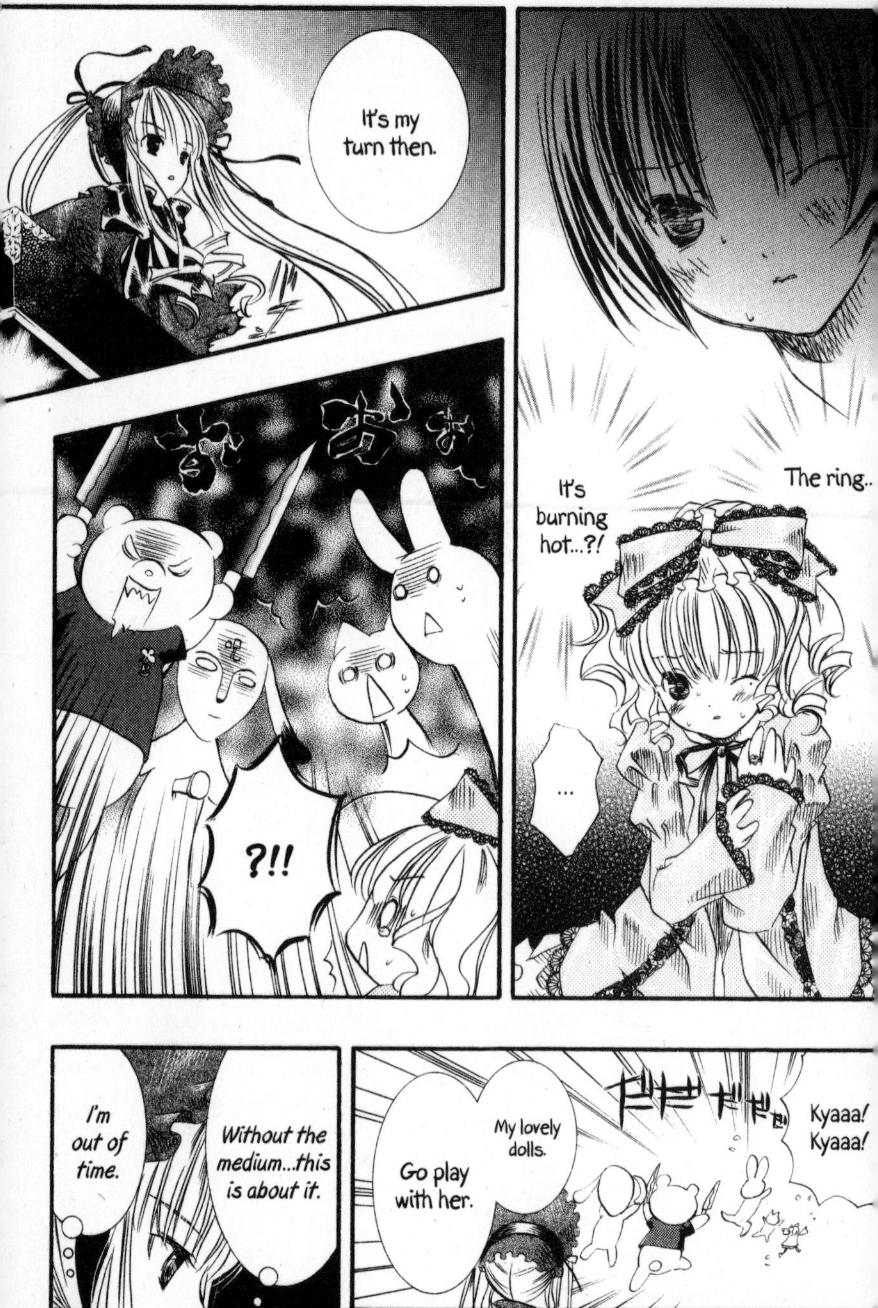
The ring..
It's burning hot...?!
...
It's my turn then.
?!!
My lovely dolls.
Go play with her.
Kyaaa! Kyaaa!
Without the medium...this is about it.
I'm out of time.

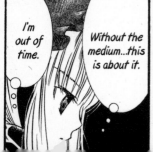

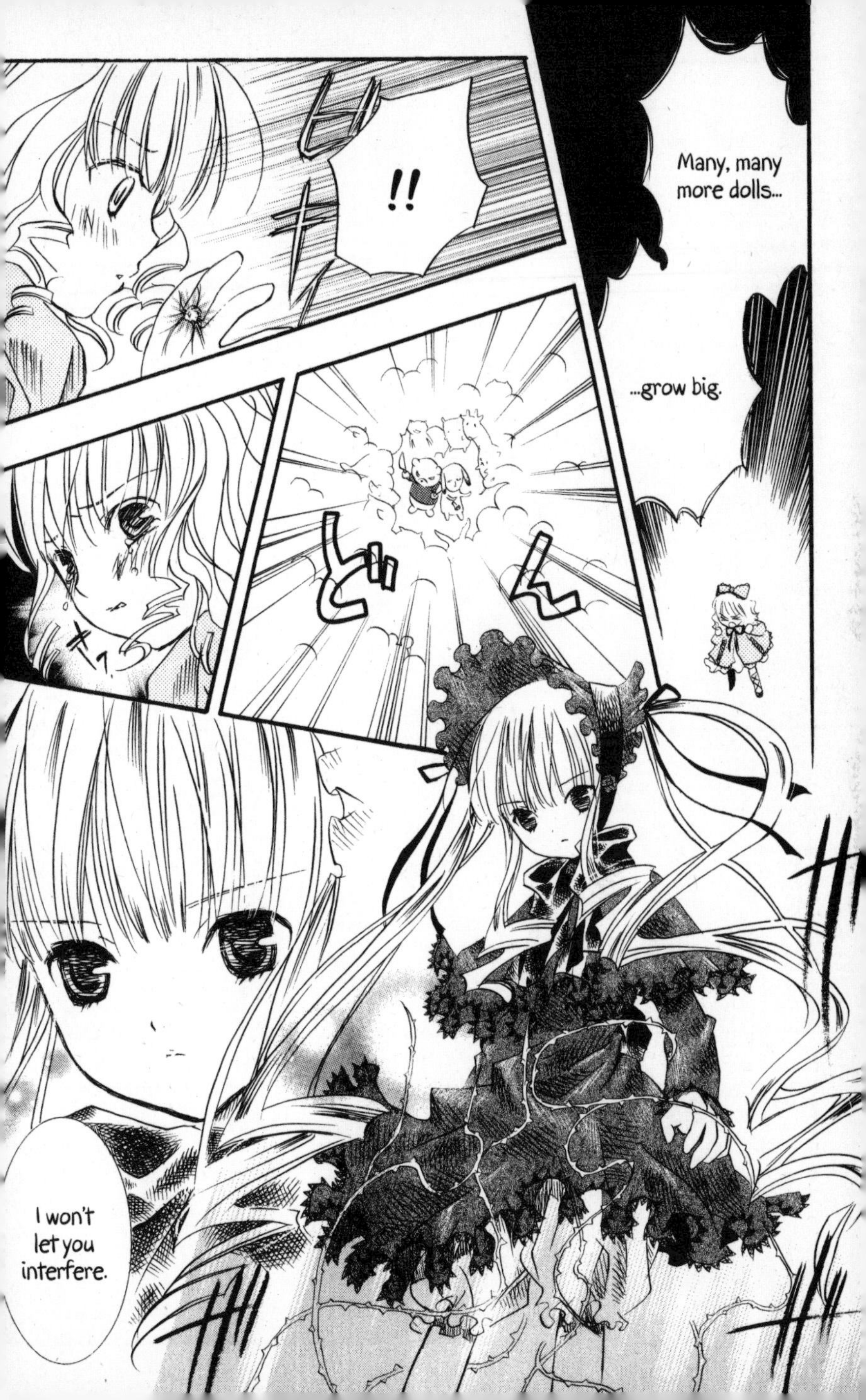
Many, many more dolls...
...grow big.
!!
どん
I won't let you interfere.

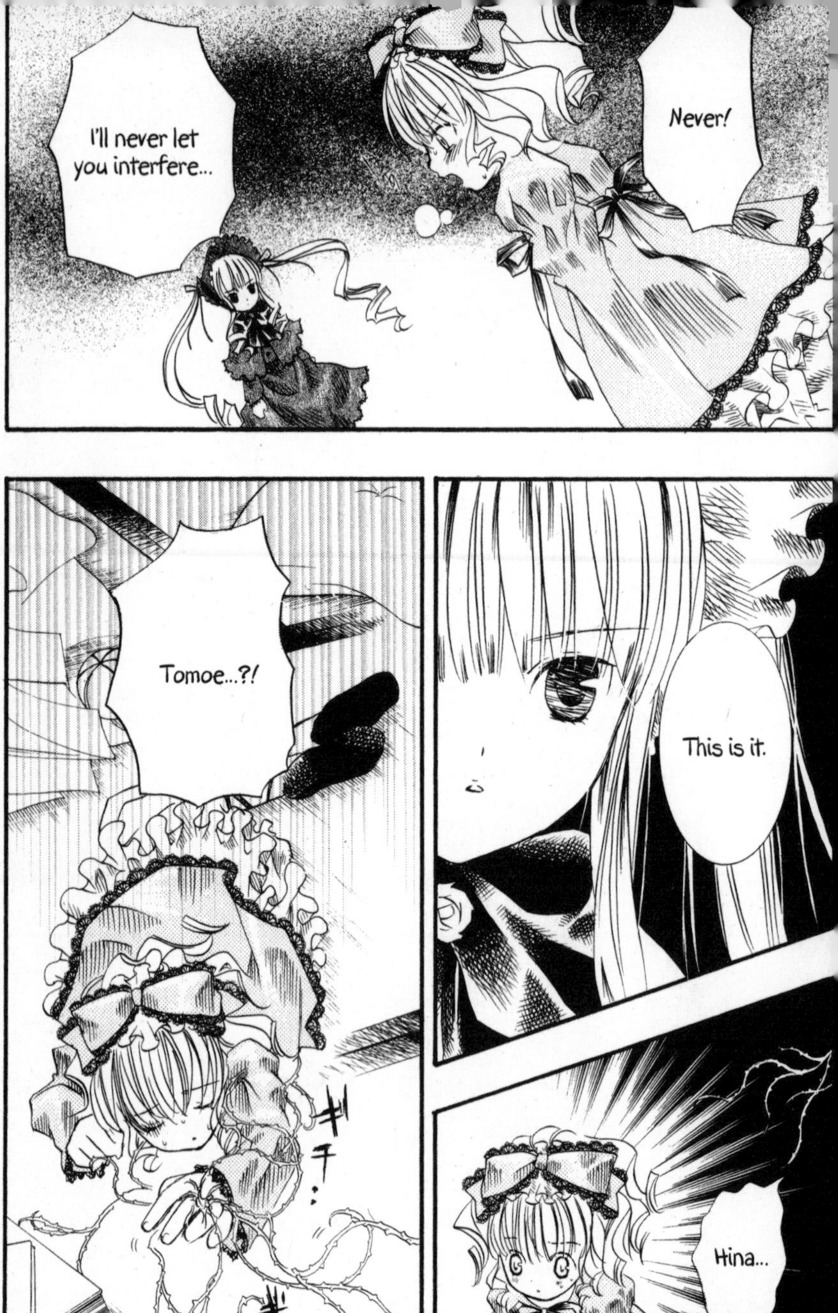

Never!
I'll never let you interfere...
This is it.
Hina...
Tomoe...?!
ギチ
ギチ

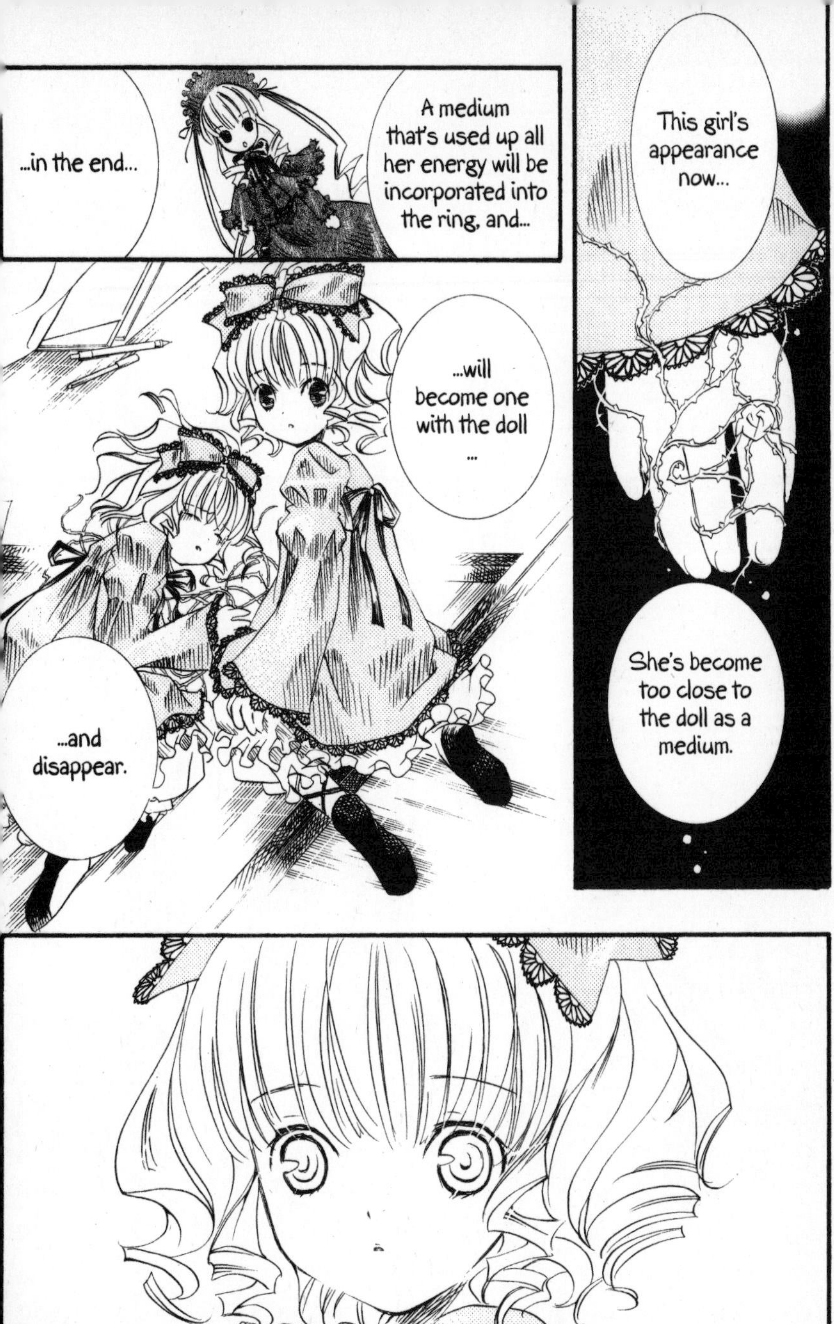
This girl's appearance now...
She's become too close to the doll as a medium.
A medium that's used up all her energy will be incorporated into the ring, and...
...in the end...
...will become one with the doll ...
...and disappear.

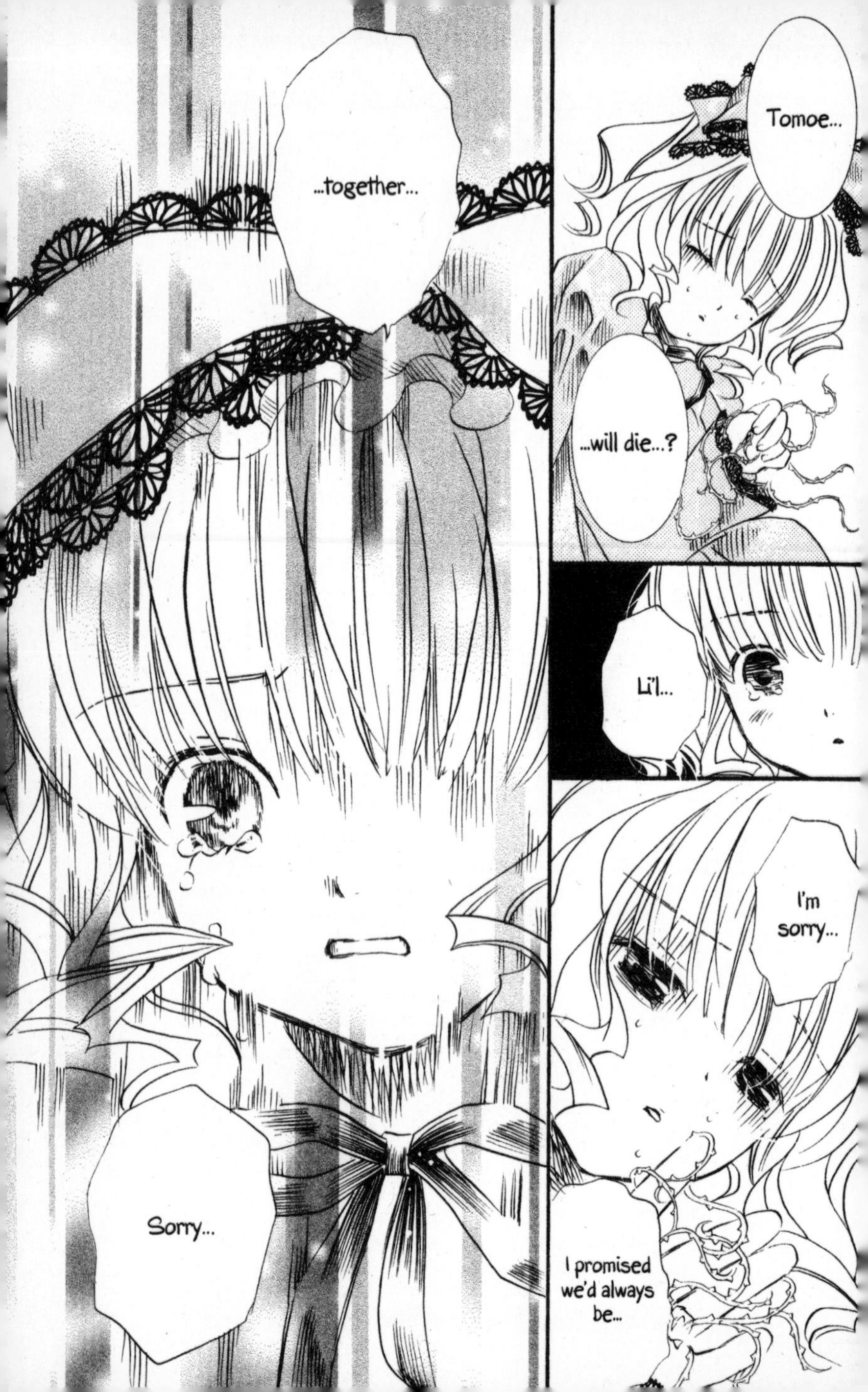
Tomoe...
...will die...?
Li'l...
I'm sorry...
I promised we'd always be...
...together...
Sorry...

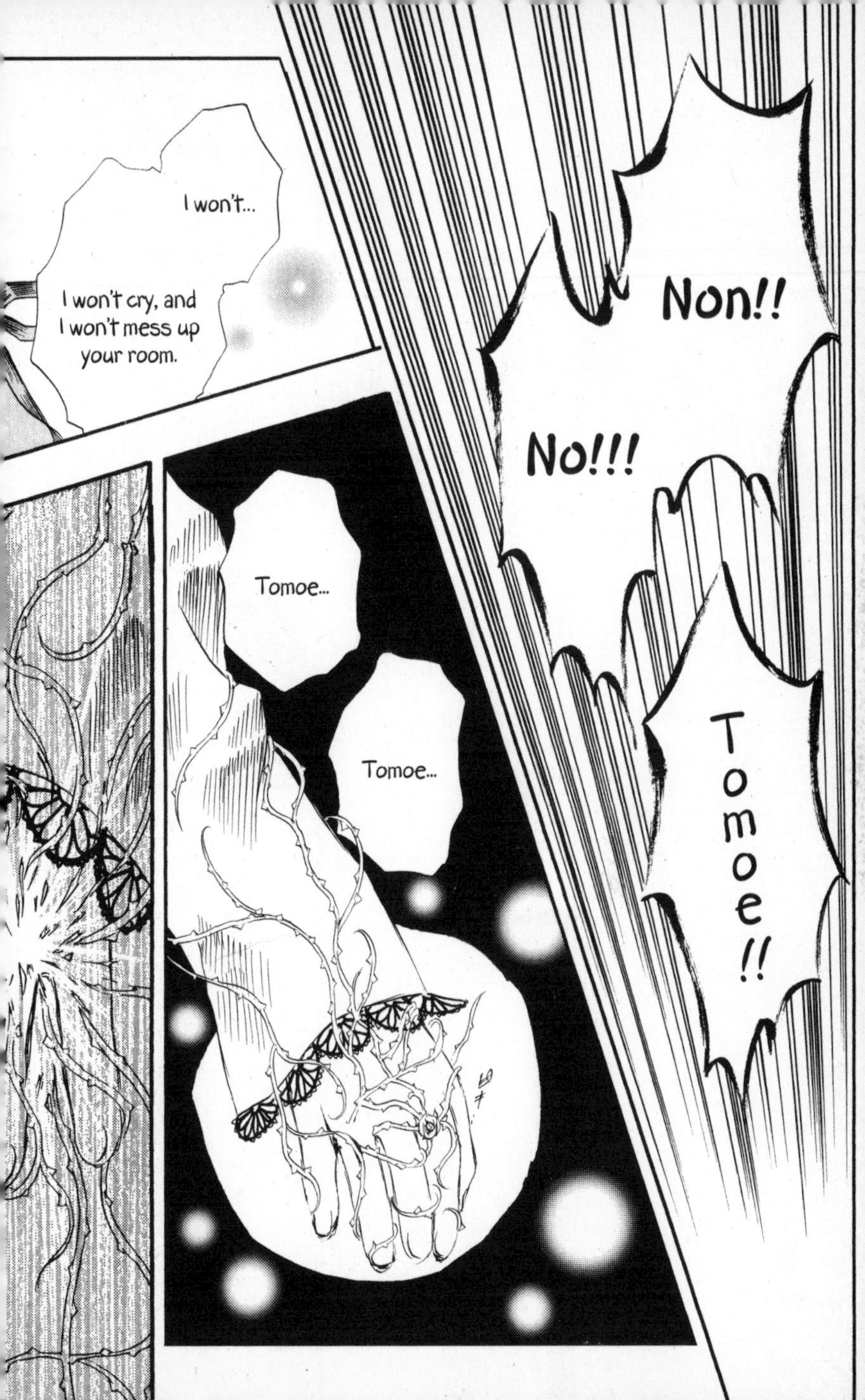
Non!!
No!!!
Tomoe!!
I won't...
I won't cry, and I won't mess up your room.
Tomoe...
Tomoe...

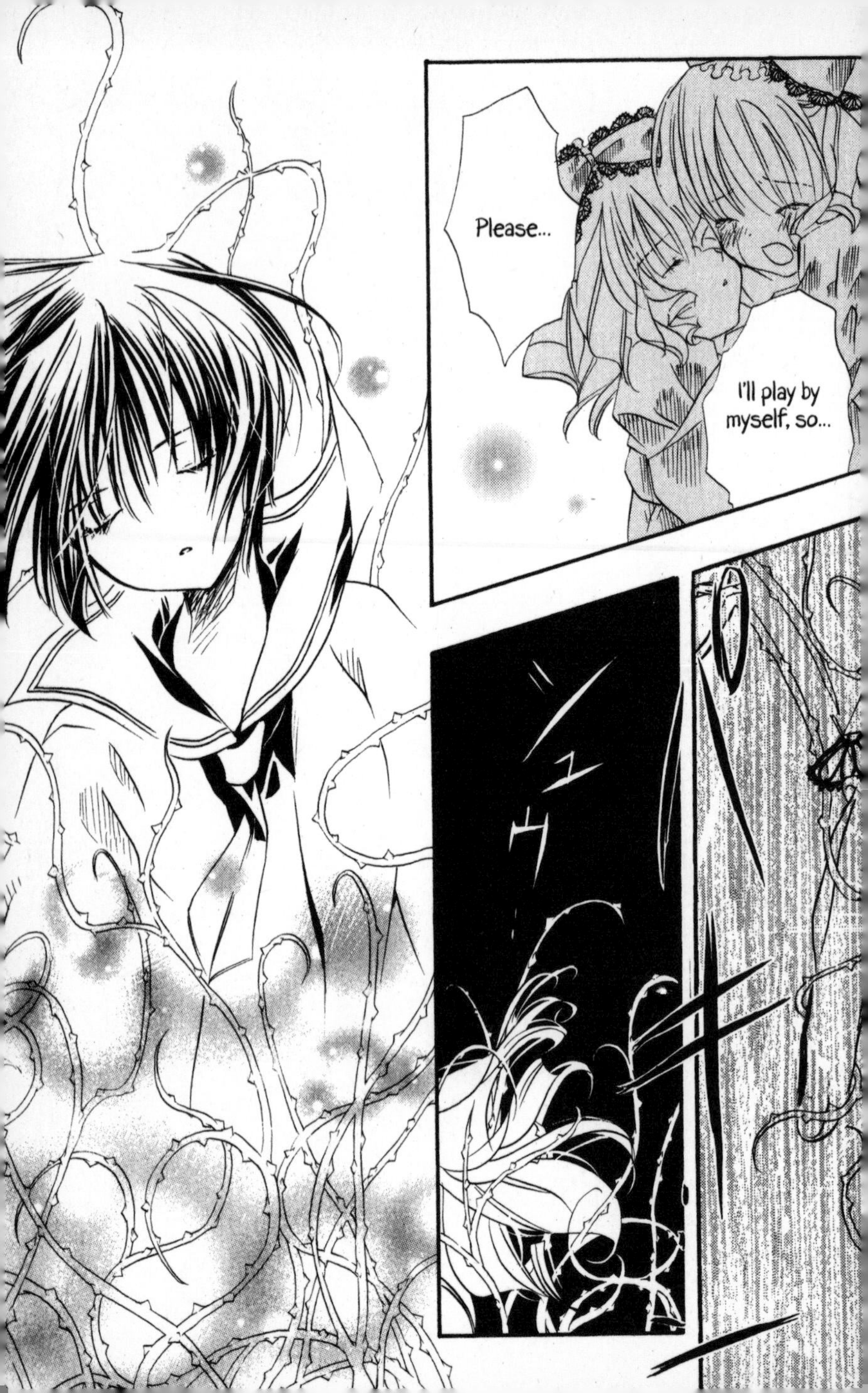
Please...
I'll play by myself, so...

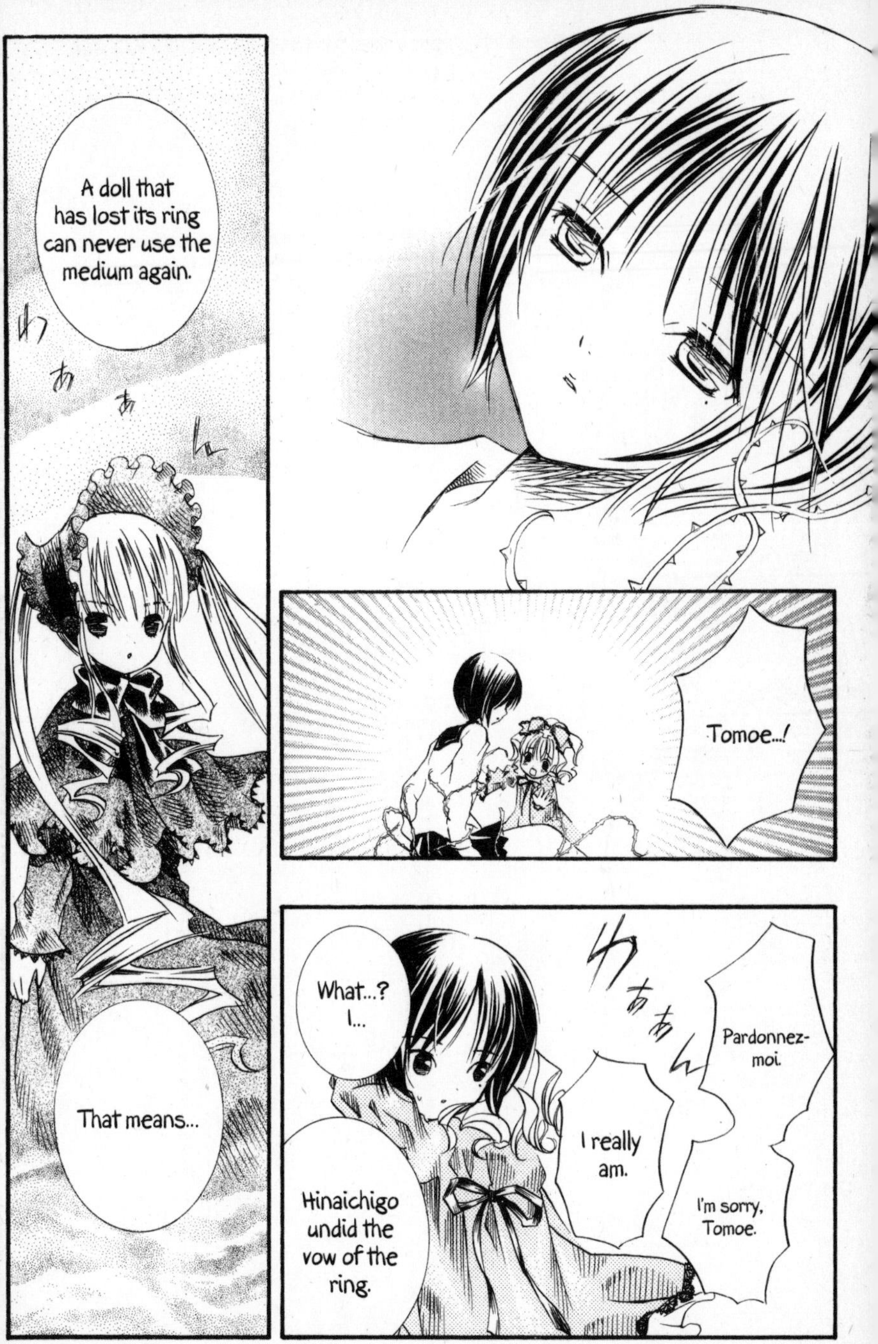
Tomoe...!
Pardonnez-moi.
わあぁん
I'm sorry, Tomoe.
I really am.
What...? I...
Hinaichigo undid the vow of the ring.
A doll that has lost its ring can never use the medium again.
わあぁん
That means...

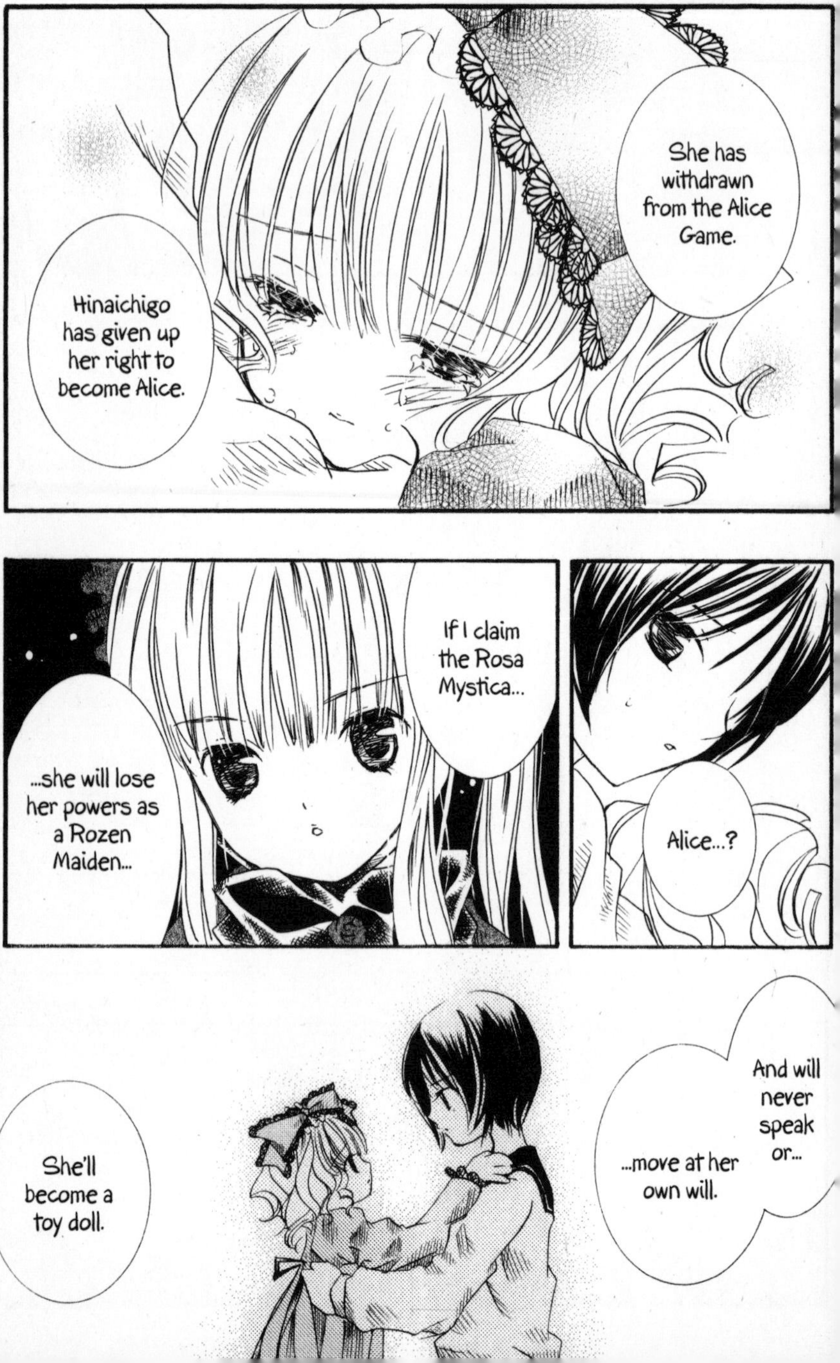
She has withdrawn from the Alice Game.
Hinaichigo has given up her right to become Alice.
Alice...?
If I claim the Rosa Mystica...
...she will lose her powers as a Rozen Maiden...
And will never speak or...
...move at her own will.
She'll become a toy doll.

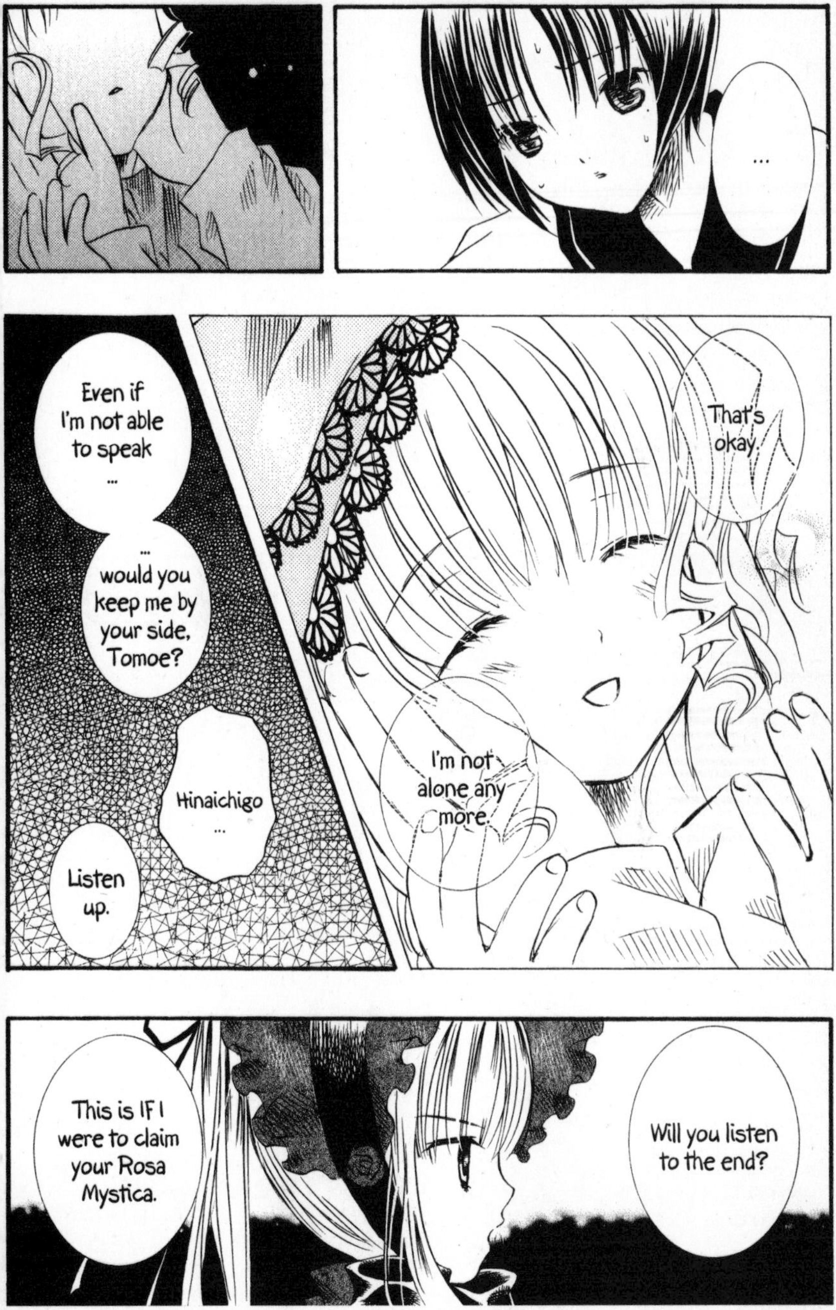
...
That's okay.
I'm not alone any more.
Even if I'm not able to speak ...
... would you keep me by your side, Tomoe?
Hinaichigo ...
Listen up.
Will you listen to the end?
This is IF I were to claim your Rosa Mystica.

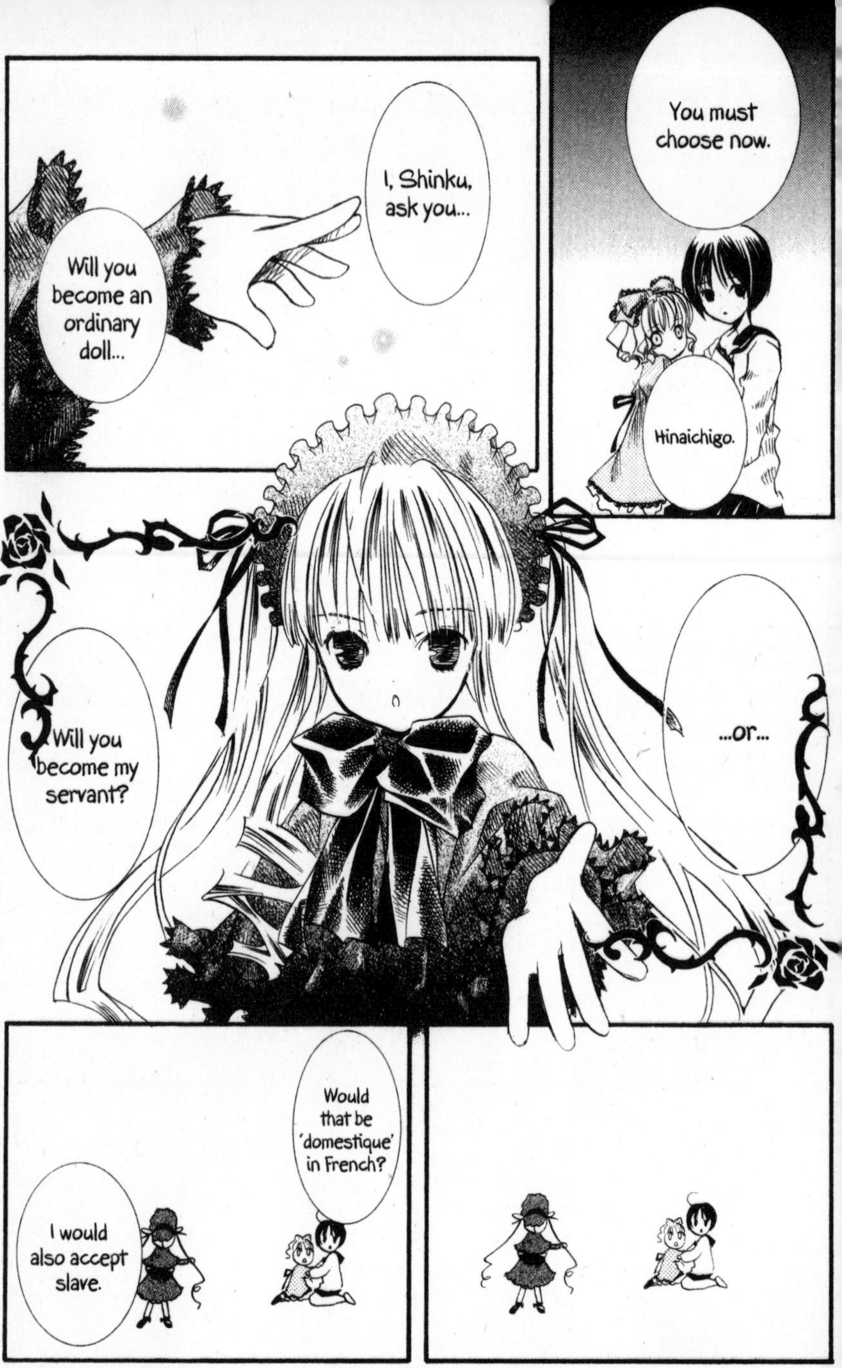
You must choose now.
Hinaichigo.
I, Shinku, ask you...
Will you become an ordinary doll...
...or...
Will you become my servant?
Would that be 'domestique' in French?
I would also accept slave.

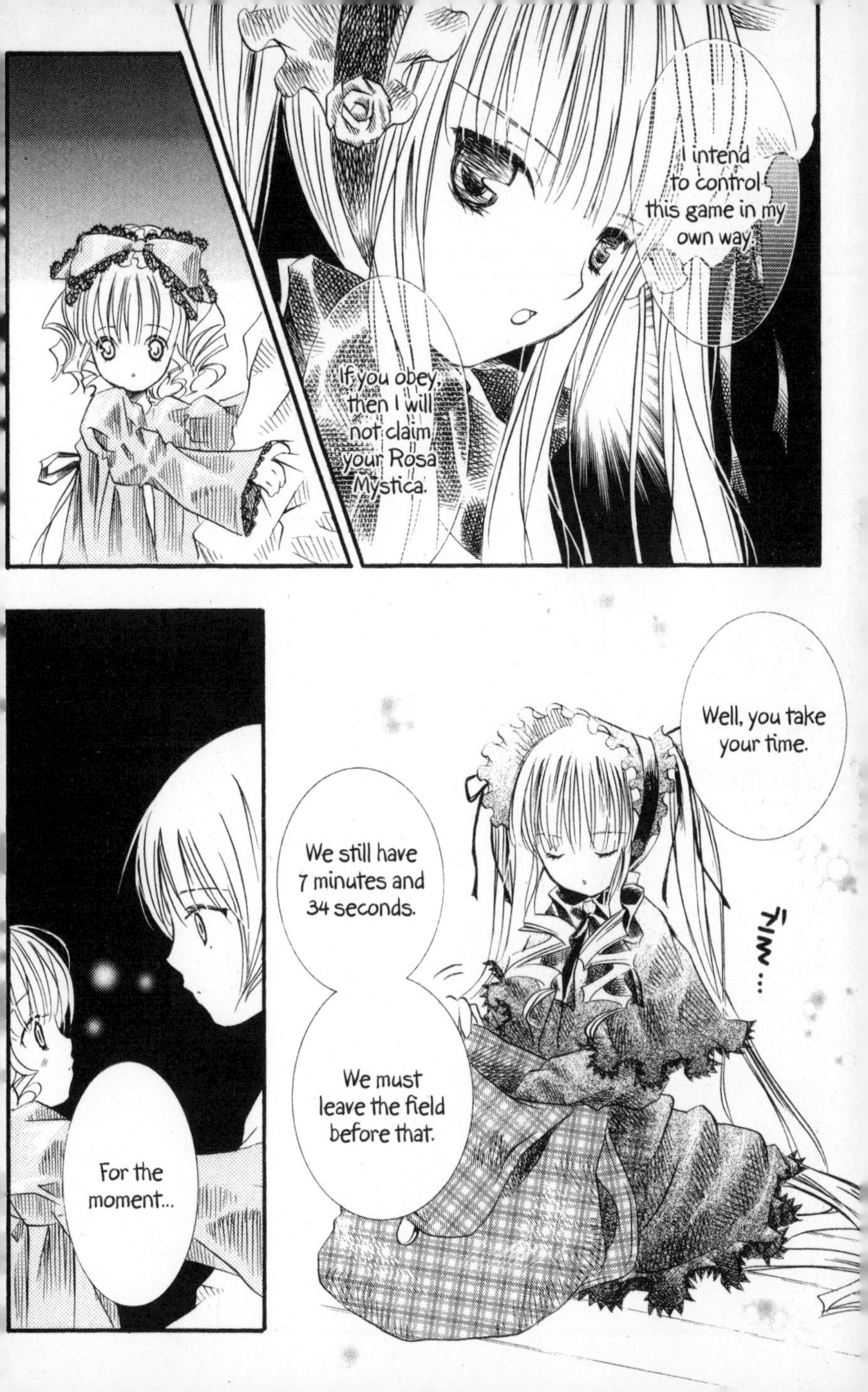
I intend to control this game in my own way.
If you obey, then I will not claim your Rosa Mystica.
Well, you take your time.
We still have 7 minutes and 34 seconds.
We must leave the field before that.
For the moment...

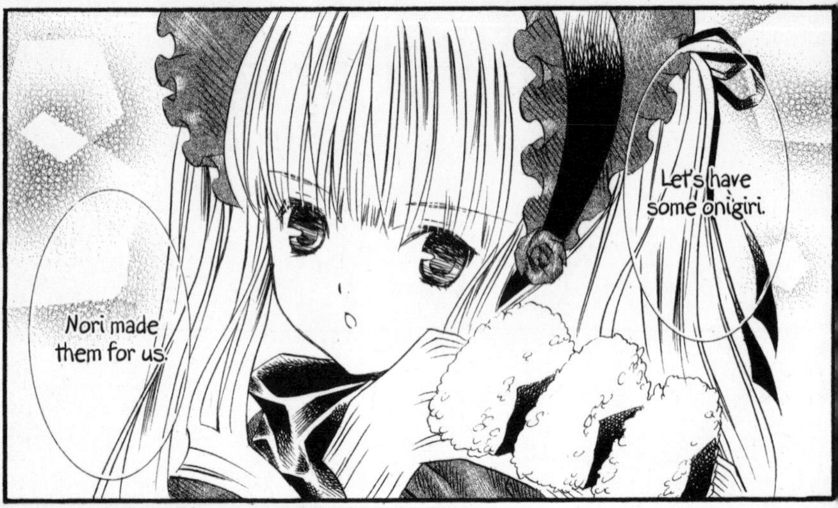
Let's have some onigiri.
Nori made them for us.

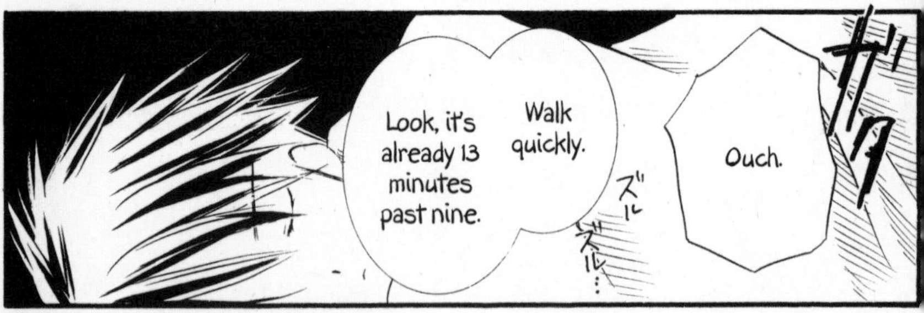
Ouch.
ズル ズル…
Walk quickly.
Look, it's already 13 minutes past nine.

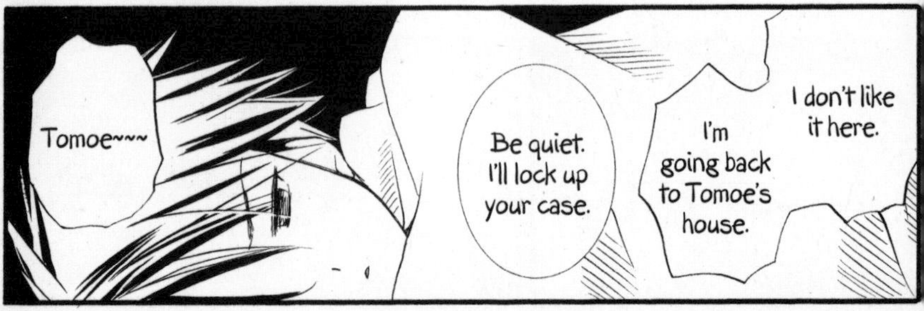
I don't like it here.
I'm going back to Tomoe's house.
Be quiet. I'll lock up your case.
Tomoe~~~

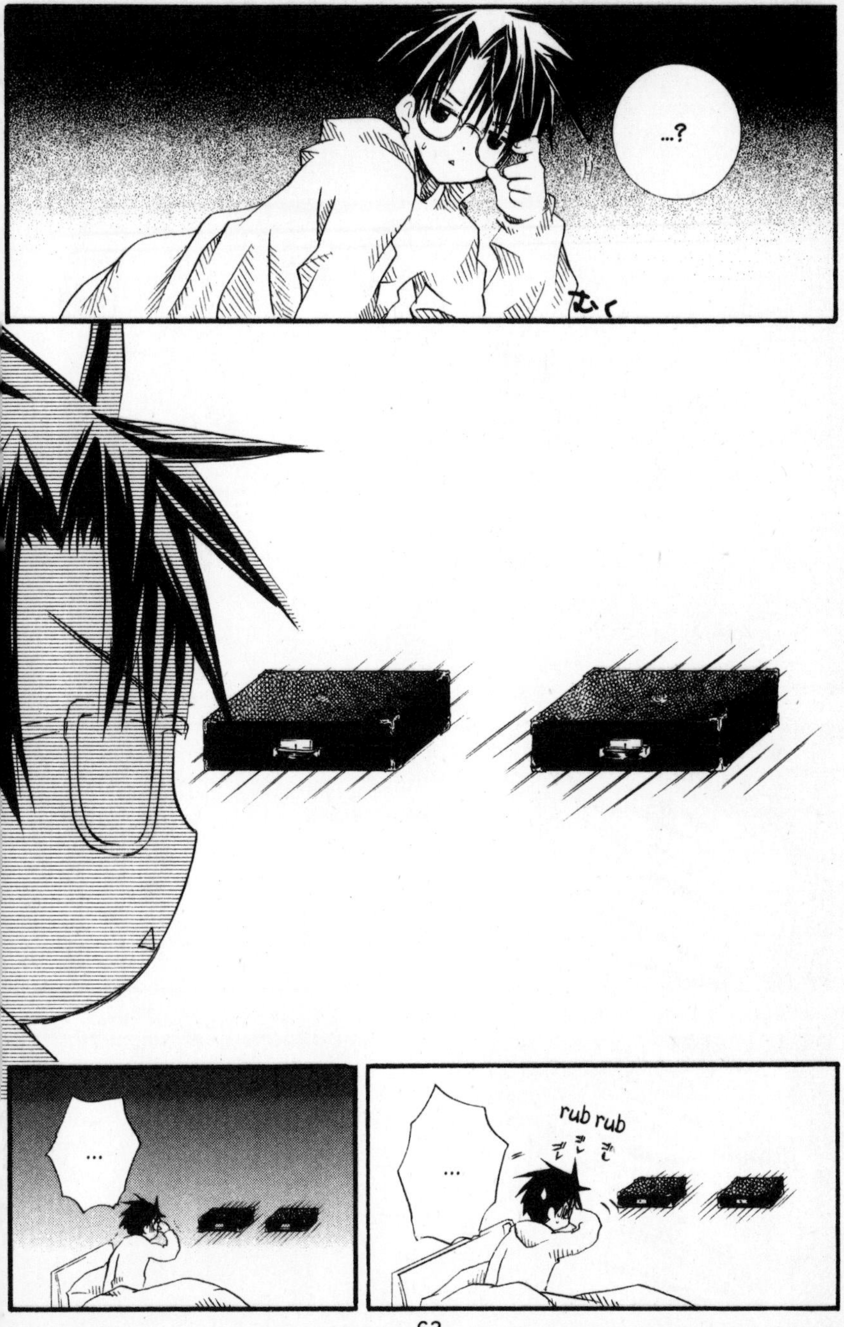
...?
むく
...
rub rub
...

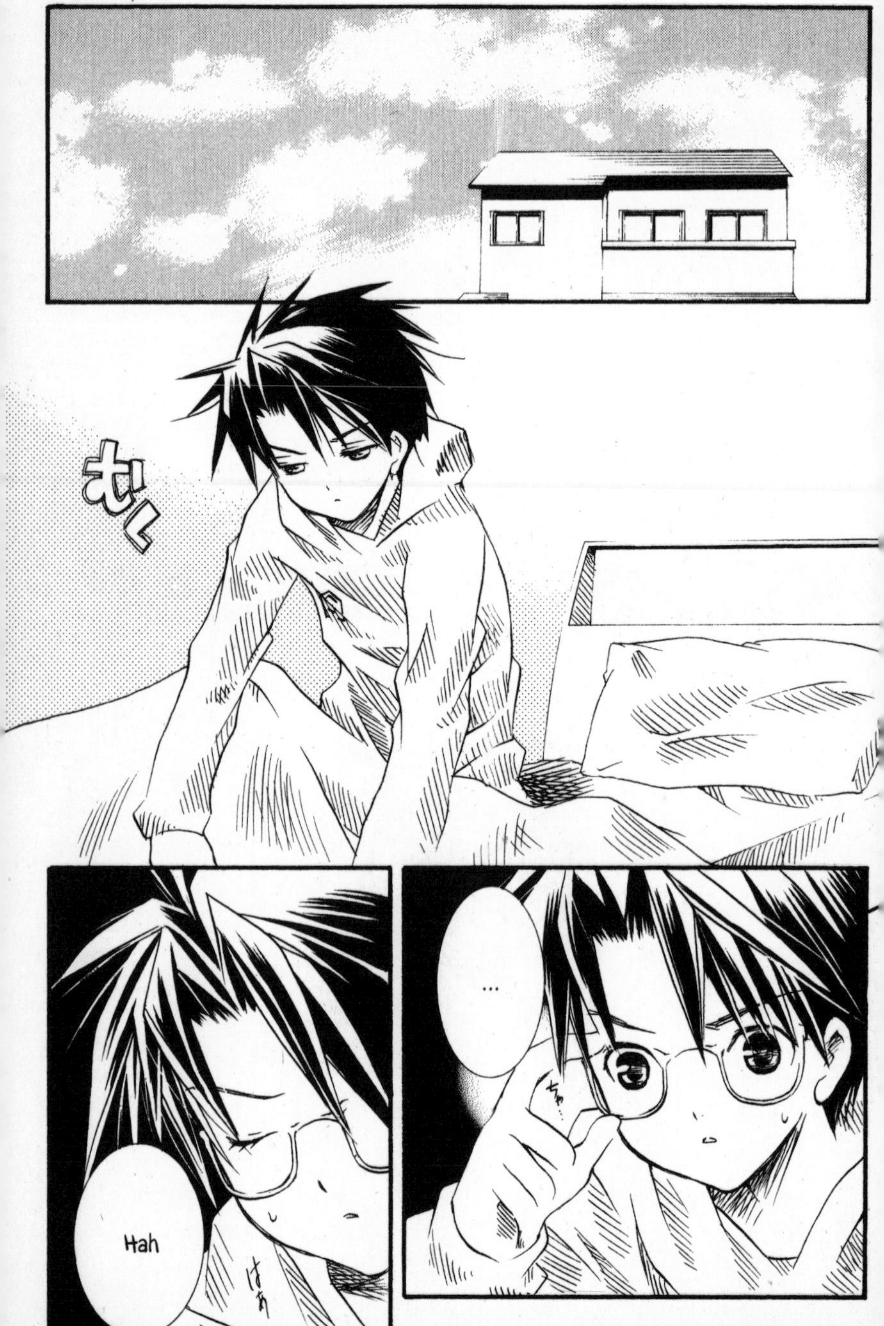
むく
...
Hah

Phase 7

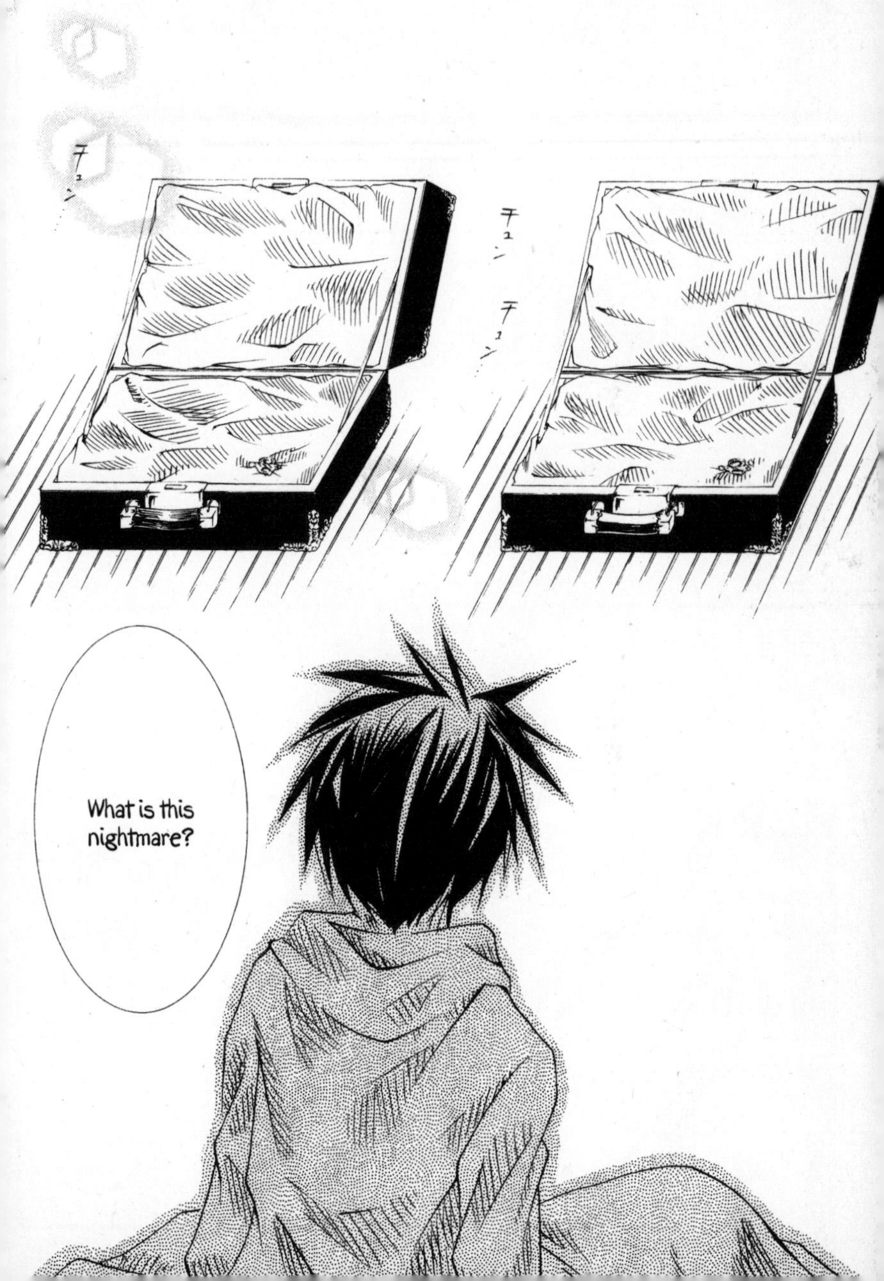

チュン
チュン
チュン
What is this nightmare?

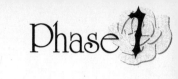

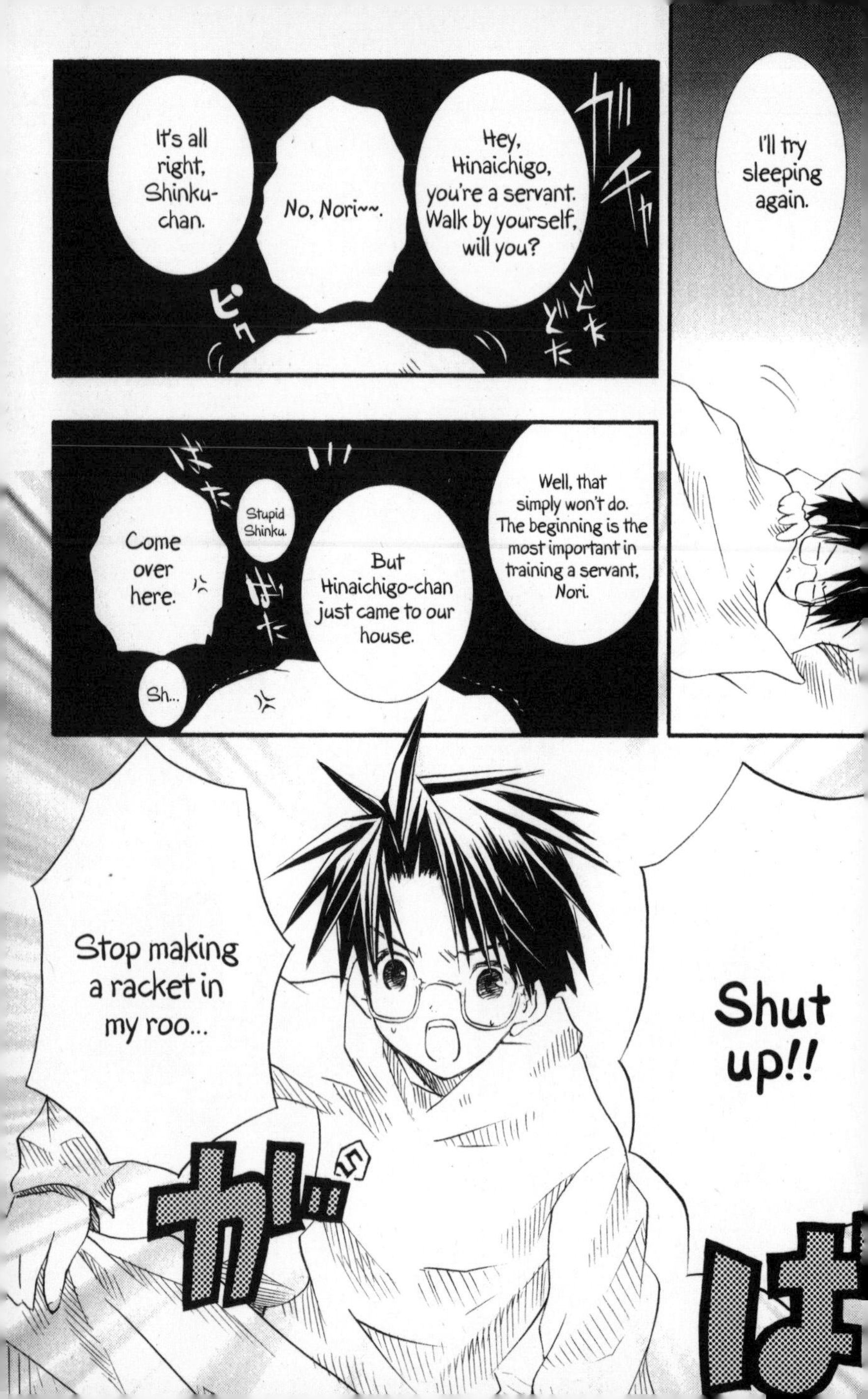
I'll try sleeping again.
Hey, Hinaichigo, you're a servant. Walk by yourself, will you?
No, Nori~~.
It's all right, Shinku-chan.
Well, that simply won't do. The beginning is the most important in training a servant, Nori.
But Hinaichigo-chan just came to our house.
Stupid Shinku.
Come over here.
Sh...
Stop making a racket in my roo...
Shut up!!

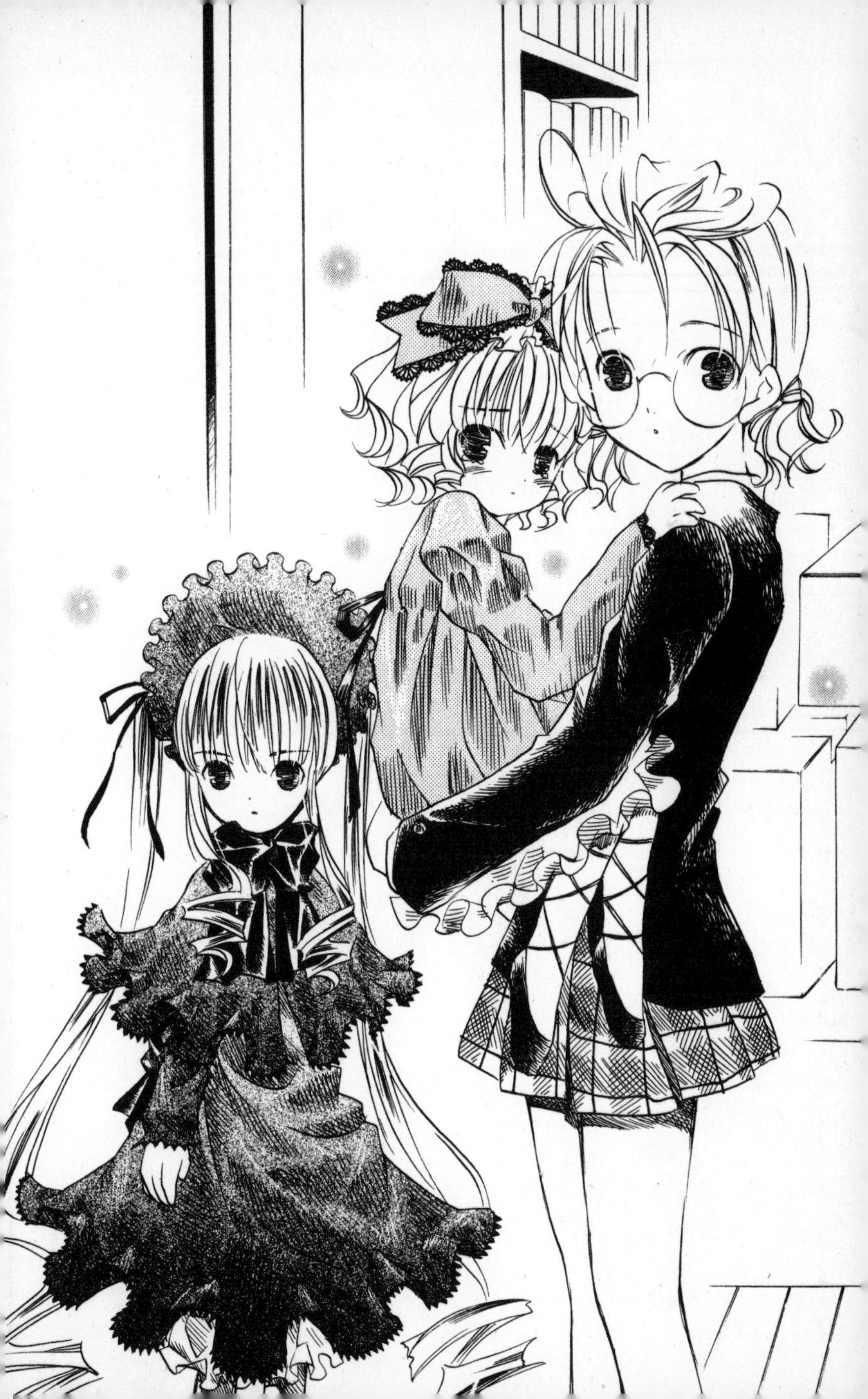

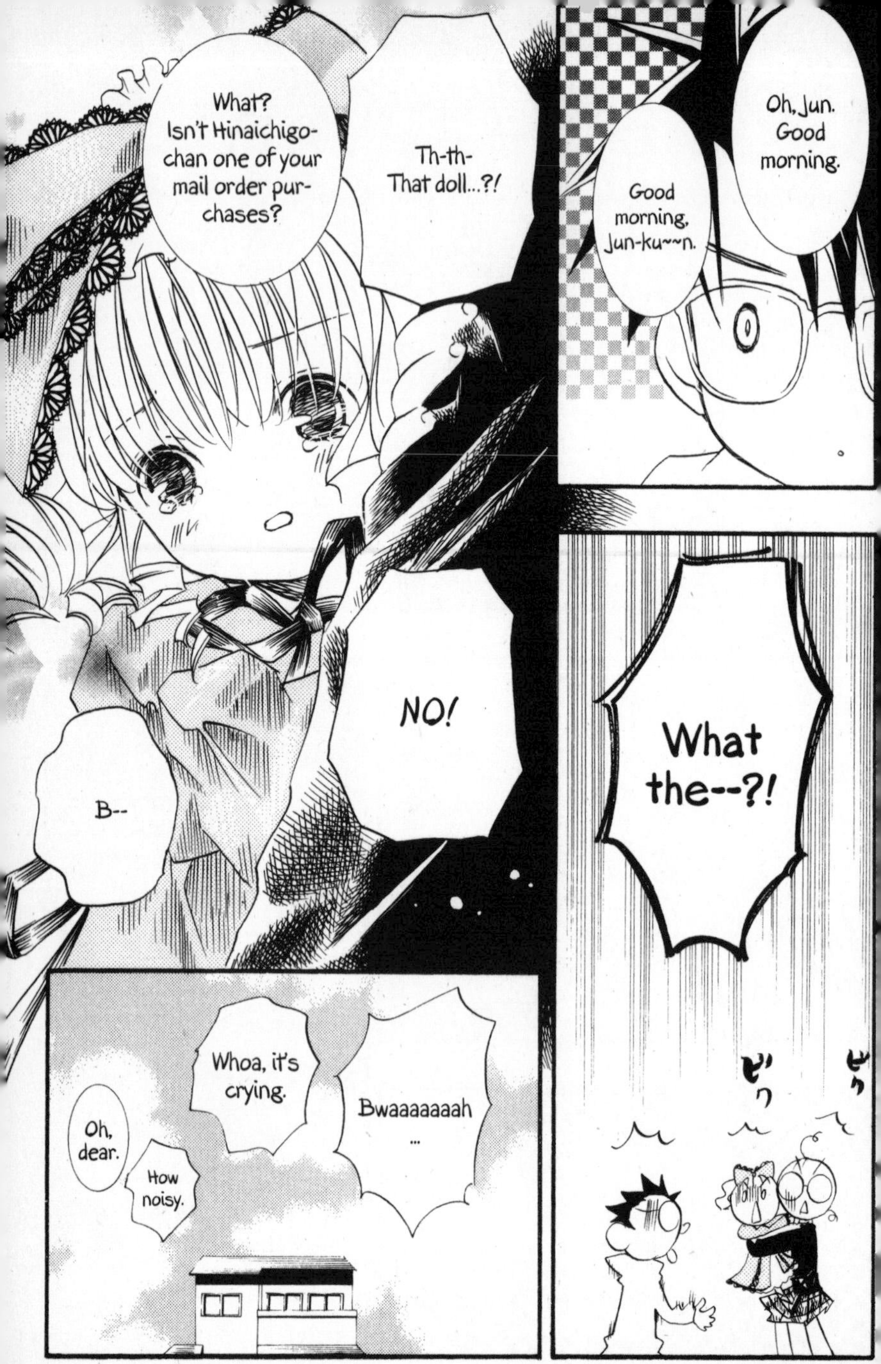
Oh, Jun. Good morning.
Good morning, Jun-ku~~n.
What the--?!
ビク
ビク
Th-th- That doll...?!
What? Isn't Hinaichigo-chan one of your mail order pur-chases?
NO!
B--
Bwaaaaaaah ...
Whoa, it's crying.
Oh, dear.
How noisy.

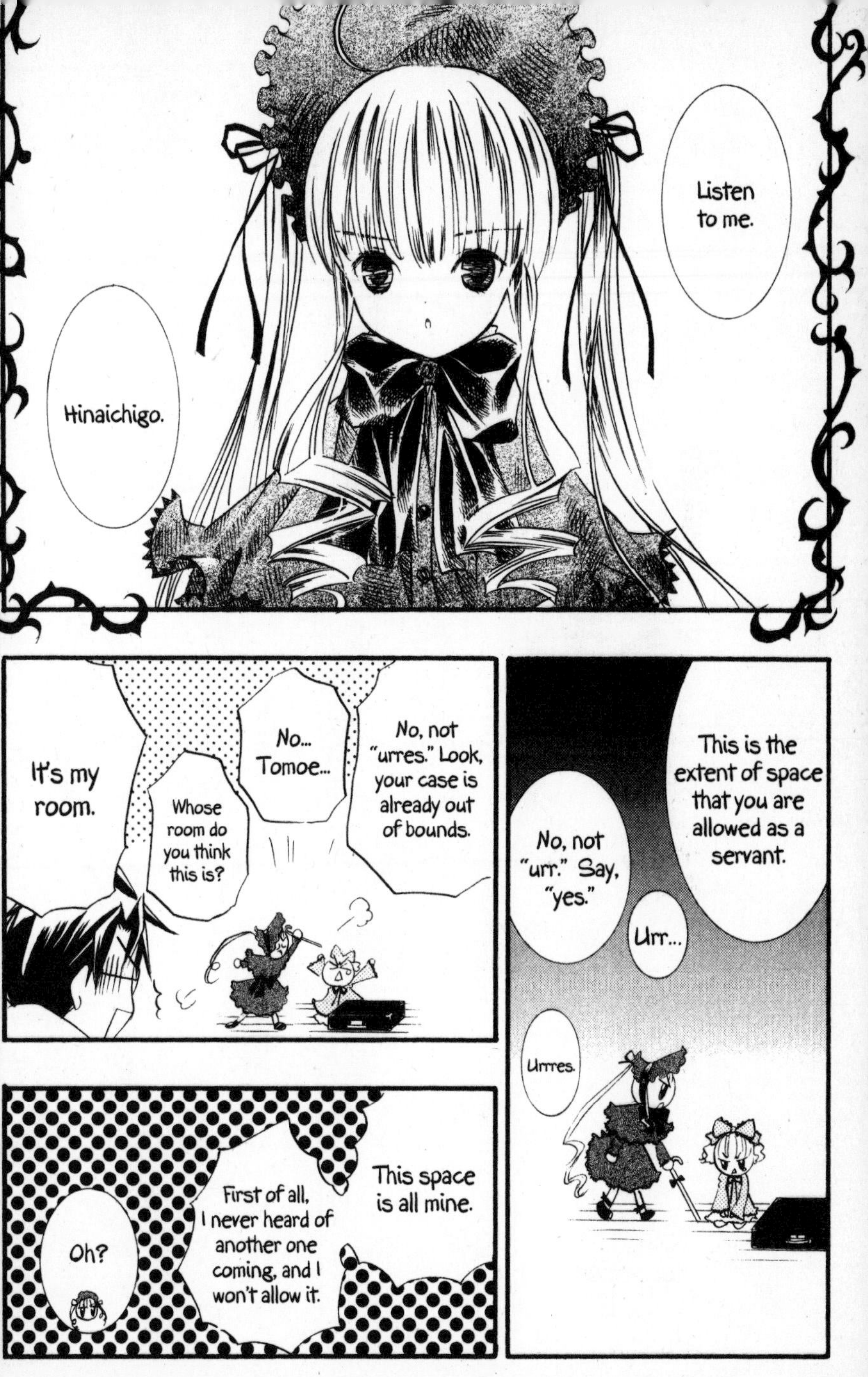
Listen to me.
Hinaichigo.
This is the extent of space that you are allowed as a servant.
Urr...
No, not "urr." Say, "yes."
Urrres.
No, not "urres." Look, your case is already out of bounds.
No... Tomoe...
Whose room do you think this is?
It's my room.
This space is all mine.
First of all, I never heard of another one coming, and I won't allow it.
Oh?

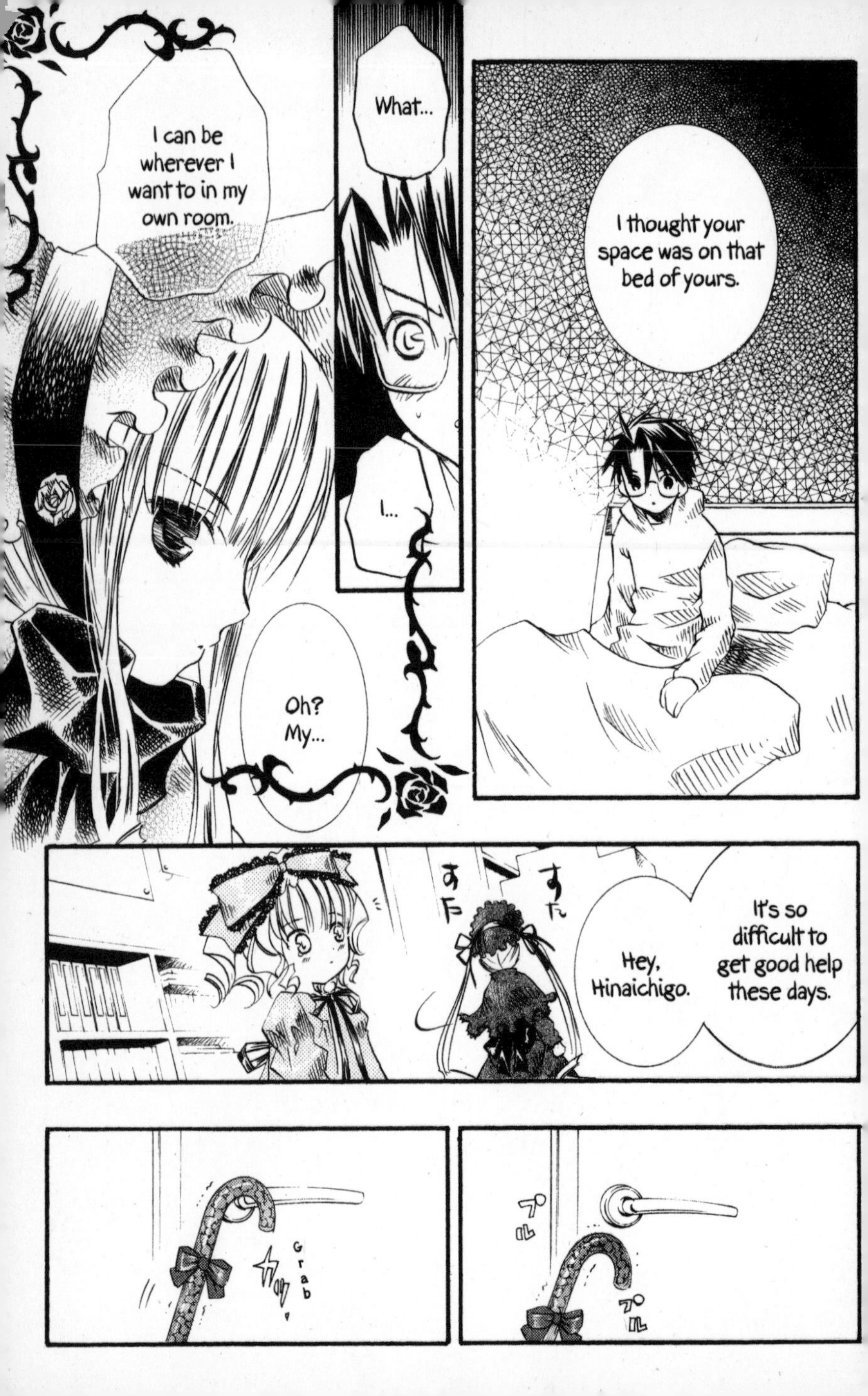
I thought your space was on that bed of yours.
What...
I...
I can be wherever I want to in my own room.
Oh? My...
It's so difficult to get good help these days.
Hey, Hinaichigo.
すた
すた
プル
プル
Grab

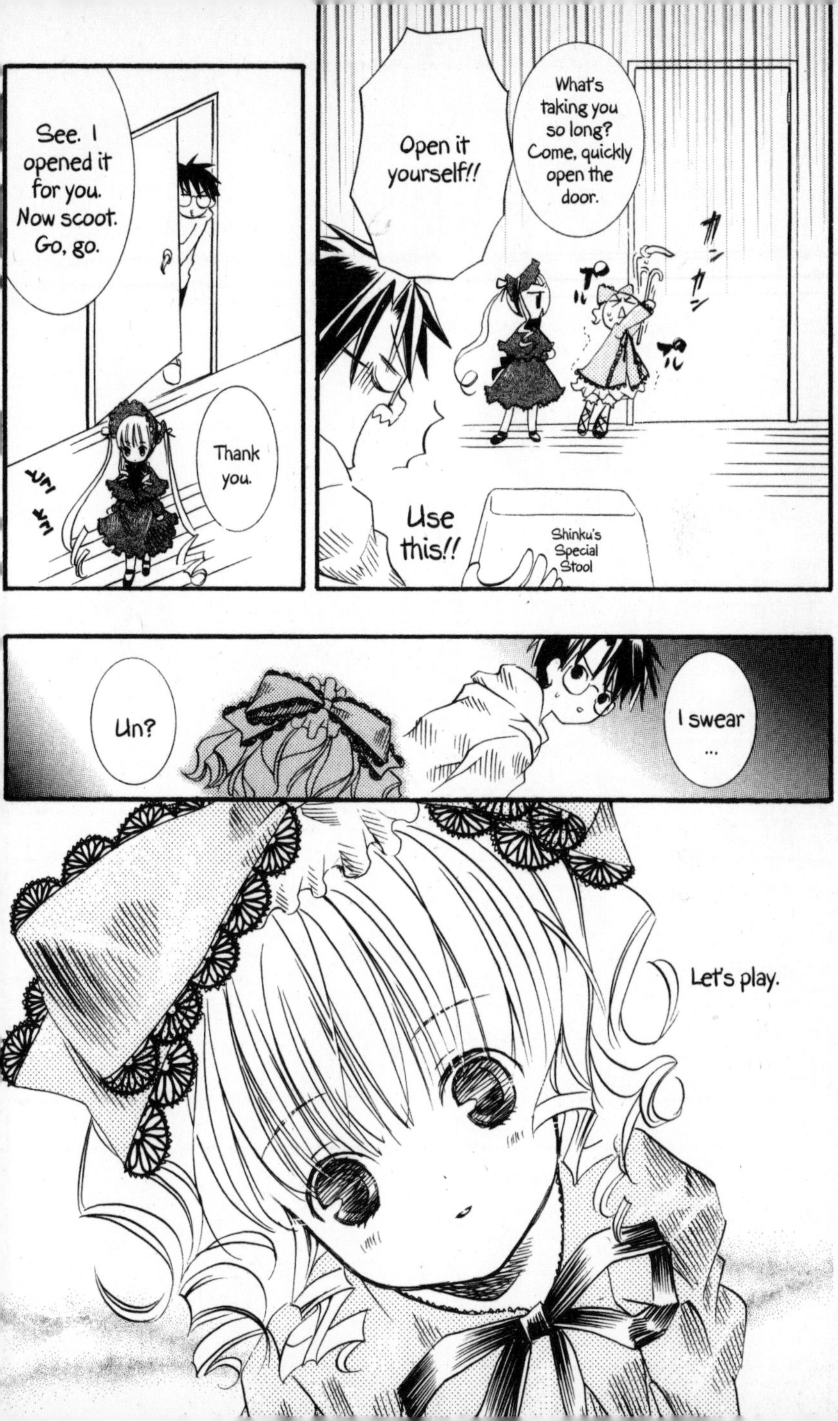
What's taking you so long? Come, quickly open the door.
カン カン
プル プル
Open it yourself!!
Use this!!
Shinku's Special Stool
See. I opened it for you. Now scoot. Go, go.
Thank you.
I swear ...
Un?
Let's play.

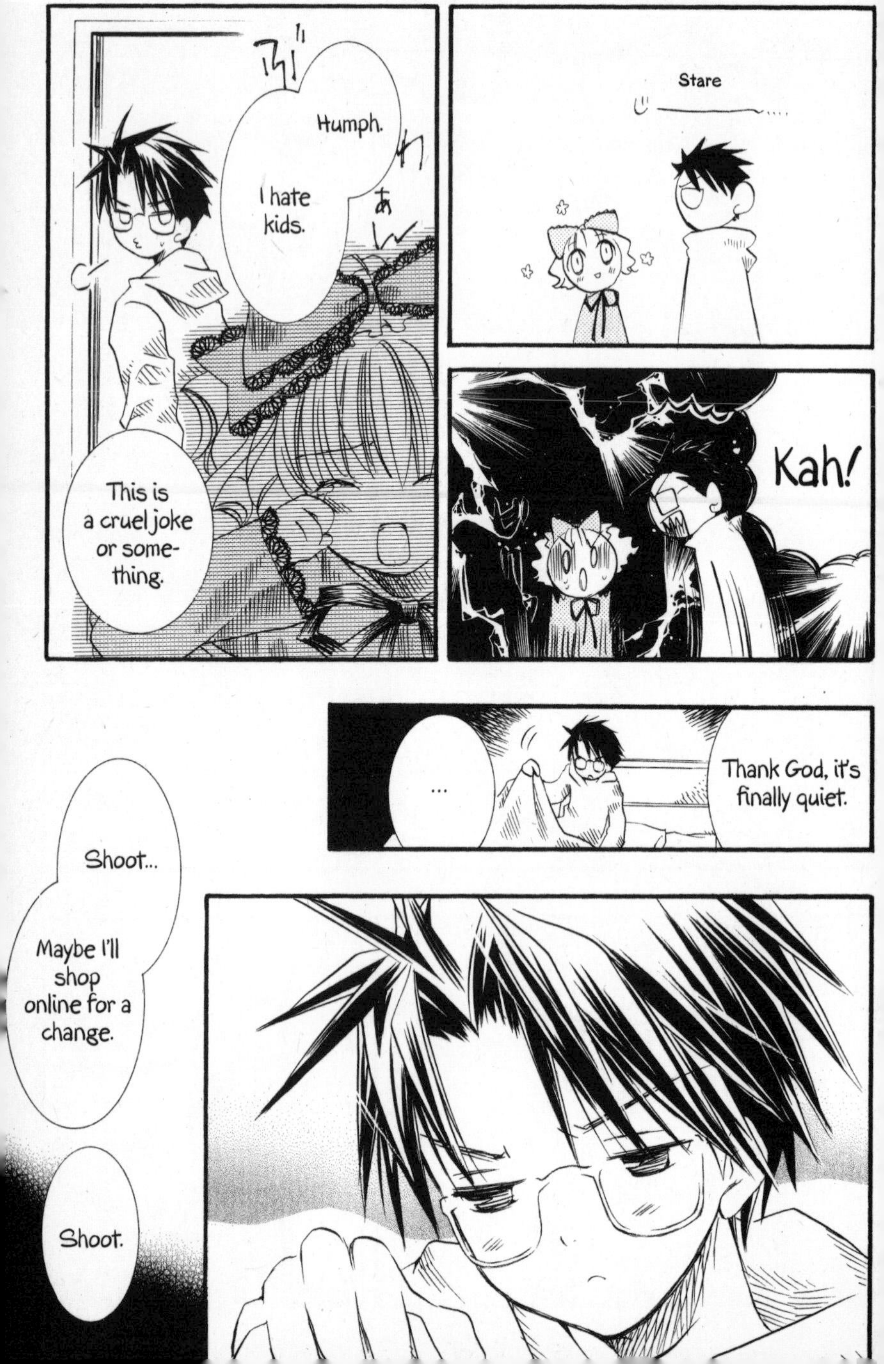

Stare
Kah!
Humph.
I hate kids.
This is a cruel joke or something.
Thank God, it's finally quiet.
...
Shoot...
Maybe I'll shop online for a change.
Shoot.

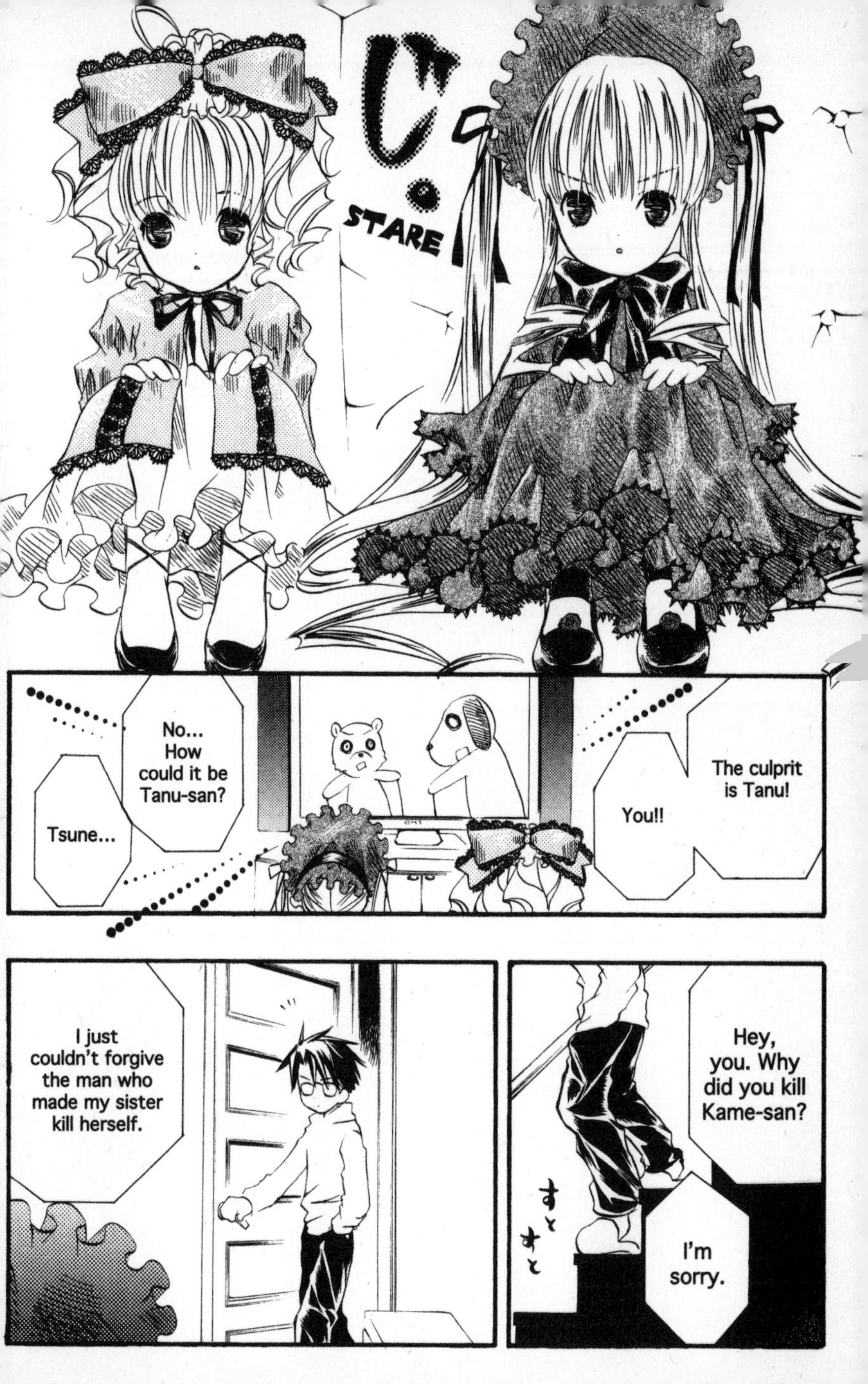
STARE
The culprit is Tanu!
You!!
No... How could it be Tanu-san?
Tsune...
Hey, you. Why did you kill Kame-san?
I'm sorry.
すと すと
I just couldn't forgive the man who made my sister kill herself.

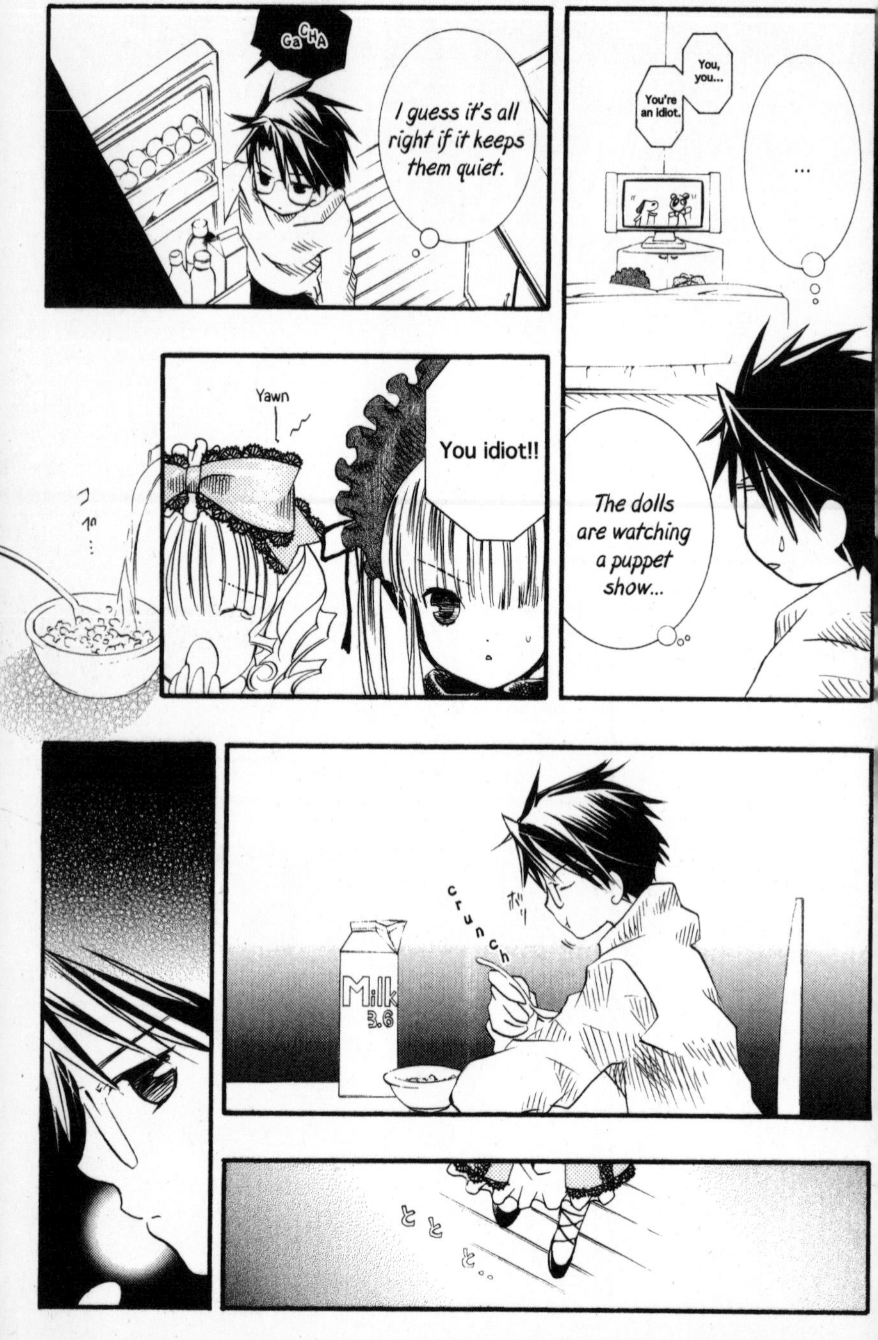
You, you...
You're an idiot.
...
The dolls are watching a puppet show...
GaCHA
I guess it's all right if it keeps them quiet.
You idiot!!
Yawn
crunch
Milk 3.6
ととと。。

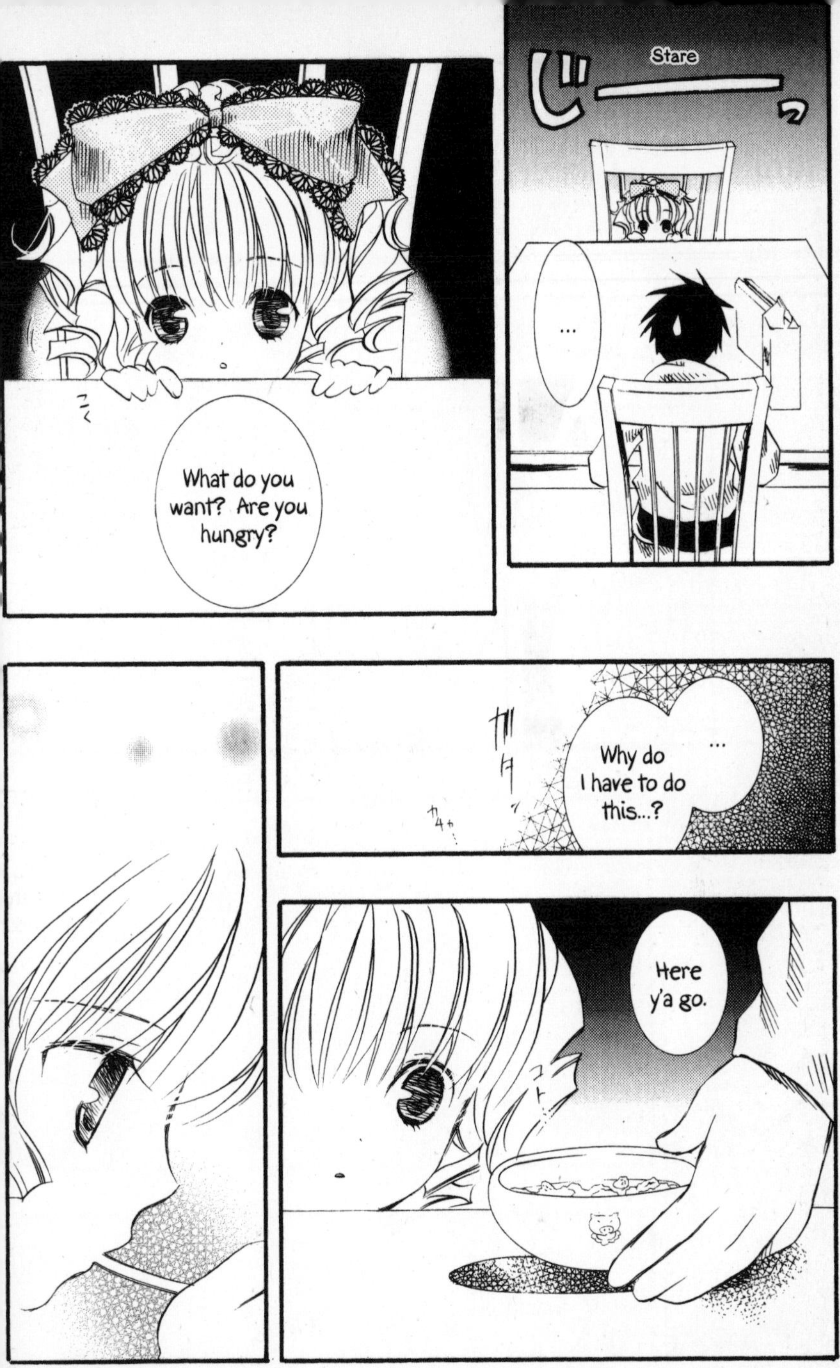
Stare
...
What do you want? Are you hungry?
...
Why do I have to do this...?
Here y'a go.

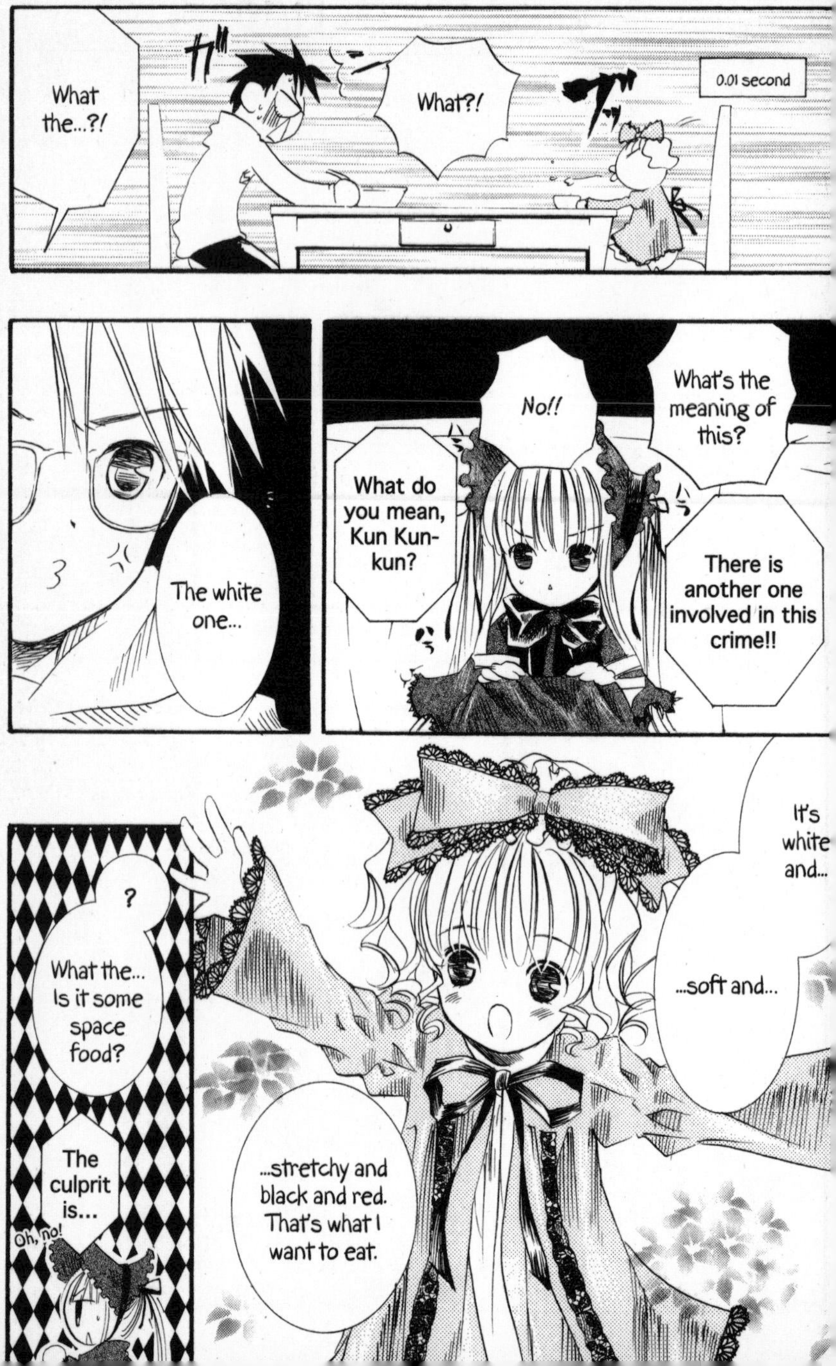
0.01 second
What?!
What the...?!
What's the meaning of this?
No!!
There is another one involved in this crime!!
What do you mean, Kun Kun-kun?
The white one...
It's white and...
...soft and...
...stretchy and black and red. That's what I want to eat.
?
What the... Is it some space food?
The culprit is...
Oh, no!

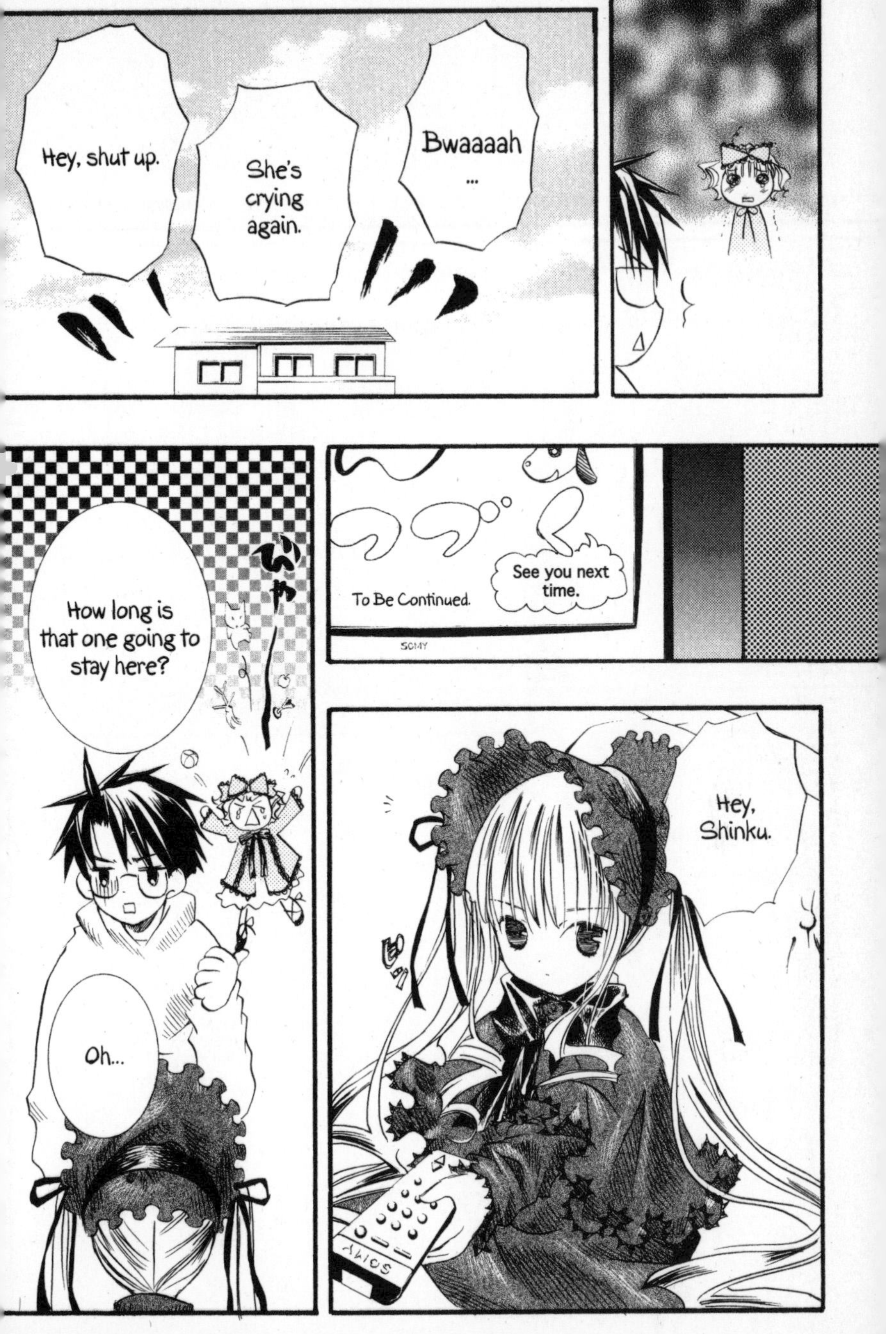
Bwaaaah ...
She's crying again.
Hey, shut up.
つづく
To Be Continued.
See you next time.
Hey, Shinku.
How long is that one going to stay here?
Oh...

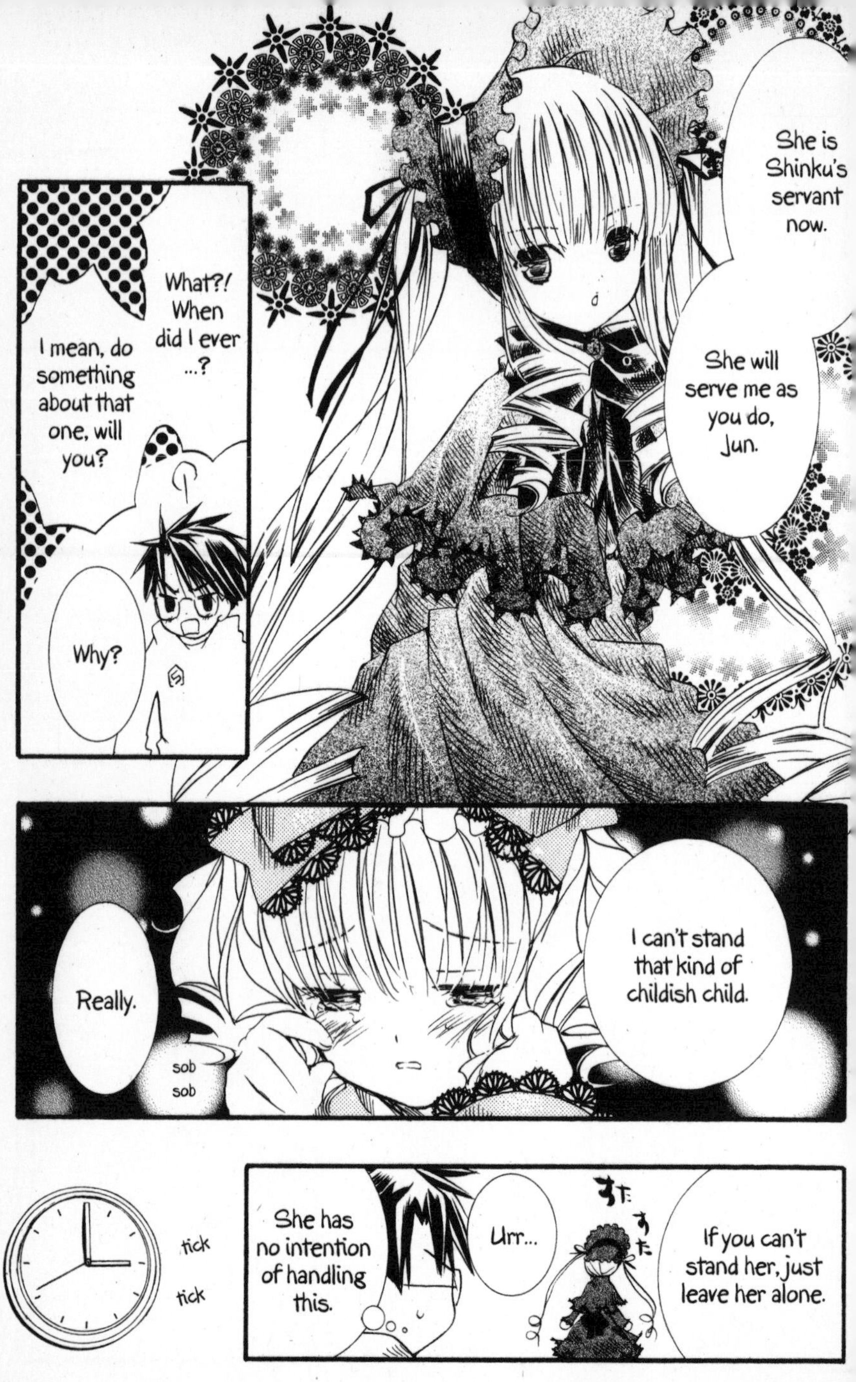

She is Shinku's servant now.
She will serve me as you do, Jun.
What?! When did I ever ...?
I mean, do something about that one, will you?
Why?
I can't stand that kind of childish child.
Really.
sob sob
If you can't stand her, just leave her alone.
すた すた
Urr...
She has no intention of handling this.
tick tick

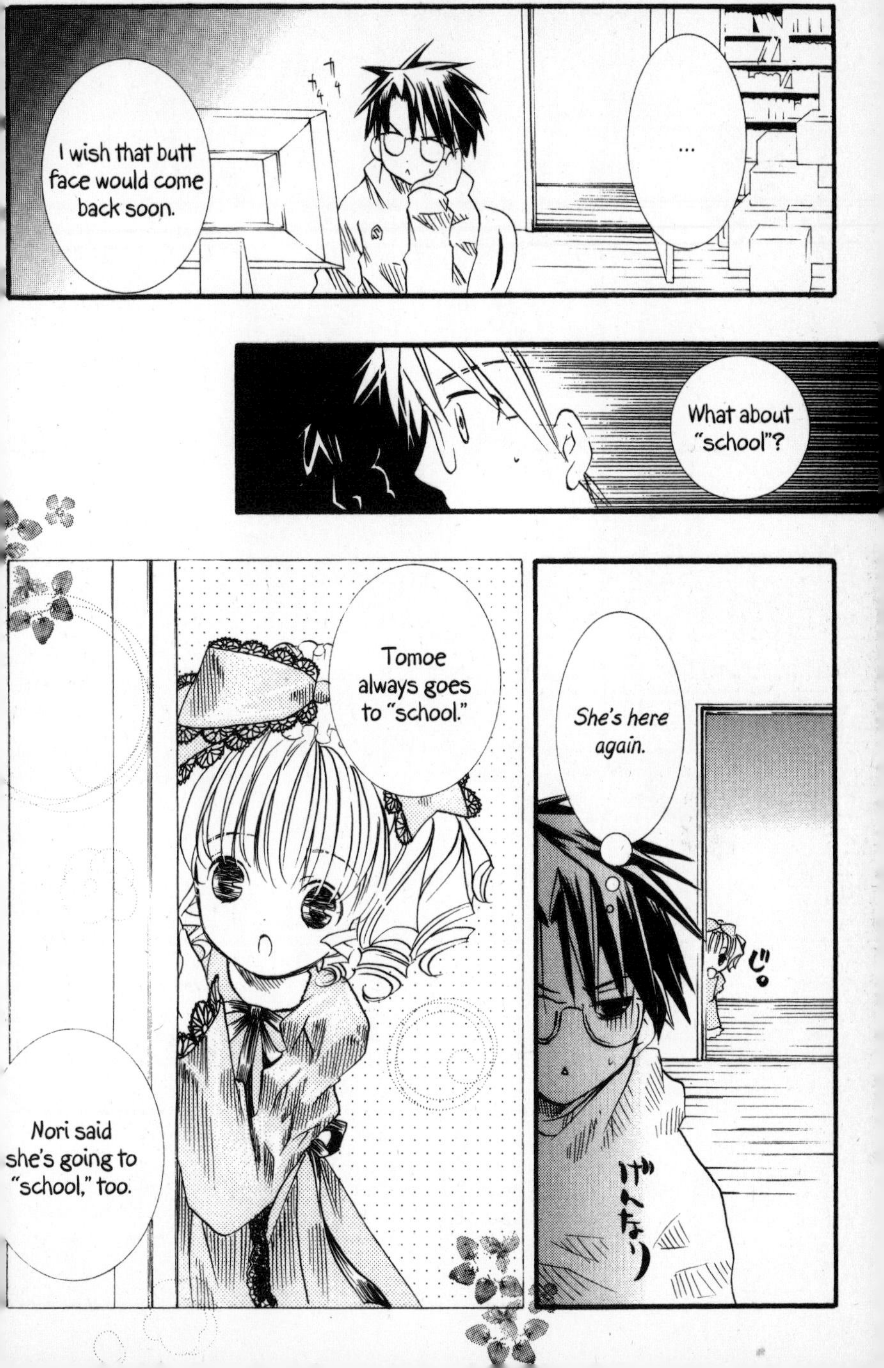
...
I wish that butt face would come back soon.
What about "school"?
She's here again.
じ。
げんなり
Tomoe always goes to "school."
Nori said she's going to "school," too.

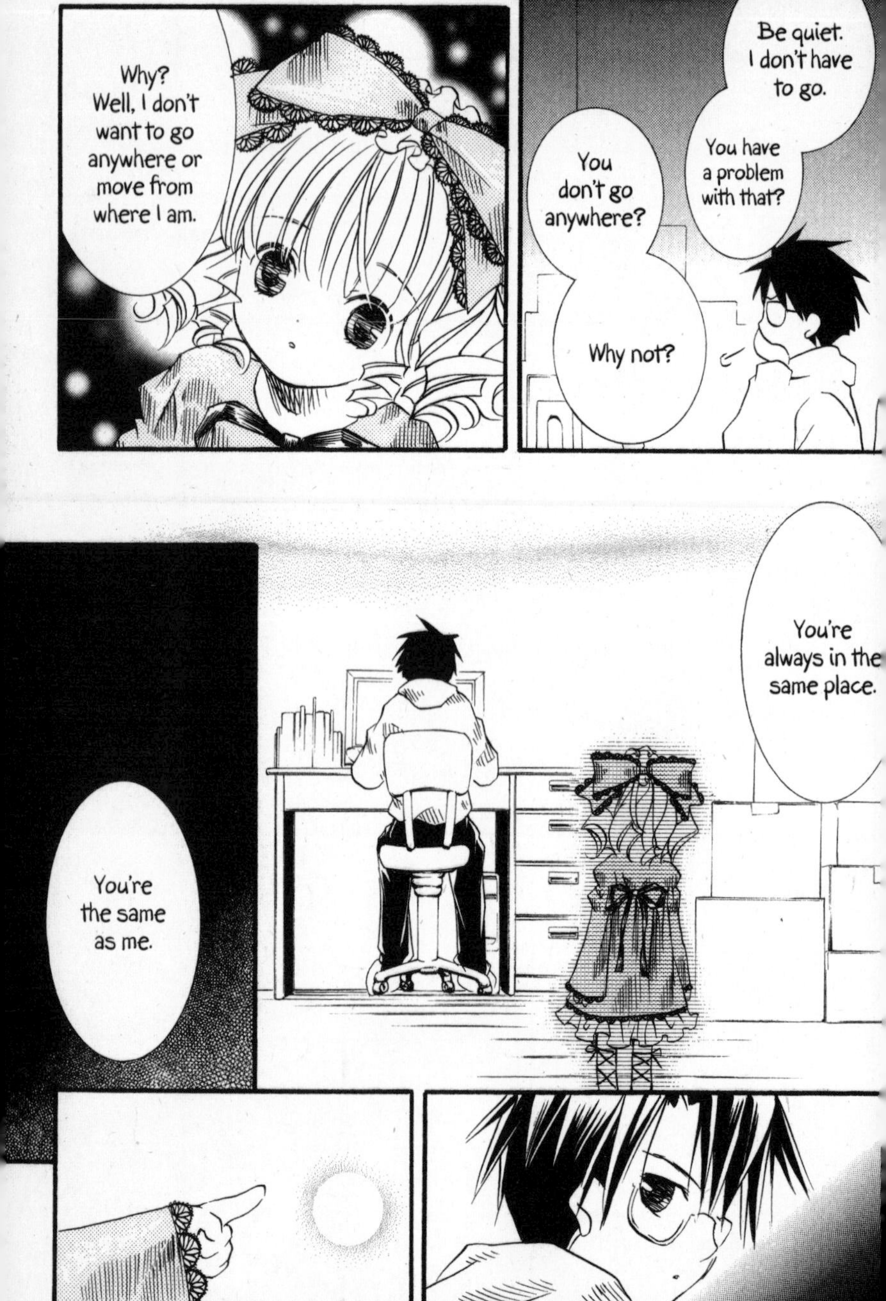
Be quiet. I don't have to go.
You have a problem with that?
You don't go anywhere?
Why not?
Why? Well, I don't want to go anywhere or move from where I am.
You're always in the same place.
You're the same as me.

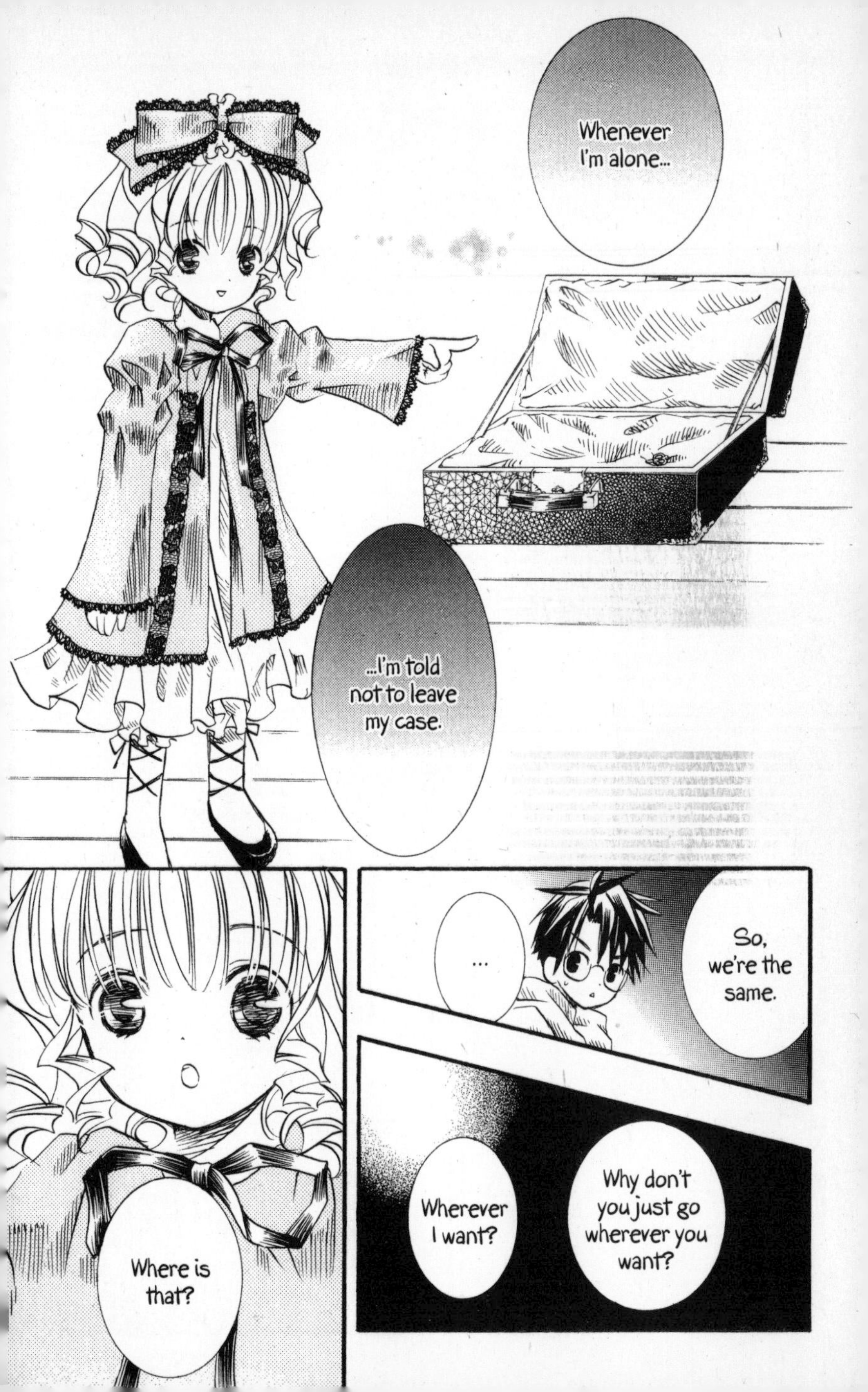
Whenever I'm alone...
...I'm told not to leave my case.
So, we're the same.
...
Why don't you just go wherever you want?
Wherever I want?
Where is that?

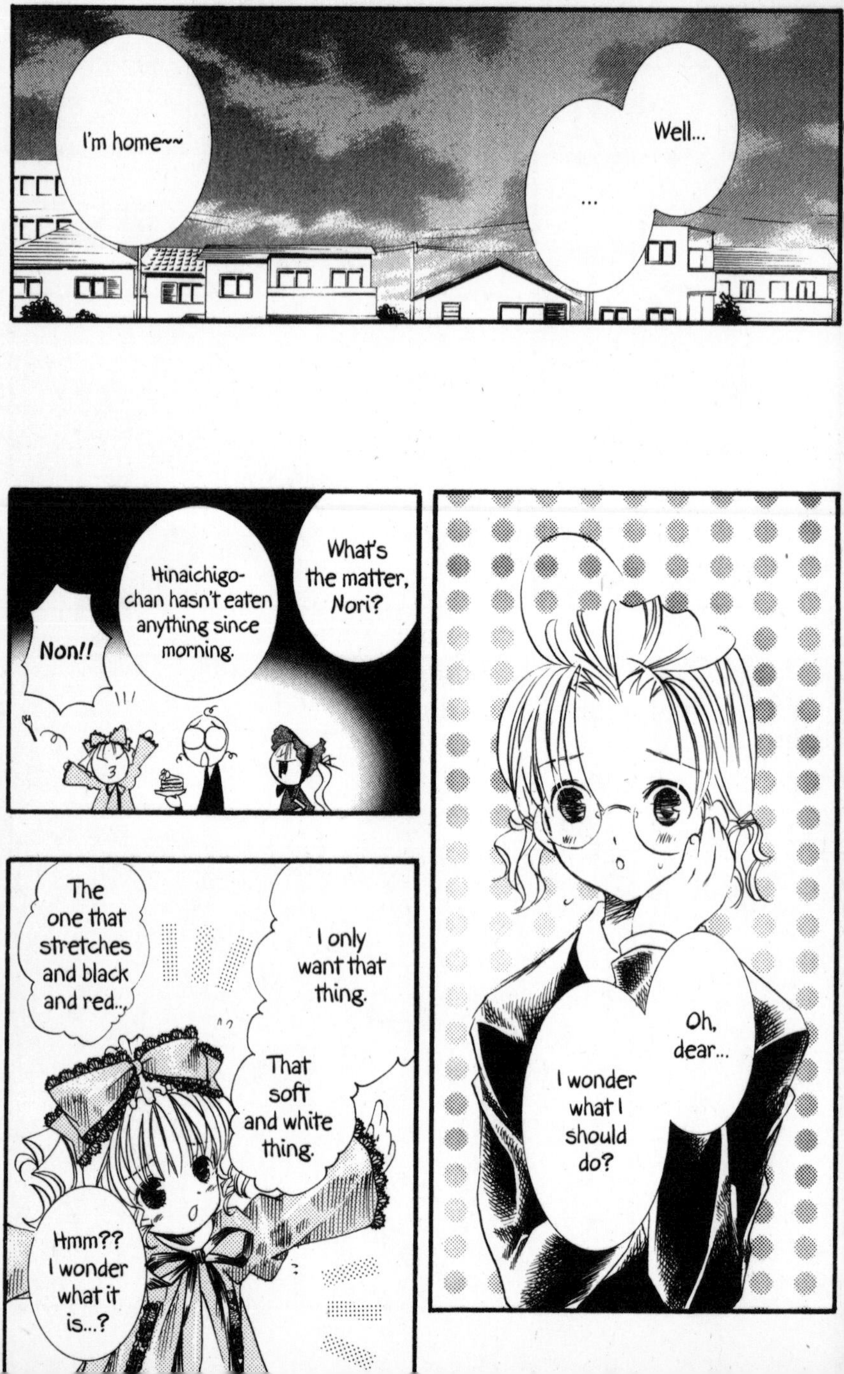
Well...
...
I'm home~~
Oh, dear...
I wonder what I should do?
What's the matter, Nori?
Hinaichigo-chan hasn't eaten anything since morning.
Non!!
I only want that thing.
The one that stretches and black and red...
That soft and white thing.
Hmm?? I wonder what it is...?

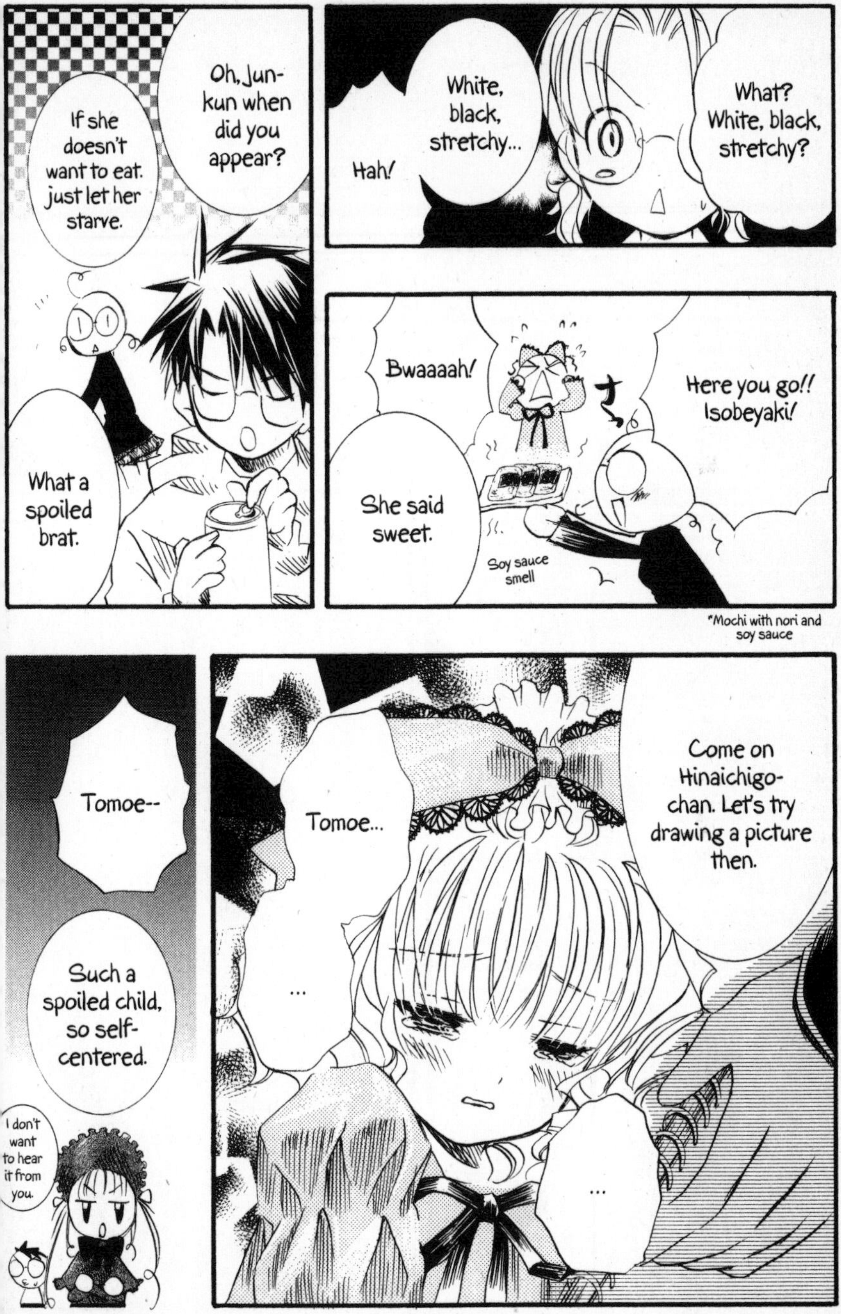
What? White, black, stretchy?
White, black, stretchy...
Hah!
Here you go!! Isobeyaki!
Bwaaaah!
She said sweet.
Soy sauce smell
Oh, Jun-kun when did you appear?
If she doesn't want to eat. just let her starve.
What a spoiled brat.
*Mochi with nori and soy sauce
Come on Hinaichigo-chan. Let's try drawing a picture then.
Tomoe...
...
...
Tomoe--
Such a spoiled child, so self-centered.
I don't want to hear it from you.

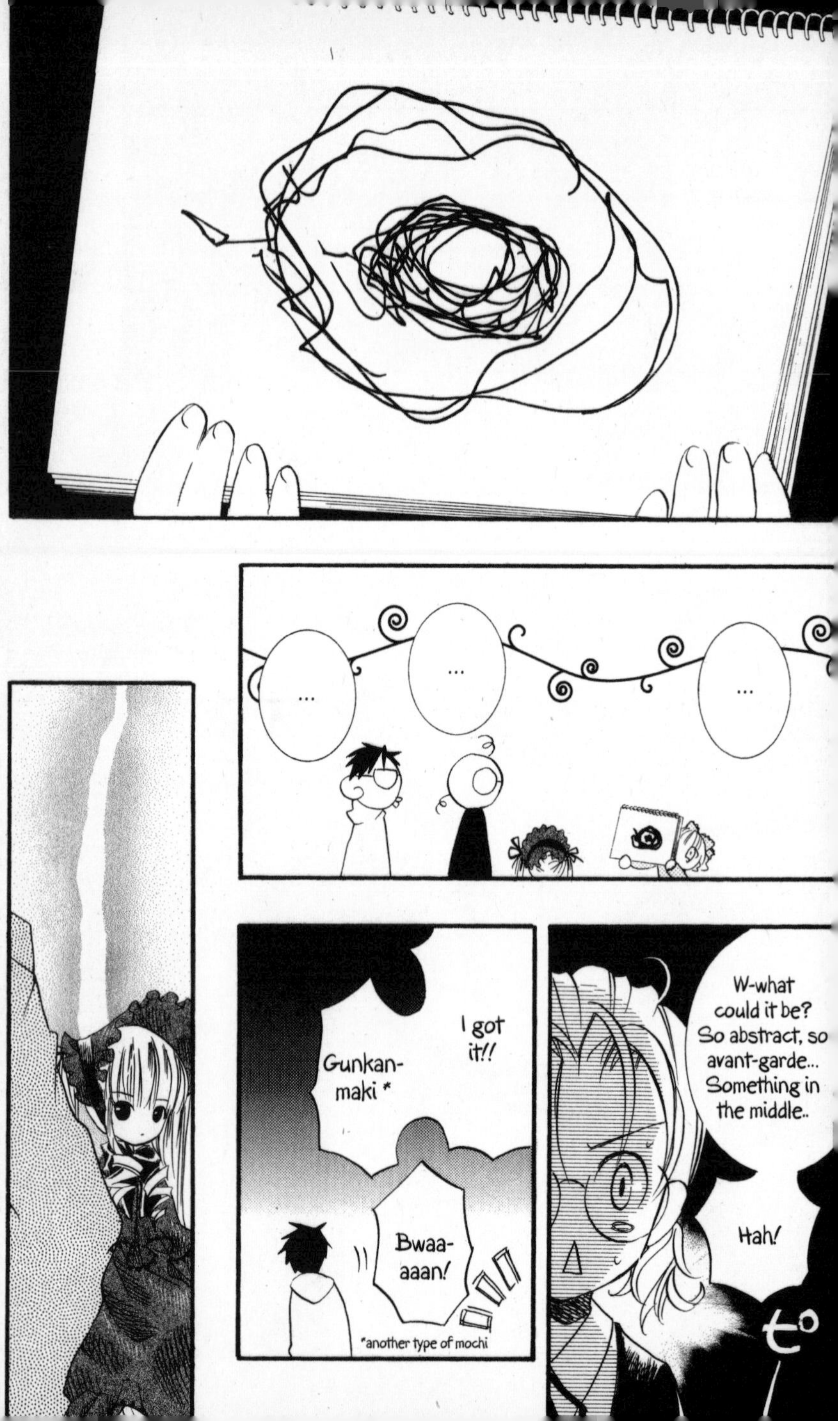
...
...
...
W-what could it be? So abstract, so avant-garde... Something in the middle..
Hah!
I got it!!
Gunkan-maki *
Bwaa-aaan!
*another type of mochi

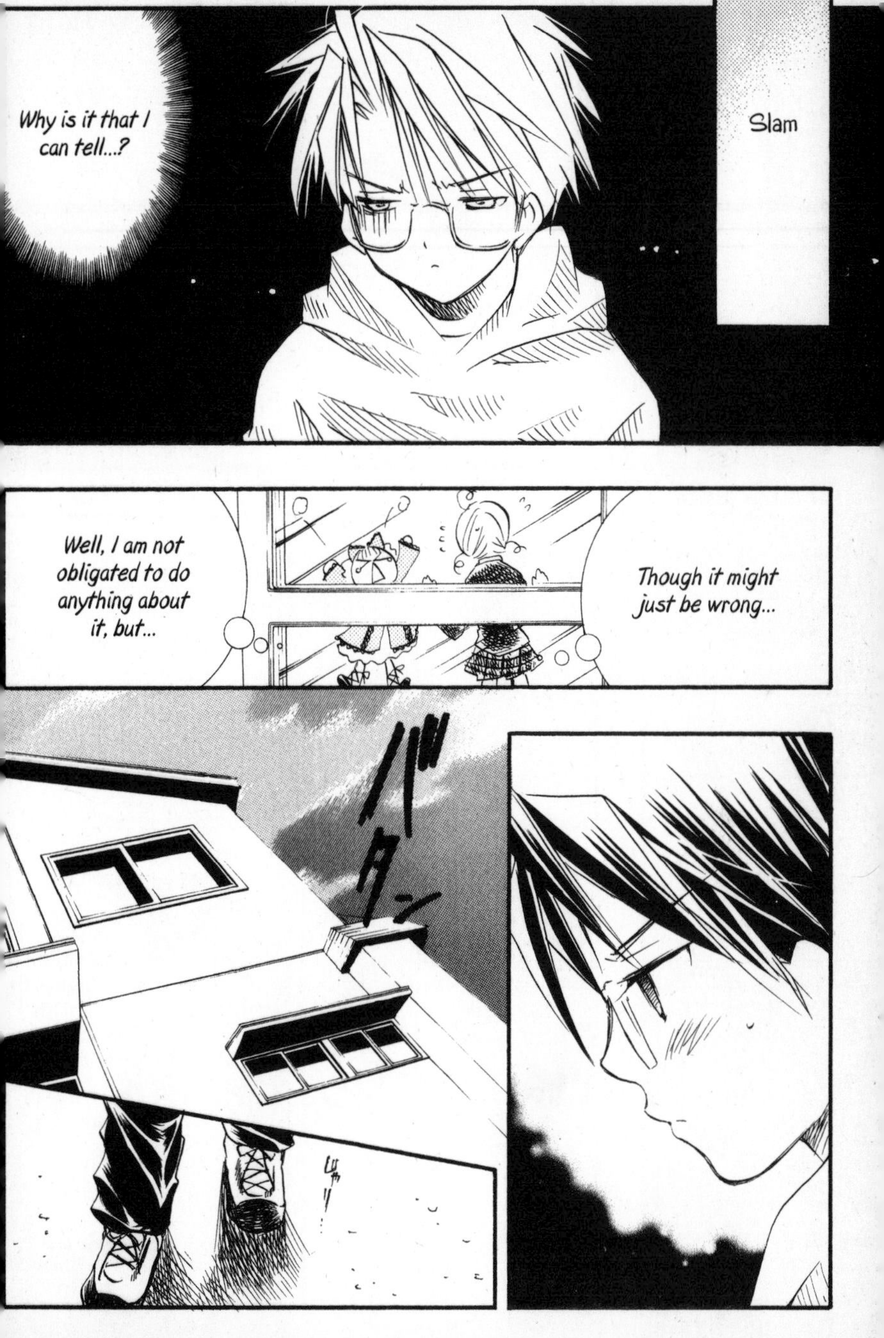
Slam
Why is it that I can tell...?
Though it might just be wrong...
Well, I am not obligated to do anything about it, but...
バタン

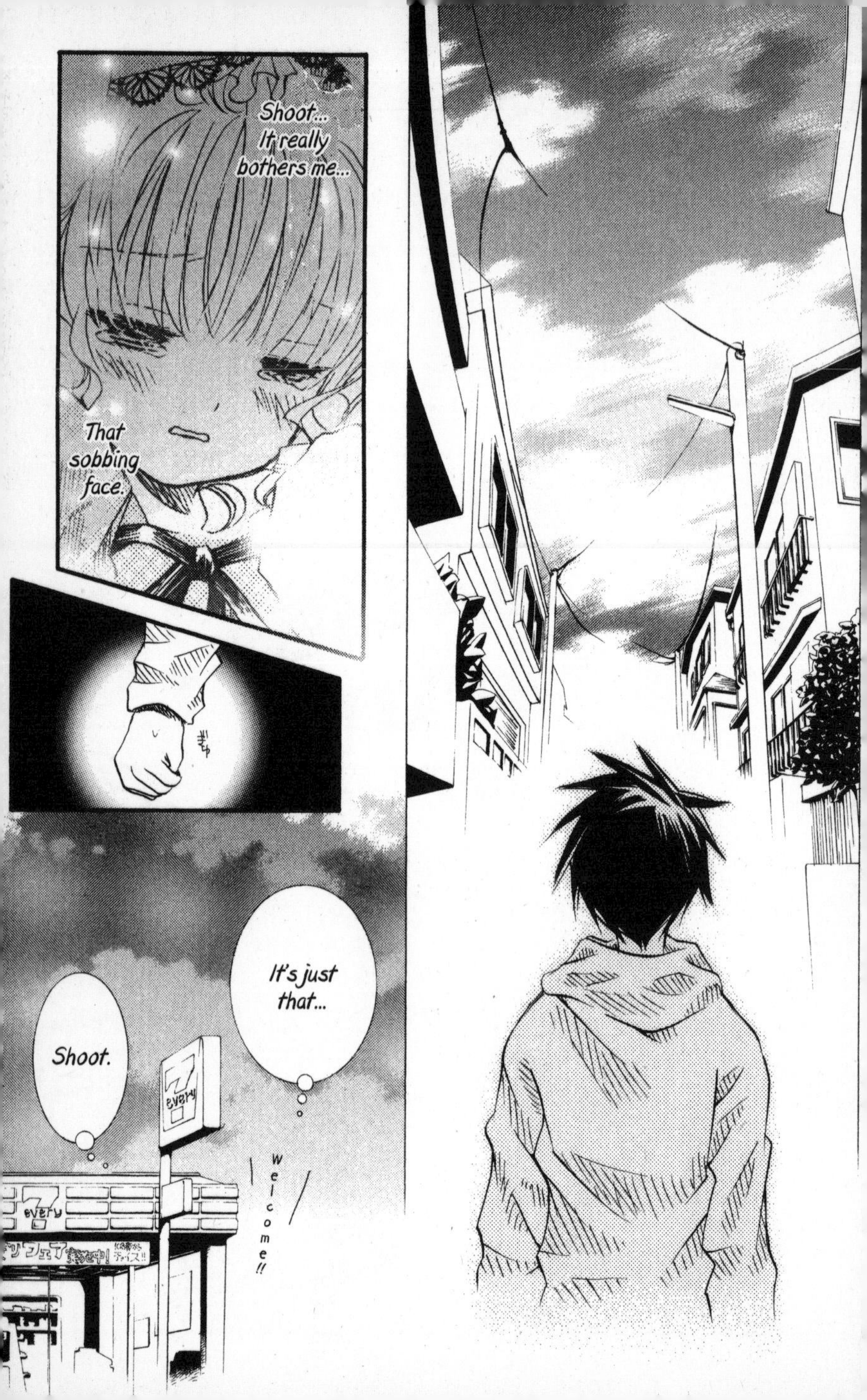
Shoot... It really bothers me...
That sobbing face.
It's just that...
Shoot.
Welcome!!

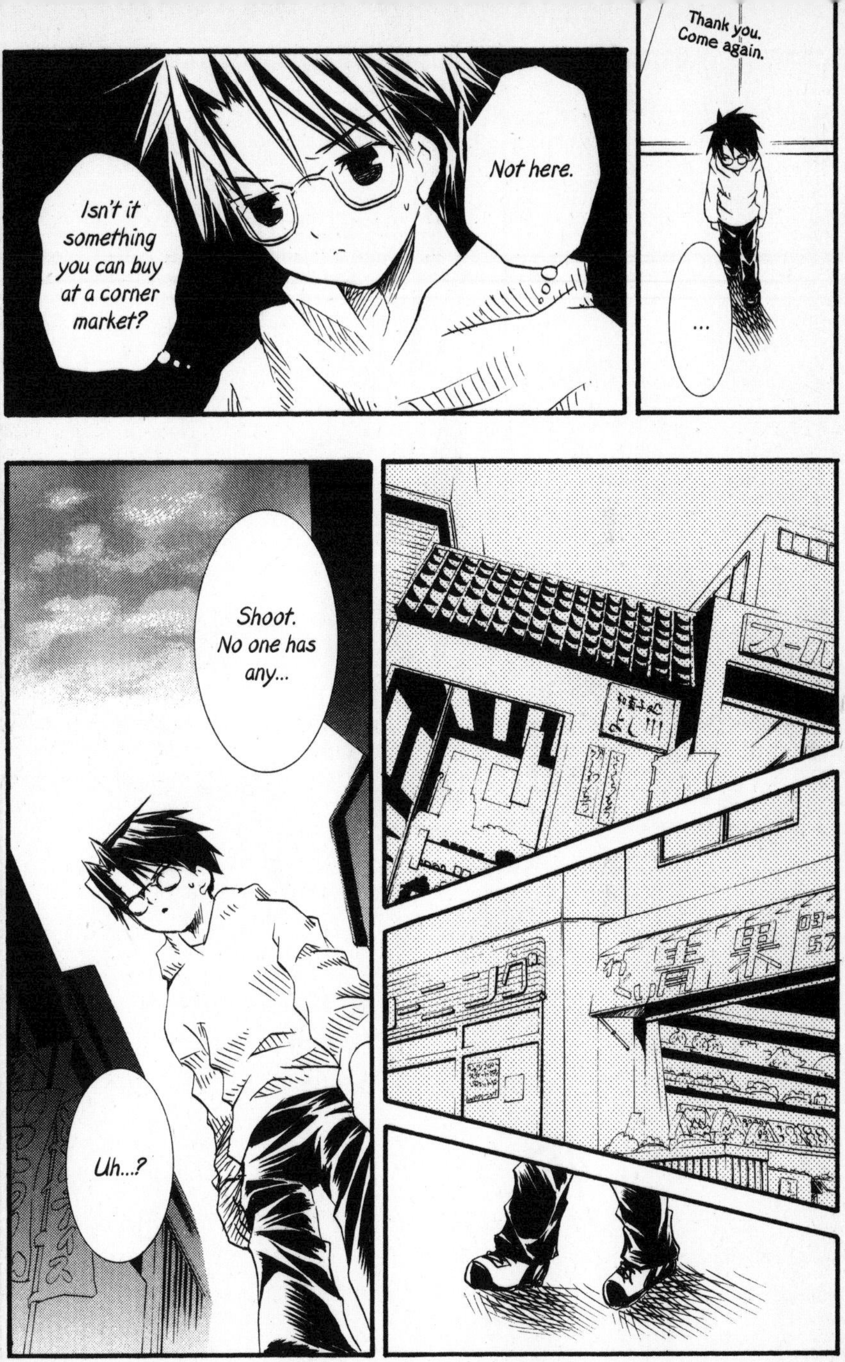
Thank you. Come again.
...
Not here.
Isn't it something you can buy at a corner market?
Shoot. No one has any...
Uh...?

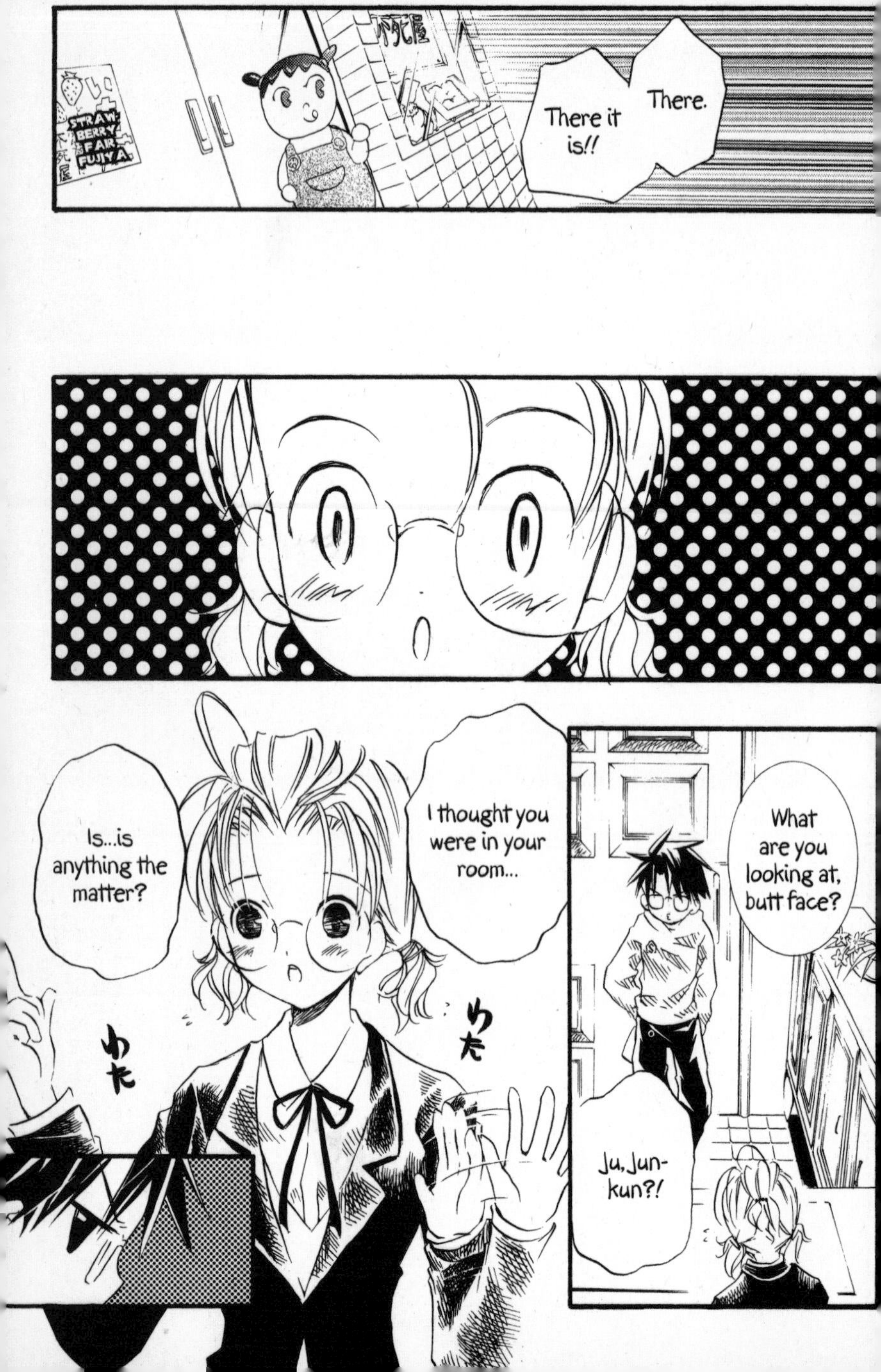
STRAW BERRY FAIR FUJIYA
There.
There it is!!
What are you looking at, butt face?
Ju, Jun-kun?!
I thought you were in your room...
わた
Is...is anything the matter?
わた

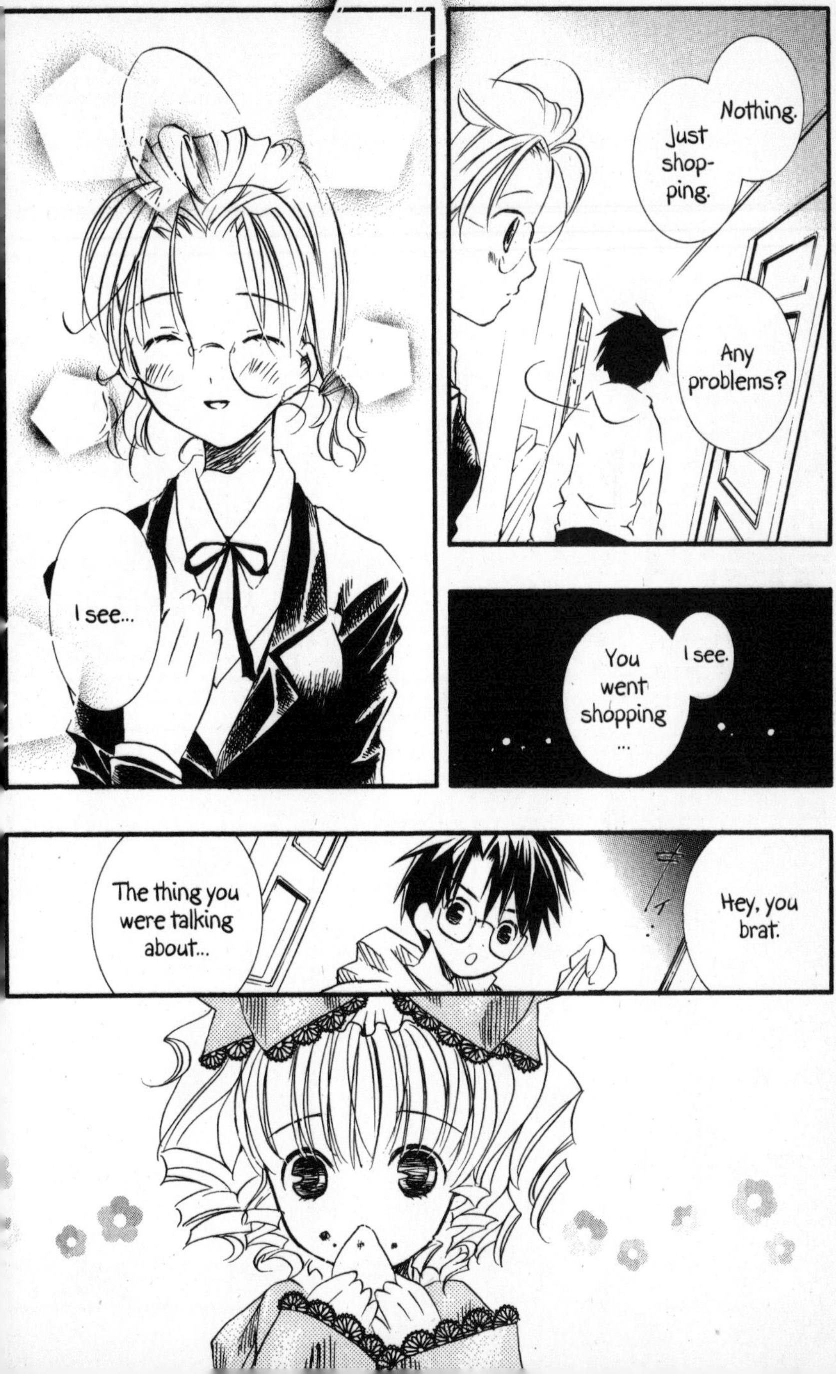
Nothing.
Just shopping.
Any problems?
I see.
You went shopping...
I see...
Hey, you brat.
The thing you were talking about...

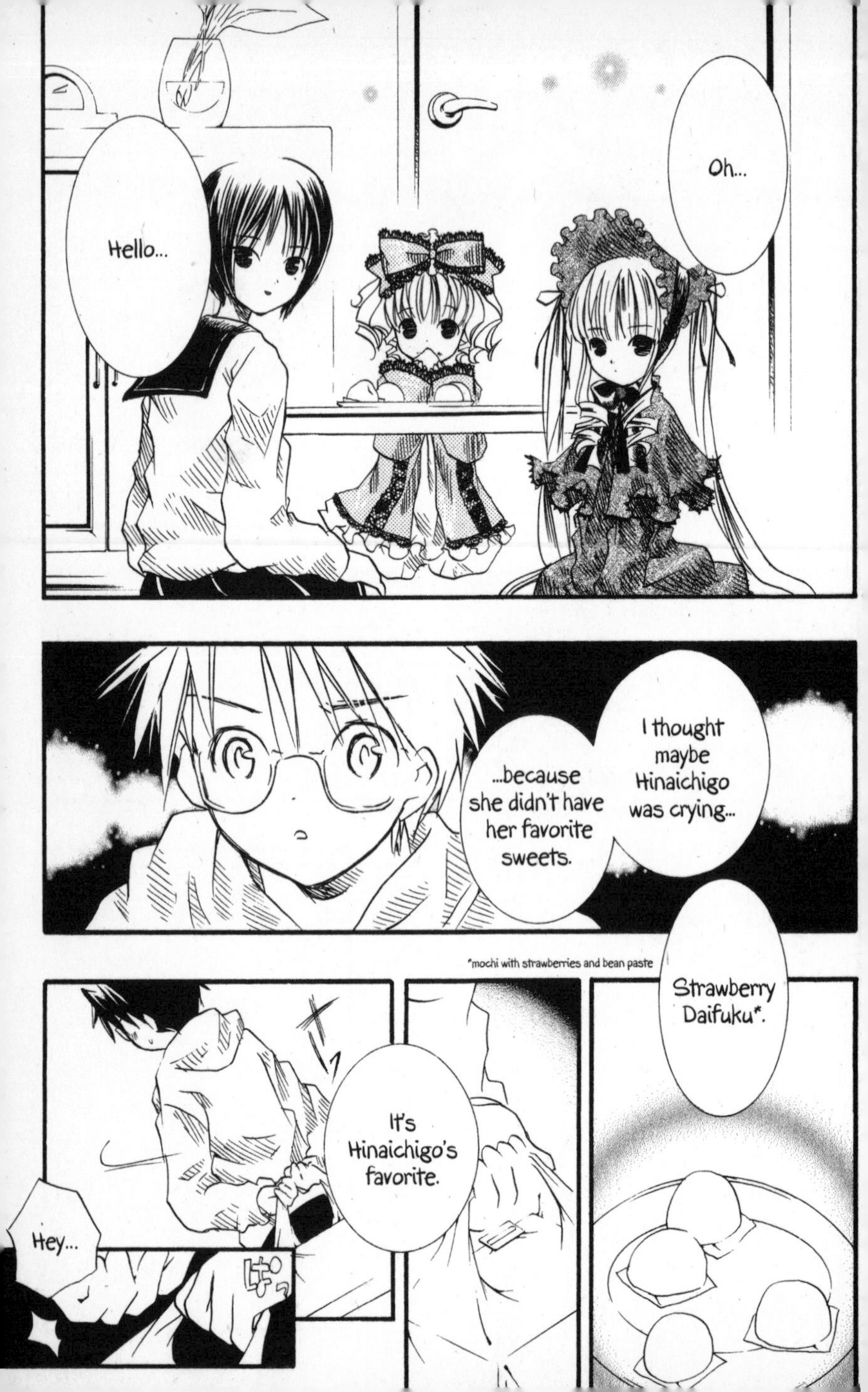
Oh...
Hello...
I thought maybe Hinaichigo was crying...
...because she didn't have her favorite sweets.
*mochi with strawberries and bean paste
Strawberry Daifuku*.
It's Hinaichigo's favorite.
Hey...
ぽっ

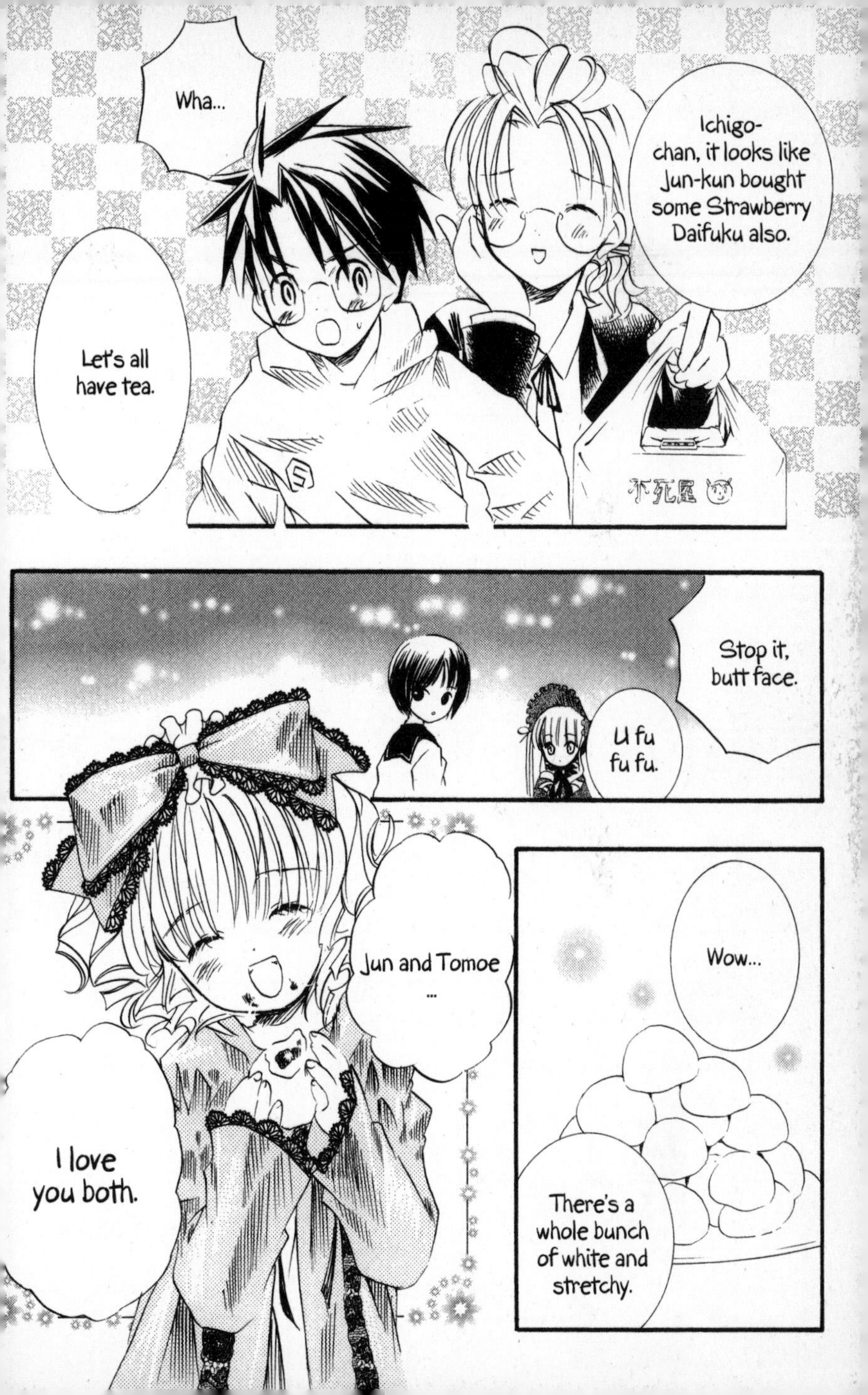
Ichigo-chan, it looks like Jun-kun bought some Strawberry Daifuku also.
Wha...
Let's all have tea.
不死屋
Stop it, butt face.
U fu fu fu.
Wow...
There's a whole bunch of white and stretchy.
Jun and Tomoe ...
I love you both.

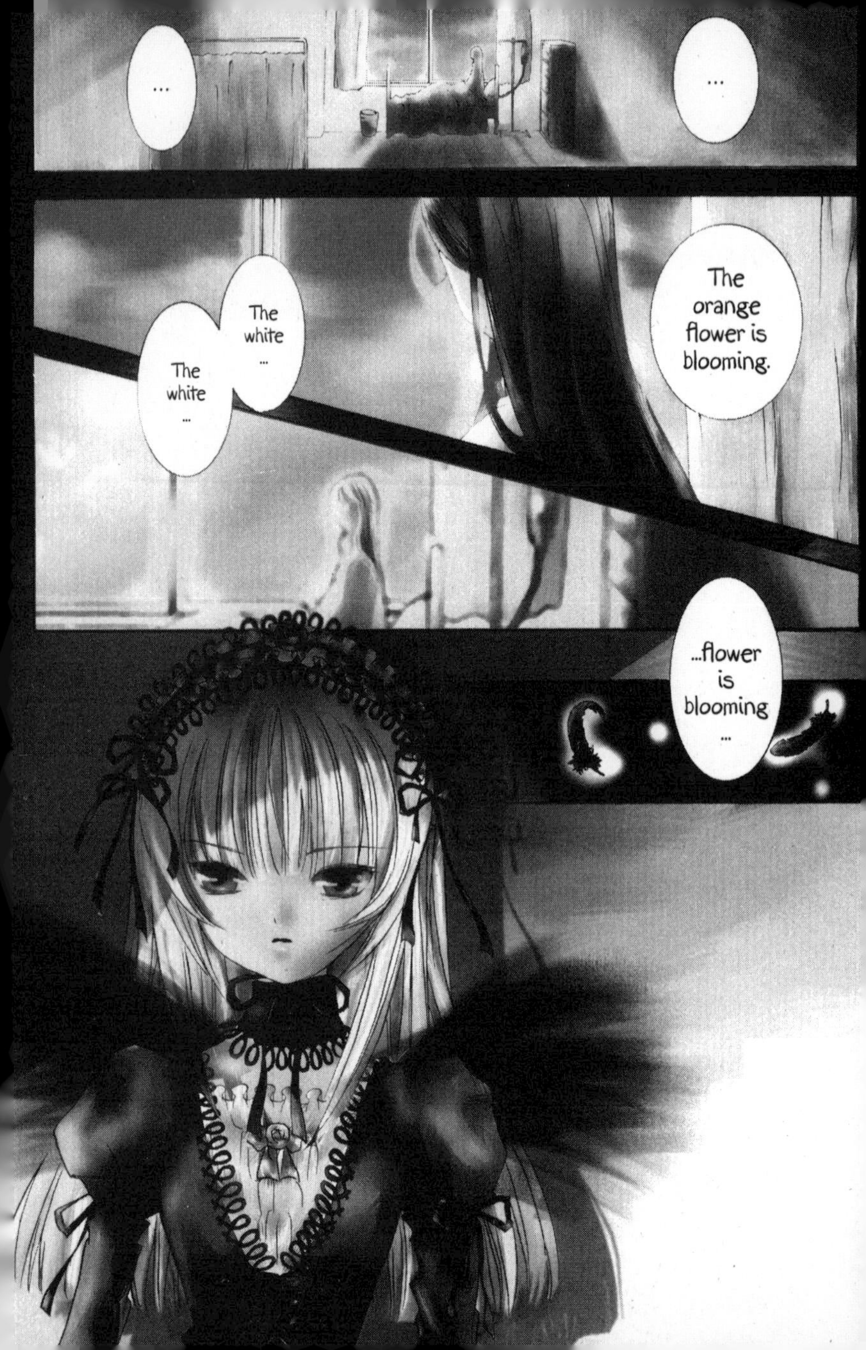
...
...
The orange flower is blooming.
The white ...
The white ...
...flower is blooming ...

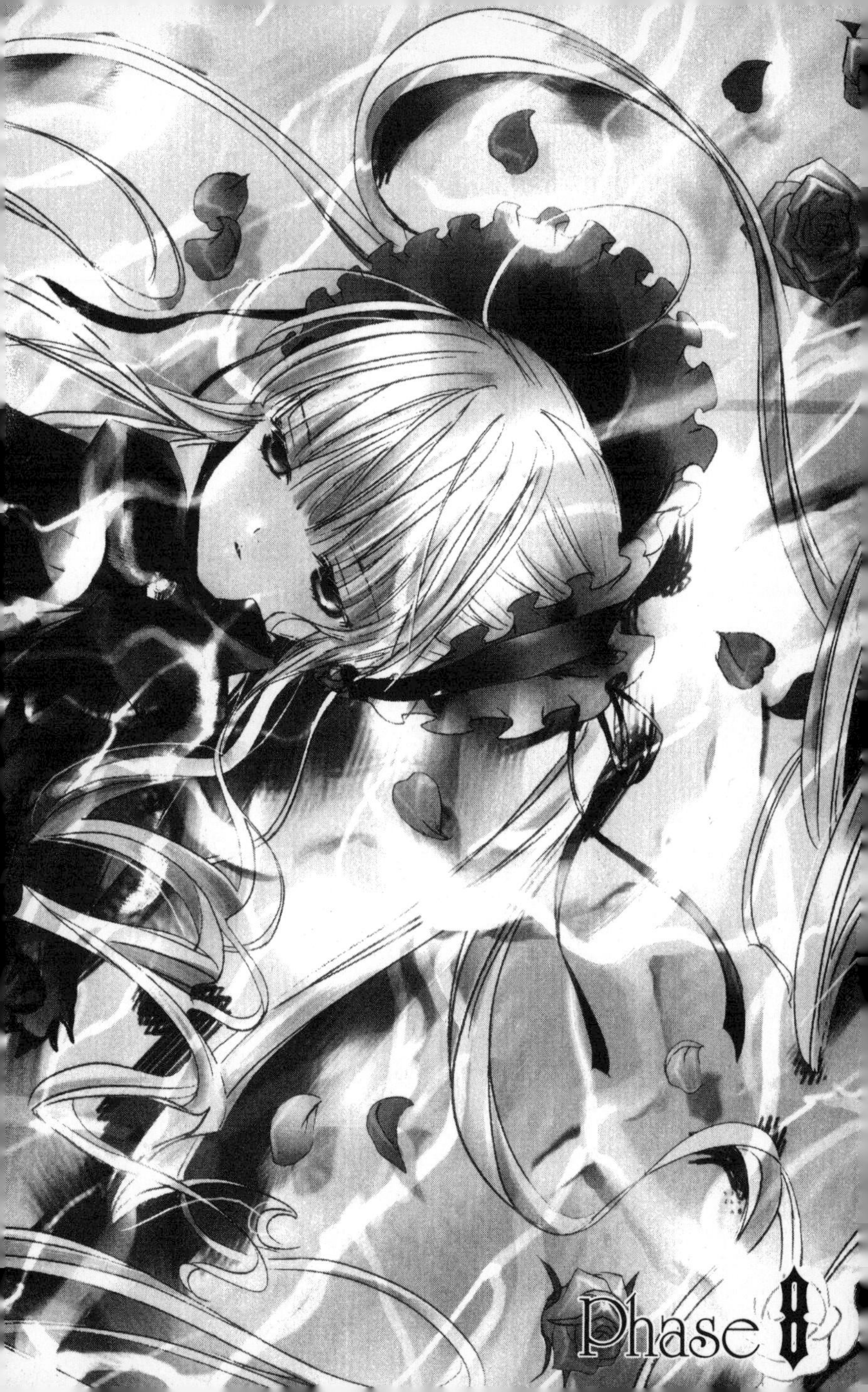
Phase 8

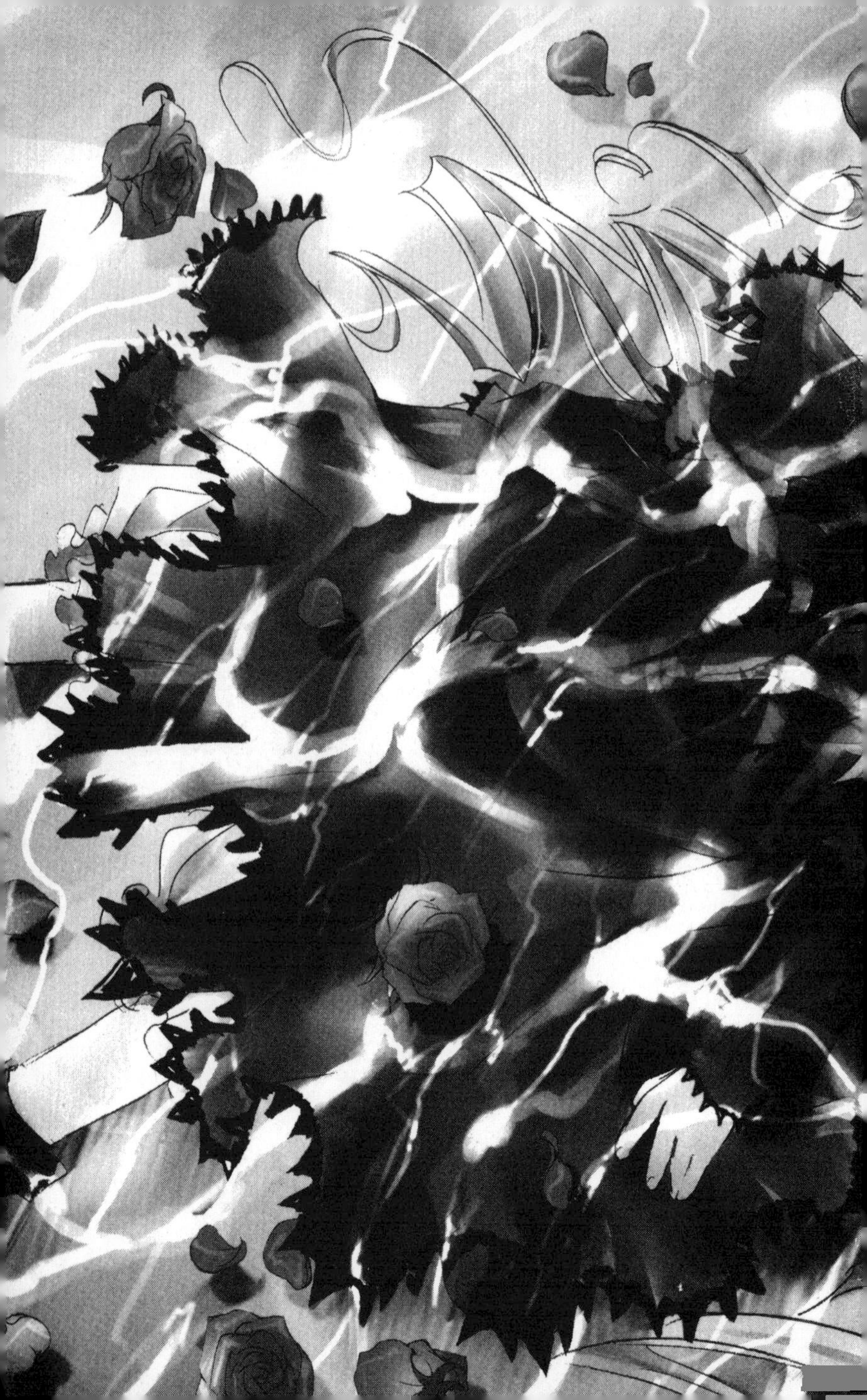

ローゼン メイデン
Rozen Maiden

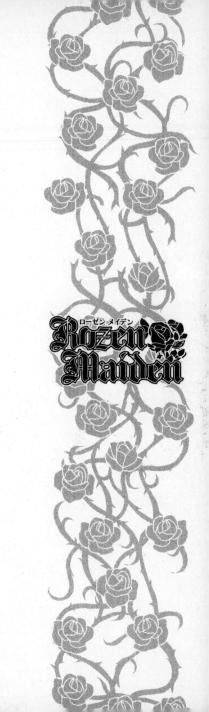

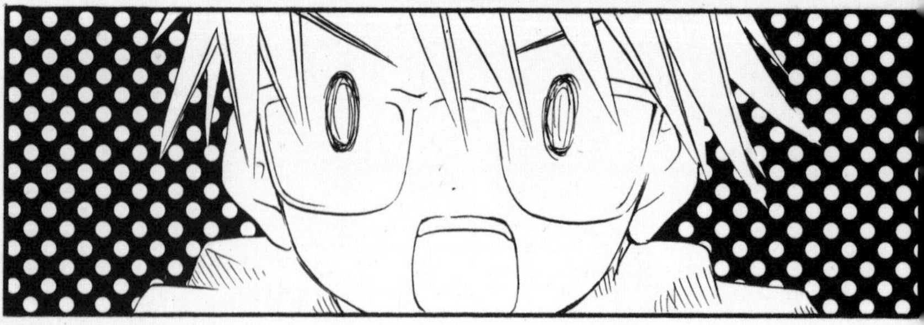

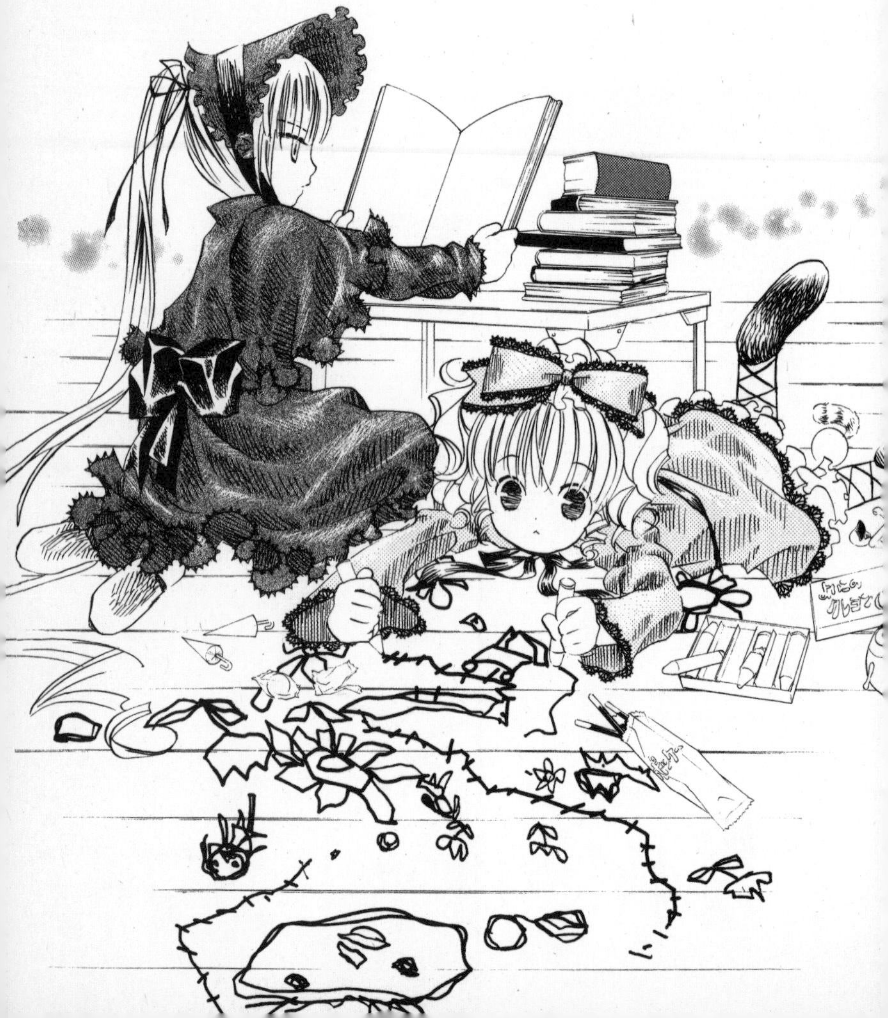

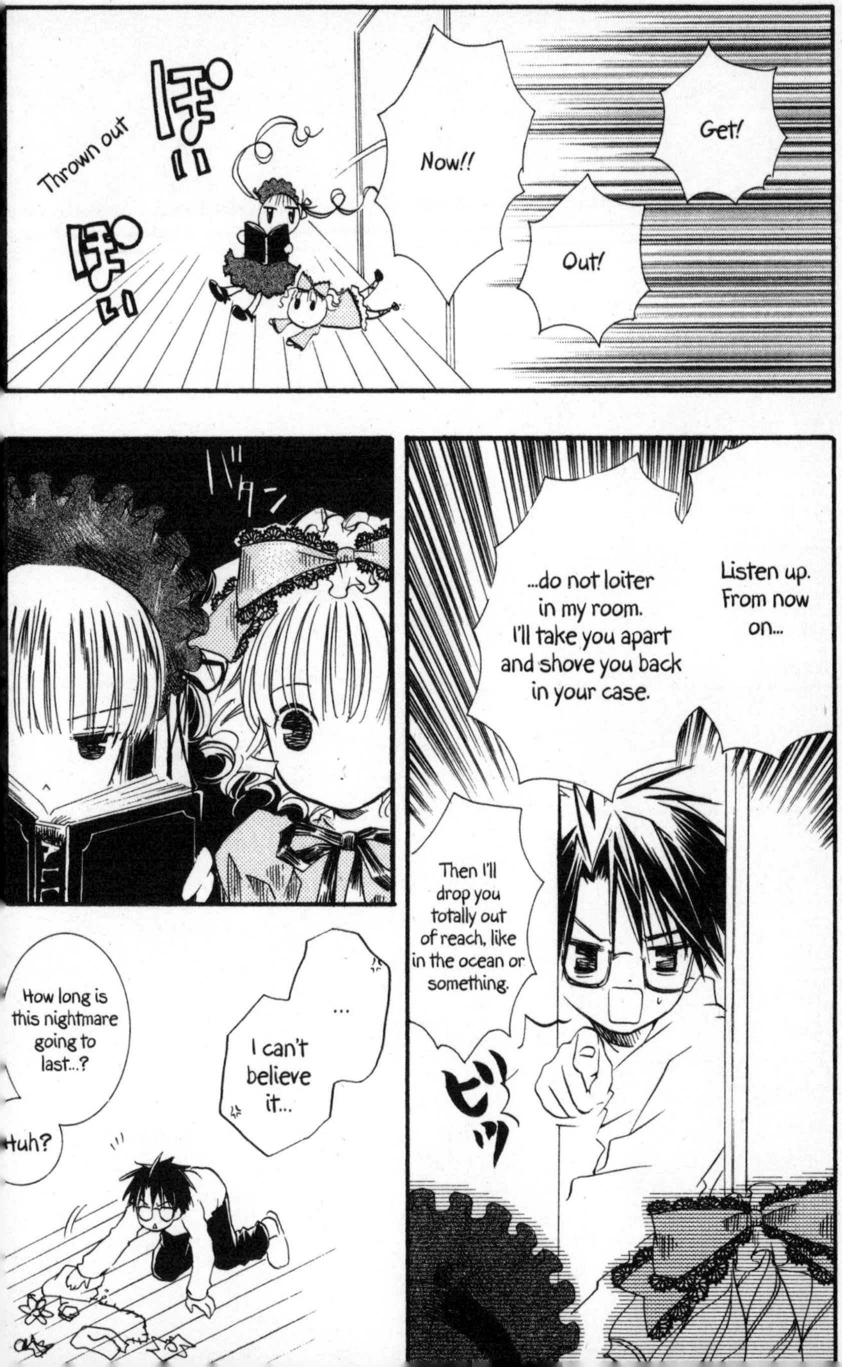
Get!
Out!
Now!!
Thrown out
ぽい
ぽい
Listen up. From now on...
...do not loiter in my room. I'll take you apart and shove you back in your case.
Then I'll drop you totally out of reach, like in the ocean or something.
ピッ
バタン
...
I can't believe it...
How long is this nightmare going to last...?
Huh?

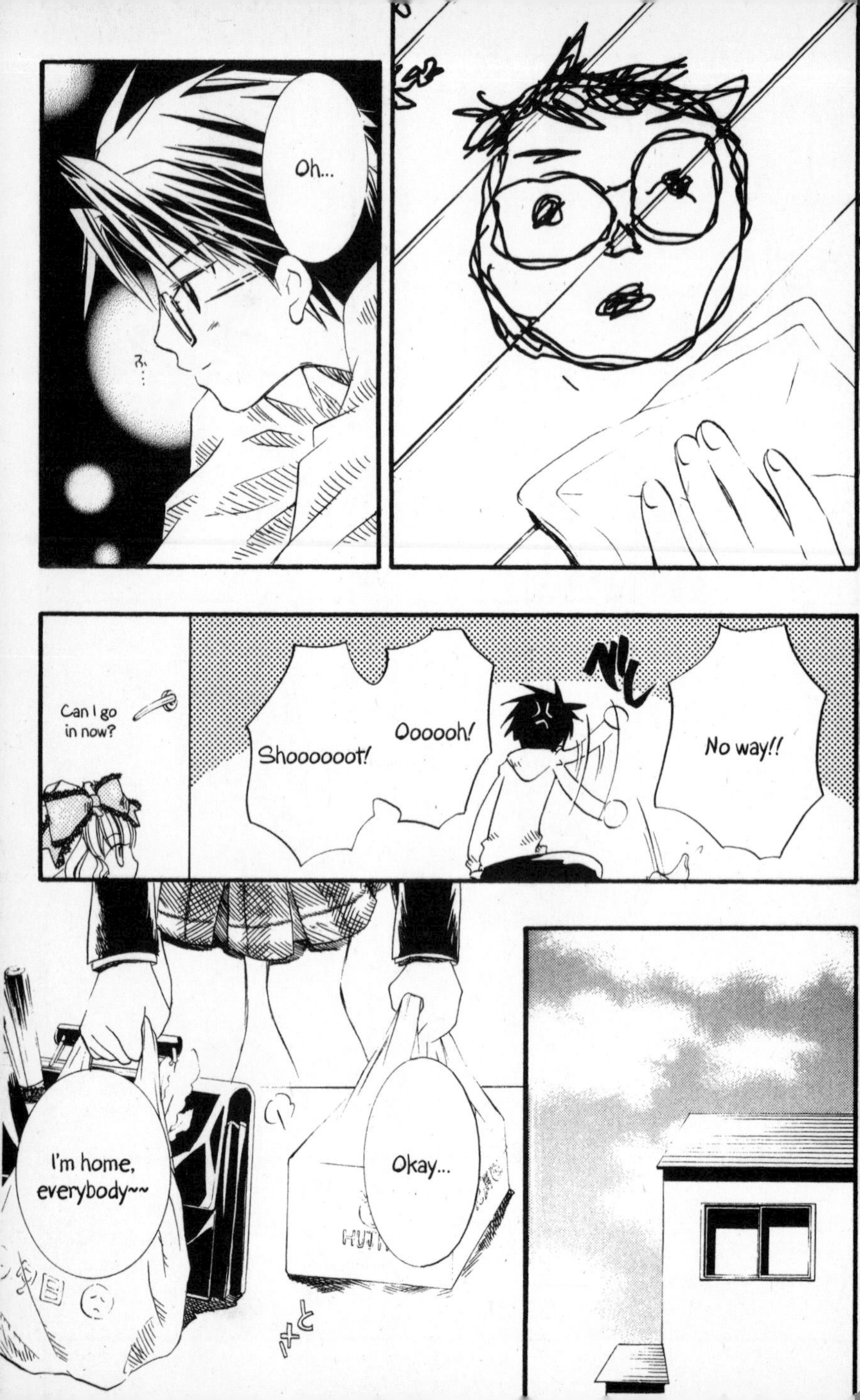
Oh...
No way!!
Ooooh!
Shoooooot!
Can I go in now?
Okay...
I'm home, everybody~~

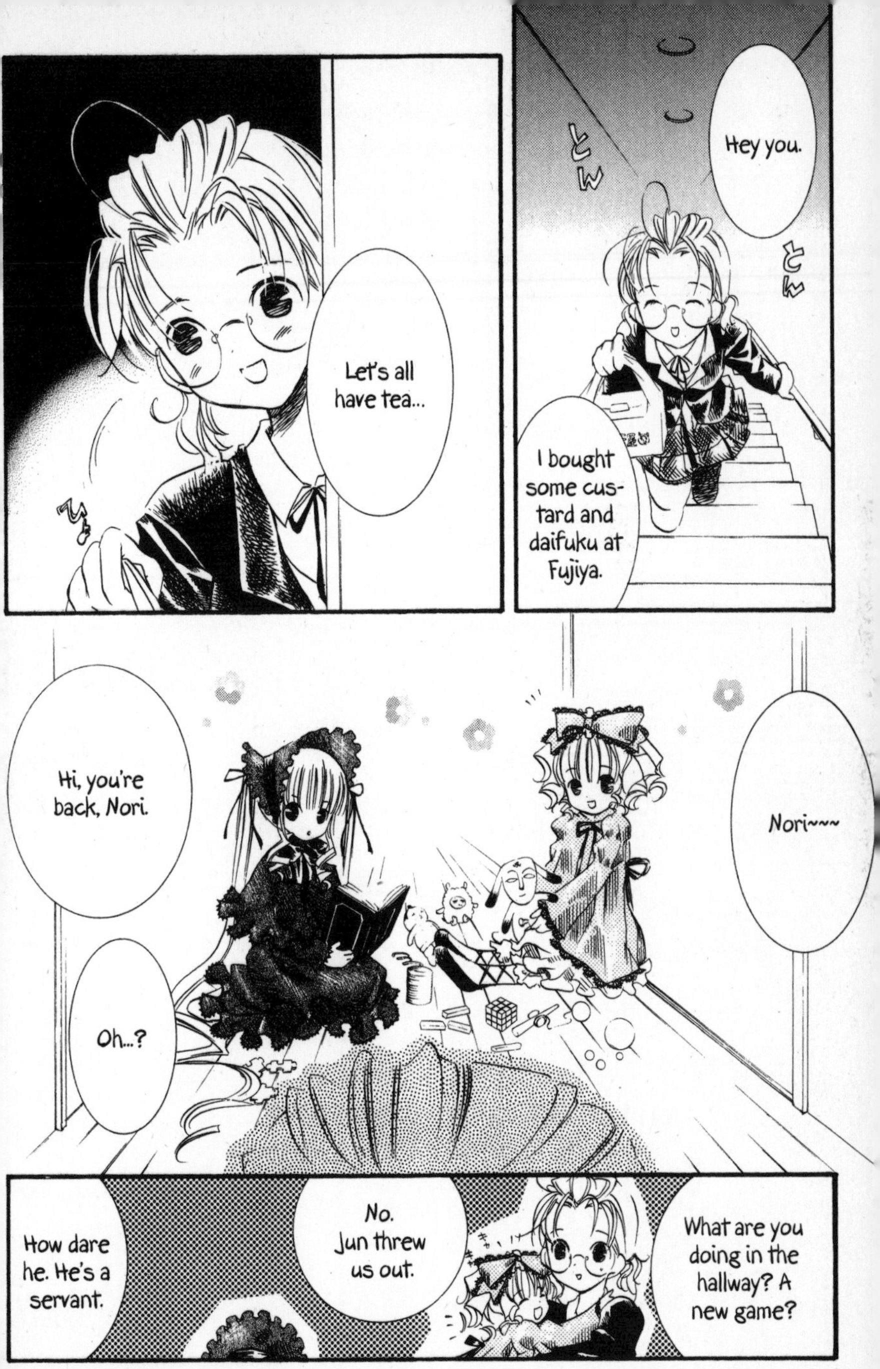
Hey you.
とん
とん
I bought some custard and daifuku at Fujiya.
Let's all have tea...
Nori~~~
Hi, you're back, Nori.
Oh...?
What are you doing in the hallway? A new game?
No. Jun threw us out.
How dare he. He's a servant.

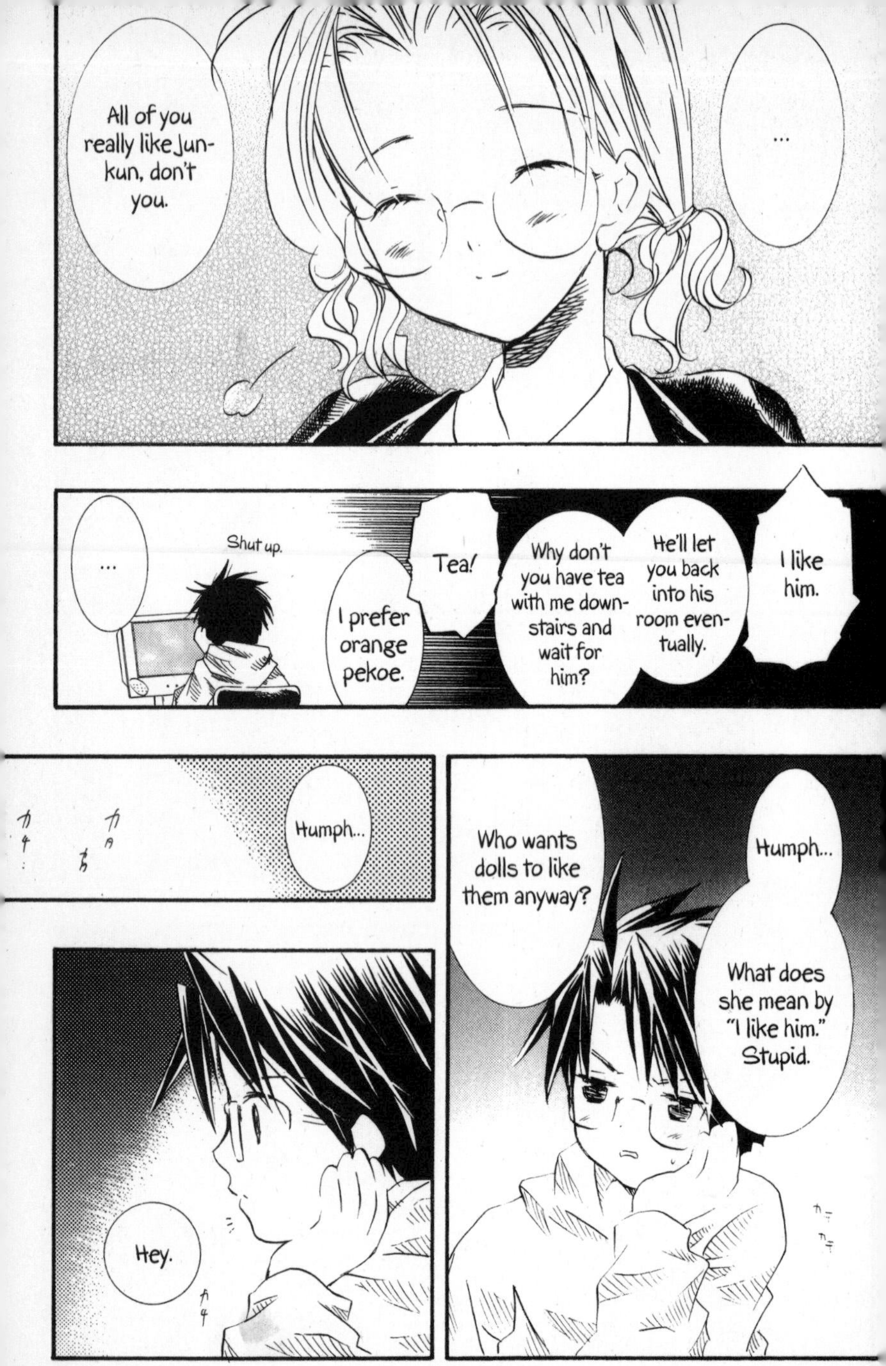
...
All of you really like Jun-kun, don't you.
I like him.
He'll let you back into his room eventually.
Why don't you have tea with me downstairs and wait for him?
Tea!
I prefer orange pekoe.
Shut up.
...
Humph...
Who wants dolls to like them anyway?
What does she mean by "I like him." Stupid.
Humph...
Hey.

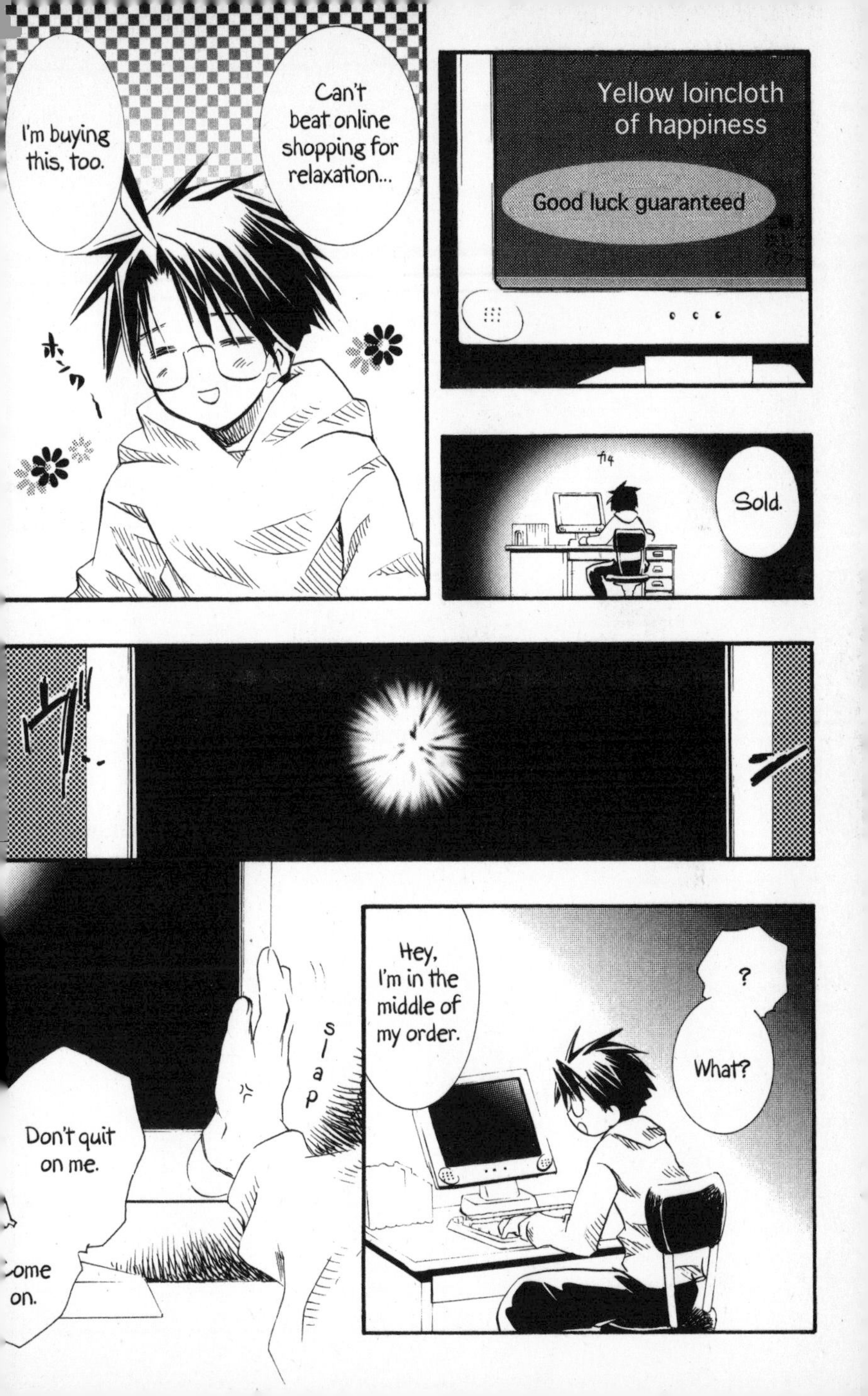
Yellow loincloth of happiness
Good luck guaranteed
Sold.
Can't beat online shopping for relaxation...
I'm buying this, too.
?
What?
Hey, I'm in the middle of my order.
slap
Don't quit on me.
ome on.

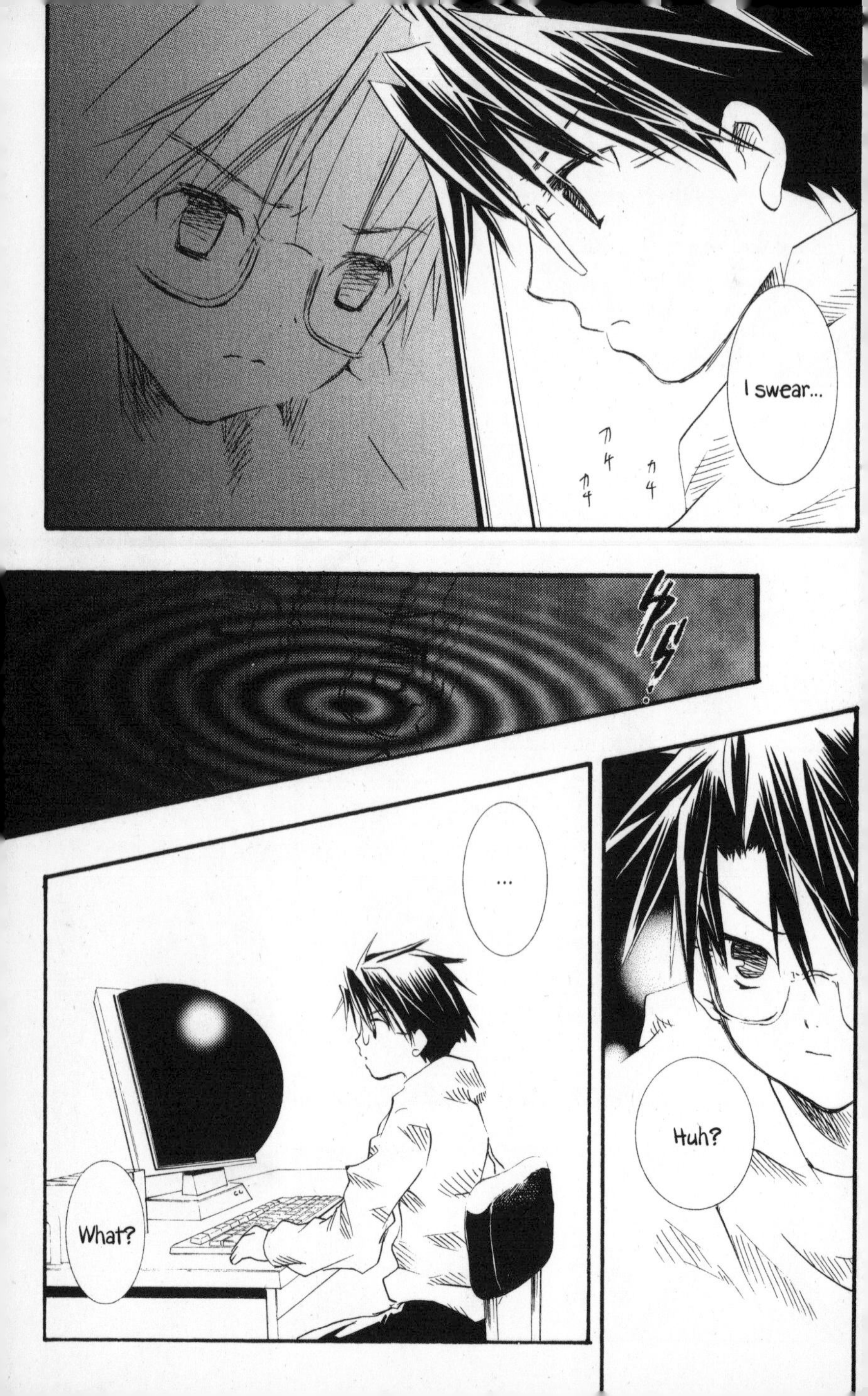
I swear...
カチ
カチ
カチ
Huh?
...
What?

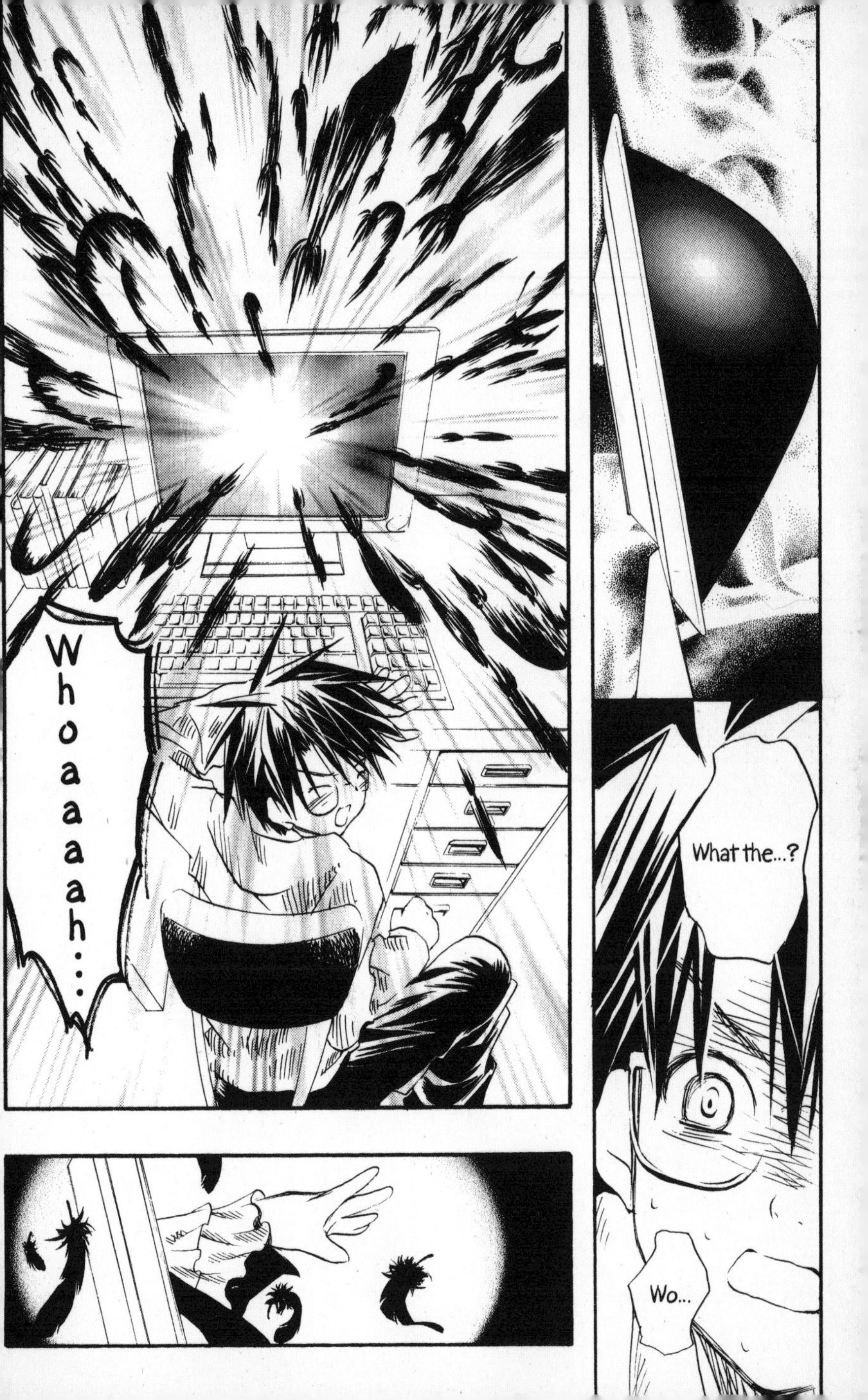
What the...?
Wo...
Whoaaaaah...

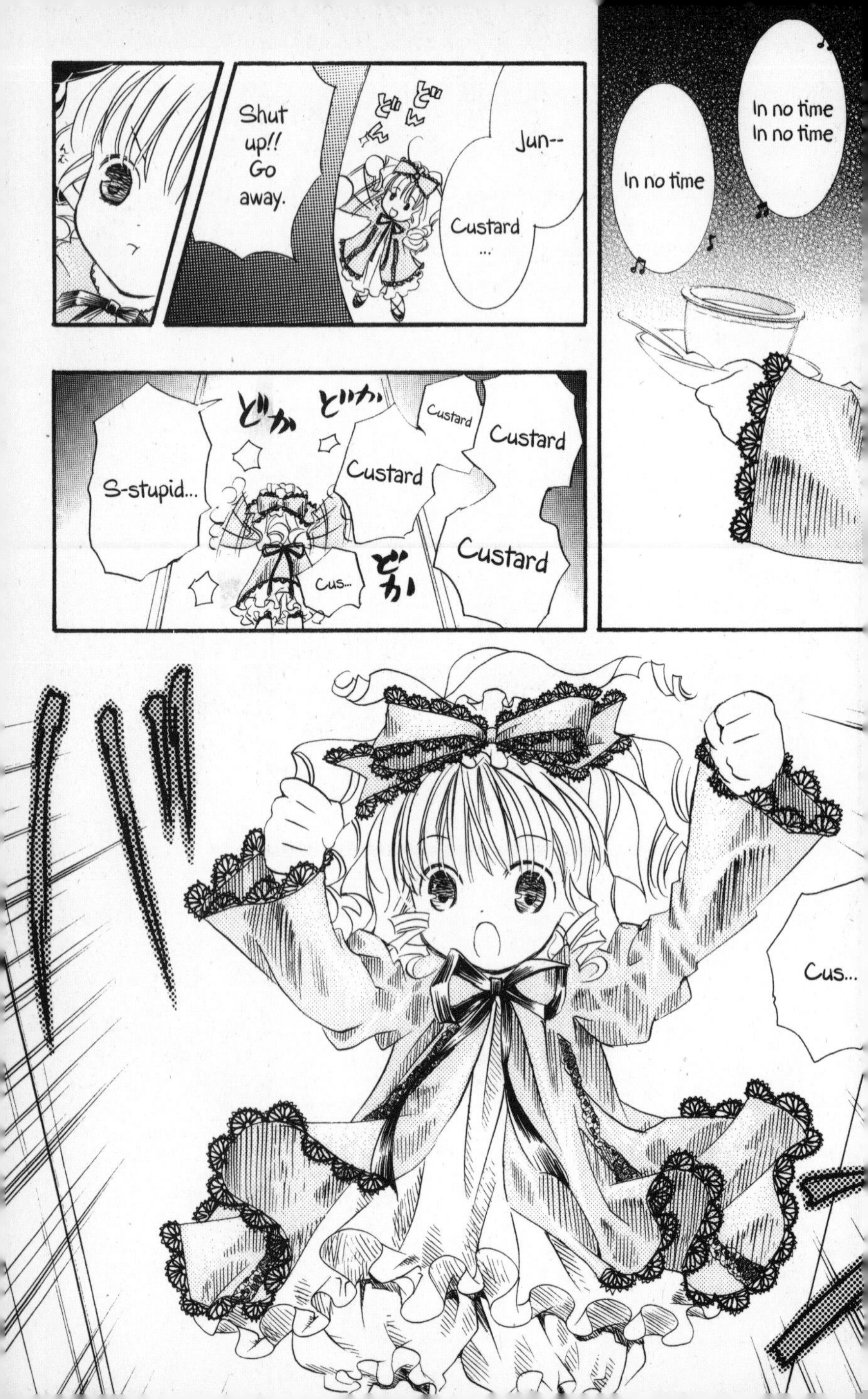
In no time
In no time
In no time
Jun--
Custard
...
Shut up!!
Go away.
Custard
Custard
Custard
Custard
Cus...
S-stupid...
Cus...

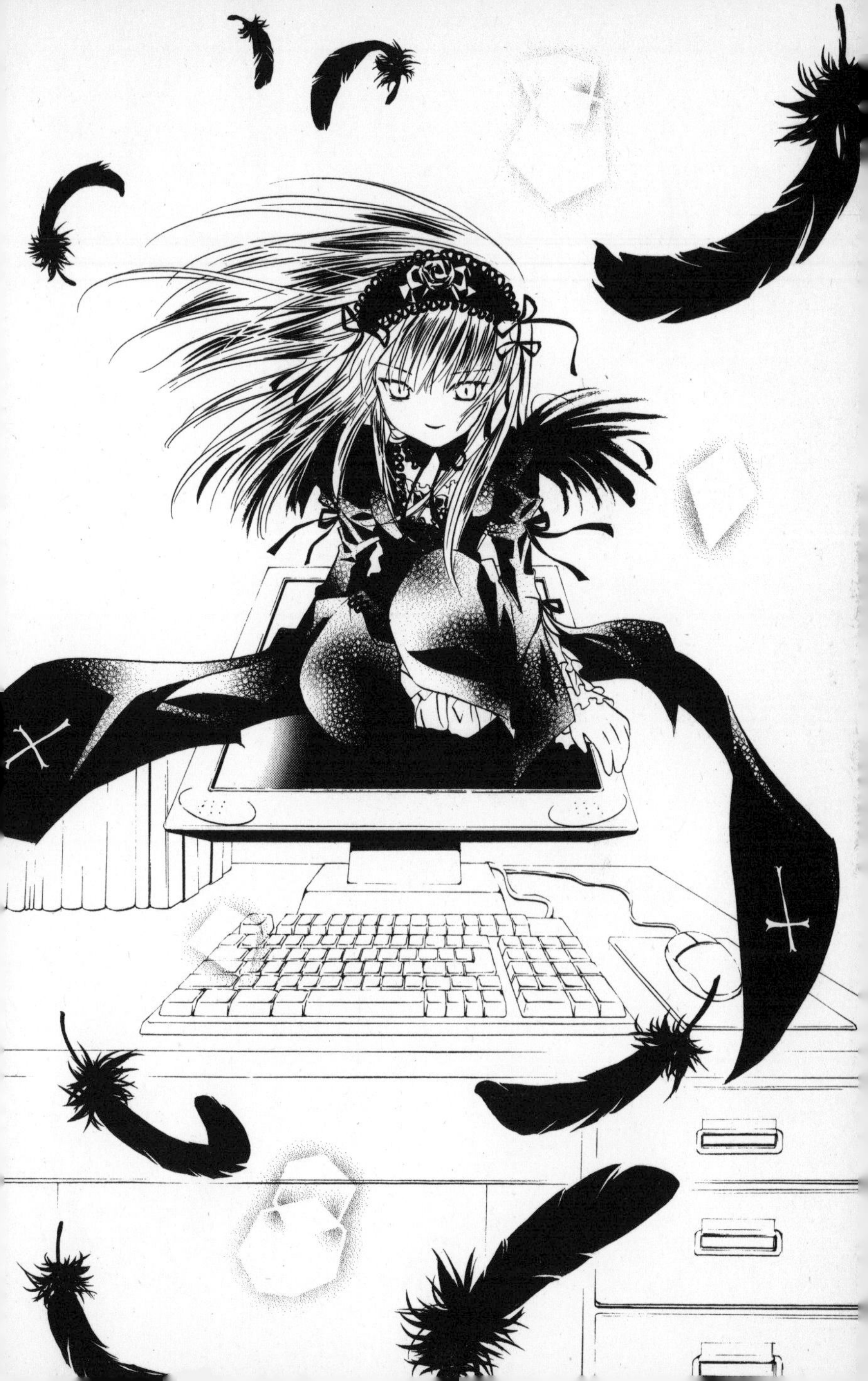

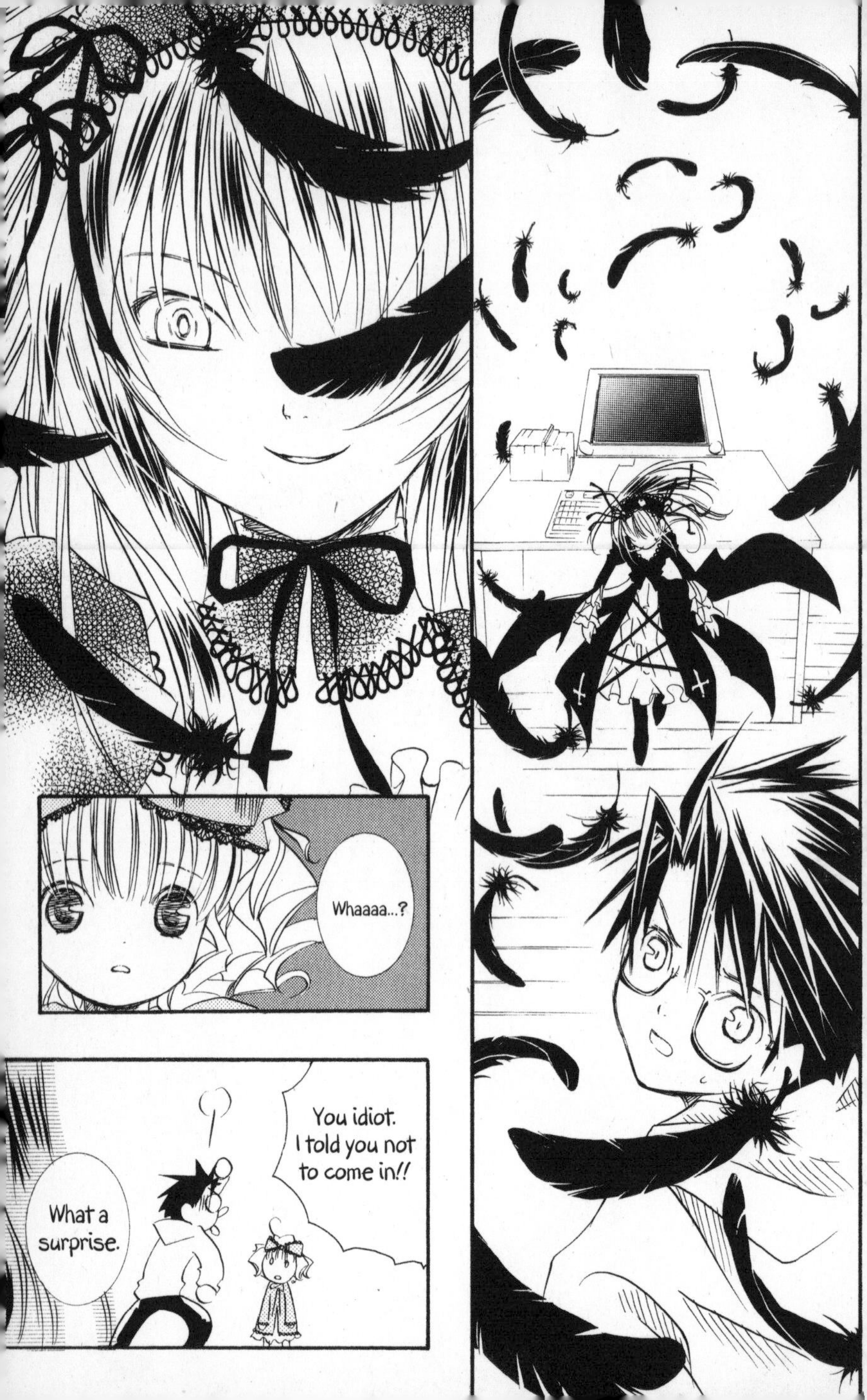
Whaaaa...?
You idiot. I told you not to come in!!
What a surprise.

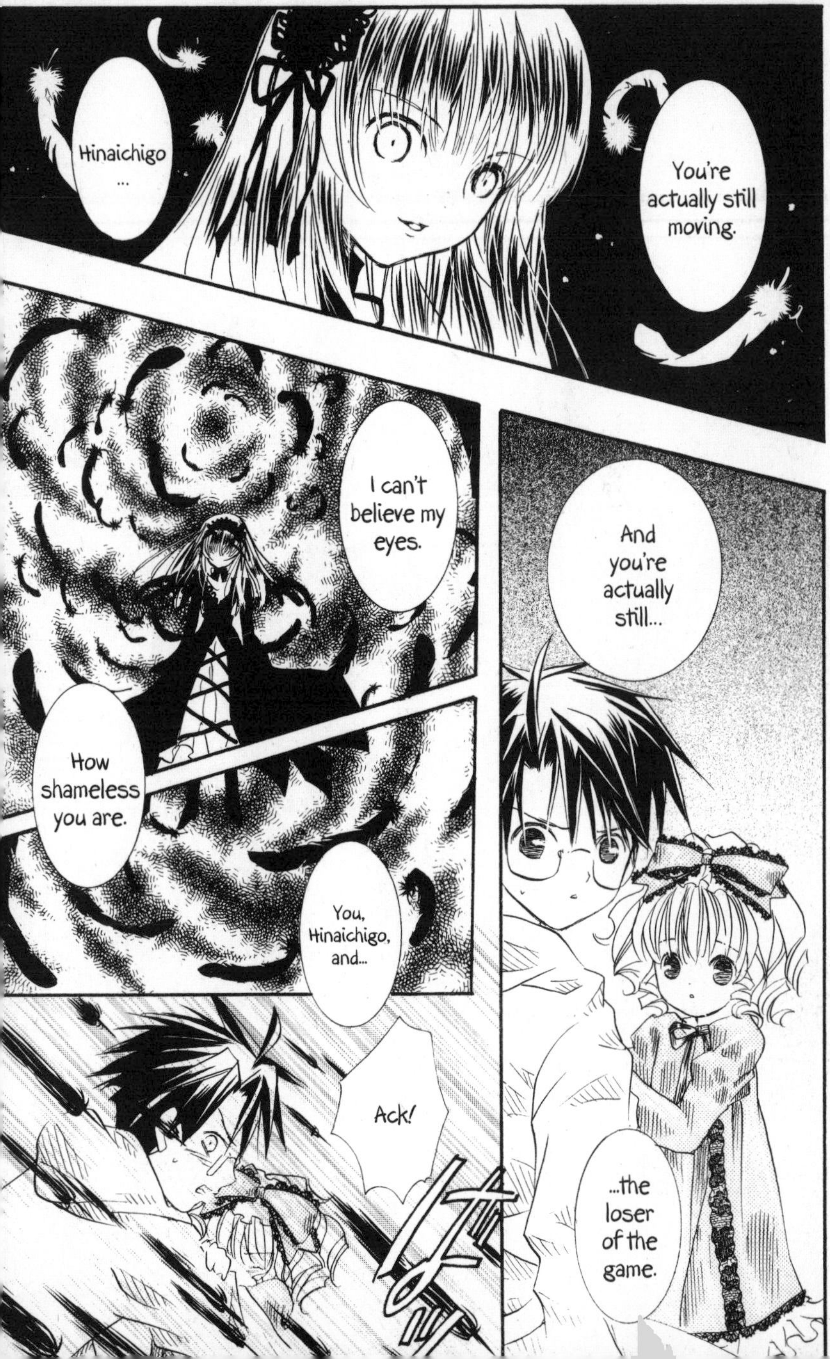
You're actually still moving.
Hinaichigo ...
And you're actually still...
...the loser of the game.
I can't believe my eyes.
How shameless you are.
You, Hinaichigo, and...
Ack!

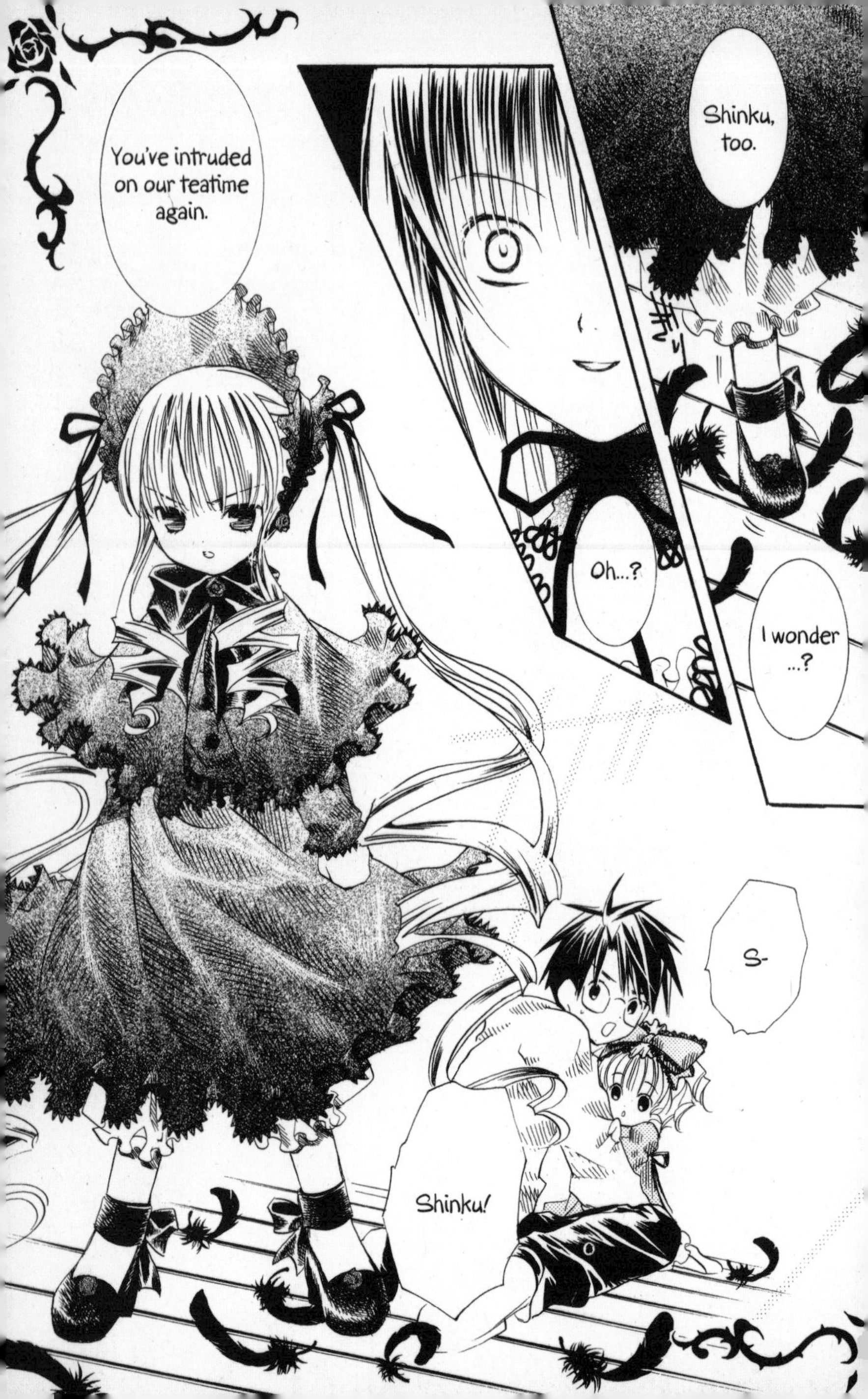
Shinku, too.
I wonder ...?
Oh...?
You've intruded on our teatime again.
S-
Shinku!

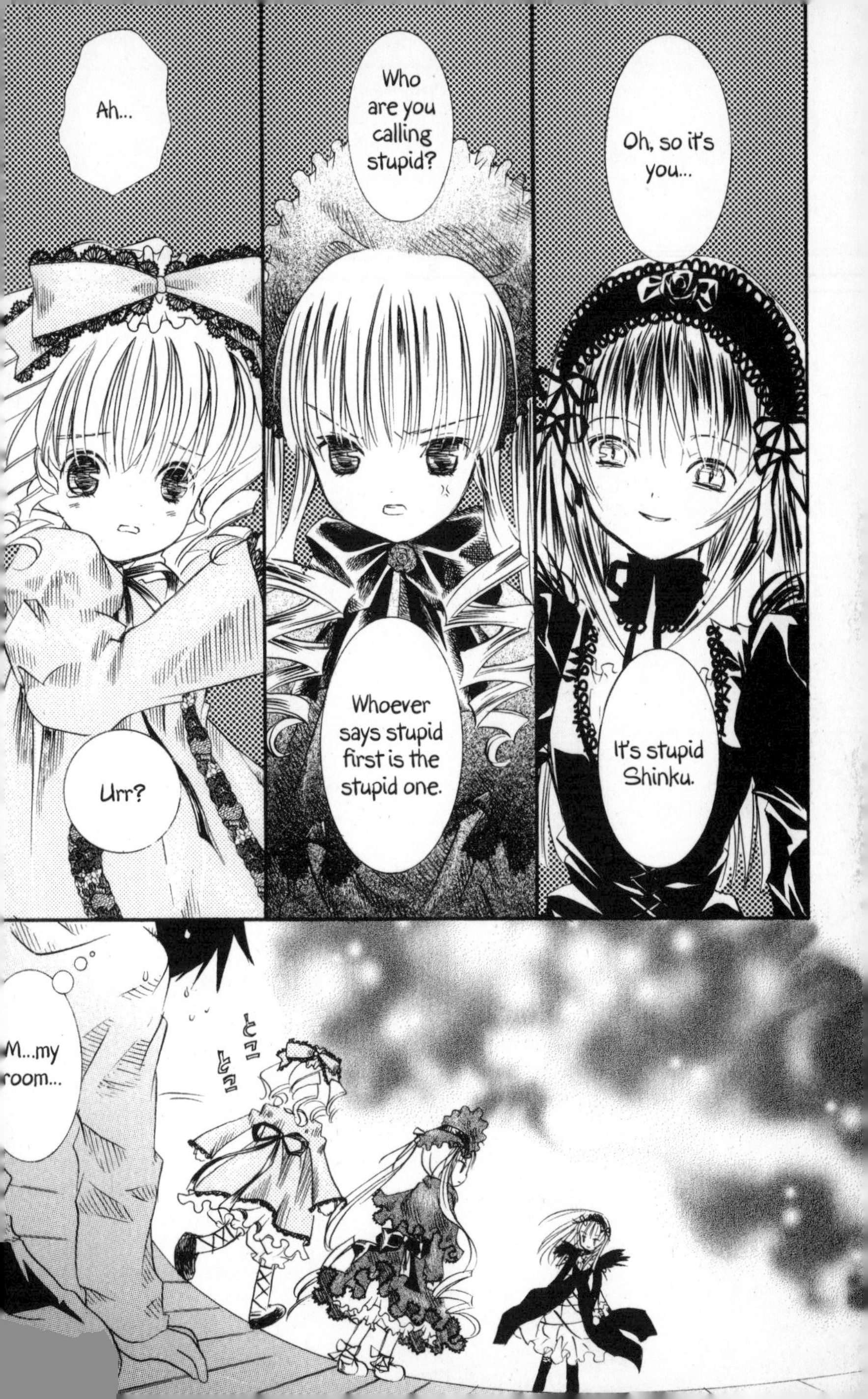
Oh, so it's you...
It's stupid Shinku.
Who are you calling stupid?
Whoever says stupid first is the stupid one.
Ah...
Urr?
M...my room...

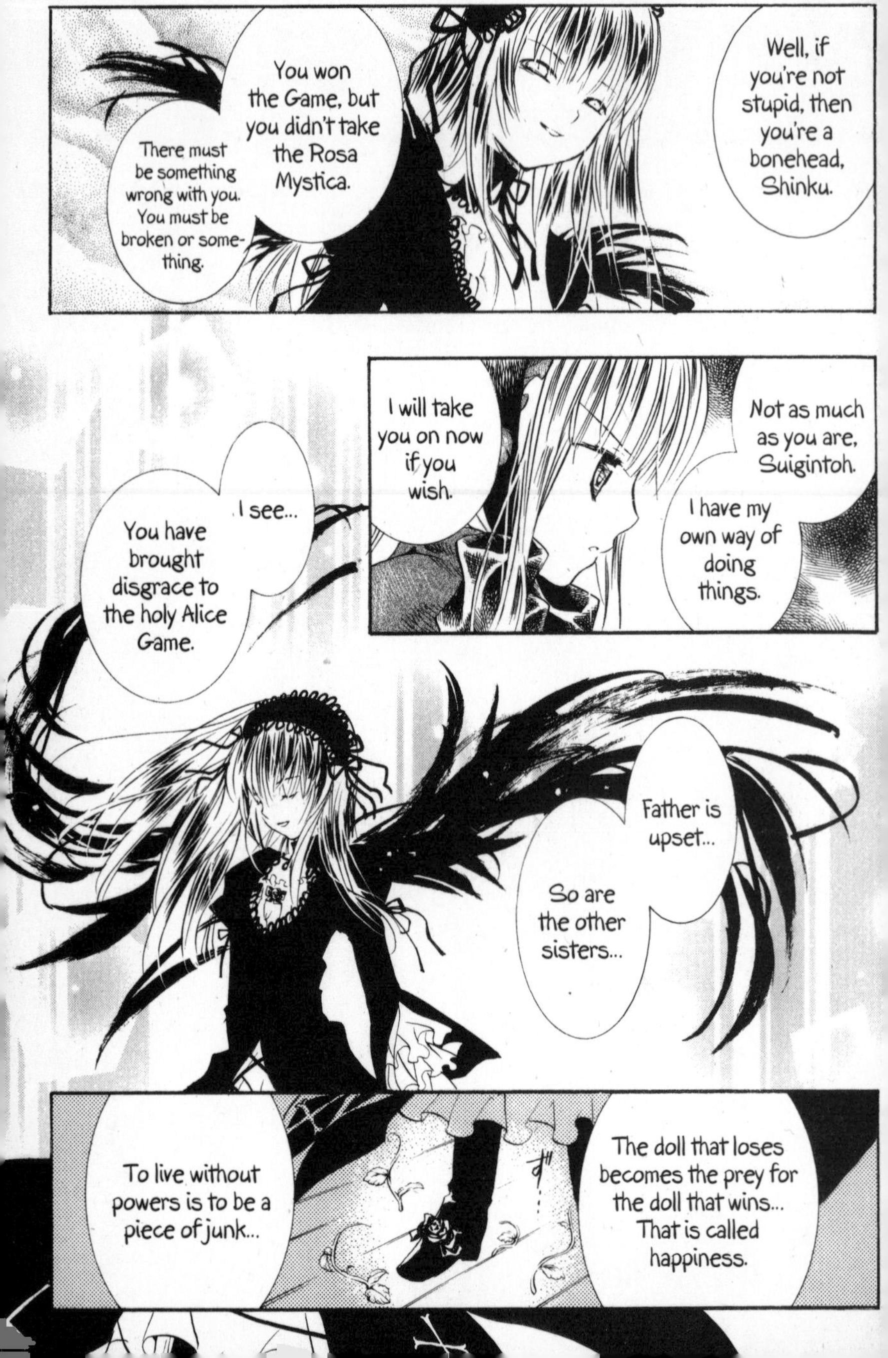
Well, if you're not stupid, then you're a bonehead, Shinku.
You won the Game, but you didn't take the Rosa Mystica.
There must be something wrong with you. You must be broken or something.
Not as much as you are, Suigintoh.
I have my own way of doing things.
I will take you on now if you wish.
I see...
You have brought disgrace to the holy Alice Game.
Father is upset...
So are the other sisters...
The doll that loses becomes the prey for the doll that wins... That is called happiness.
ず
To live without powers is to be a piece of junk...

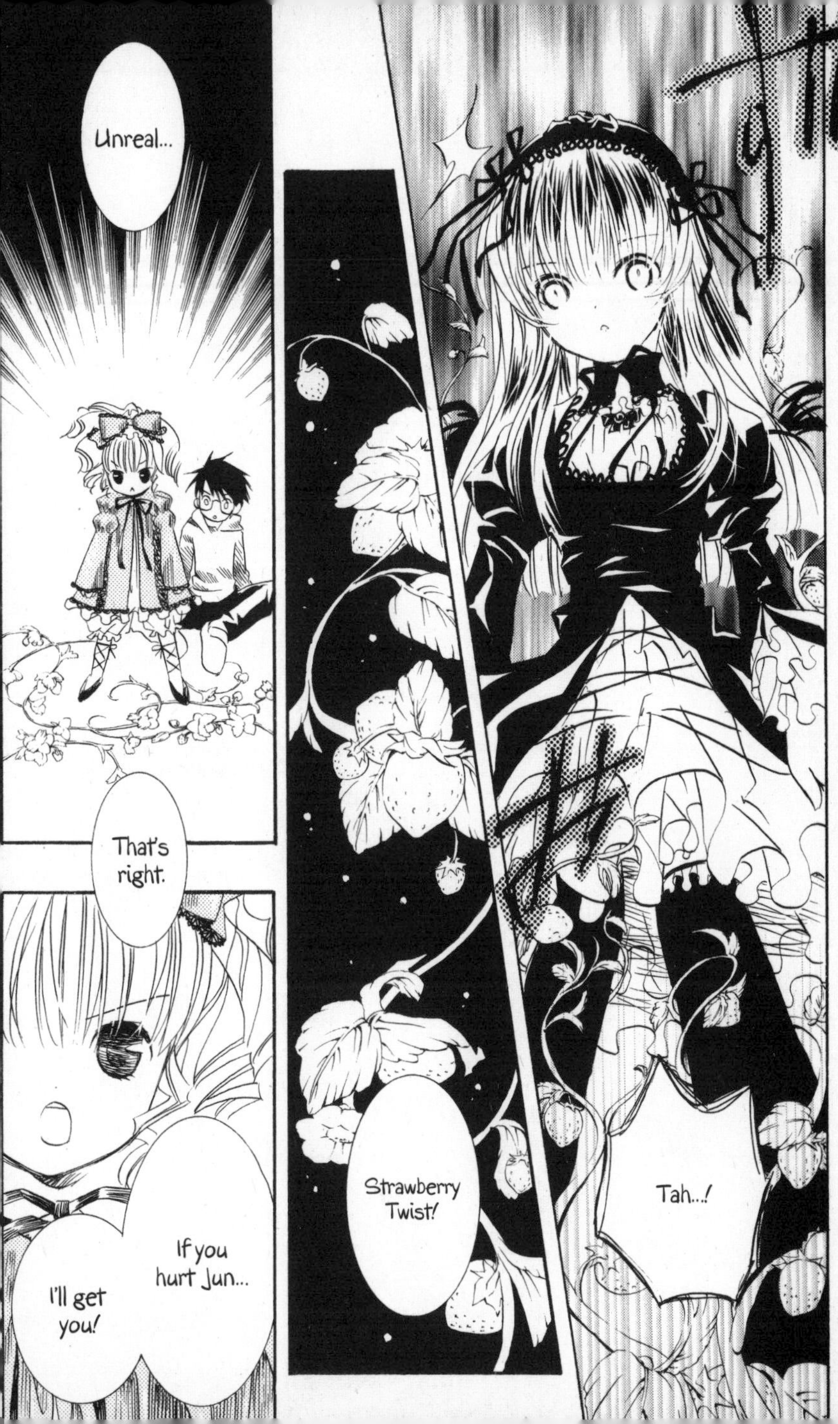
Tah...!
Strawberry Twist!
Unreal...
That's right.
If you hurt Jun...
I'll get you!

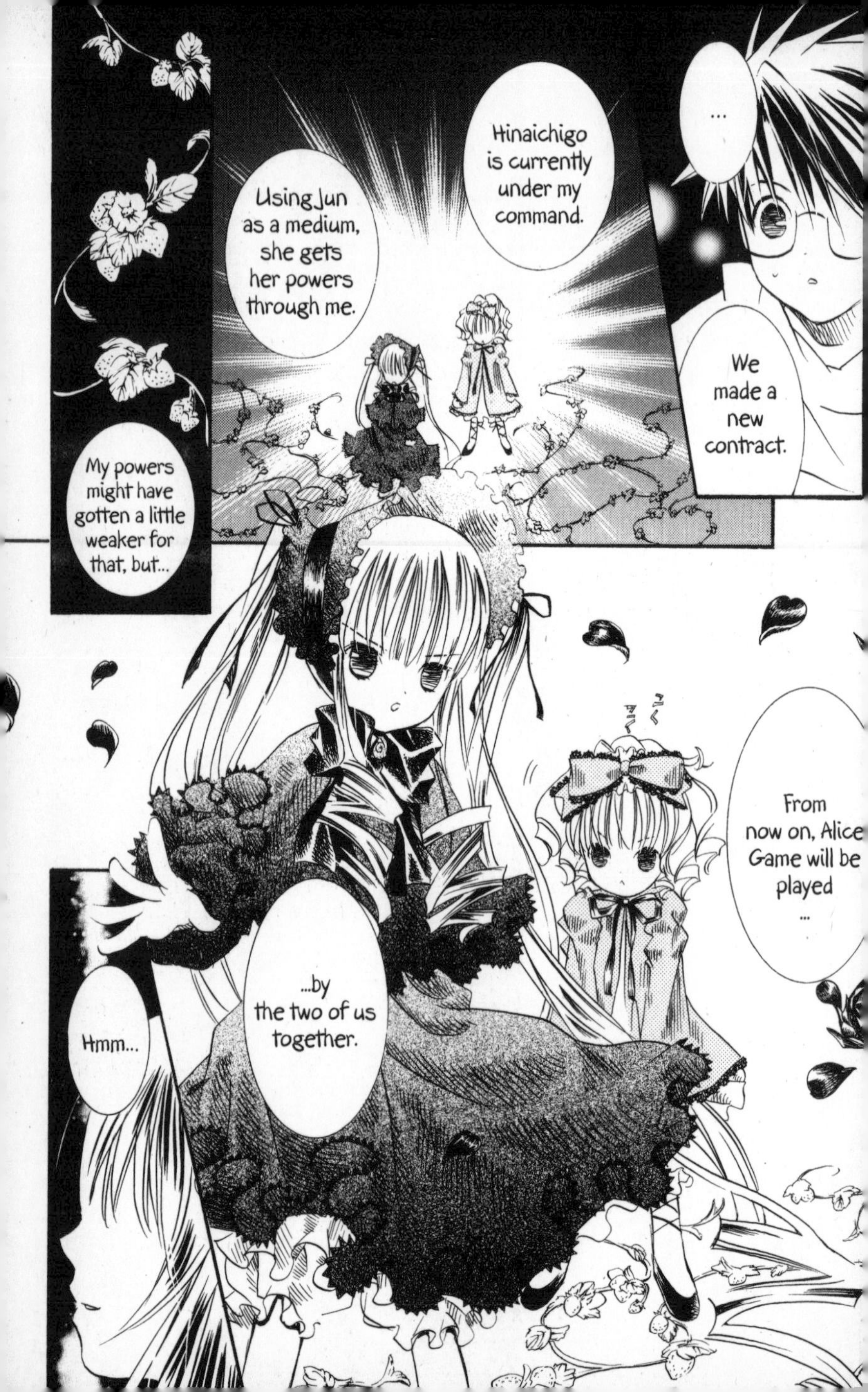
...
We made a new contract.
Hinaichigo is currently under my command.
Using Jun as a medium, she gets her powers through me.
My powers might have gotten a little weaker for that, but...
From now on, Alice Game will be played ...
...by the two of us together.
Hmm...

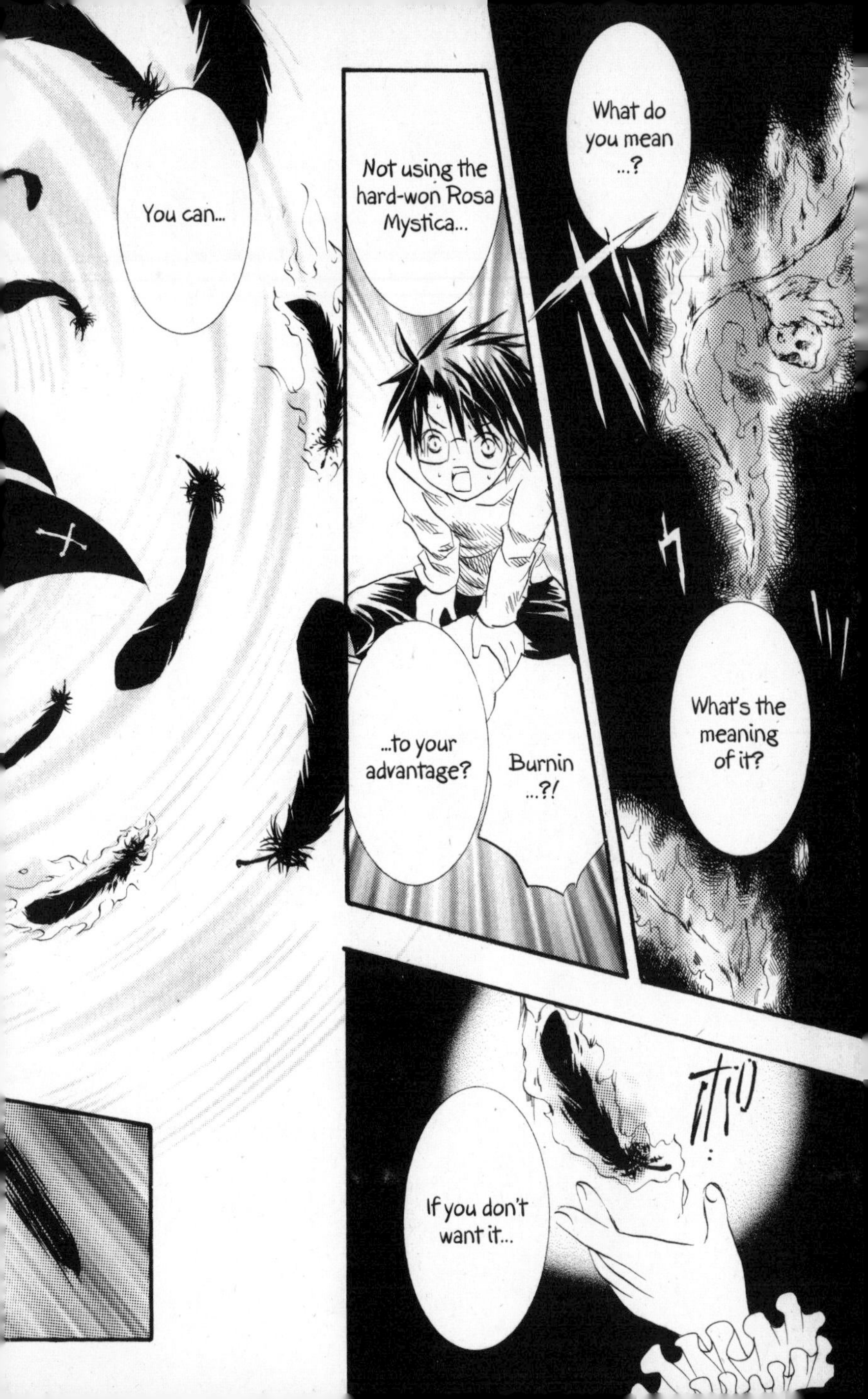
What do you mean ...?
What's the meaning of it?
Not using the hard-won Rosa Mystica...
...to your advantage?
Burnin ...?!
You can...
If you don't want it...

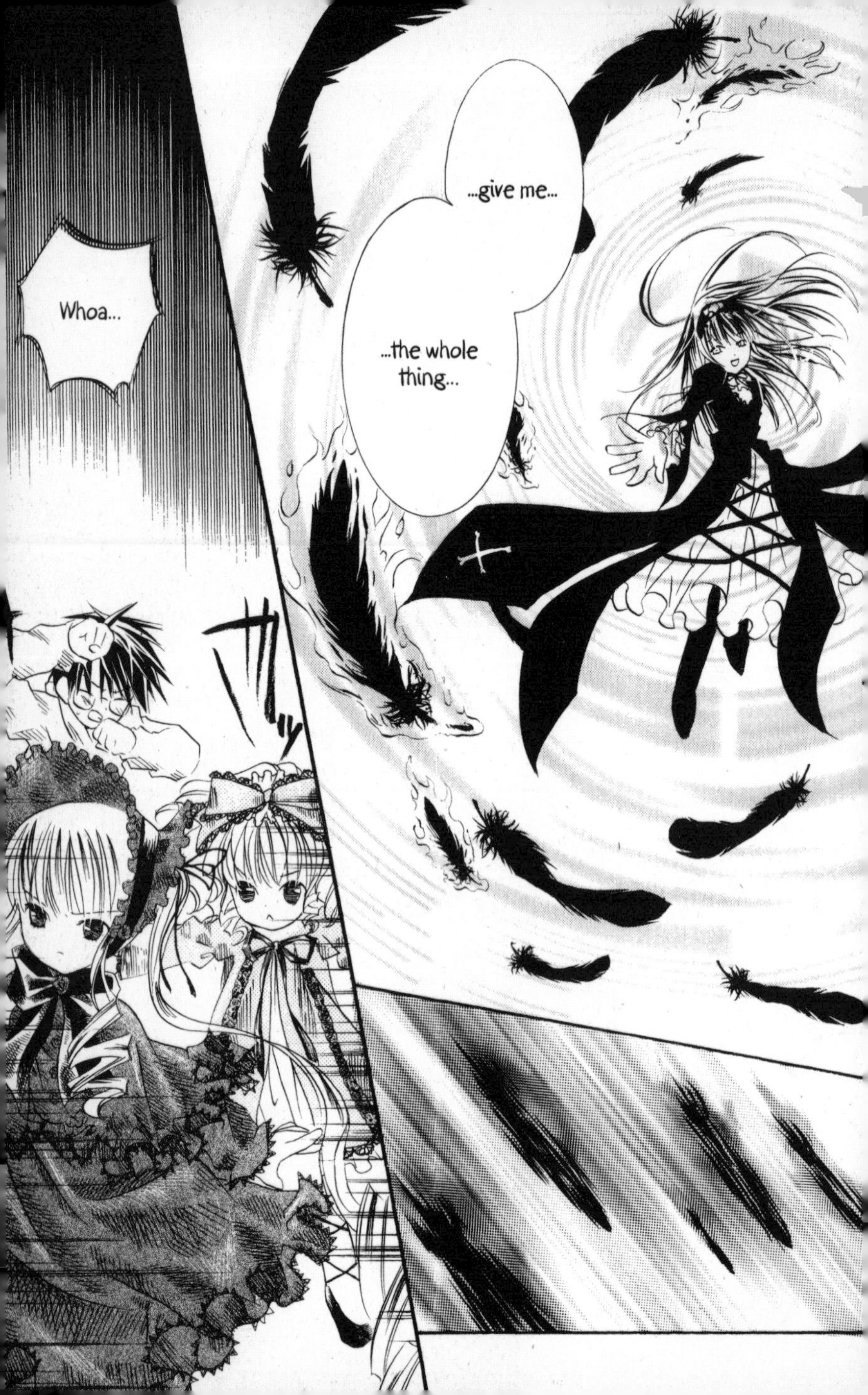

...give me...
...the whole thing...
Whoa...

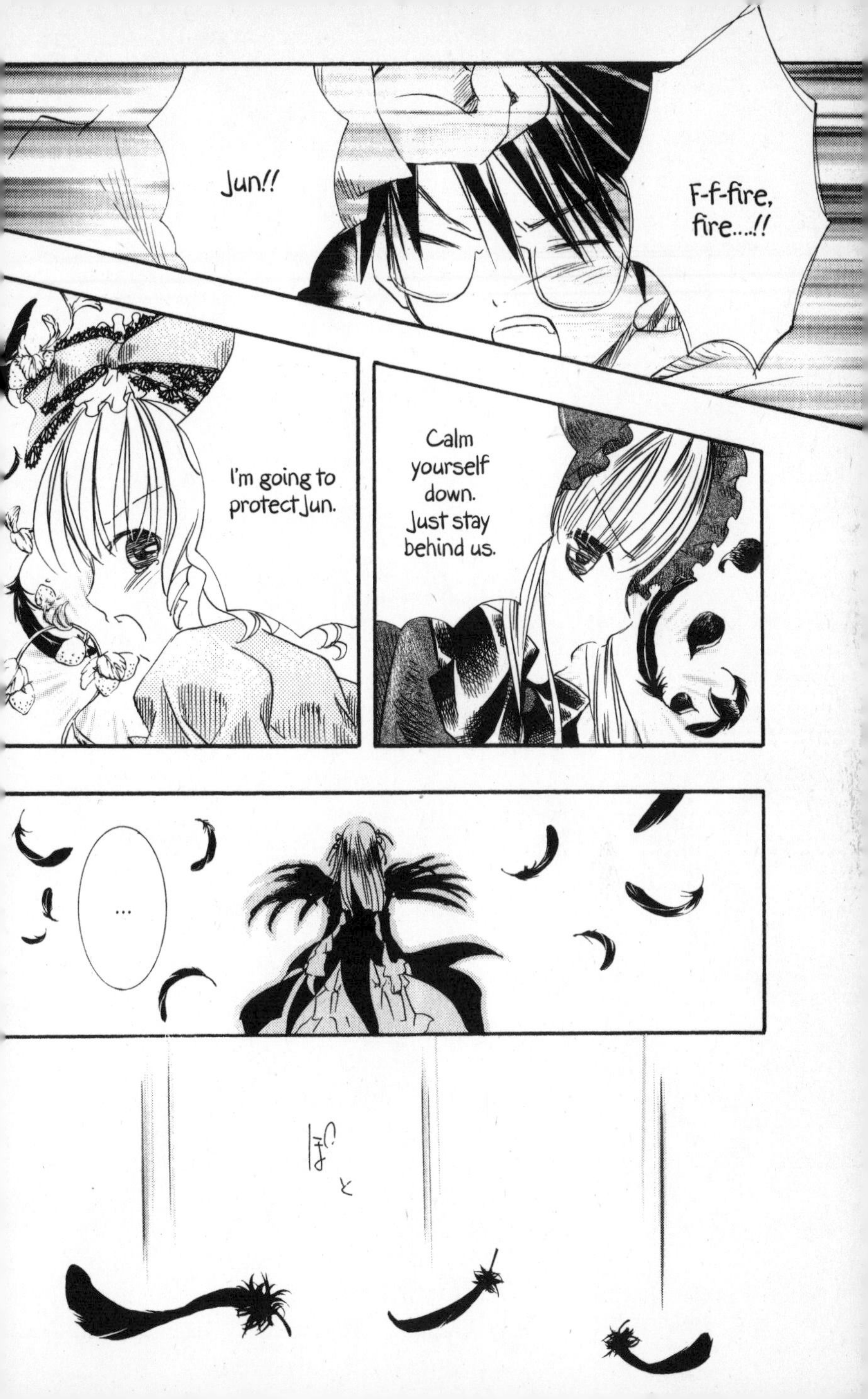
F-f-fire, fire....!!
Jun!!
Calm yourself down. Just stay behind us.
I'm going to protect Jun.
...
ぽと

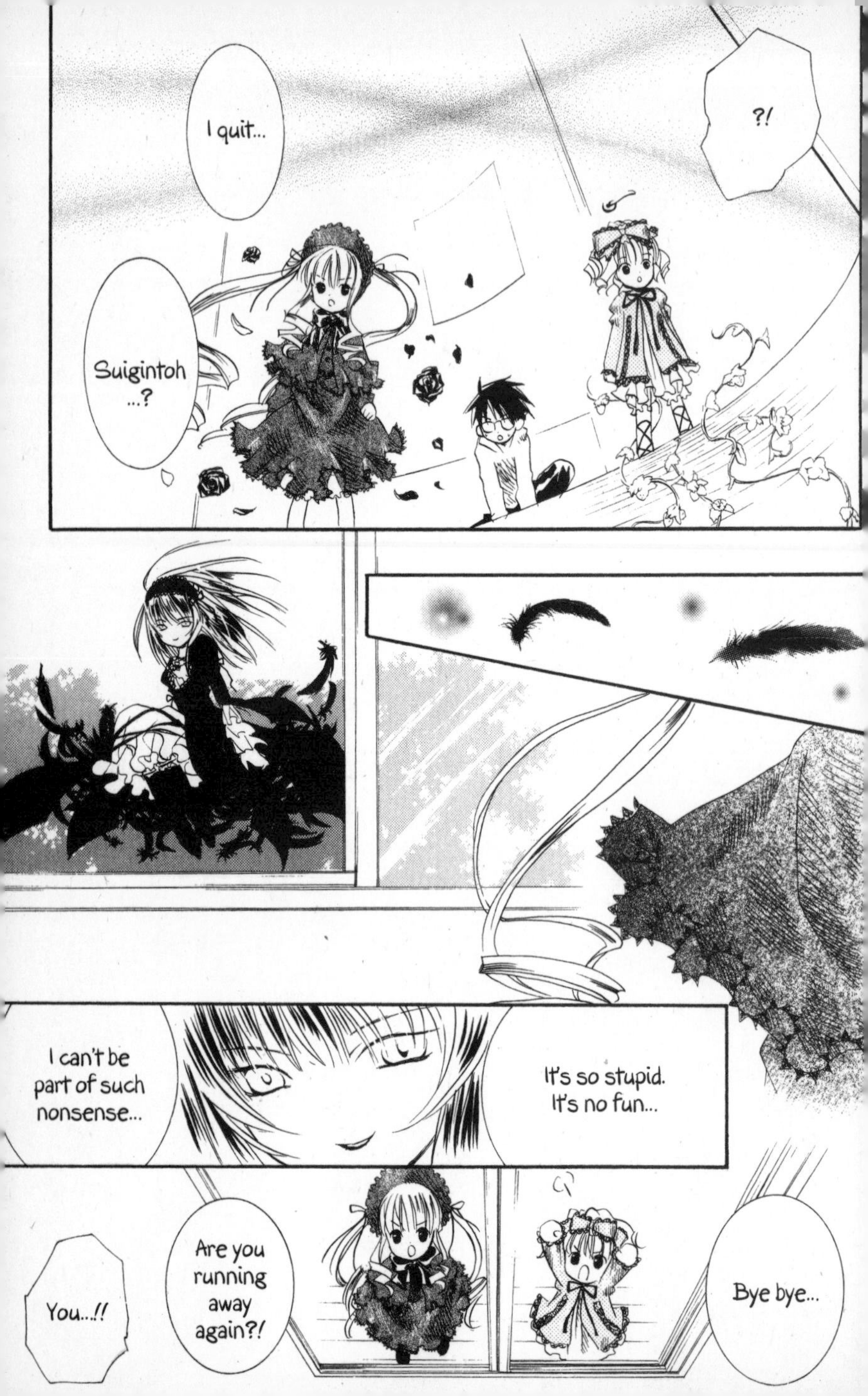
?!
I quit...
Suigintoh ...?
It's so stupid. It's no fun...
I can't be part of such nonsense...
Bye bye...
Are you running away again?!
You...!!

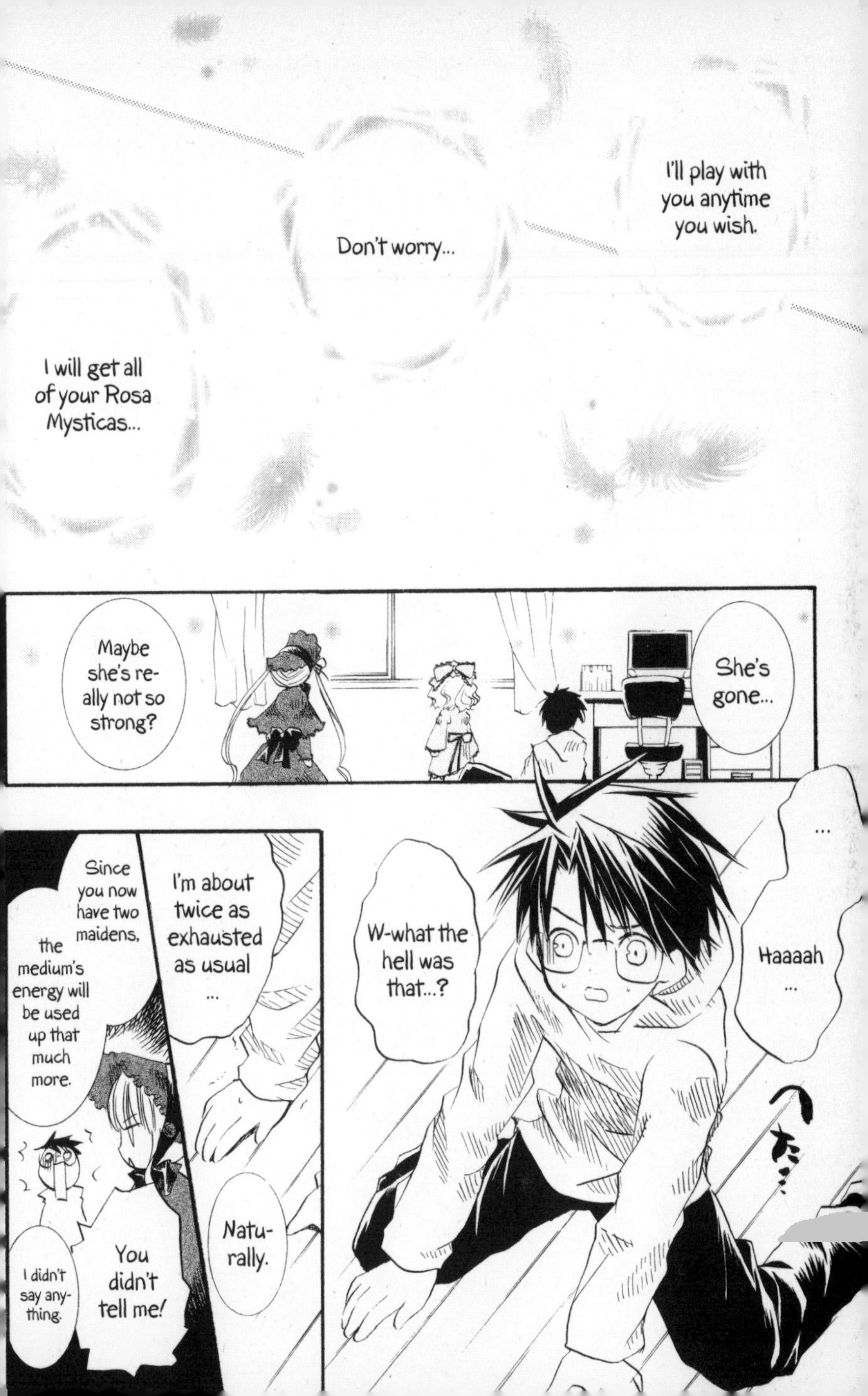
I'll play with you anytime you wish.
Don't worry...
I will get all of your Rosa Mysticas...
She's gone...
Maybe she's really not so strong?
...
Haaaah ...
W-what the hell was that...?
I'm about twice as exhausted as usual ...
Since you now have two maidens, the medium's energy will be used up that much more.
Naturally.
You didn't tell me!
I didn't say anything.

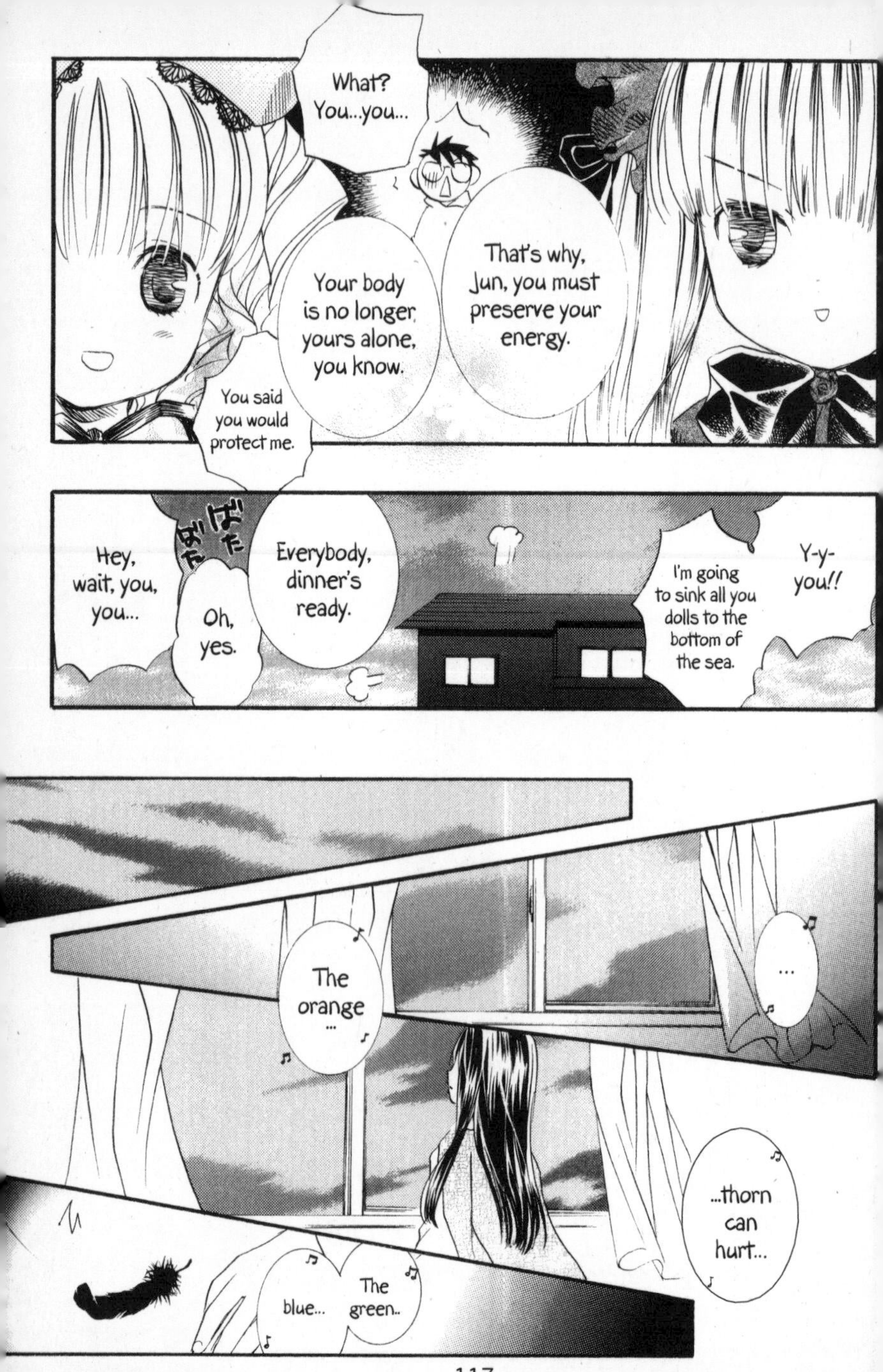
That's why, Jun, you must preserve your energy.
Your body is no longer yours alone, you know.
You said you would protect me.
What? You...you...
Y-y-you!!
I'm going to sink all you dolls to the bottom of the sea.
Everybody, dinner's ready.
ばたばた
Oh, yes.
Hey, wait, you, you...
...
The orange ...
...thorn can hurt...
The green..
blue...

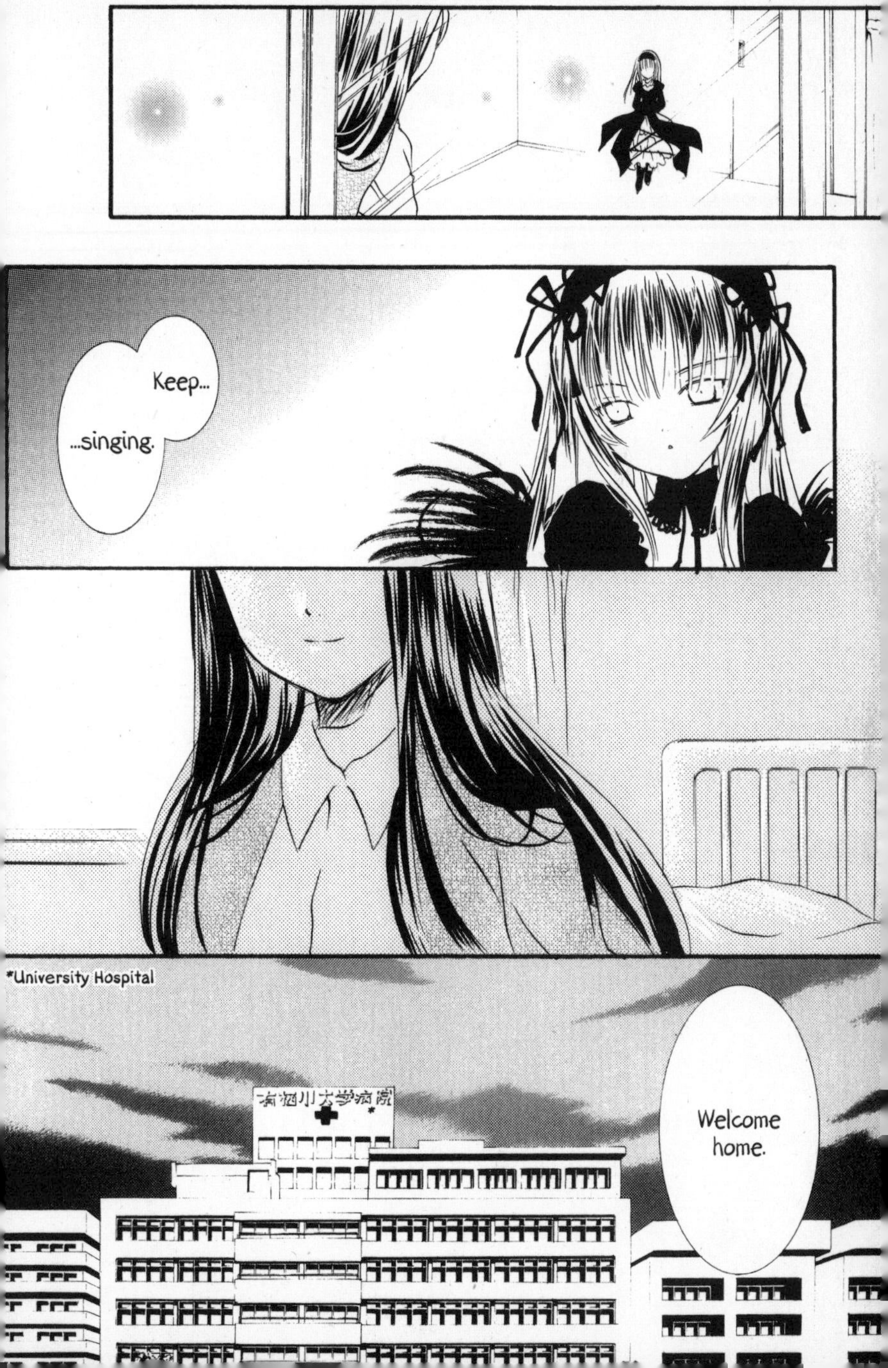
Keep...
...singing.
*University Hospital
Welcome home.

Phase 9

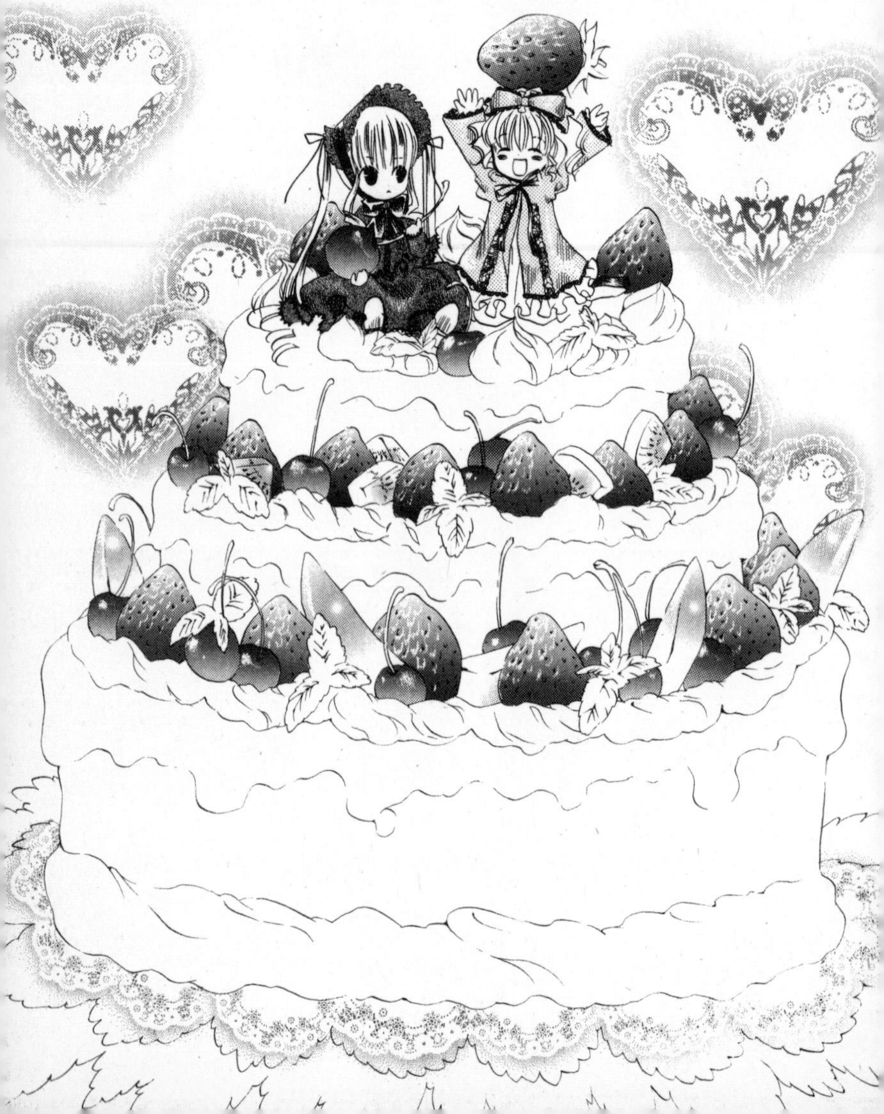

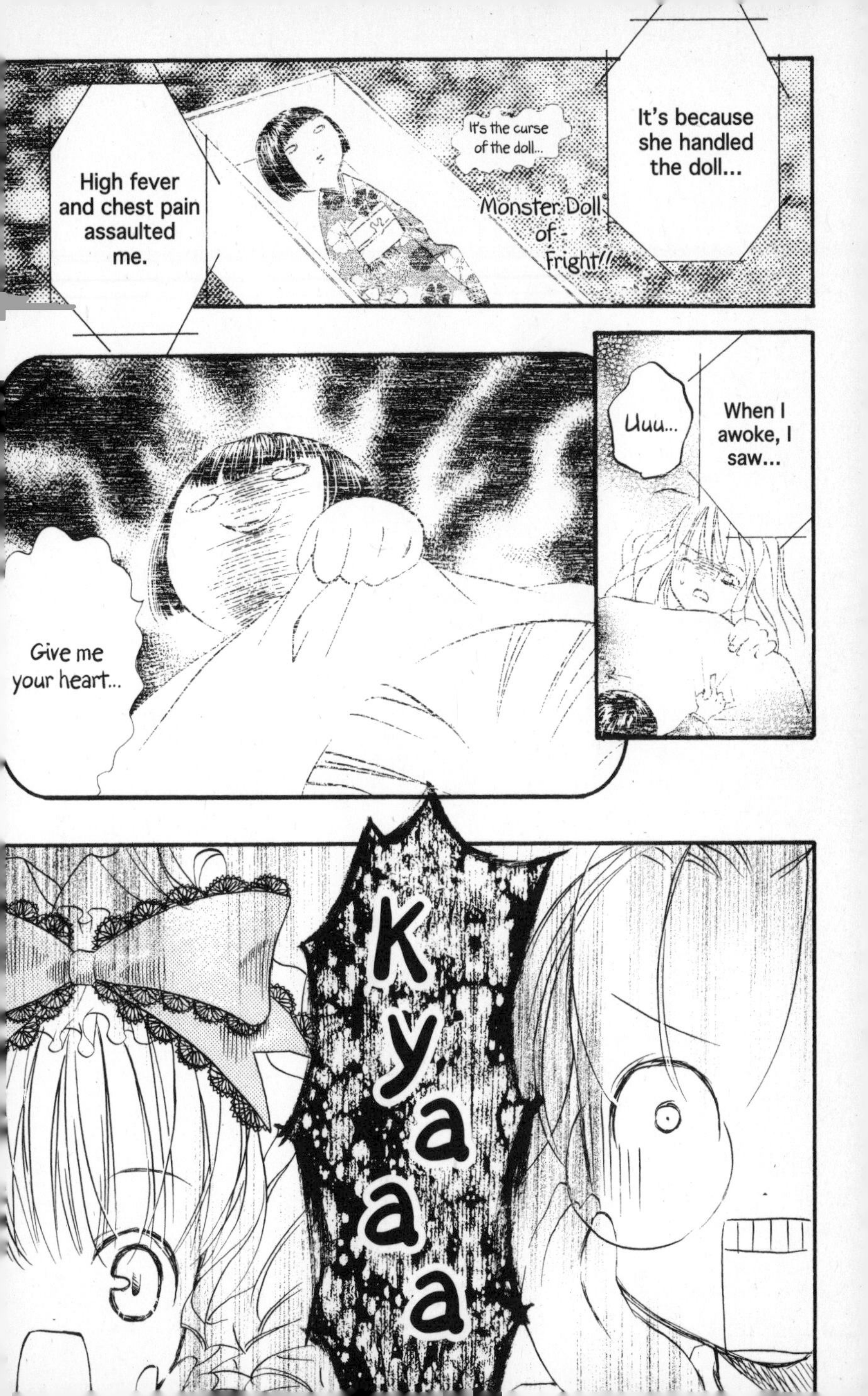
It's because she handled the doll...
It's the curse of the doll...
Monster Doll of - Fright!!
High fever and chest pain assaulted me.
When I awoke, I saw...
Uuu...
Give me your heart...
Kyaaa

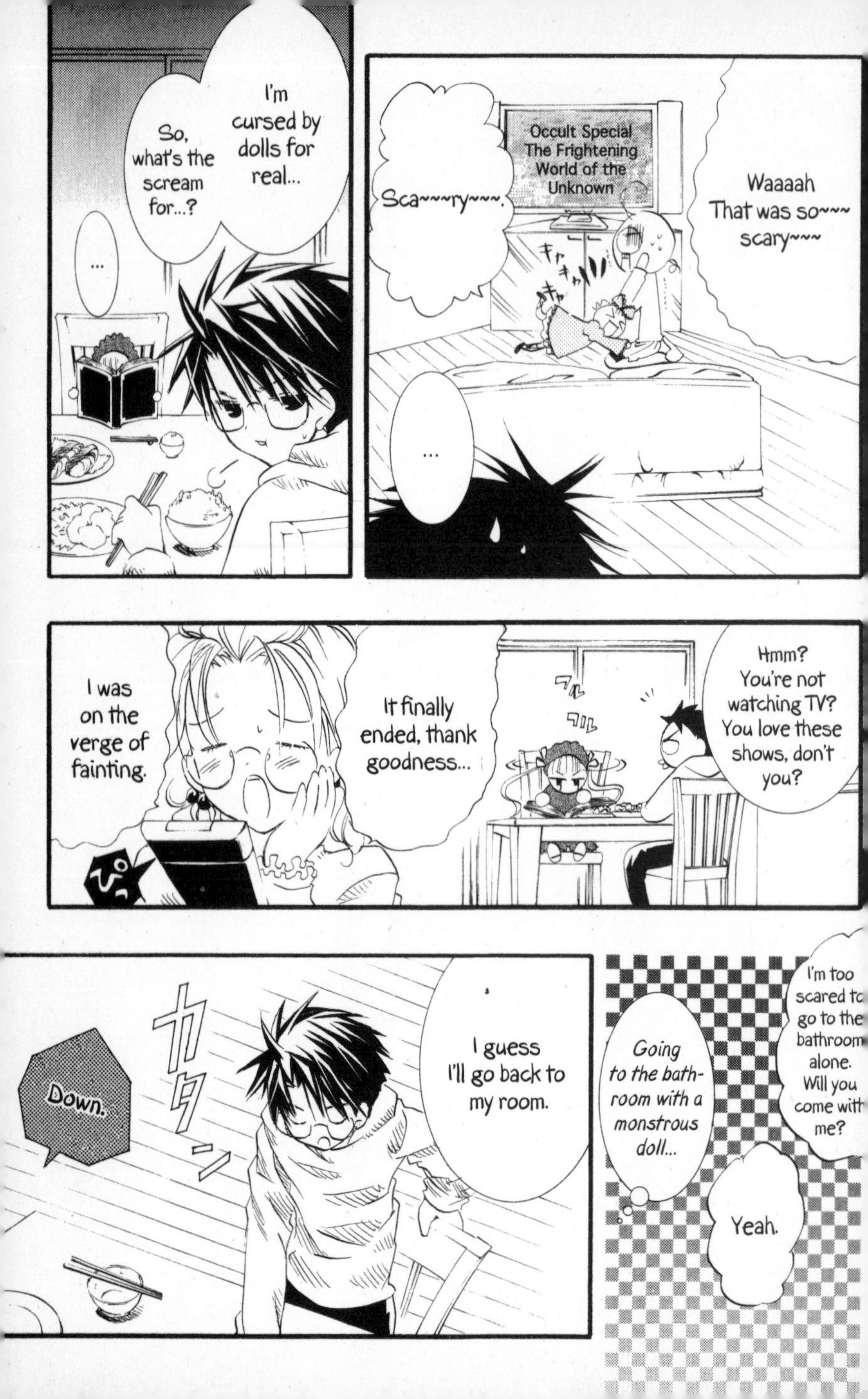
Waaaah That was so~~~ scary~~~
Occult Special The Frightening World of the Unknown
Sca~~~ry~~~.
キャキャキャ
...
I'm cursed by dolls for real...
So, what's the scream for...?
...
Hmm? You're not watching TV? You love these shows, don't you?
フルフル
It finally ended, thank goodness...
I was on the verge of fainting.
I'm too scared to go to the bathroom alone. Will you come with me?
Yeah.
Going to the bathroom with a monstrous doll...
I guess I'll go back to my room.
カタン
Down.

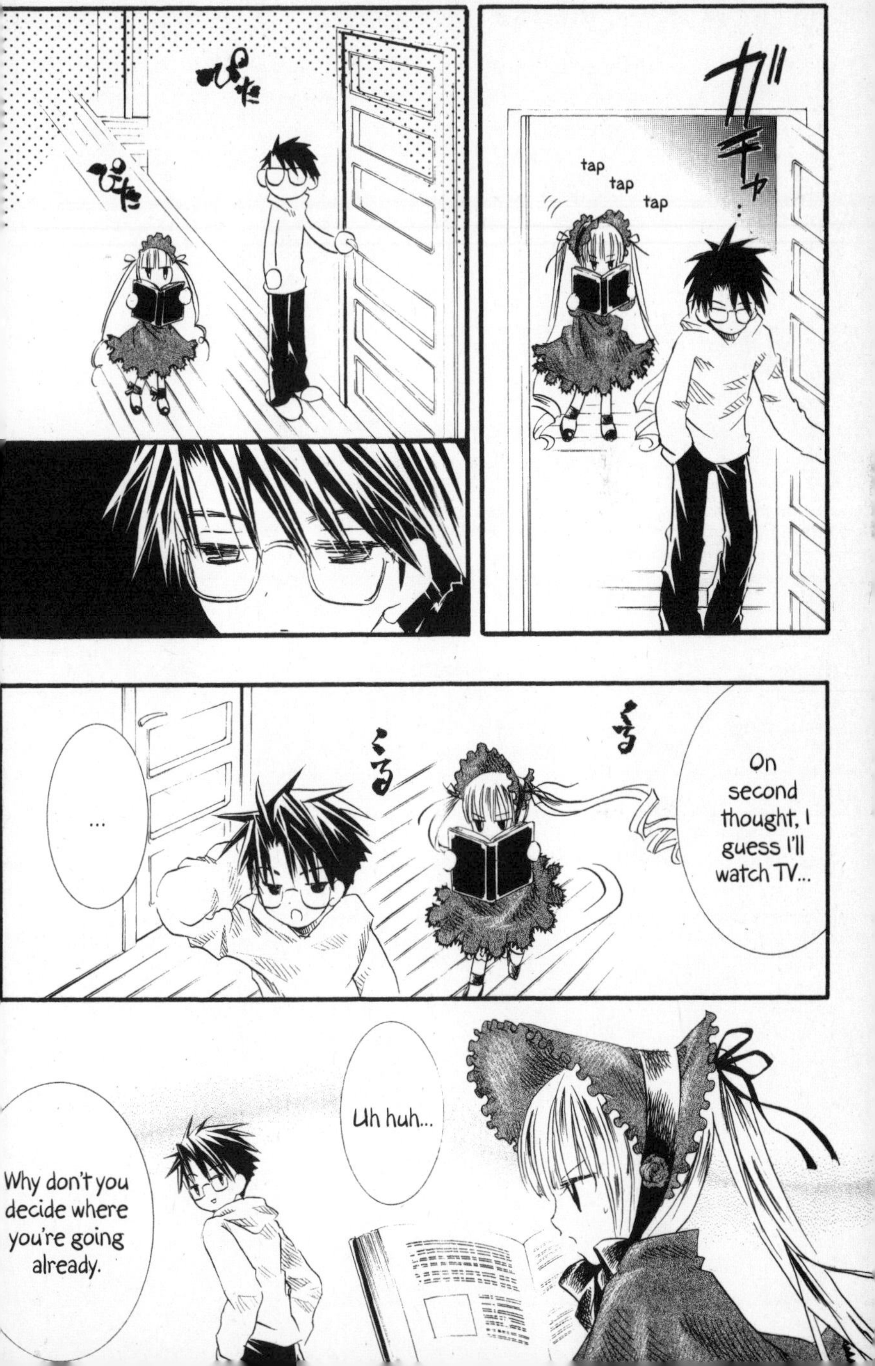
ガチャ…
tap
tap
tap
ぴた
ぴた
On second thought, I guess I'll watch TV...
くる
くる
...
Uh huh...
Why don't you decide where you're going already.

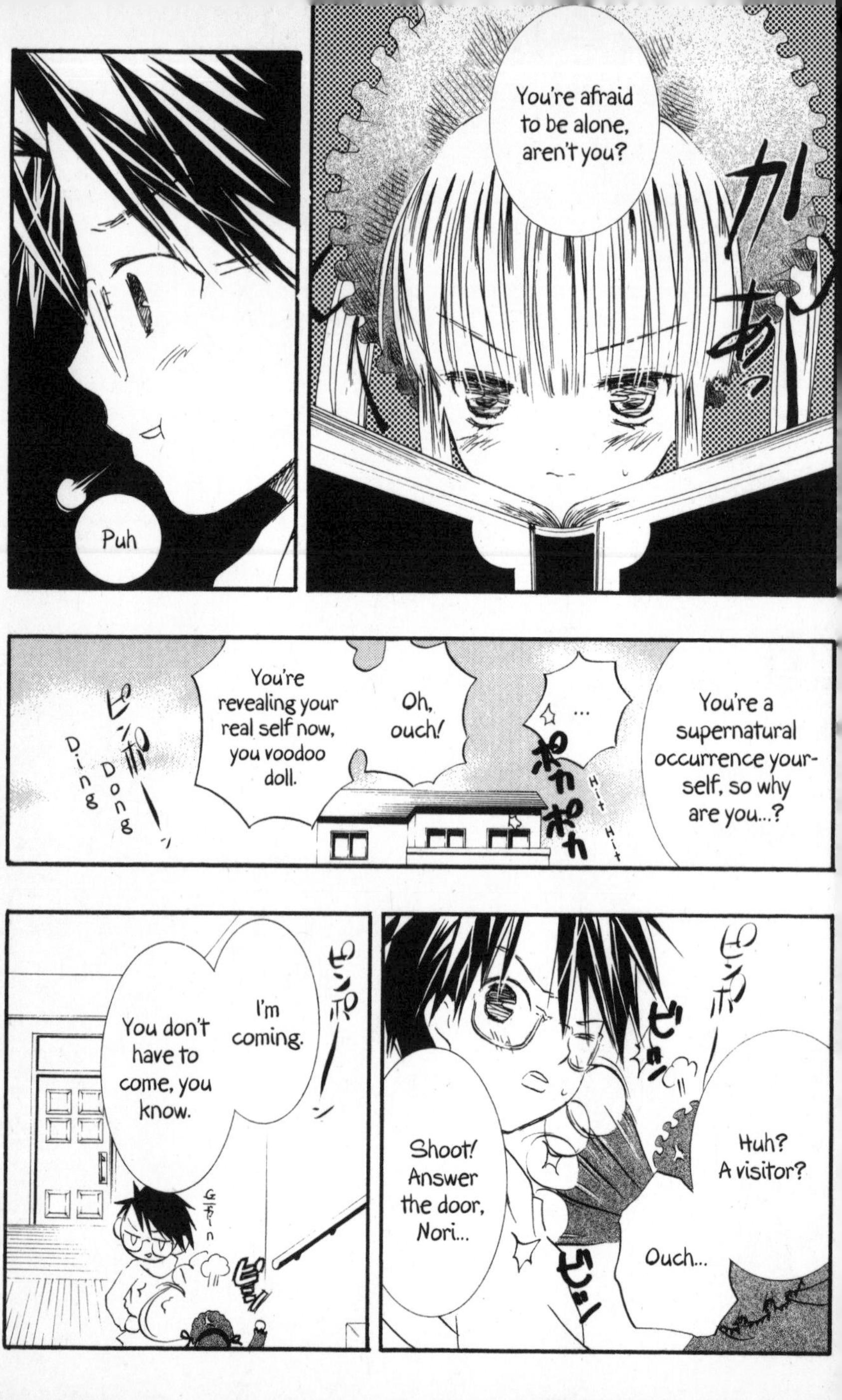
You're afraid to be alone, aren't you?
Puh
You're a supernatural occurrence your-self, so why are you...?
...
Hit Hit
Oh, ouch!
You're revealing your real self now, you voodoo doll.
Ding Dong
Huh? A visitor?
Ouch...
Shoot! Answer the door, Nori...
I'm coming.
You don't have to come, you know.
Grin

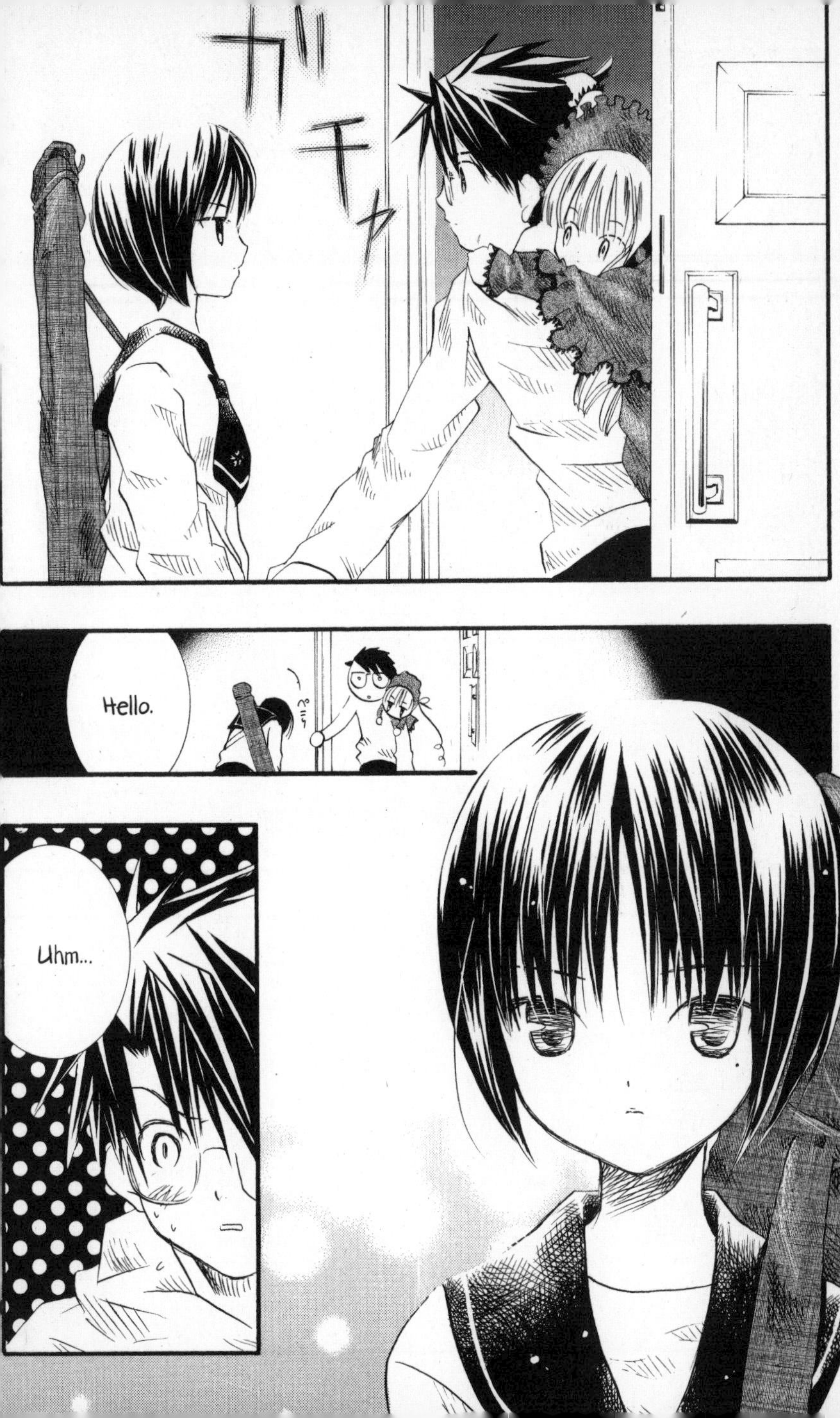
ガチャ
Hello.
Uhm...

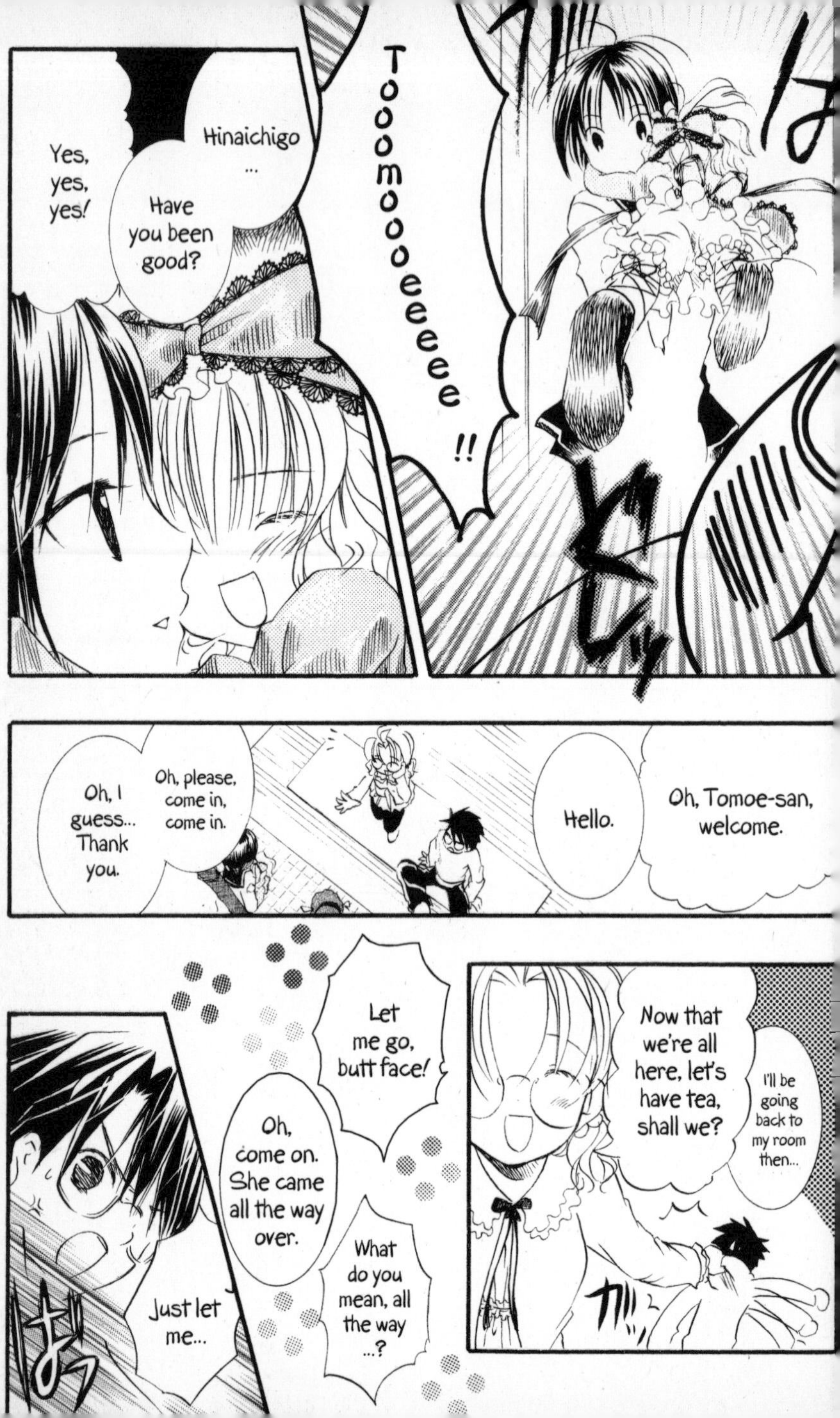
Tooooomoooeeeee!!
Hinaichigo... Have you been good?
Yes, yes, yes!
Oh, Tomoe-san, welcome.
Hello.
Oh, please, come in, come in.
Oh, I guess... Thank you.
Now that we're all here, let's have tea, shall we?
I'll be going back to my room then...
Let me go, butt face!
Oh, come on. She came all the way over.
What do you mean, all the way...?
Just let me...

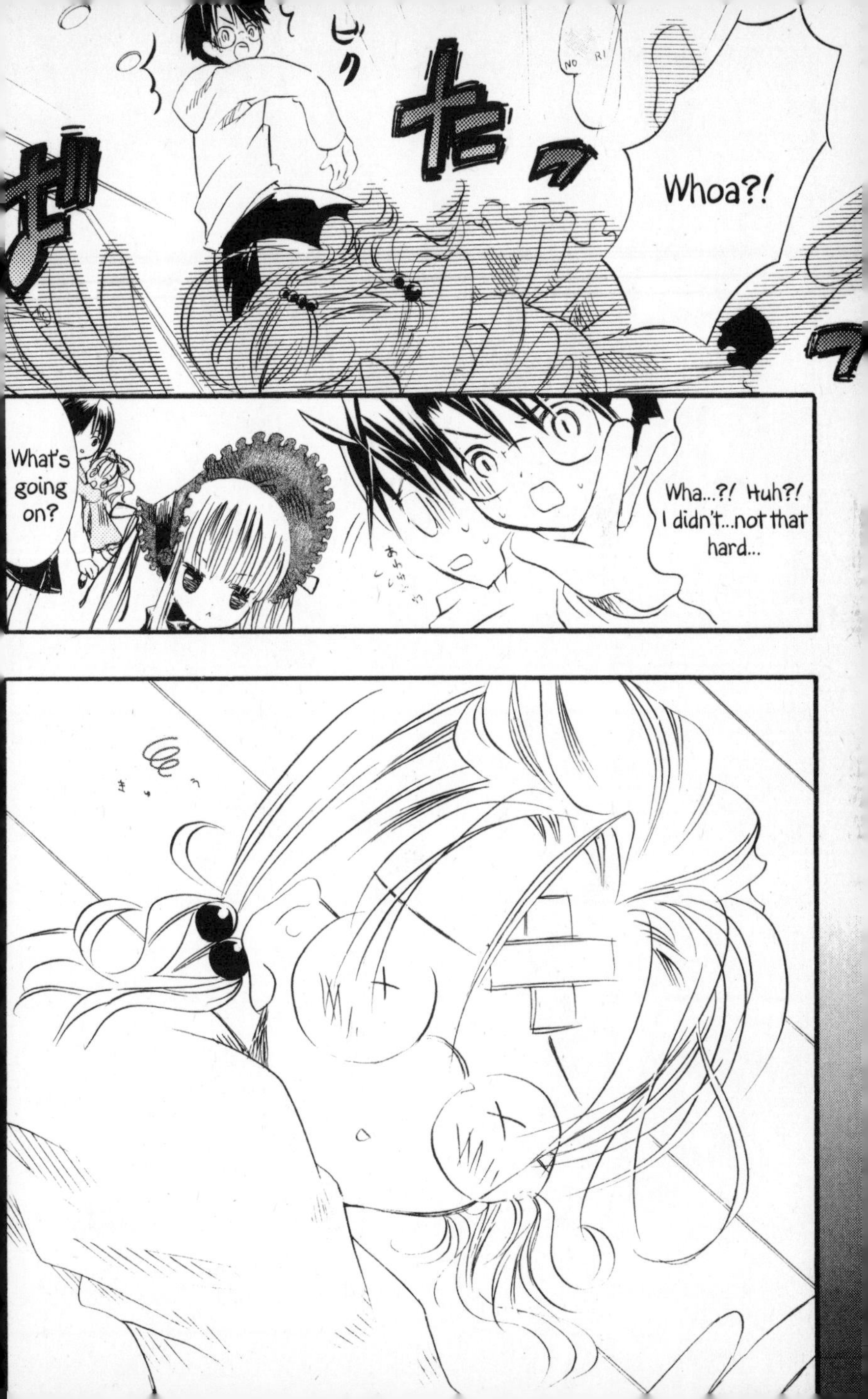
NO RI
Whoa?!
Wha...?! Huh?! I didn't...not that hard...
What's going on?

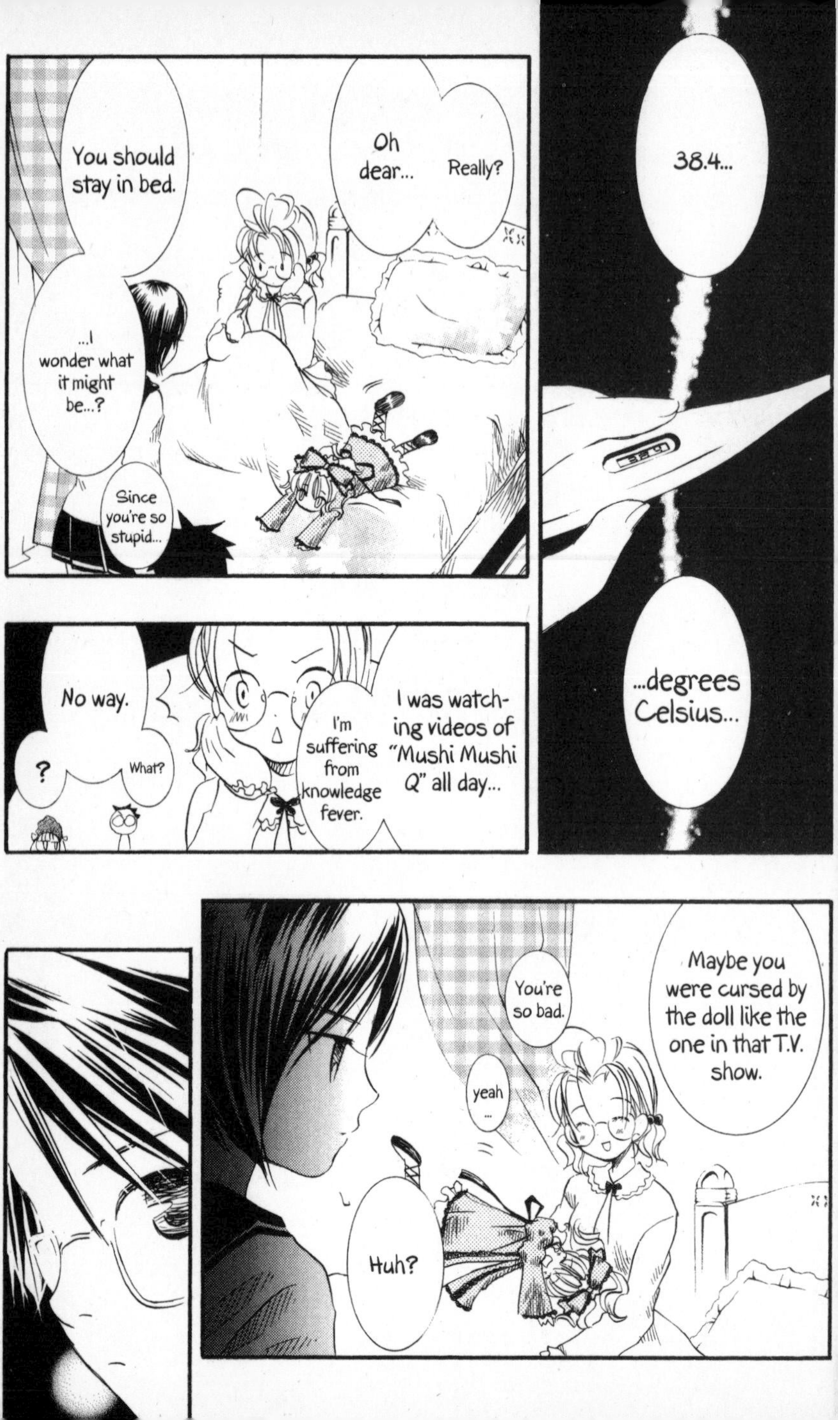
38.4...
...degrees Celsius...
Really?
Oh dear...
You should stay in bed.
...I wonder what it might be...?
Since you're so stupid...
I was watch-ing videos of "Mushi Mushi Q" all day...
I'm suffering from knowledge fever.
No way.
What?
?
Maybe you were cursed by the doll like the one in that T.V. show.
You're so bad.
yeah ...
Huh?

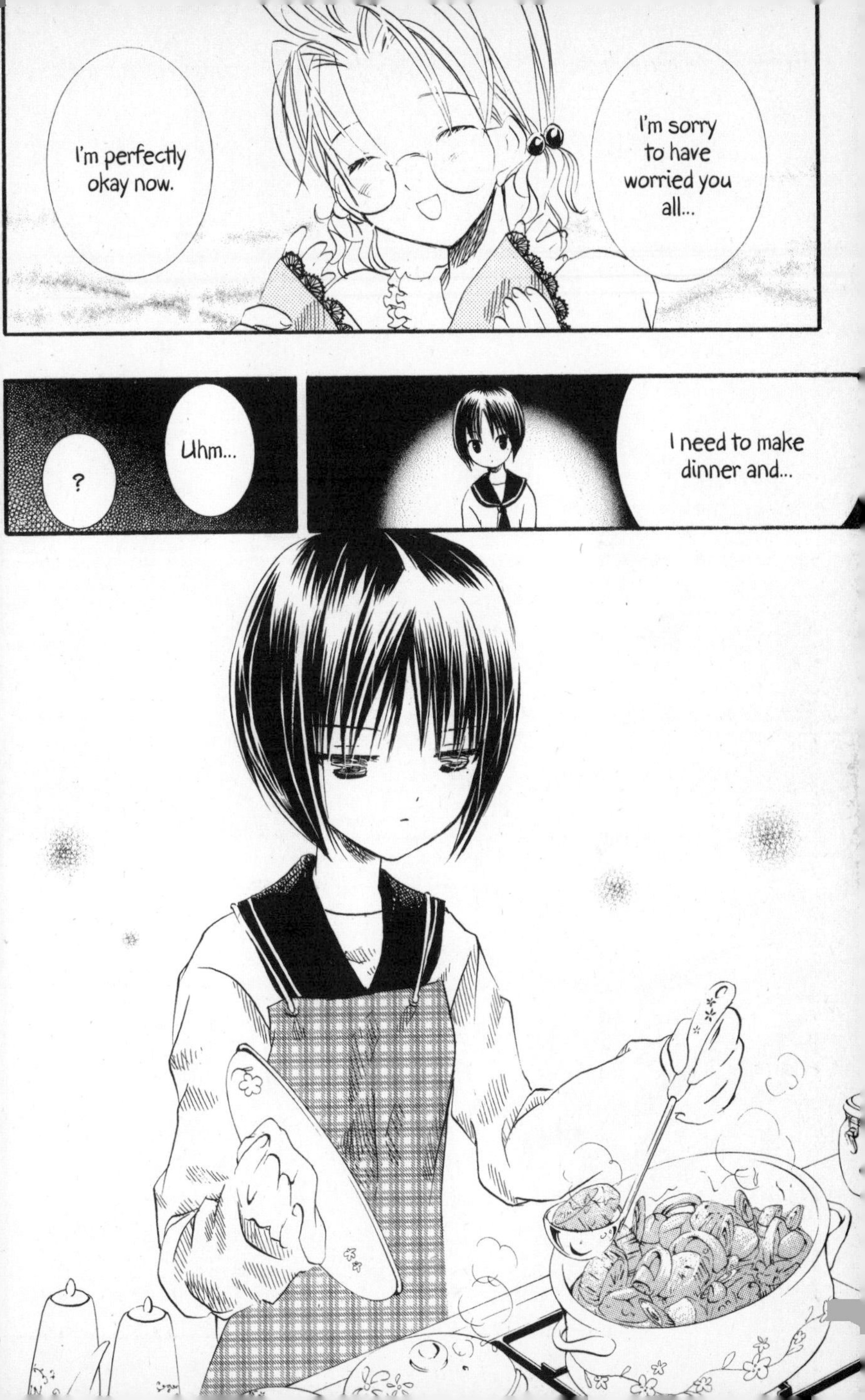
I'm sorry to have worried you all...
I'm perfectly okay now.
I need to make dinner and...
Uhm...
?

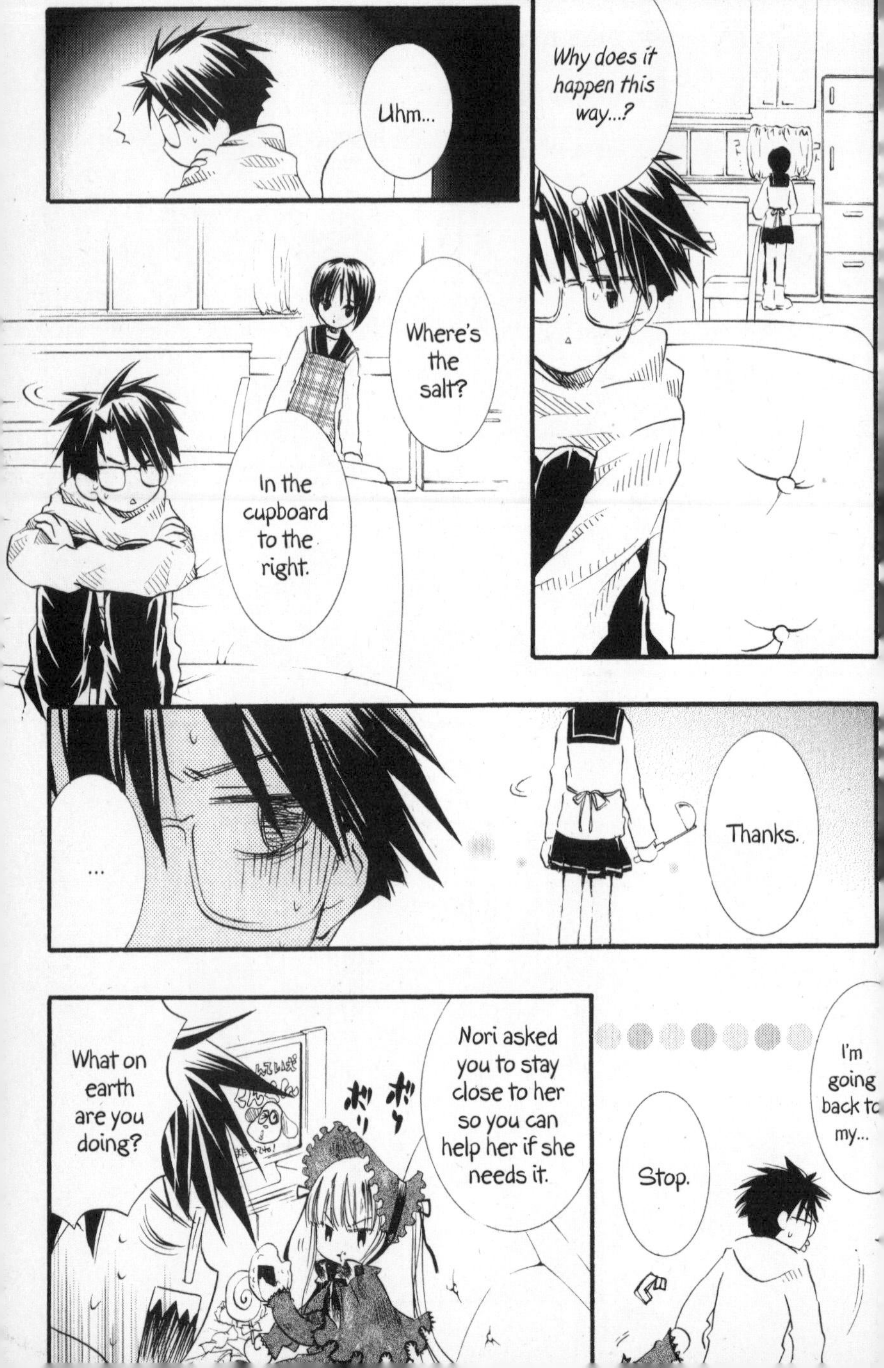
Why does it happen this way...?
Uhm...
Where's the salt?
In the cupboard to the right.
Thanks.
...
I'm going back to my...
Stop.
Nori asked you to stay close to her so you can help her if she needs it.
What on earth are you doing?

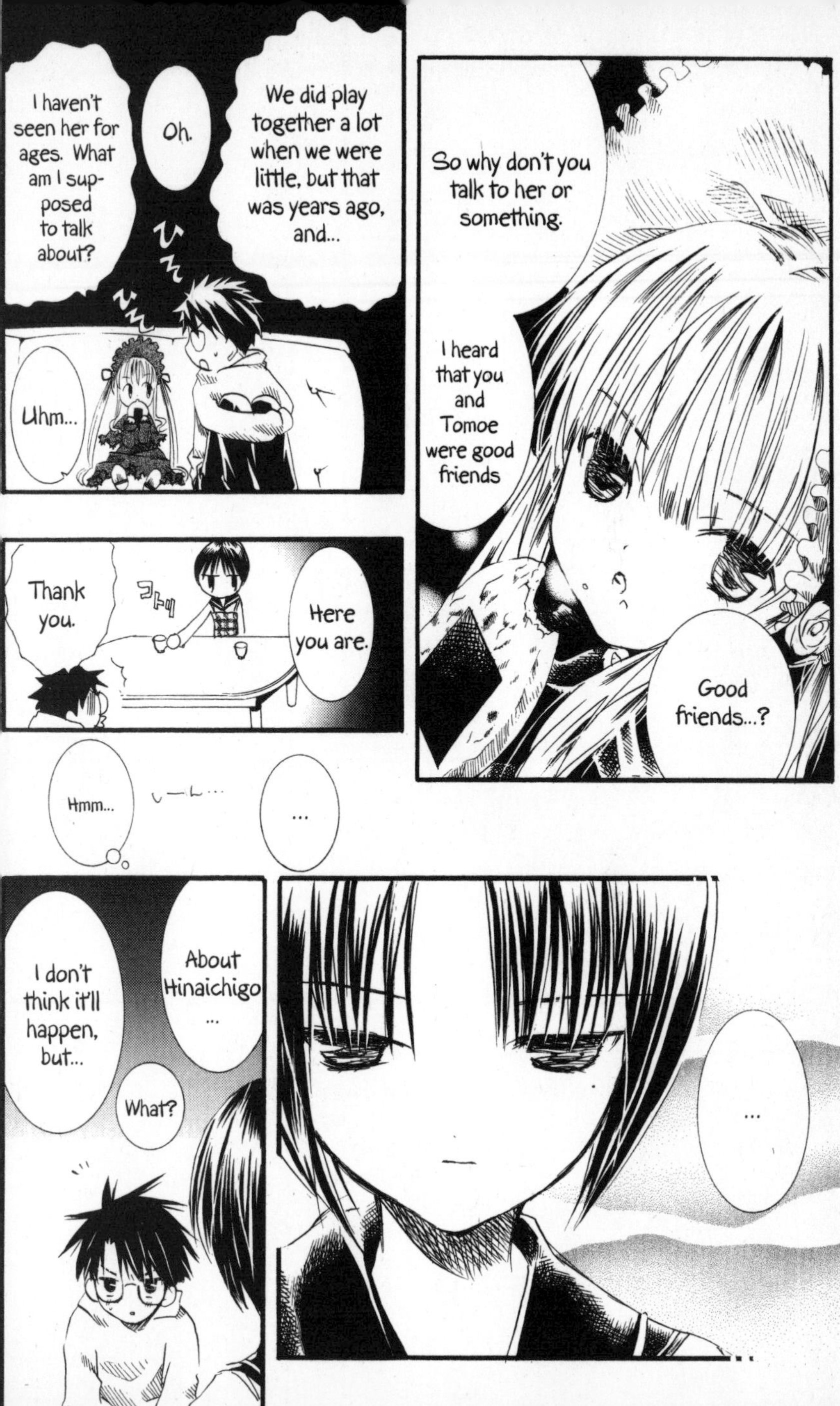
So why don't you talk to her or something.
I heard that you and Tomoe were good friends
Good friends...?
We did play together a lot when we were little, but that was years ago, and...
Oh.
I haven't seen her for ages. What am I supposed to talk about?
Uhm...
Here you are.
Thank you.
...
Hmm...
...
About Hinaichigo ...
I don't think it'll happen, but...
What?

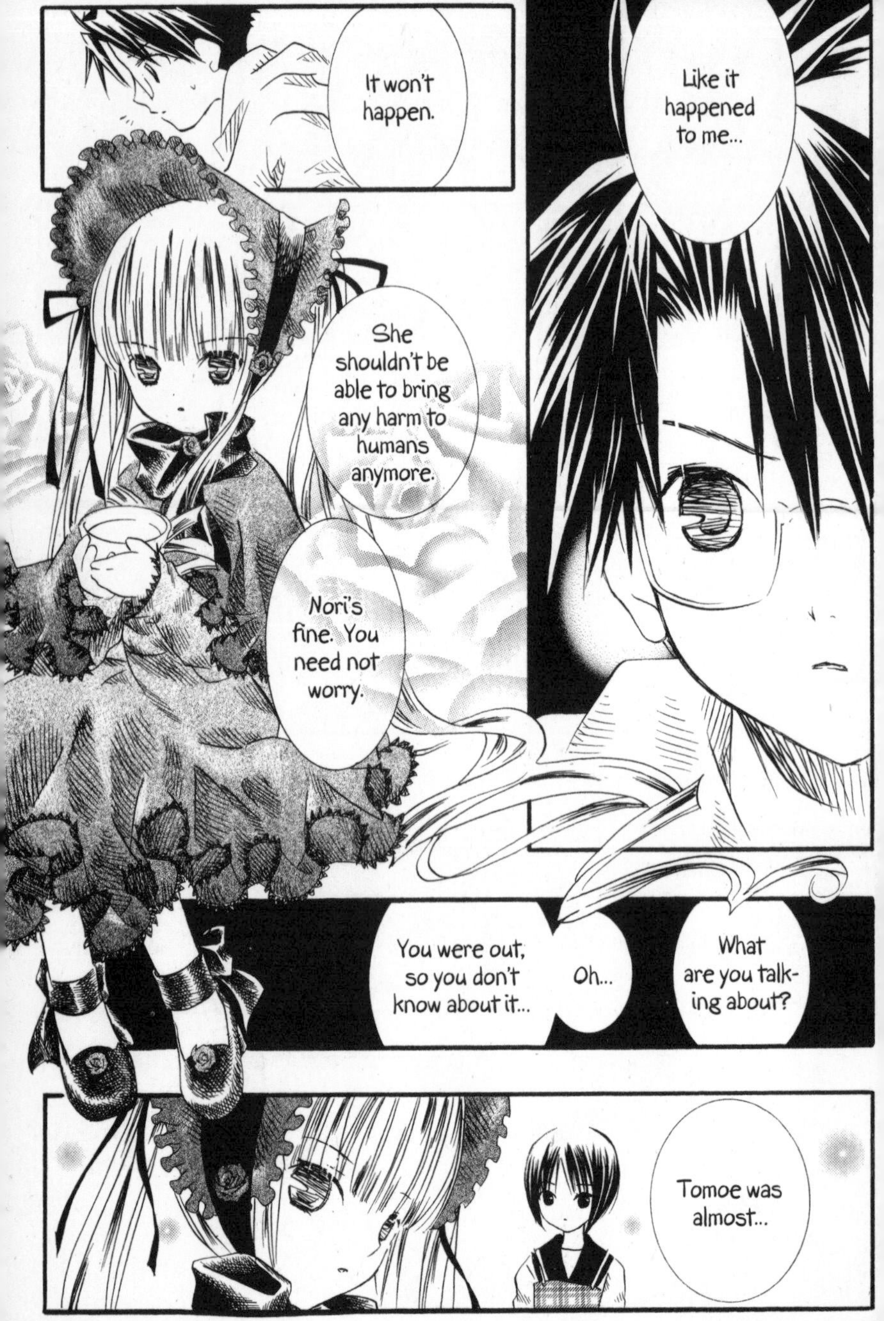
Like it happened to me...
It won't happen.
She shouldn't be able to bring any harm to humans anymore.
Nori's fine. You need not worry.
What are you talk-ing about?
Oh...
You were out, so you don't know about it...
Tomoe was almost...

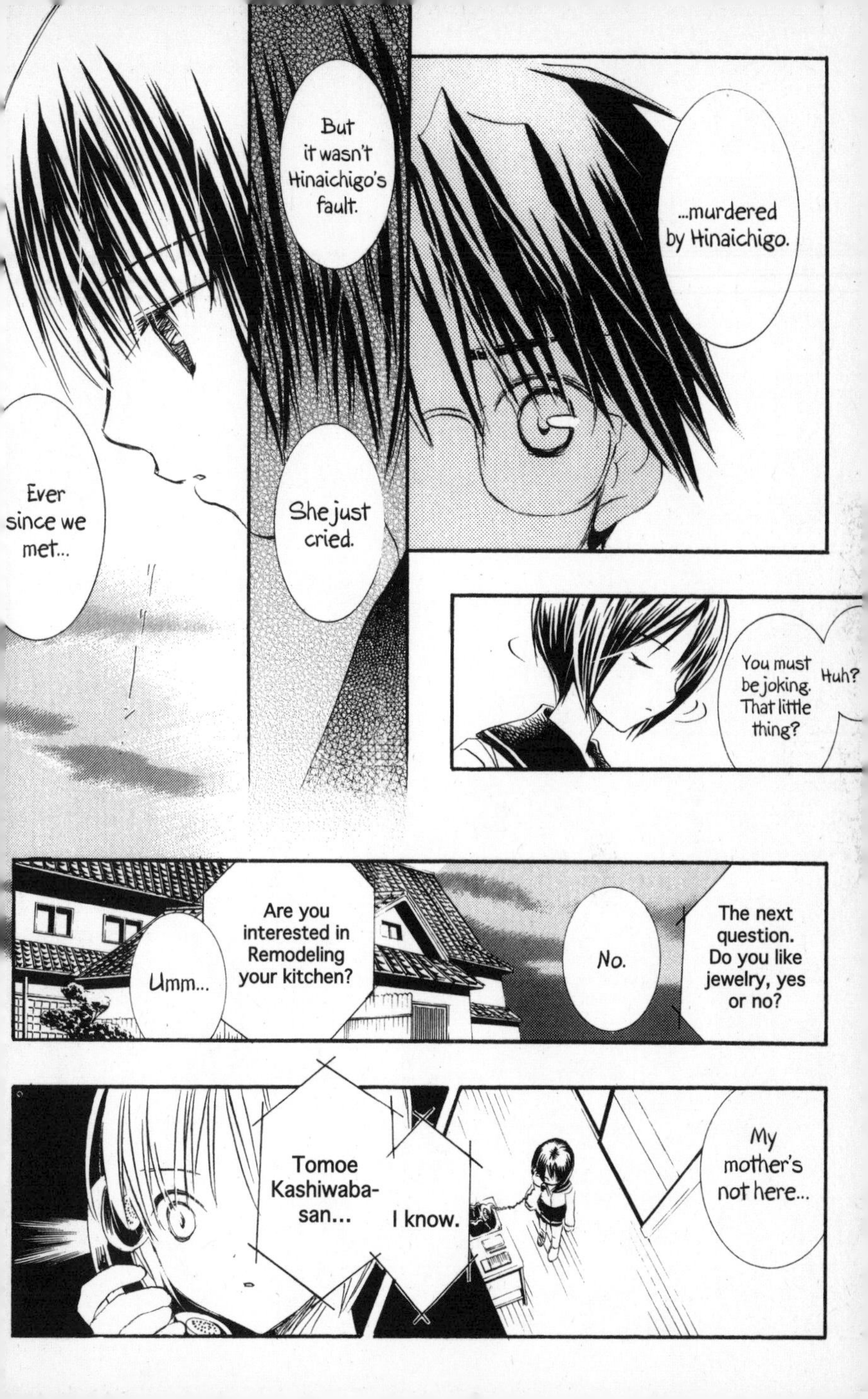
...murdered by Hinaichigo.
Huh?
You must be joking. That little thing?
But it wasn't Hinaichigo's fault.
She just cried.
Ever since we met...
The next question. Do you like jewelry, yes or no?
No.
Are you interested in Remodeling your kitchen?
Umm...
My mother's not here...
Tomoe Kashiwaba-san...
I know.

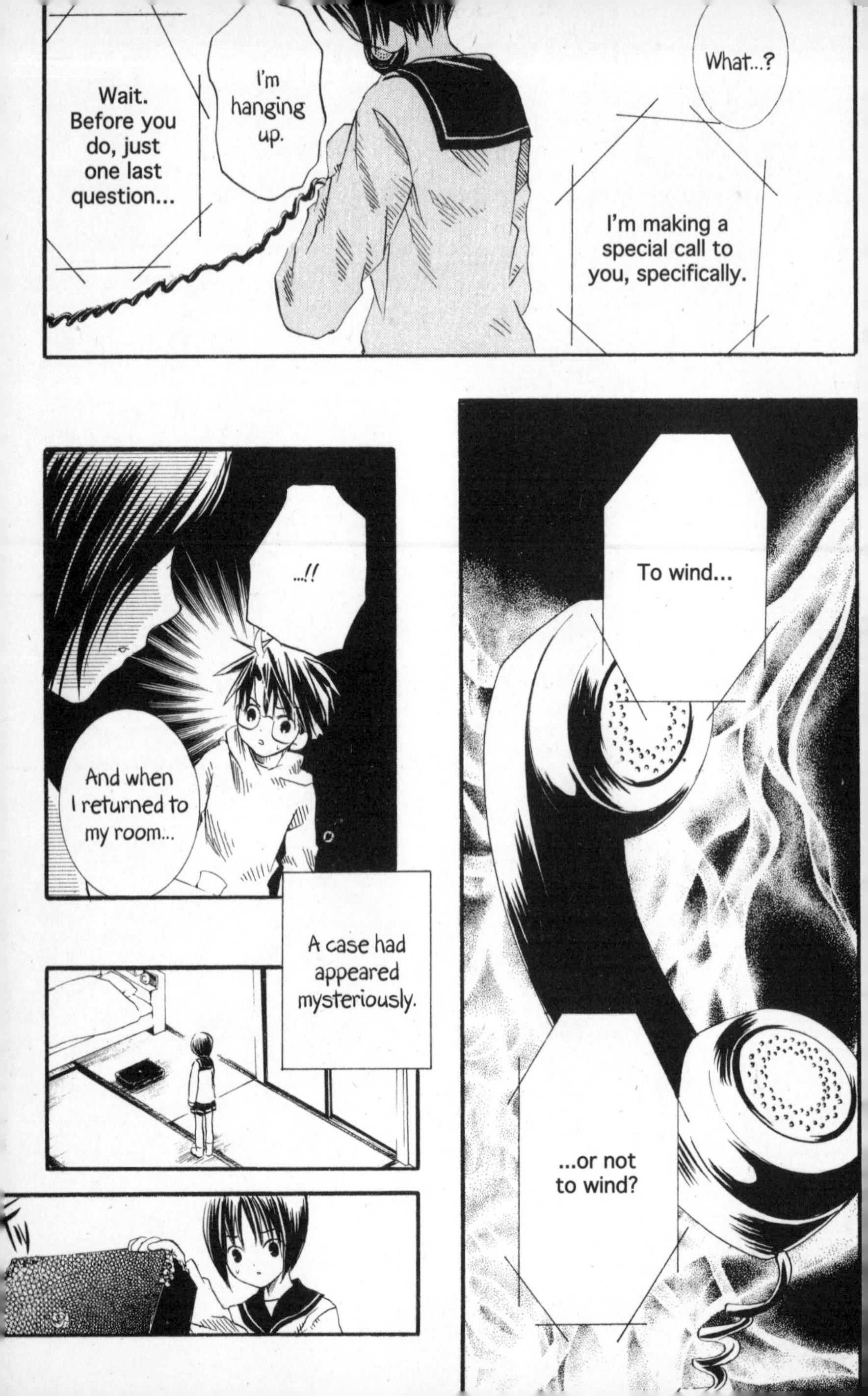
What...?
I'm making a special call to you, specifically.
I'm hanging up.
Wait. Before you do, just one last question...
To wind...
...or not to wind?
...!!
And when I returned to my room...
A case had appeared mysteriously.

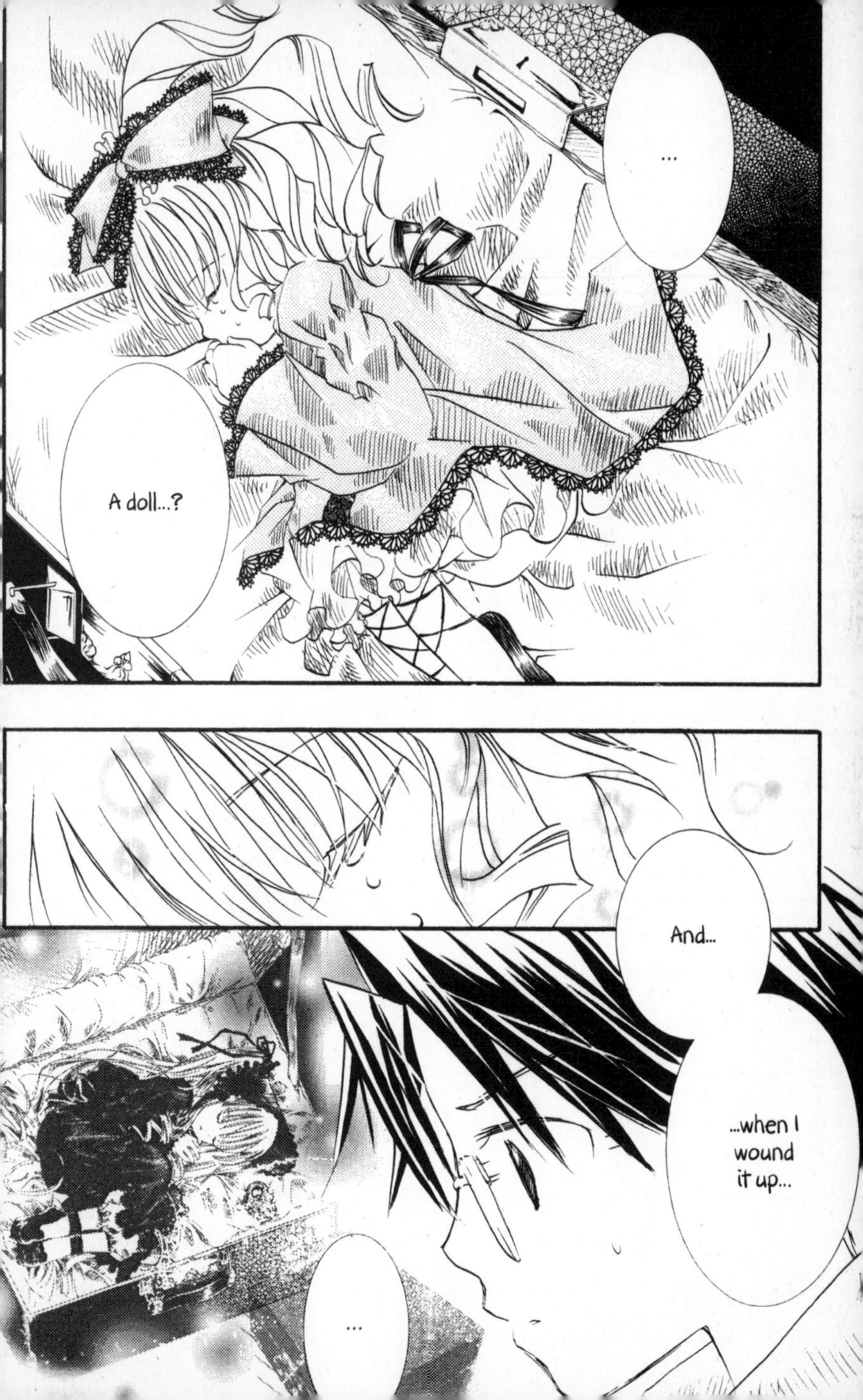
...
A doll...?
And...
...when I wound it up...
...

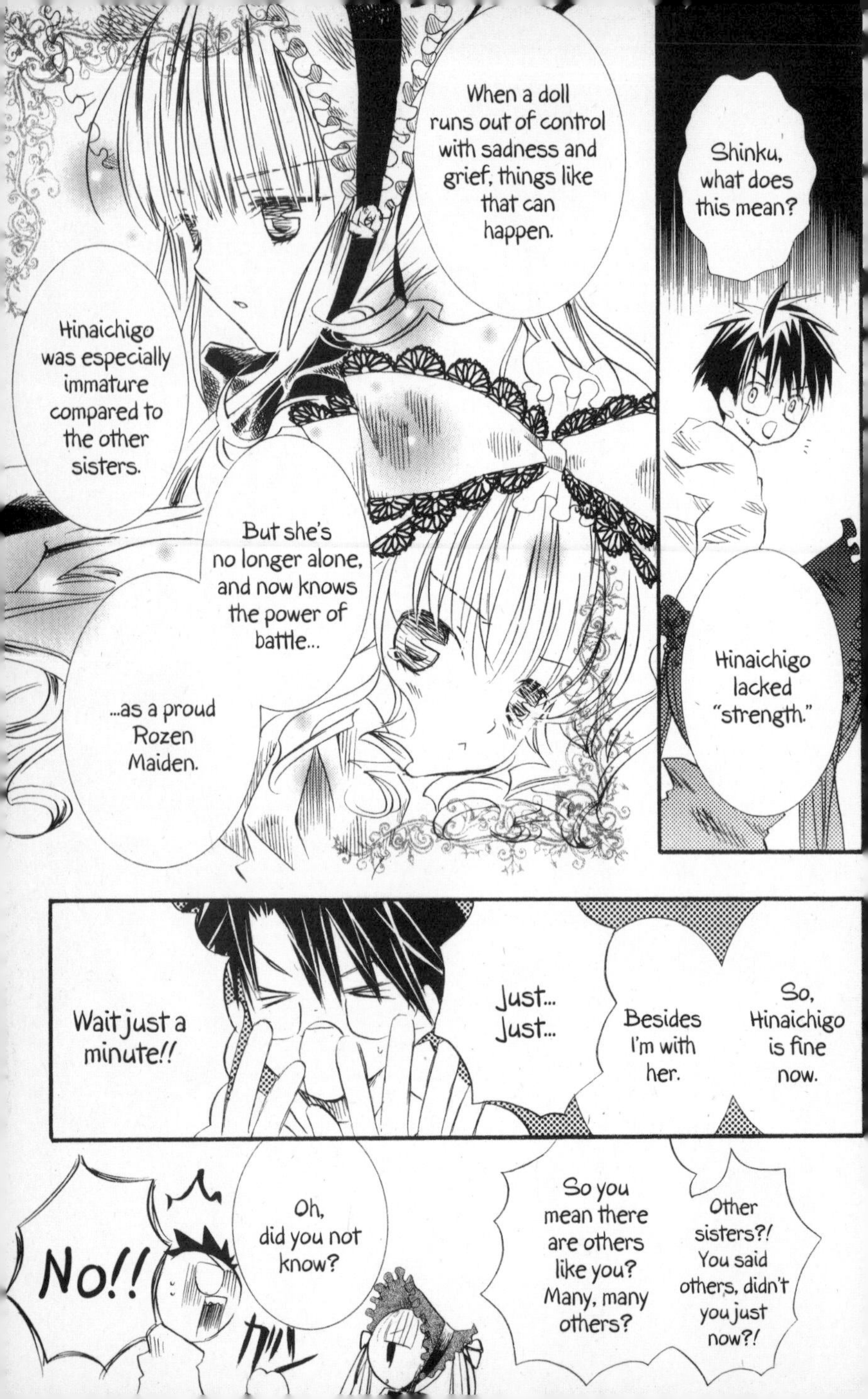
Shinku, what does this mean?
Hinaichigo lacked "strength."
When a doll runs out of control with sadness and grief, things like that can happen.
Hinaichigo was especially immature compared to the other sisters.
But she's no longer alone, and now knows the power of battle...
...as a proud Rozen Maiden.
So, Hinaichigo is fine now.
Besides I'm with her.
Just... Just...
Wait just a minute!!
Other sisters?! You said others, didn't you just now?!
So you mean there are others like you? Many, many others?
Oh, did you not know?
No!!

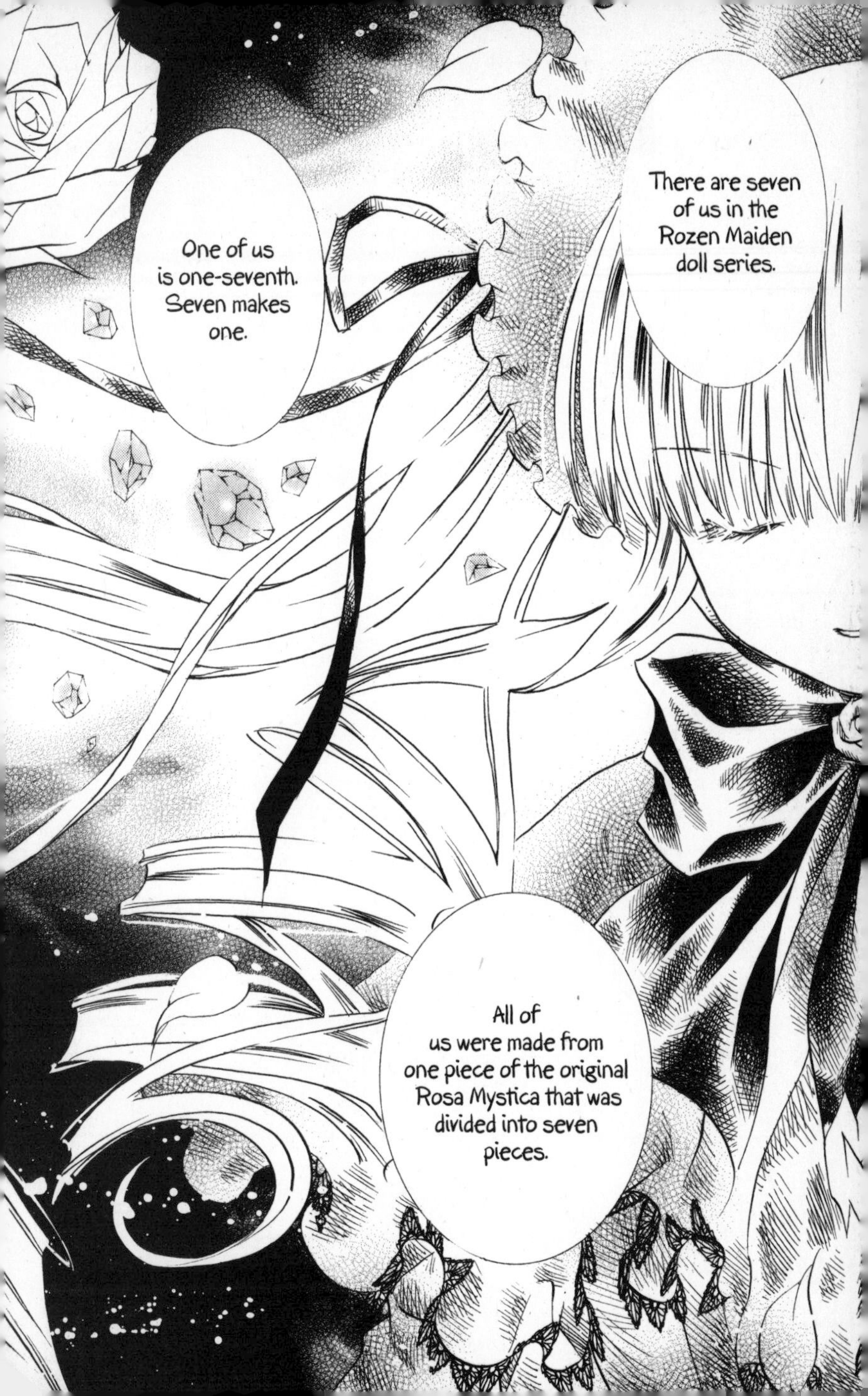
There are seven of us in the Rozen Maiden doll series.
One of us is one-seventh. Seven makes one.
All of us were made from one piece of the original Rosa Mystica that was divided into seven pieces.

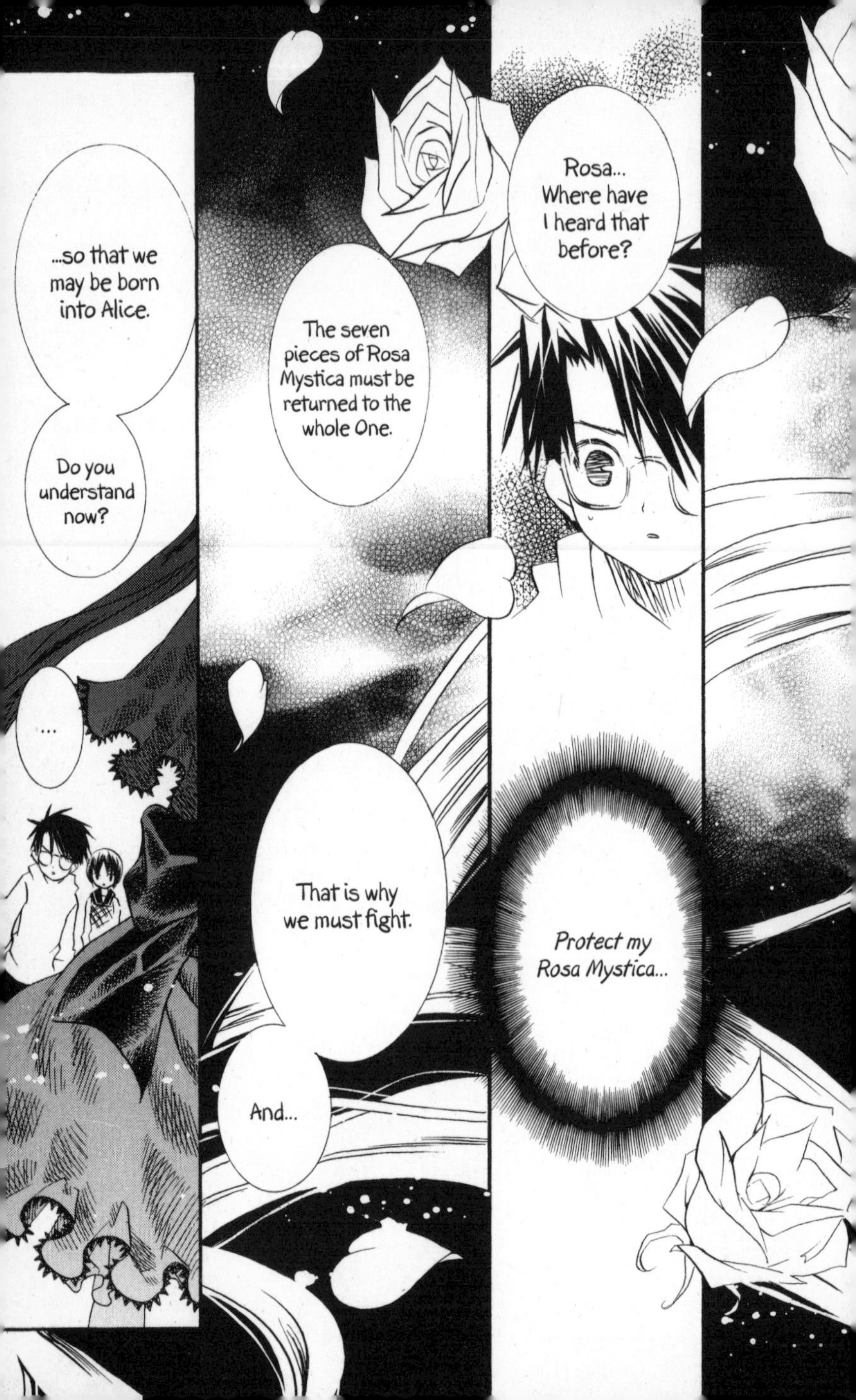
Rosa... Where have I heard that before?
Protect my Rosa Mystica...
The seven pieces of Rosa Mystica must be returned to the whole One.
That is why we must fight.
And...
...so that we may be born into Alice.
Do you understand now?
...

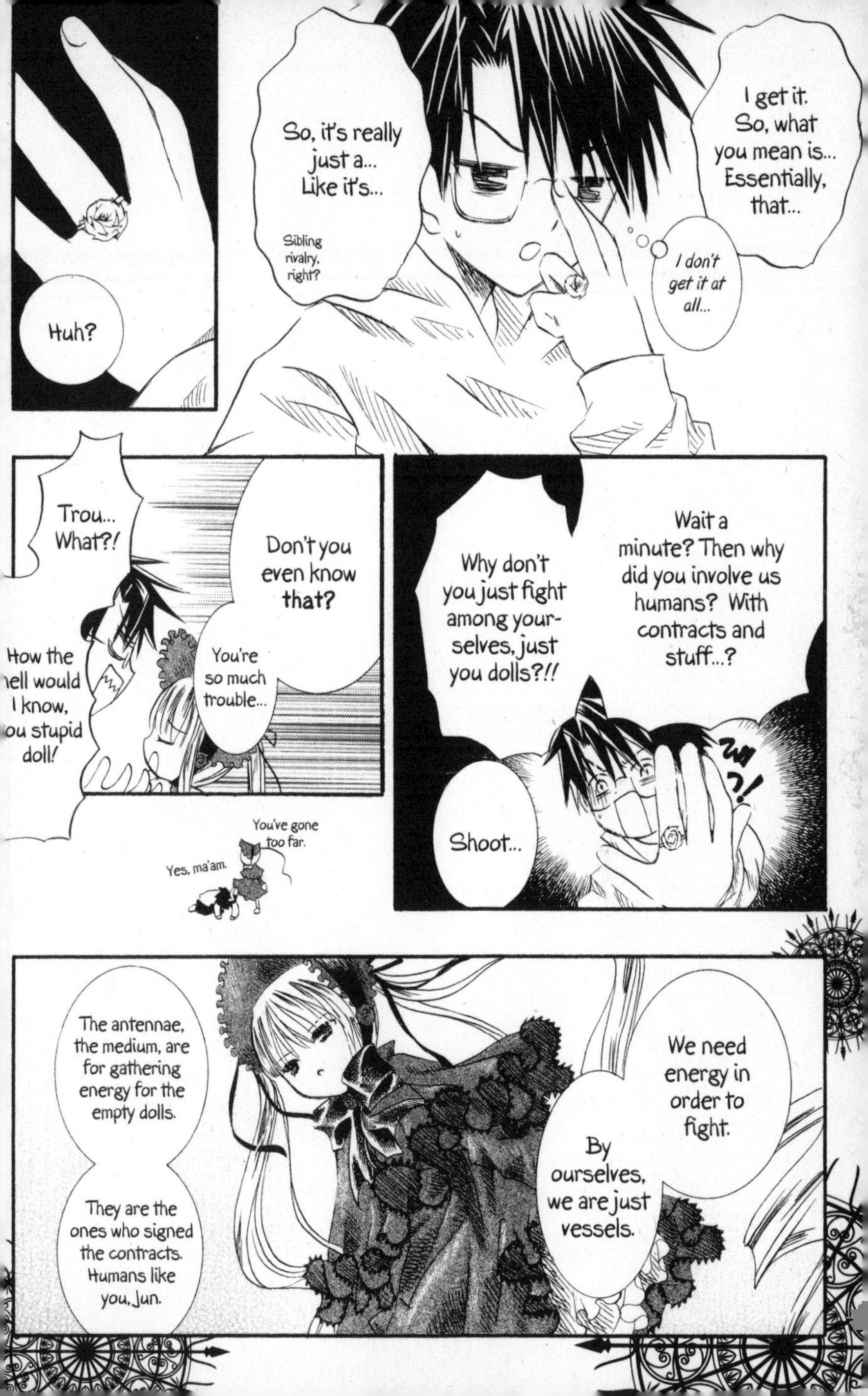
I get it. So, what you mean is... Essentially, that...
I don't get it at all...
So, it's really just a... Like it's...
Sibling rivalry, right?
Huh?
Wait a minute? Then why did you involve us humans? With contracts and stuff...?
Why don't you just fight among your-selves, just you dolls?!!
Shoot...
Don't you even know that?
You're so much trouble...
Trou... What?!
How the ell would I know, ou stupid doll!
You've gone too far.
Yes, ma'am.
We need energy in order to fight.
By ourselves, we are just vessels.
The antennae, the medium, are for gathering energy for the empty dolls.
They are the ones who signed the contracts. Humans like you, Jun.

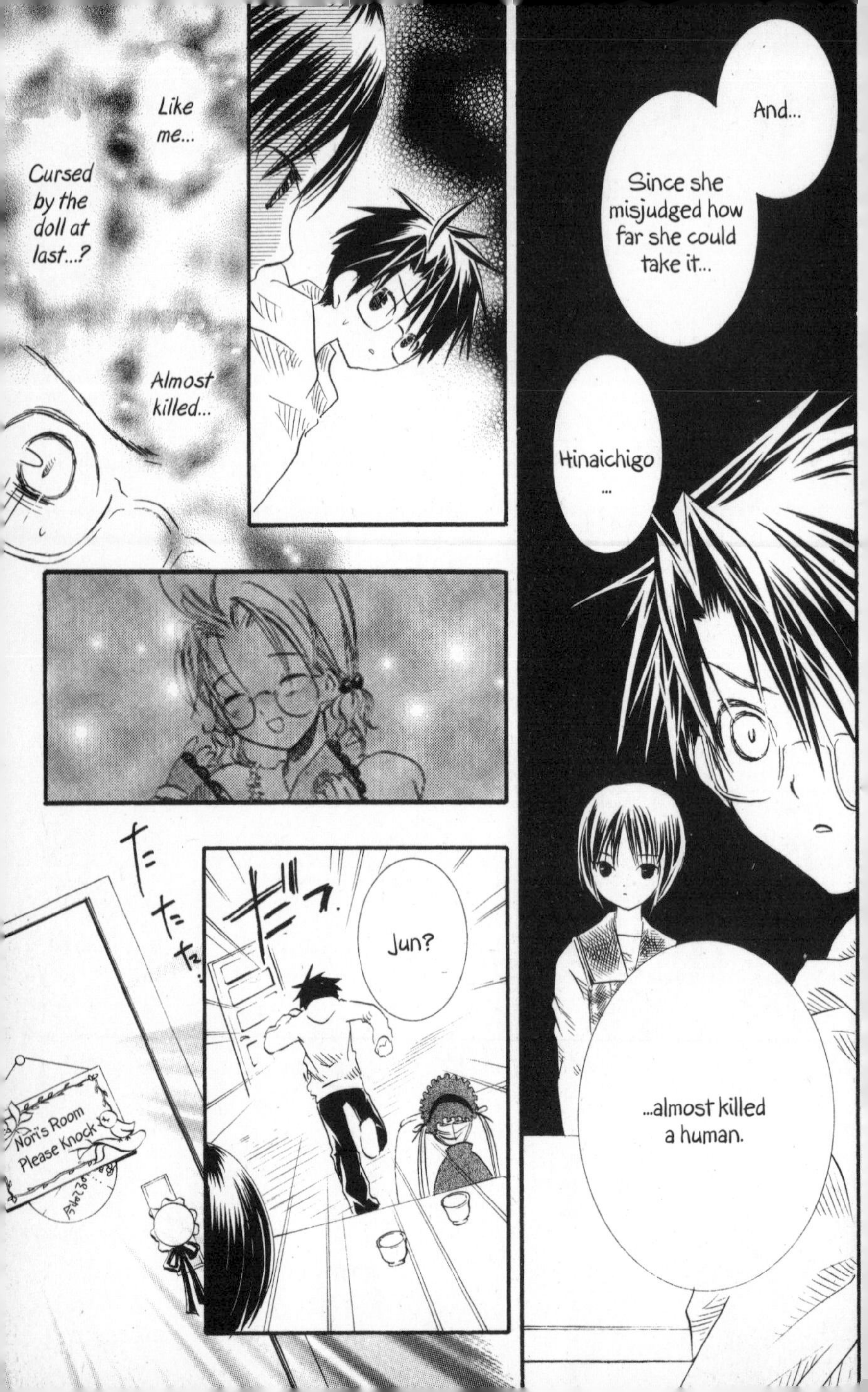
And...
Since she misjudged how far she could take it...
Hinaichigo ...
...almost killed a human.
Like me...
Cursed by the doll at last...?
Almost killed...
Jun?
Nori's Room Please Knock

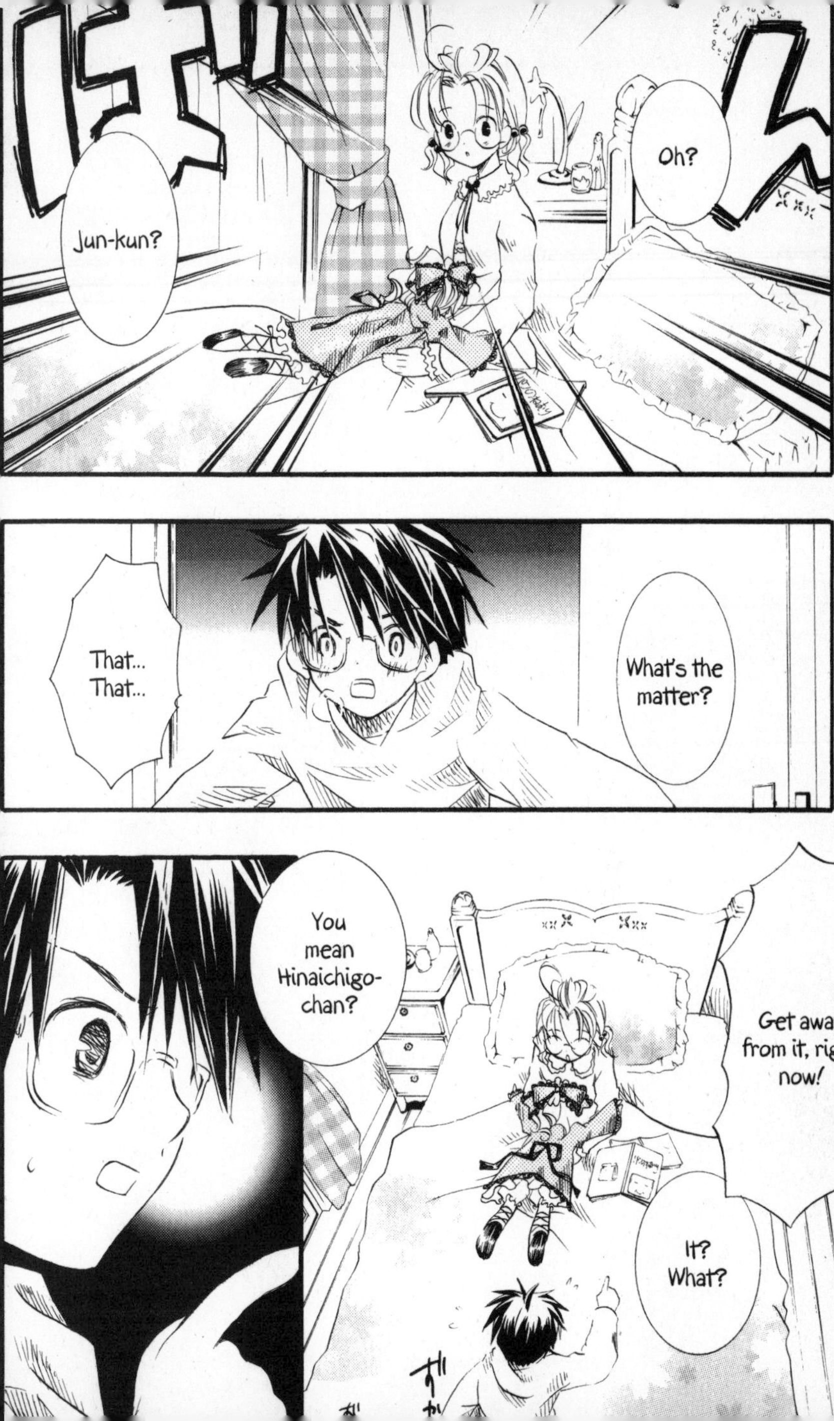
Oh?
Jun-kun?
What's the matter?
That... That...
Get away from it, right now!
It? What?
You mean Hinaichigo-chan?

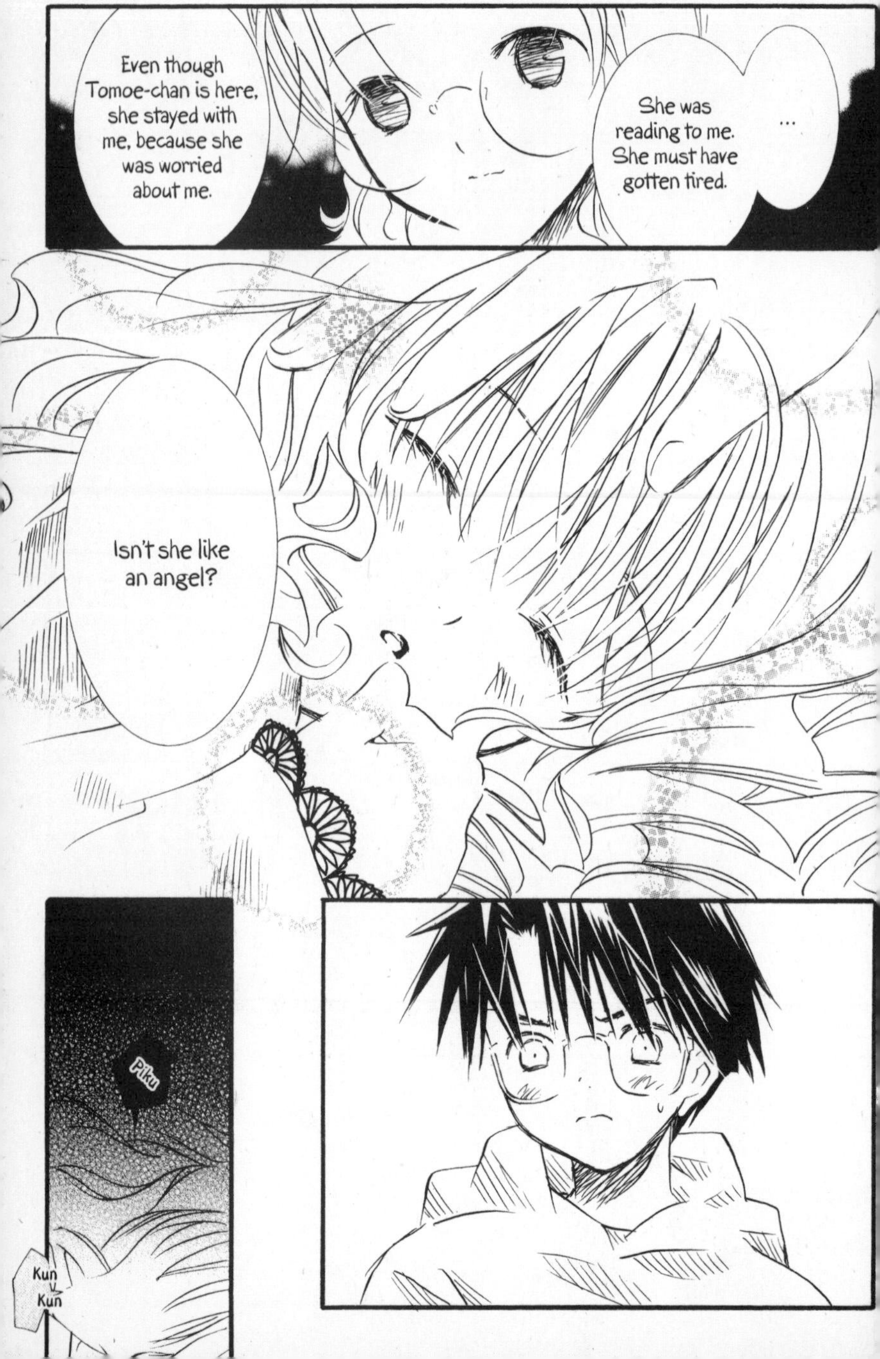
...
She was reading to me. She must have gotten tired.
Even though Tomoe-chan is here, she stayed with me, because she was worried about me.
Isn't she like an angel?
Piku
Kun Kun

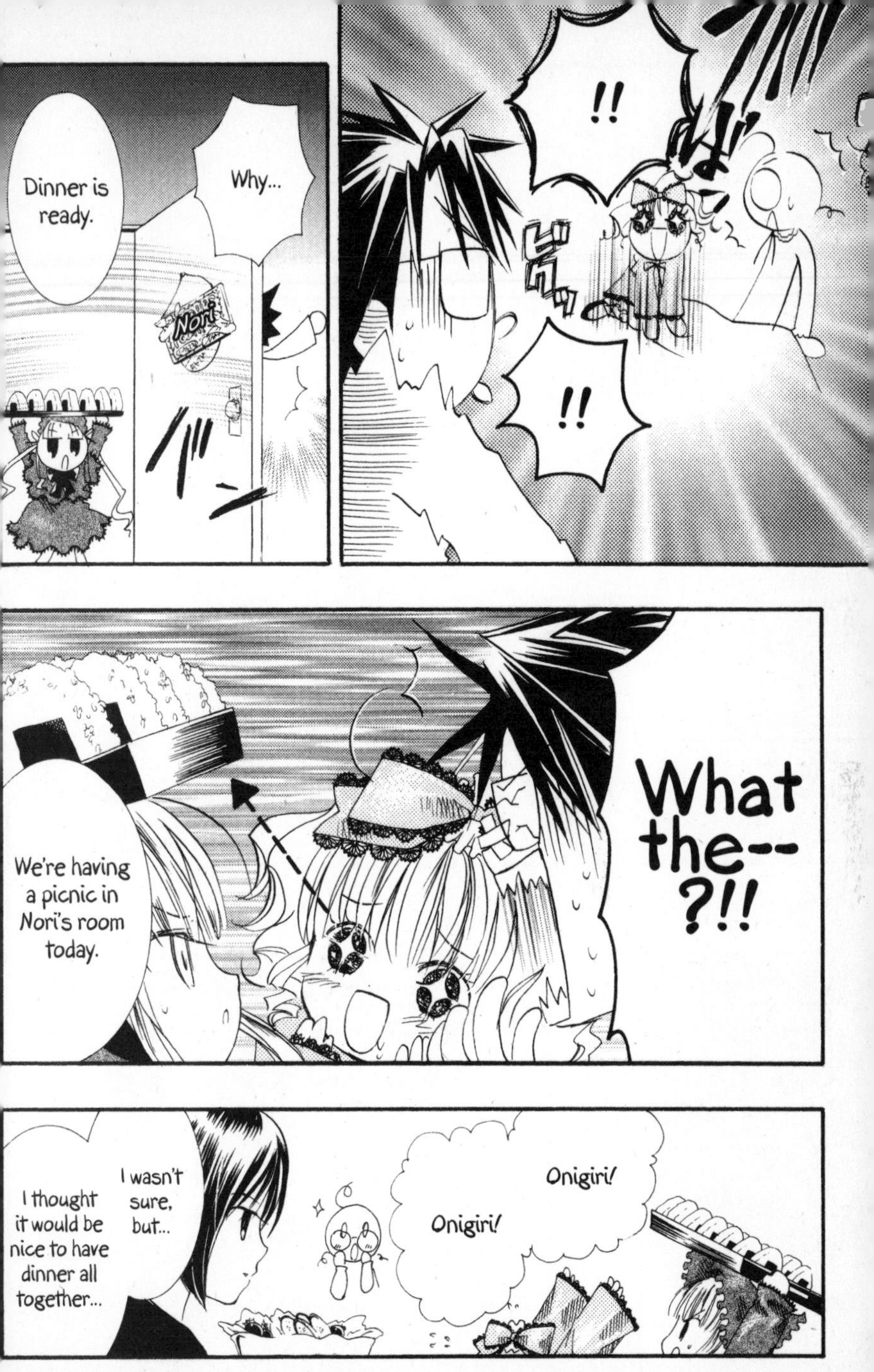
!!
!!
Why...
Dinner is ready.
Nori
What the--?!!
We're having a picnic in Nori's room today.
Onigiri!
Onigiri!
I wasn't sure, but...
I thought it would be nice to have dinner all together...

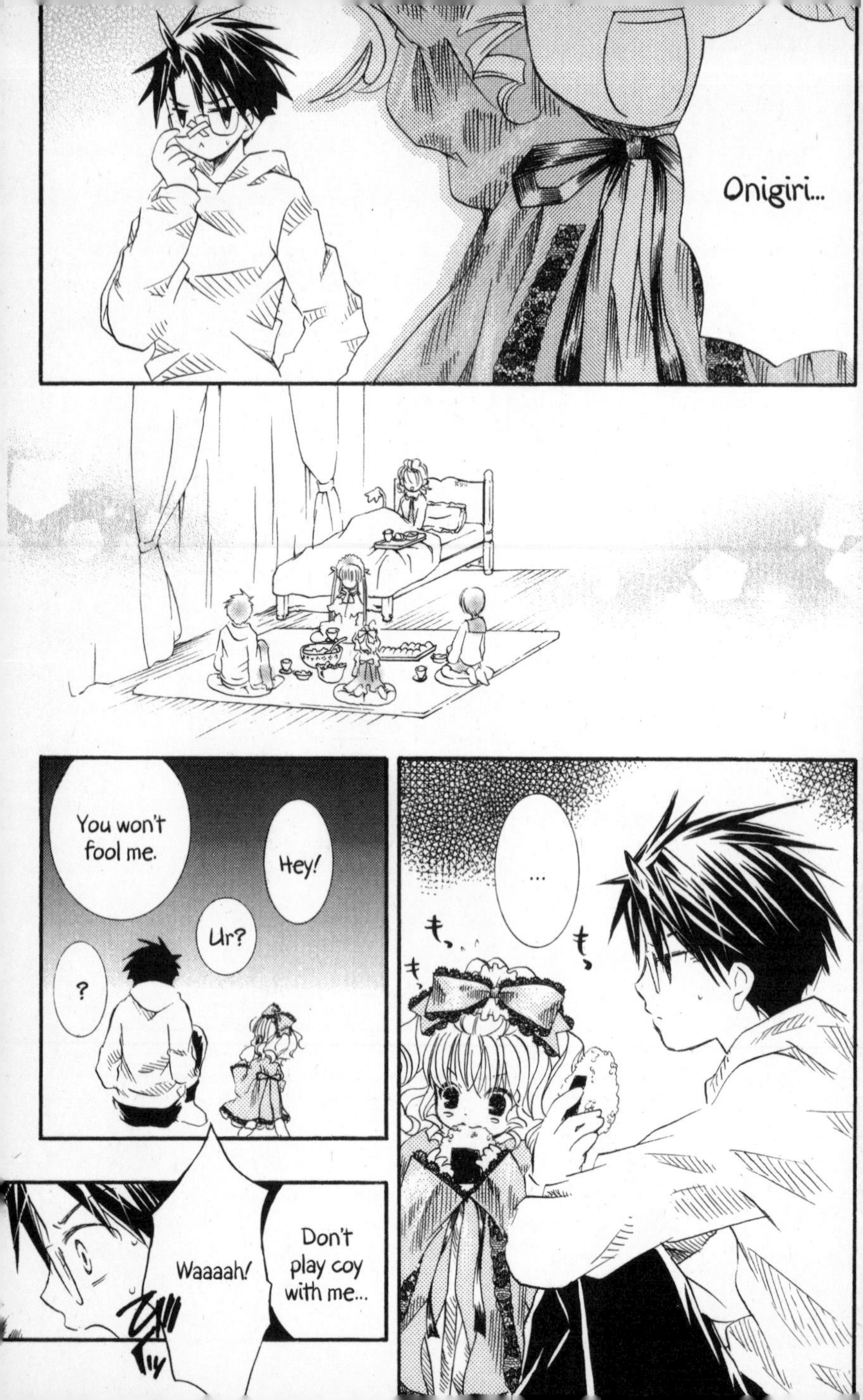
Onigiri...
...
Hey!
You won't fool me.
Ur?
?
Don't play coy with me...
Waaaah!

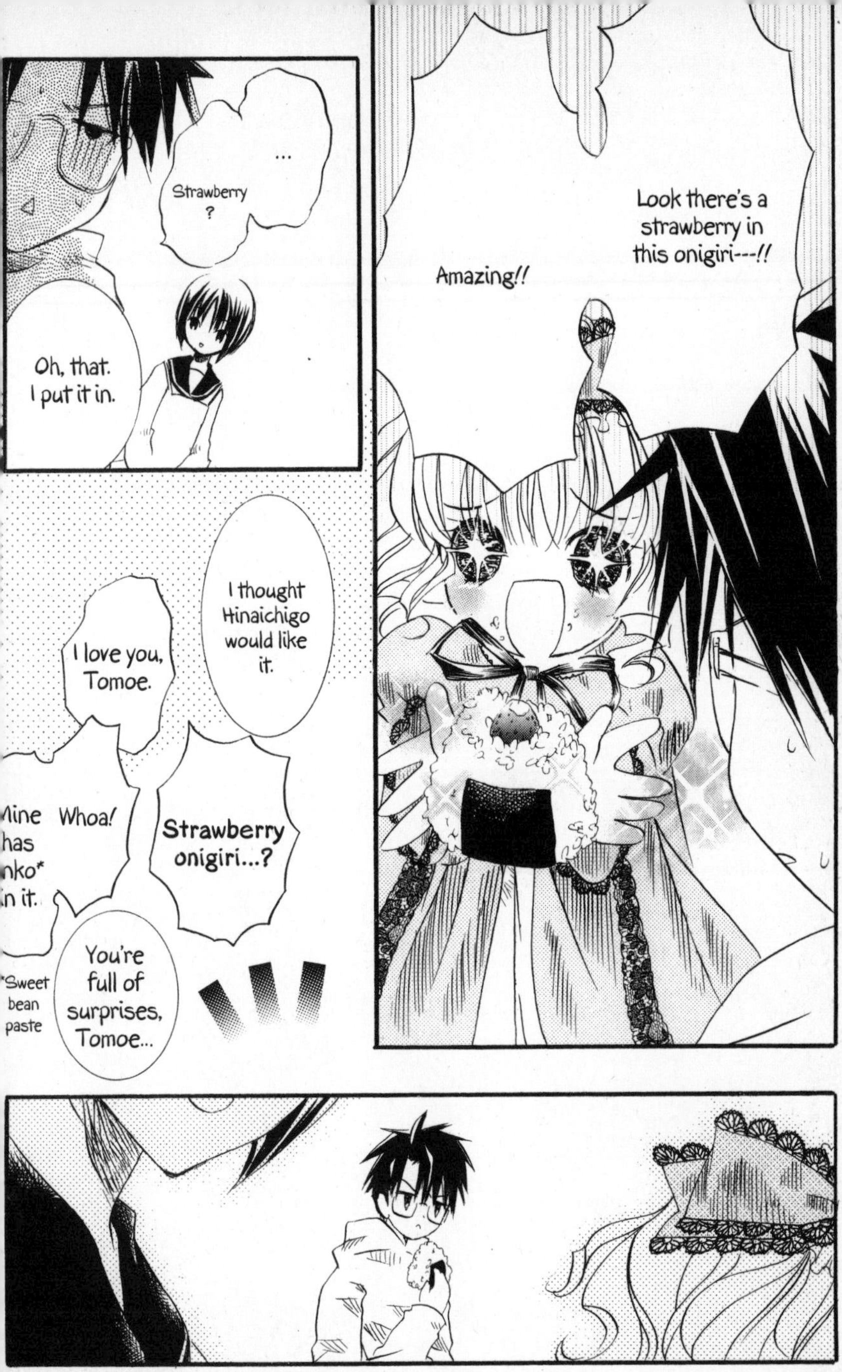

Look there's a strawberry in this onigiri---!!
Amazing!!
...
Strawberry ?
Oh, that. I put it in.
I thought Hinaichigo would like it.
I love you, Tomoe.
Strawberry onigiri...?
Whoa! Mine has nko* in it.
You're full of surprises, Tomoe...
*Sweet bean paste

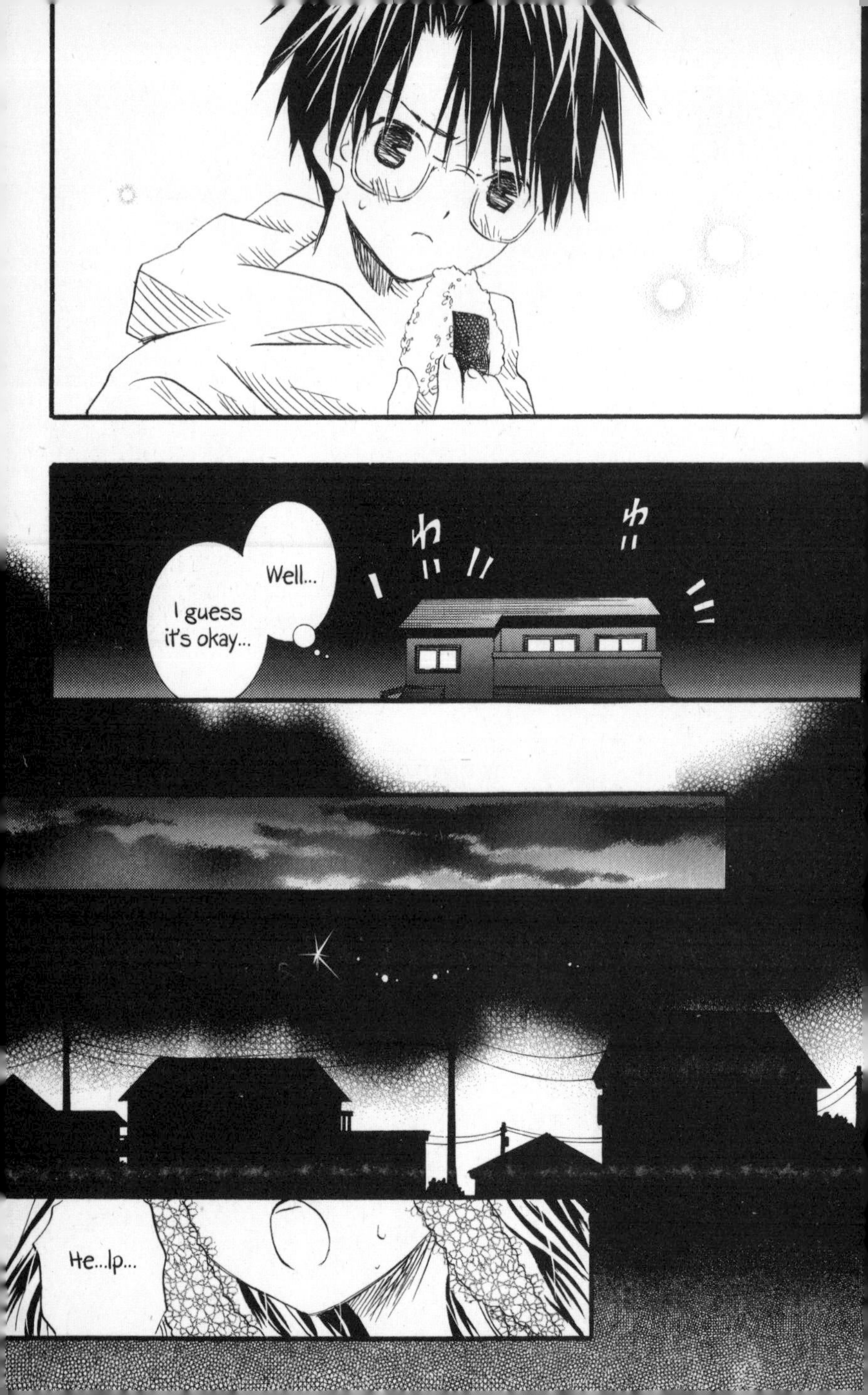
Well...
I guess it's okay...
He...lp...

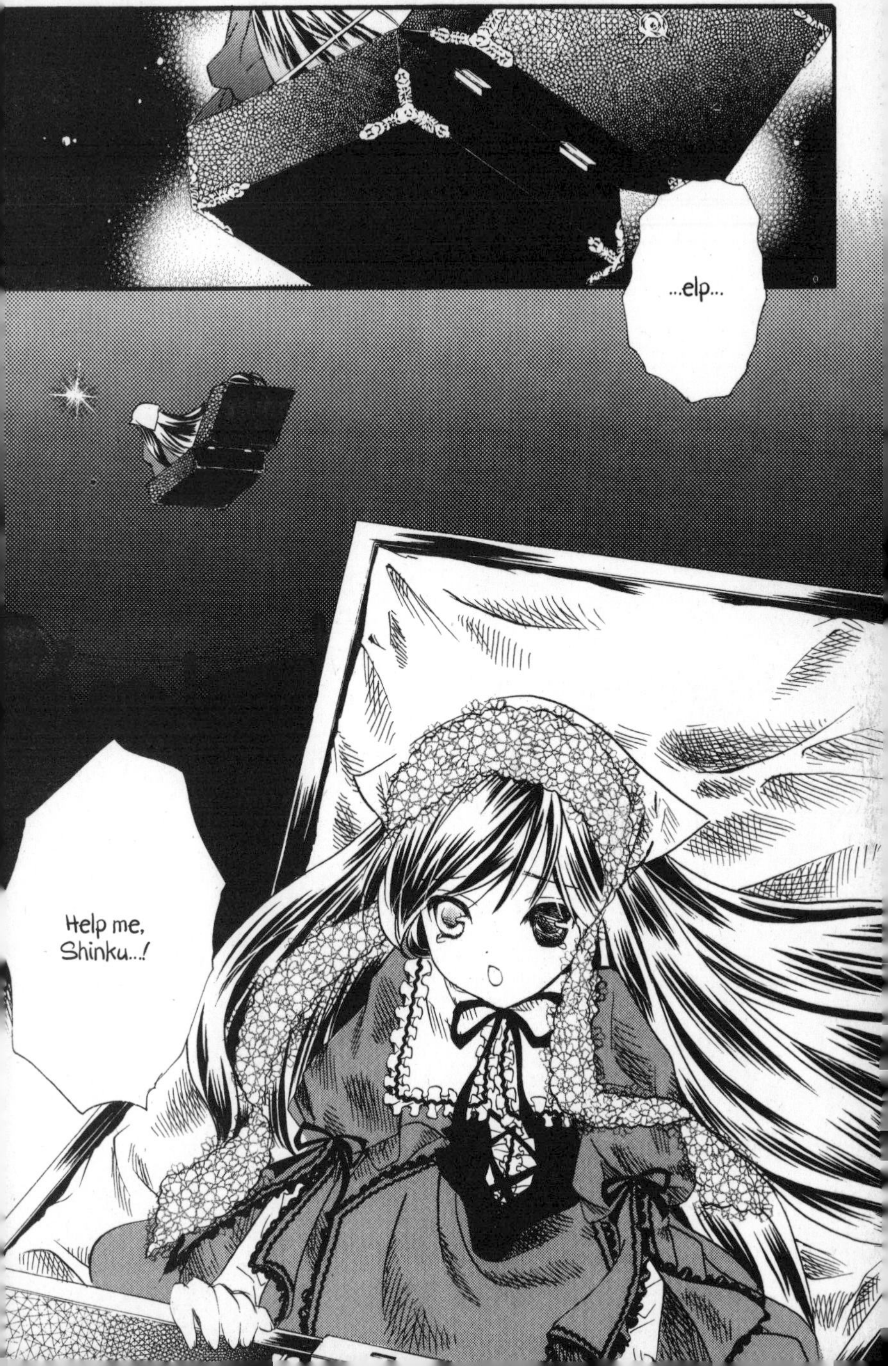
...elp...
Help me, Shinku...!

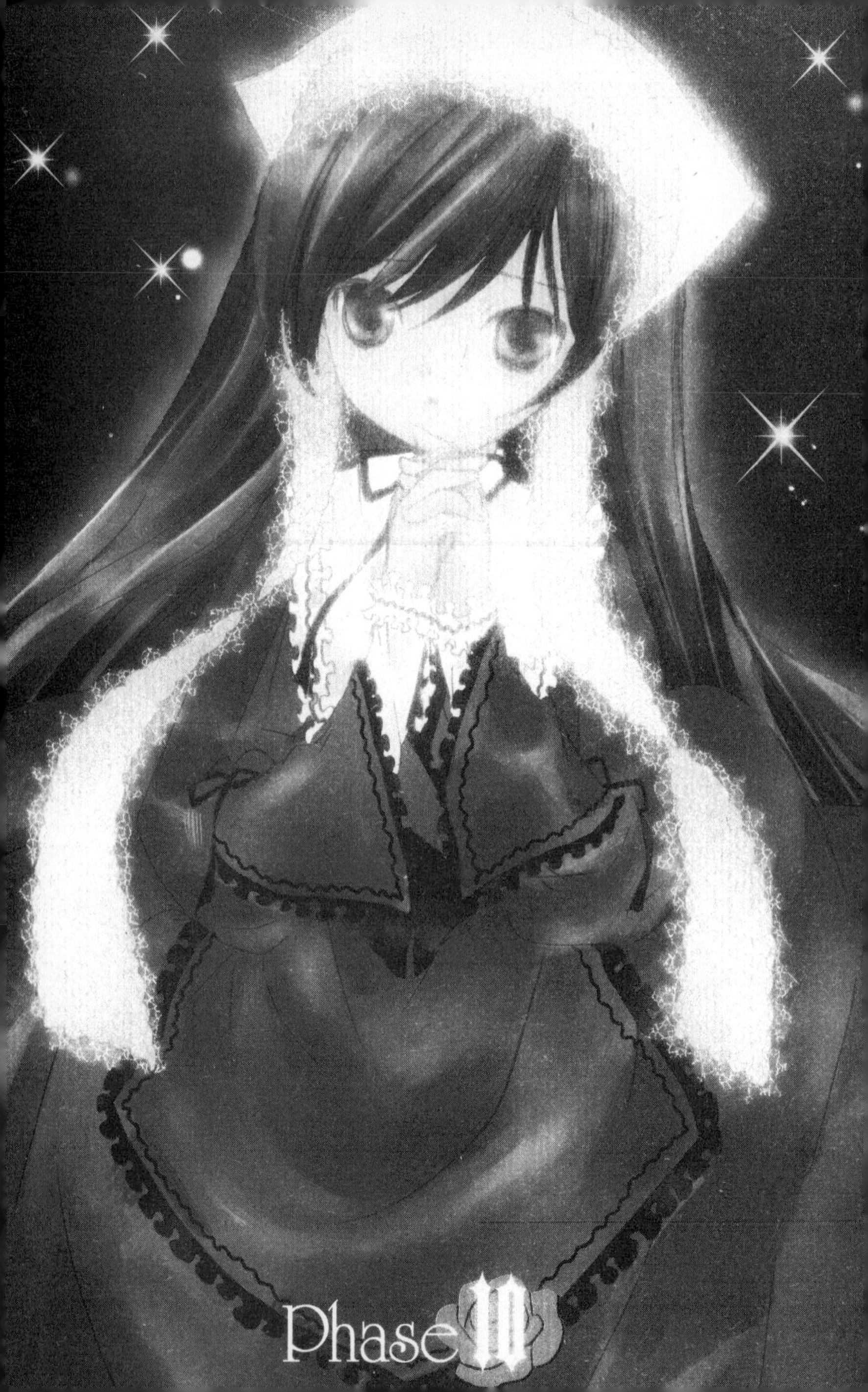
Phase 10

ローゼン メイデン
Rozen Maiden

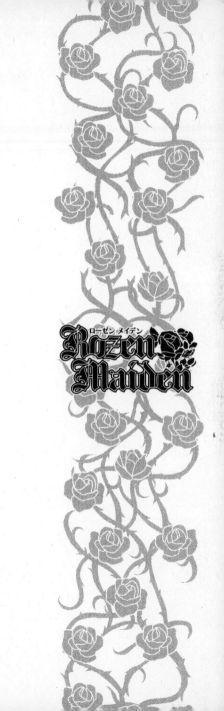

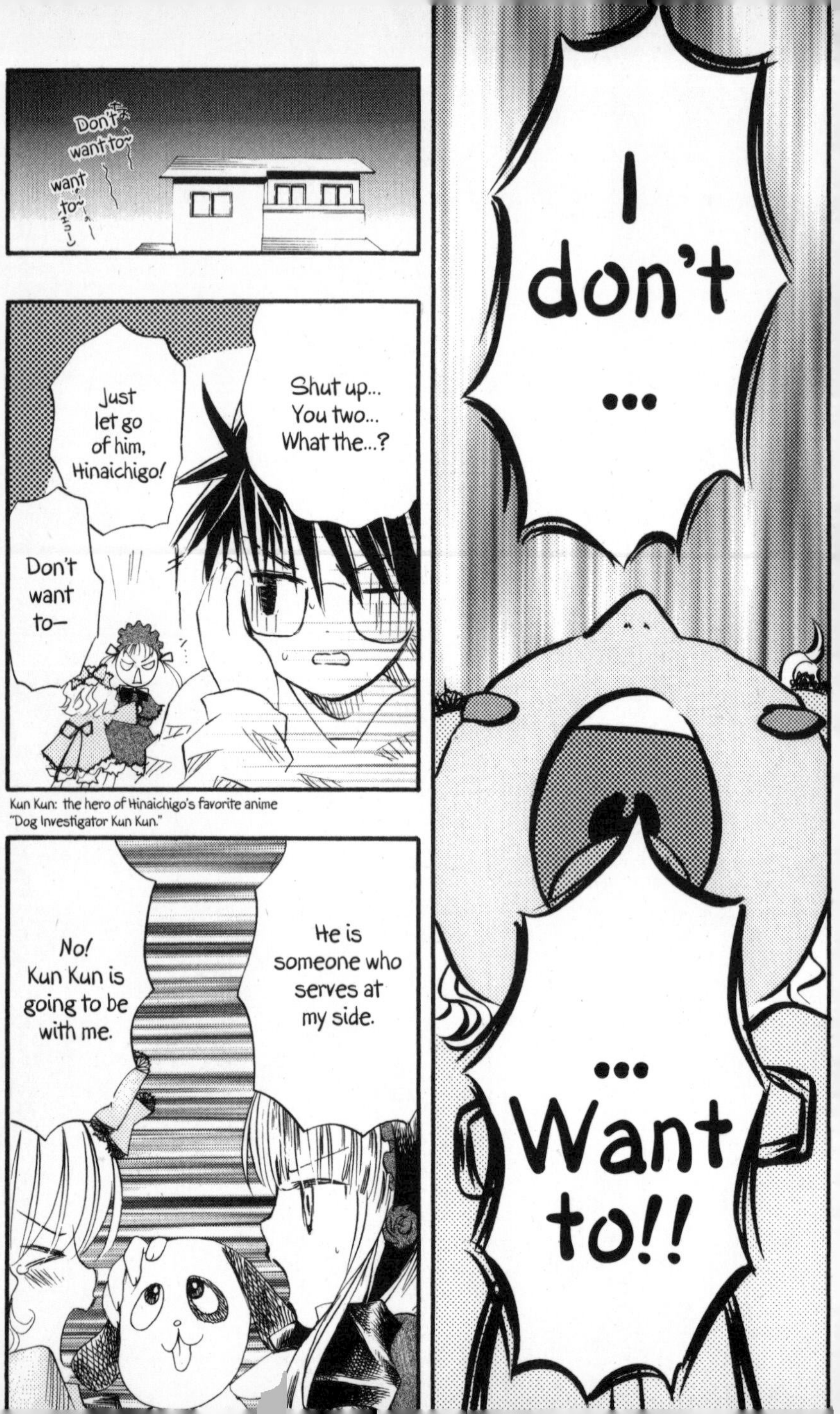
I don't ...
... Want to!!
Don't want to~
want to~
Shut up... You two... What the...?
Just let go of him, Hinaichigo!
Don't want to—
He is someone who serves at my side.
No! Kun Kun is going to be with me.

Kun Kun: the hero of Hinaichigo's favorite anime "Dog Investigator Kun Kun."

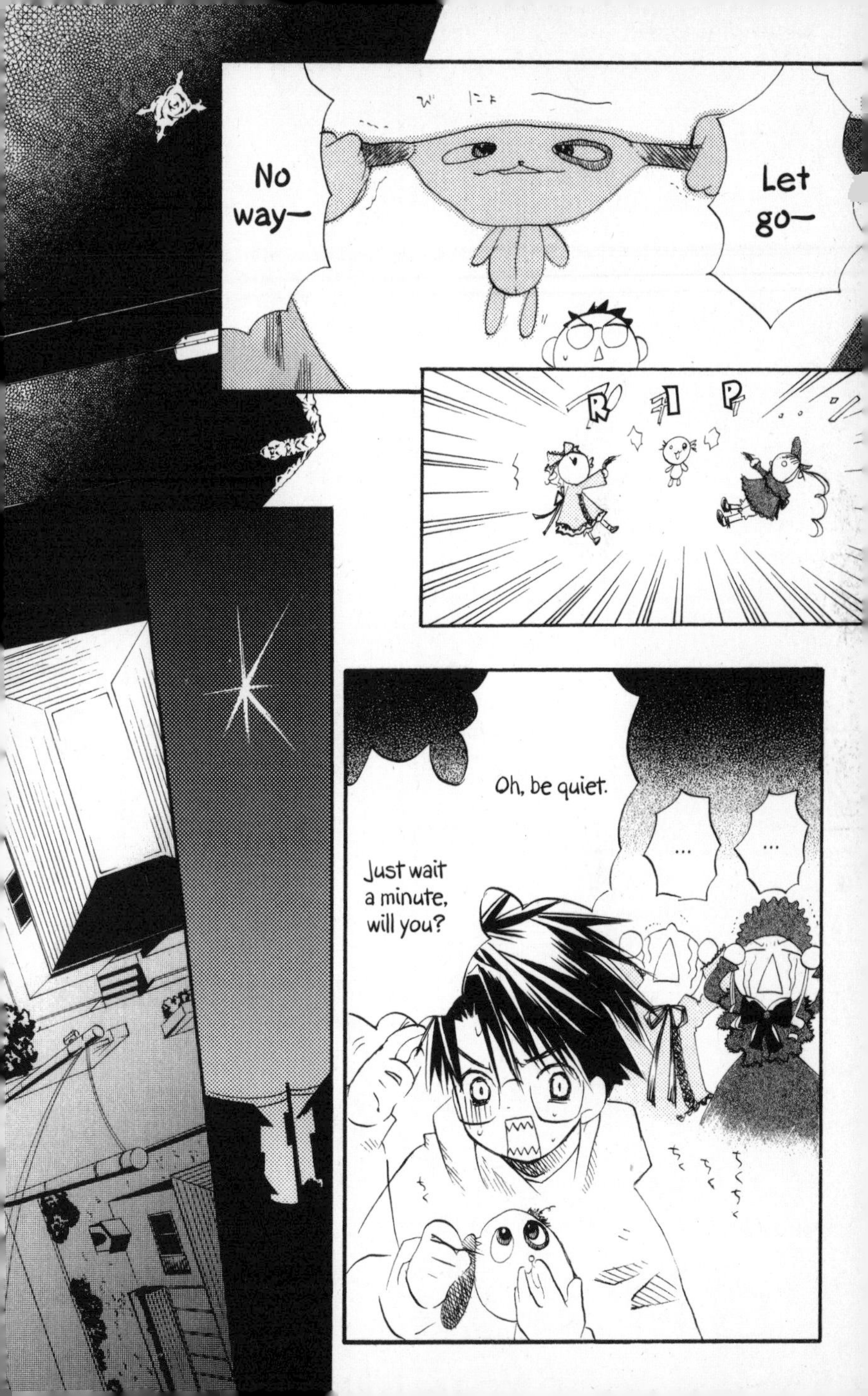
Let go—
No way—
RIP
Oh, be quiet.
...
...
Just wait a minute, will you?

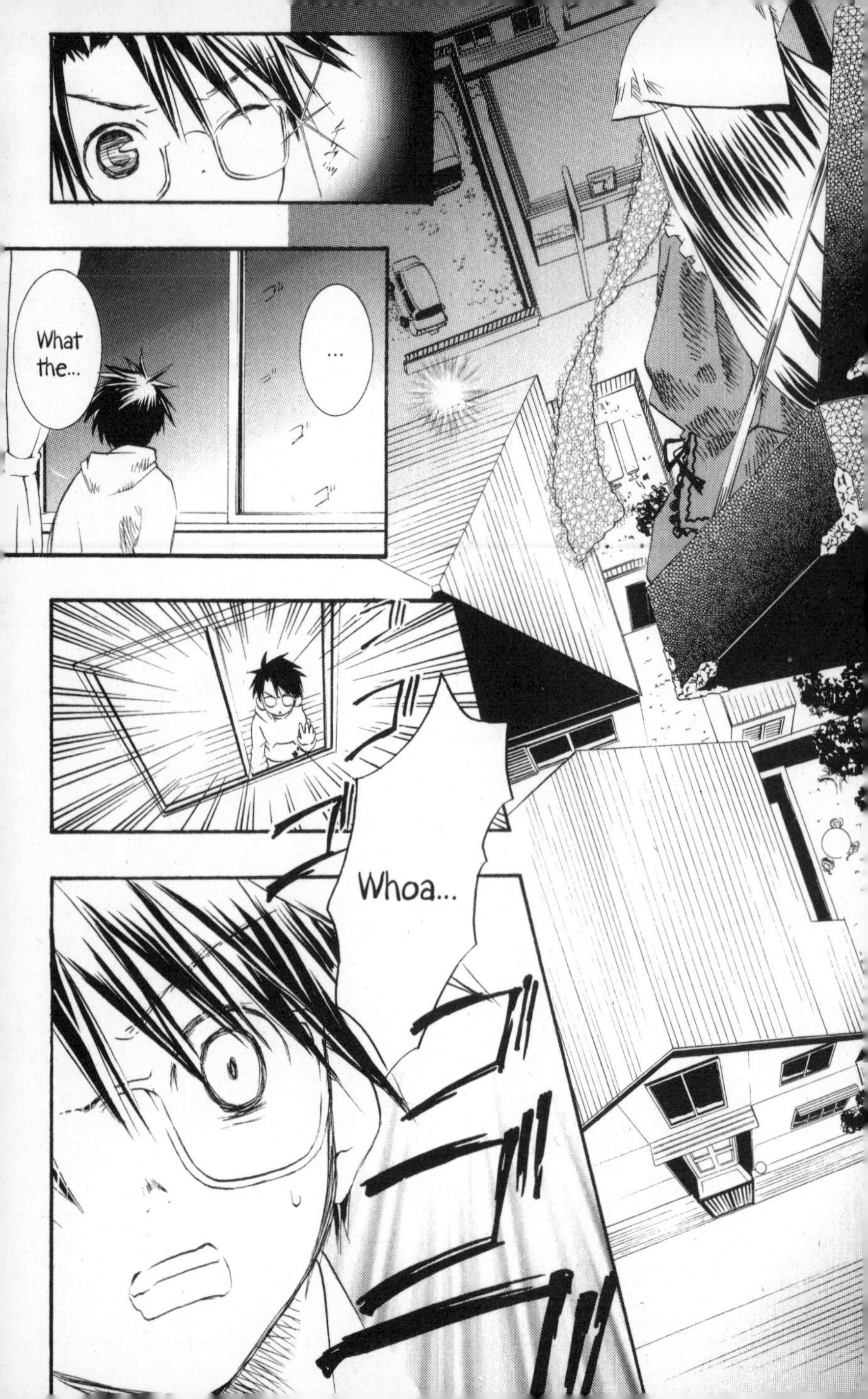
...
What the...
Whoa...

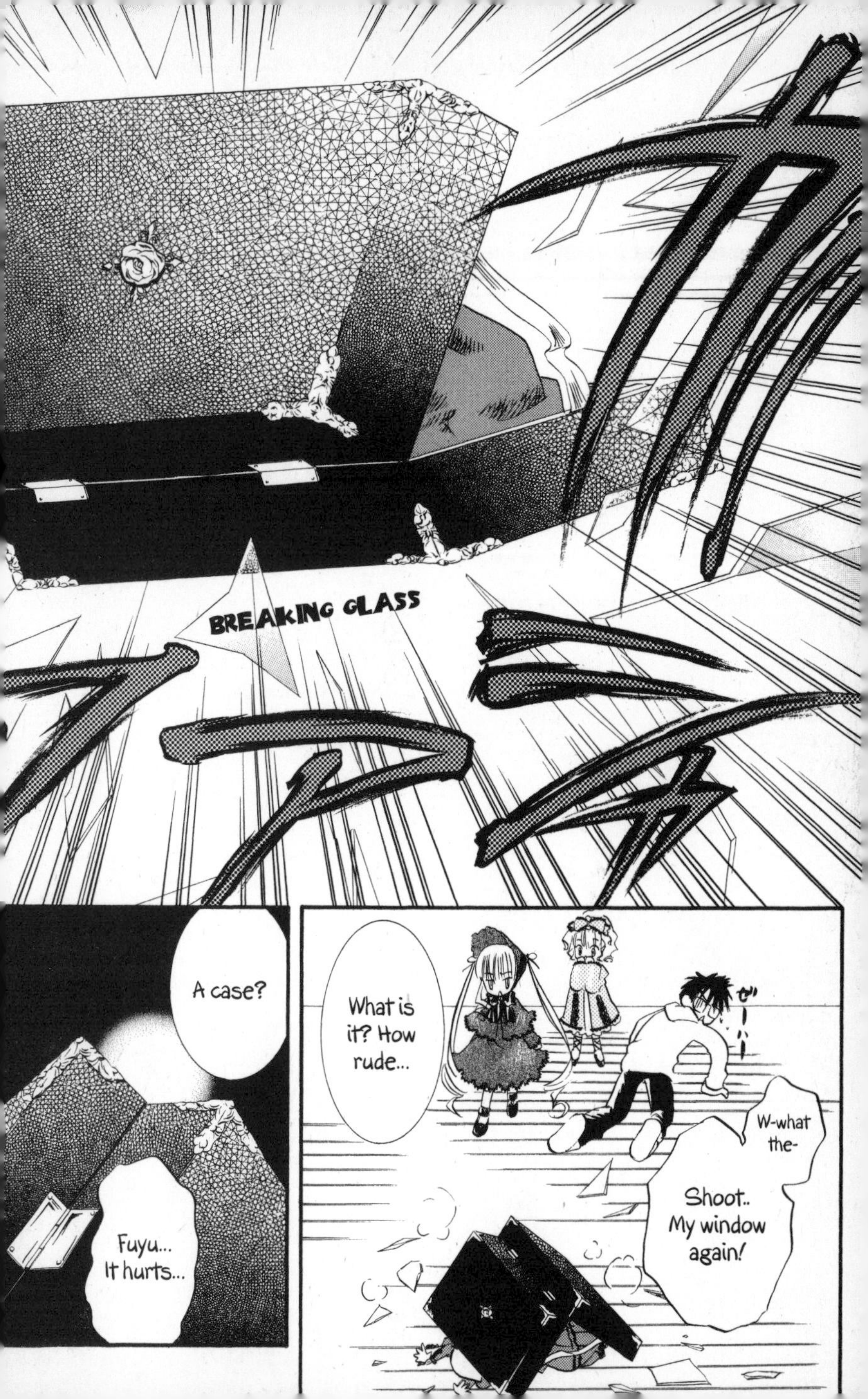
BREAKING GLASS
What is it? How rude...
W-what the-
Shoot.. My window again!
A case?
Fuyu... It hurts...

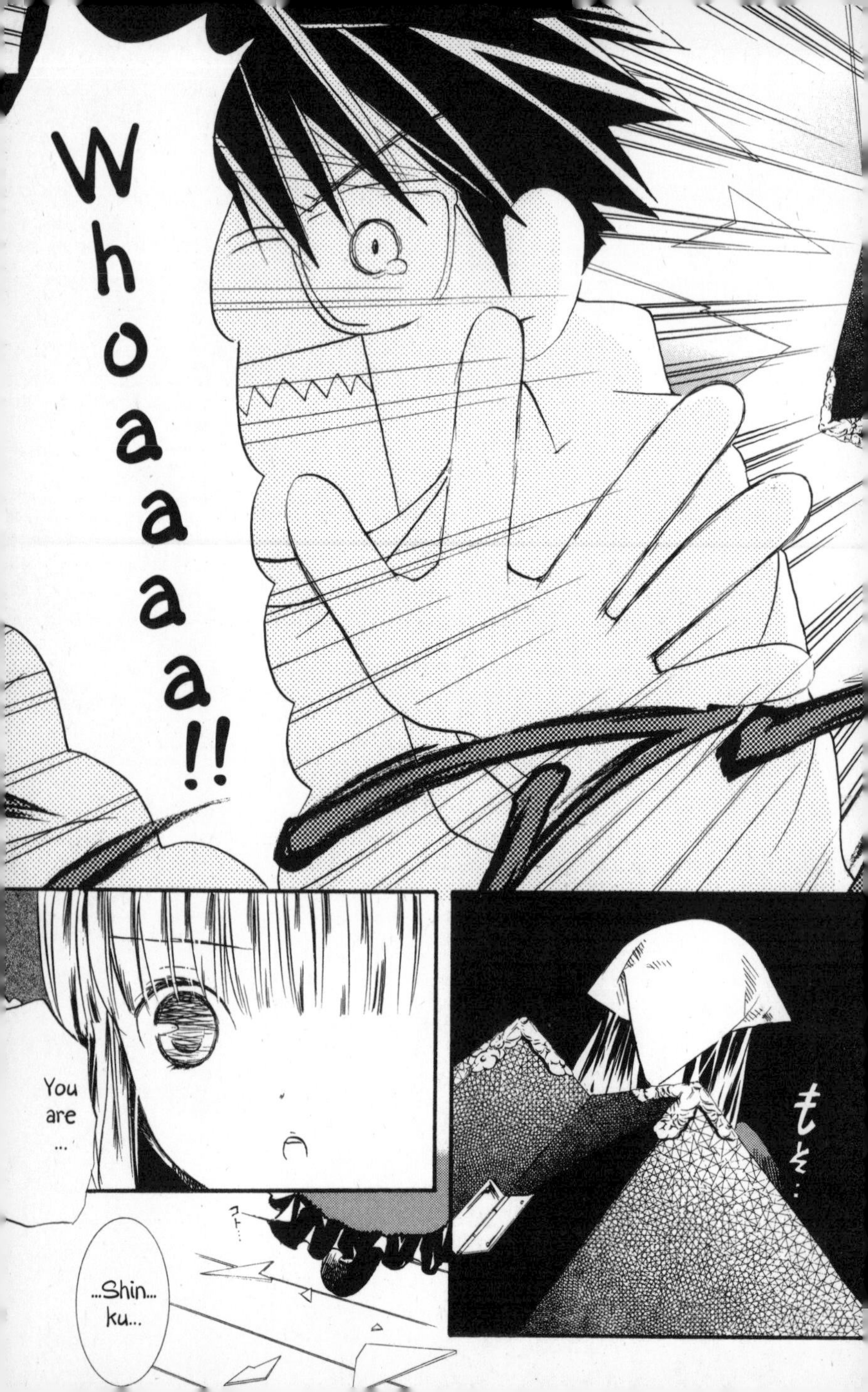
Whoaaaa!!
もそ…
You are ...
コト…
...Shin... ku...

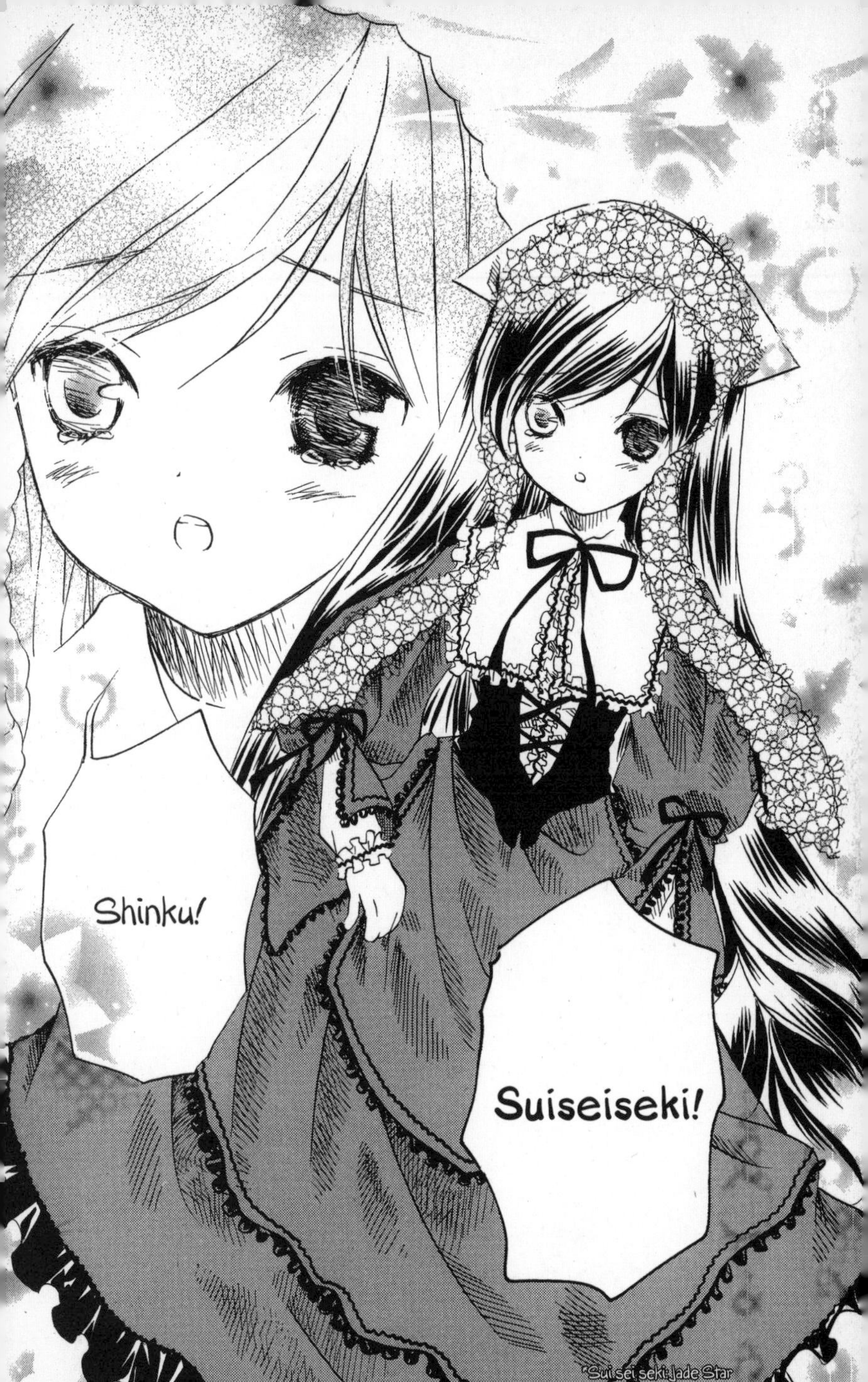
Shinku!
Suiseiseki!

*Sui sei seki: Jade Star

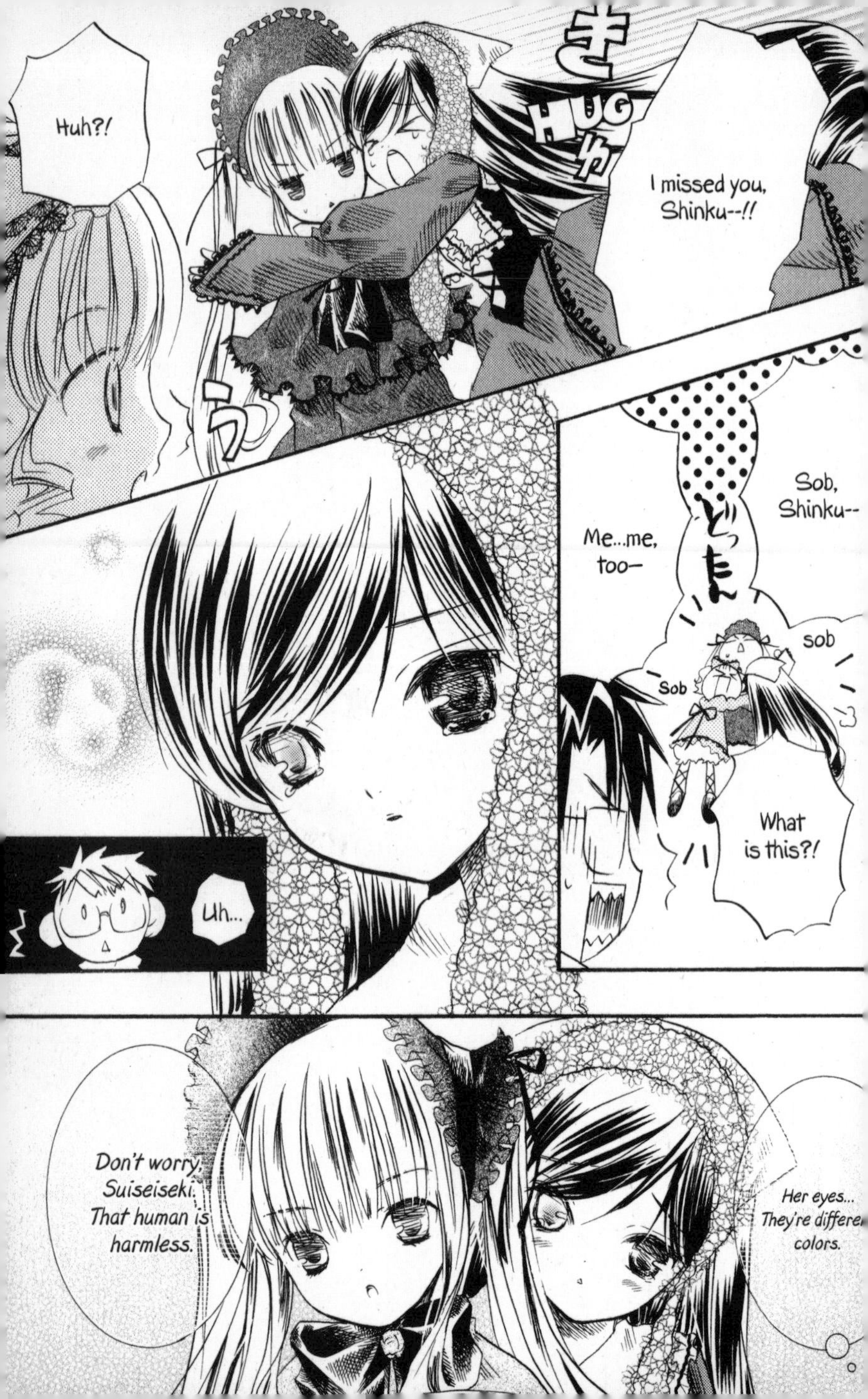
HUG
I missed you, Shinku--!!
Huh?!
Sob, Shinku--
Me...me, too–
sob
Sob
What is this?!
Uh...
Her eyes... They're differe colors.
Don't worry, Suiseiseki. That human is harmless.

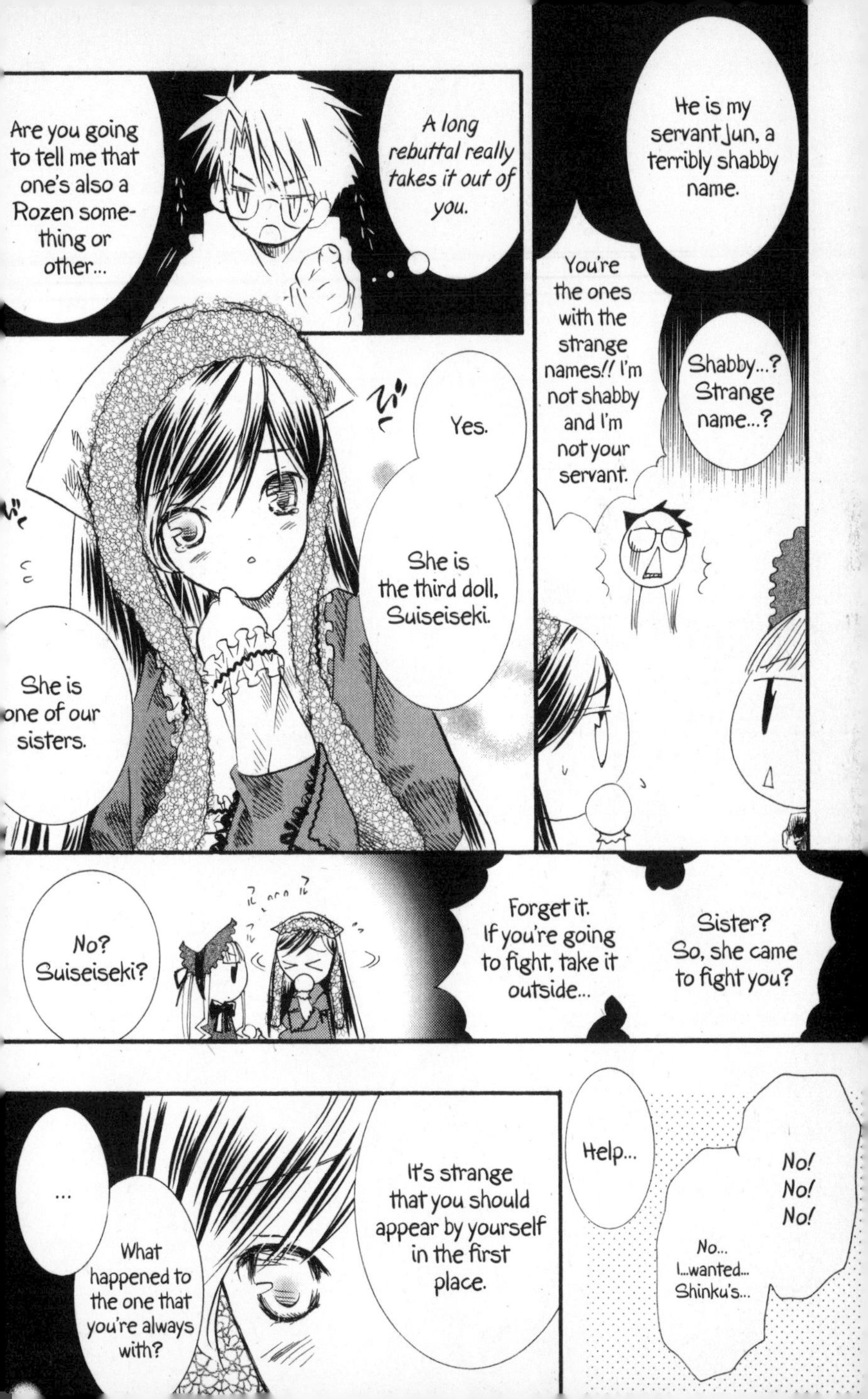
He is my servant Jun, a terribly shabby name.
Shabby...? Strange name...?
You're the ones with the strange names!! I'm not shabby and I'm not your servant.
A long rebuttal really takes it out of you.
Are you going to tell me that one's also a Rozen some-thing or other...
Yes.
She is the third doll, Suiseiseki.
She is one of our sisters.
Sister? So, she came to fight you?
Forget it. If you're going to fight, take it outside...
No? Suiseiseki?
No! No! No!
Help...
No... I...wanted... Shinku's...
It's strange that you should appear by yourself in the first place.
...
What happened to the one that you're always with?

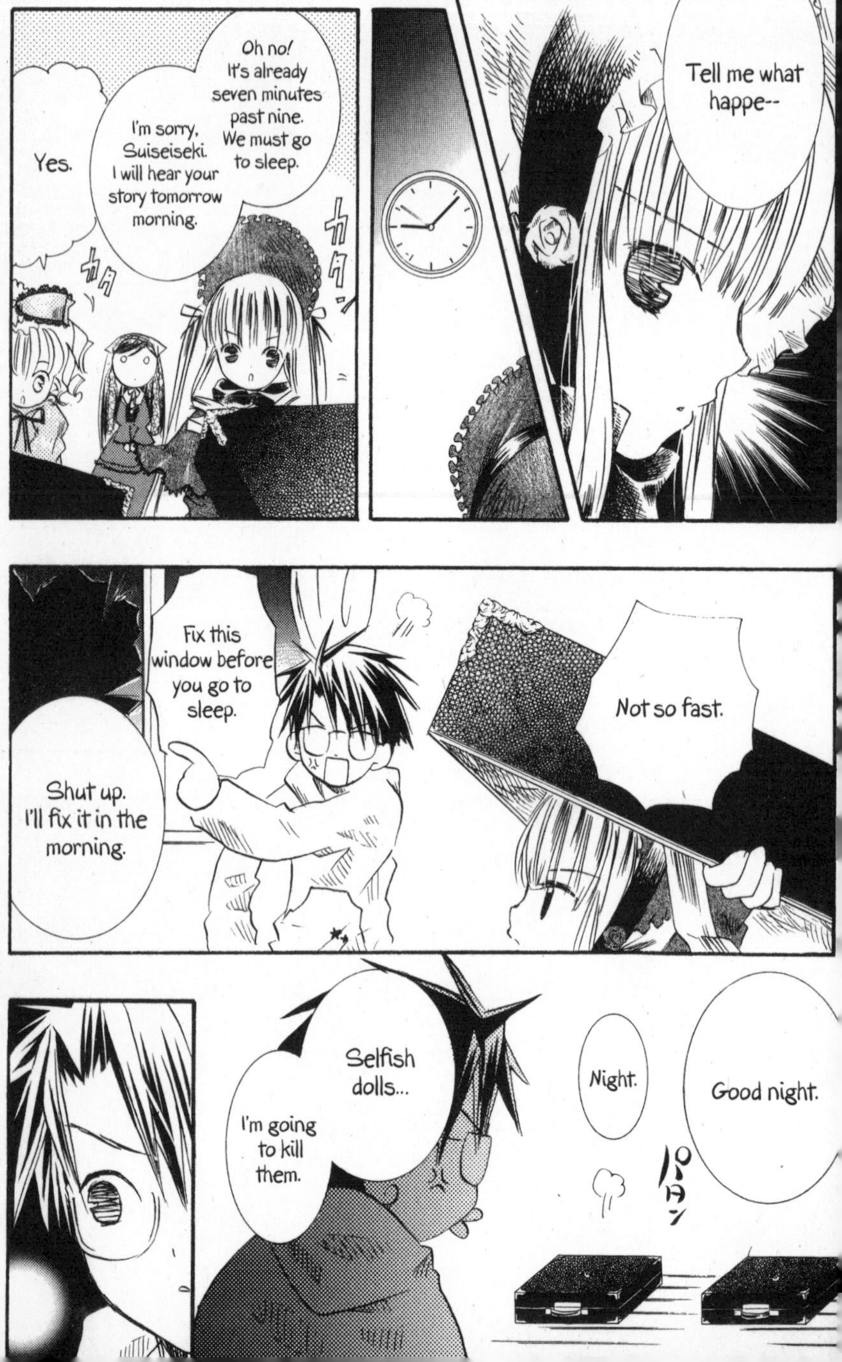
Tell me what happe--
Oh no! It's already seven minutes past nine. We must go to sleep.
I'm sorry, Suiseiseki. I will hear your story tomorrow morning.
Yes.
Not so fast.
Fix this window before you go to sleep.
Shut up. I'll fix it in the morning.
Good night.
Night.
パタン
Selfish dolls...
I'm going to kill them.

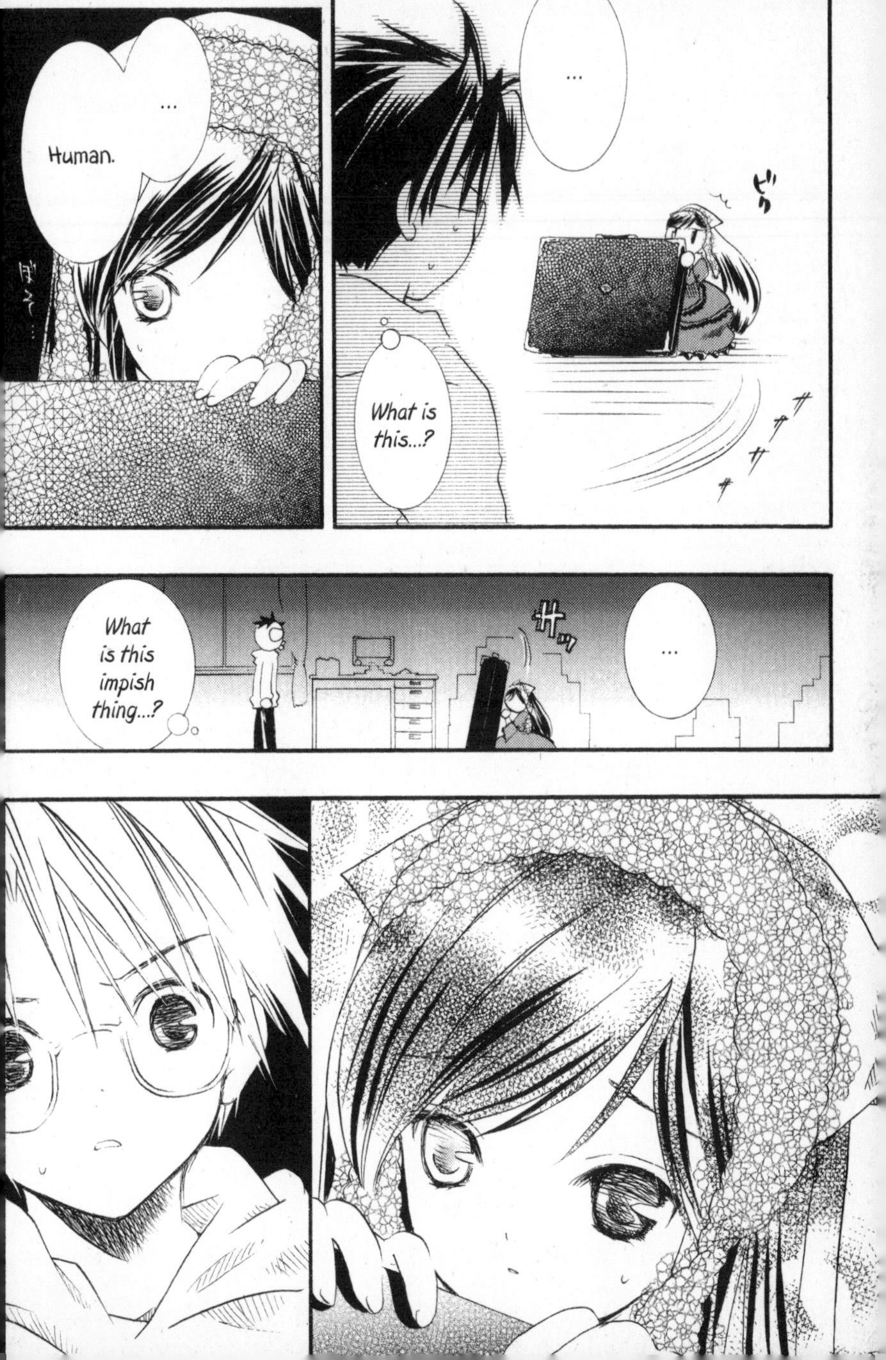
...
ビク
サササ
What is this...?
...
Human.
...
サッ
What is this impish thing...?

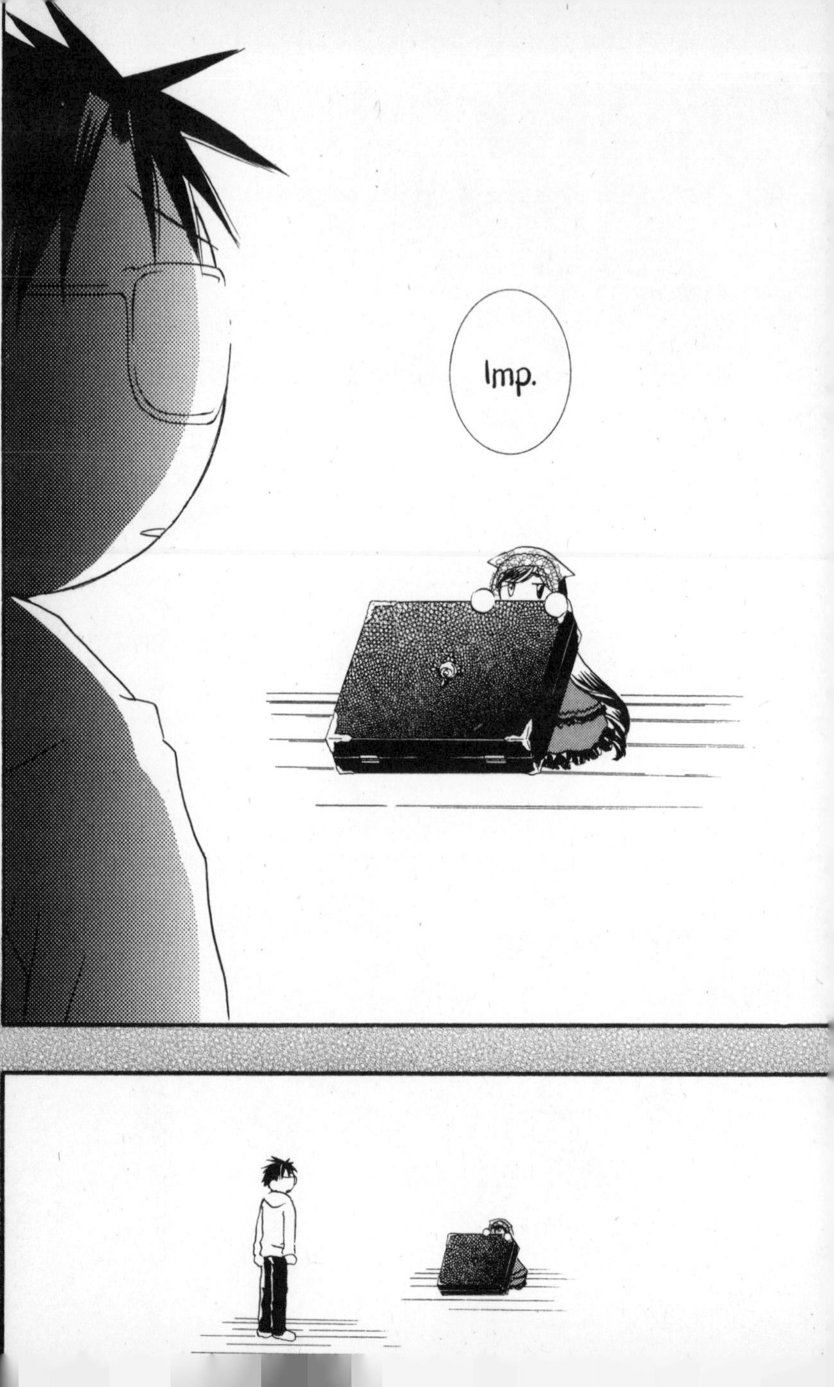
Imp.

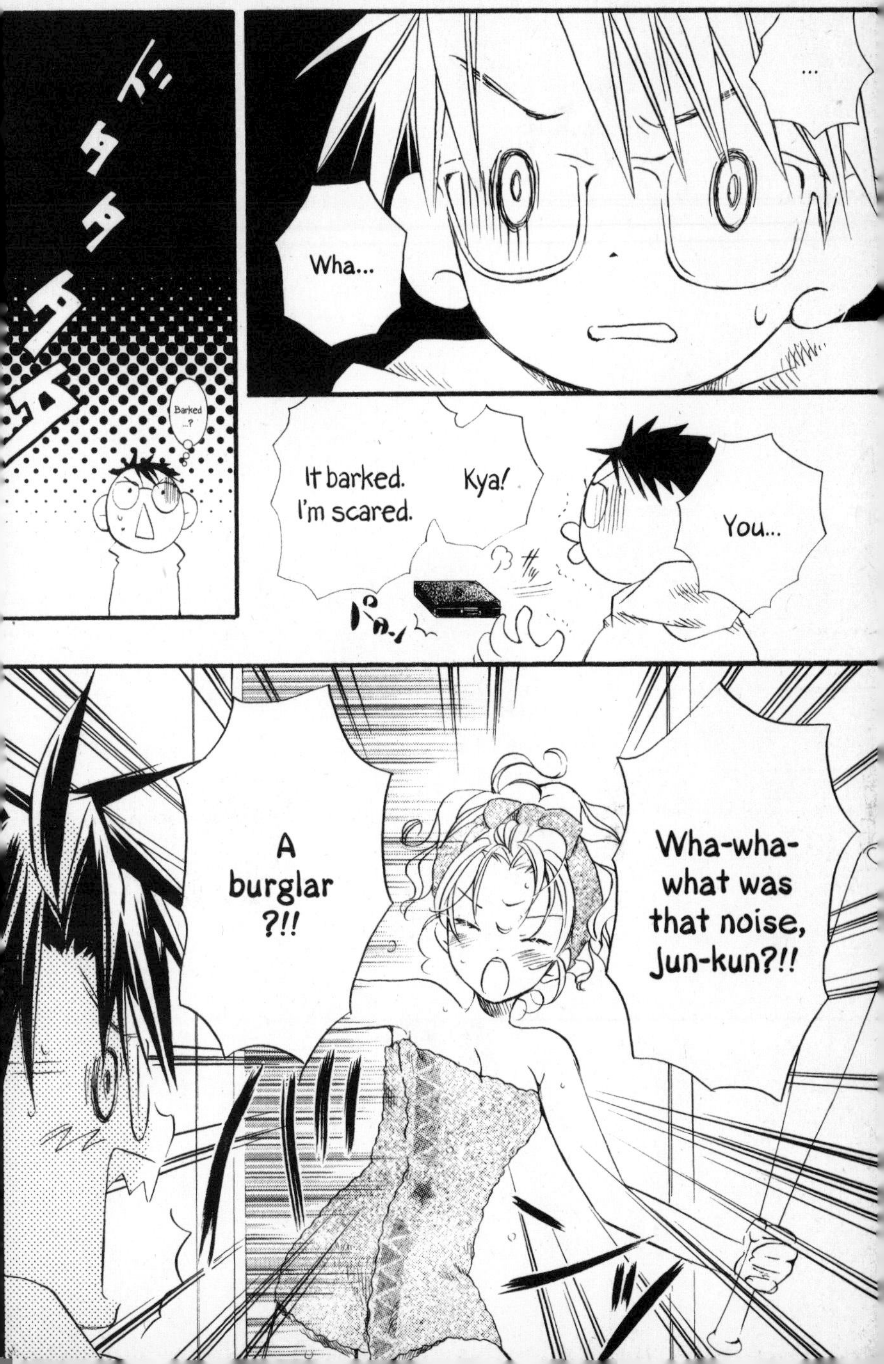
...
Wha...
You...
Kya!
It barked. I'm scared.
ドタタタタ
Barked ...?
Wha-wha-what was that noise, Jun-kun?!!
A burglar ?!!

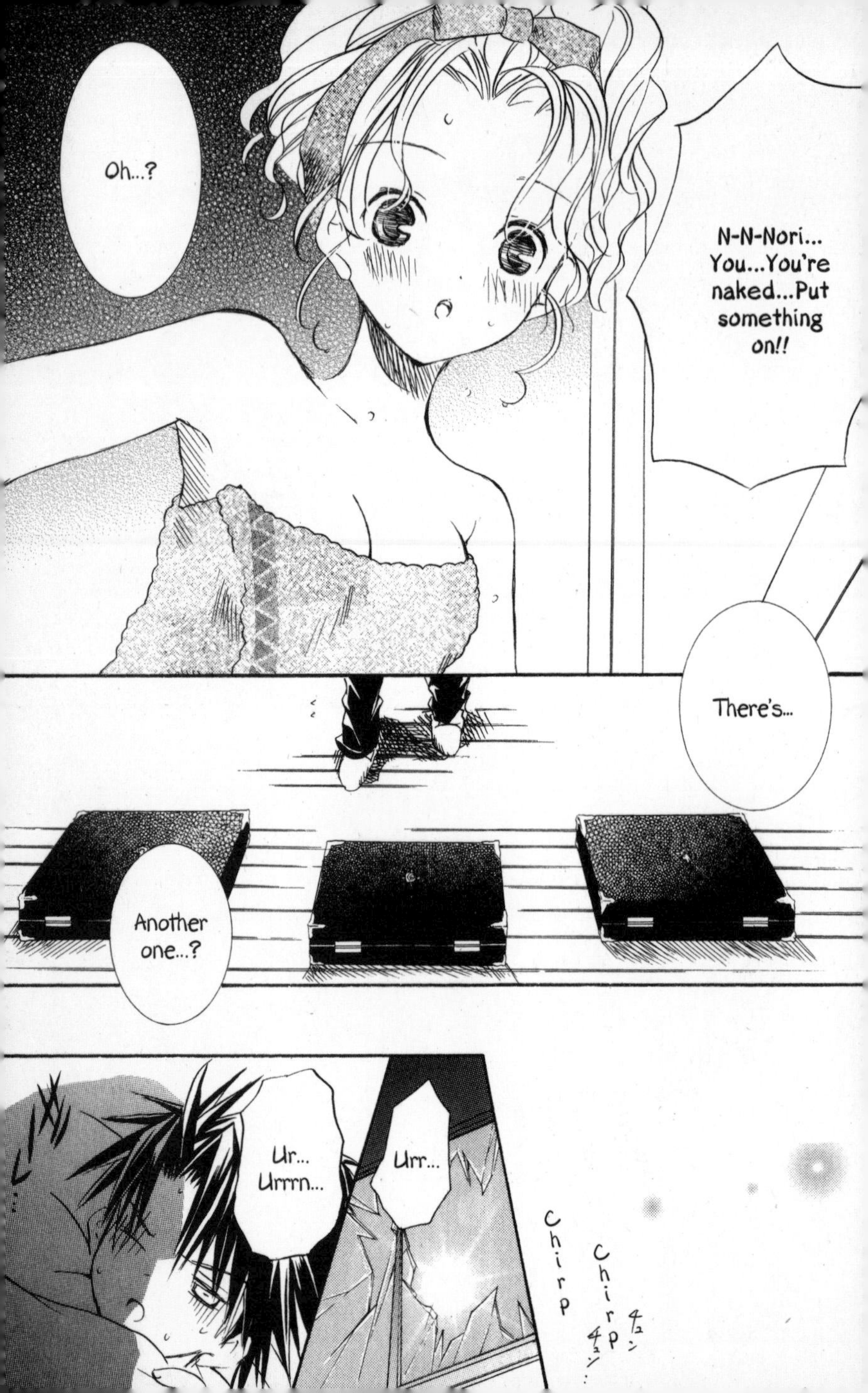
N-N-Nori... You...You're naked...Put something on!!
Oh...?
There's...
Another one...?
Chirp Chirp
Urr...
Ur... Urrrn...

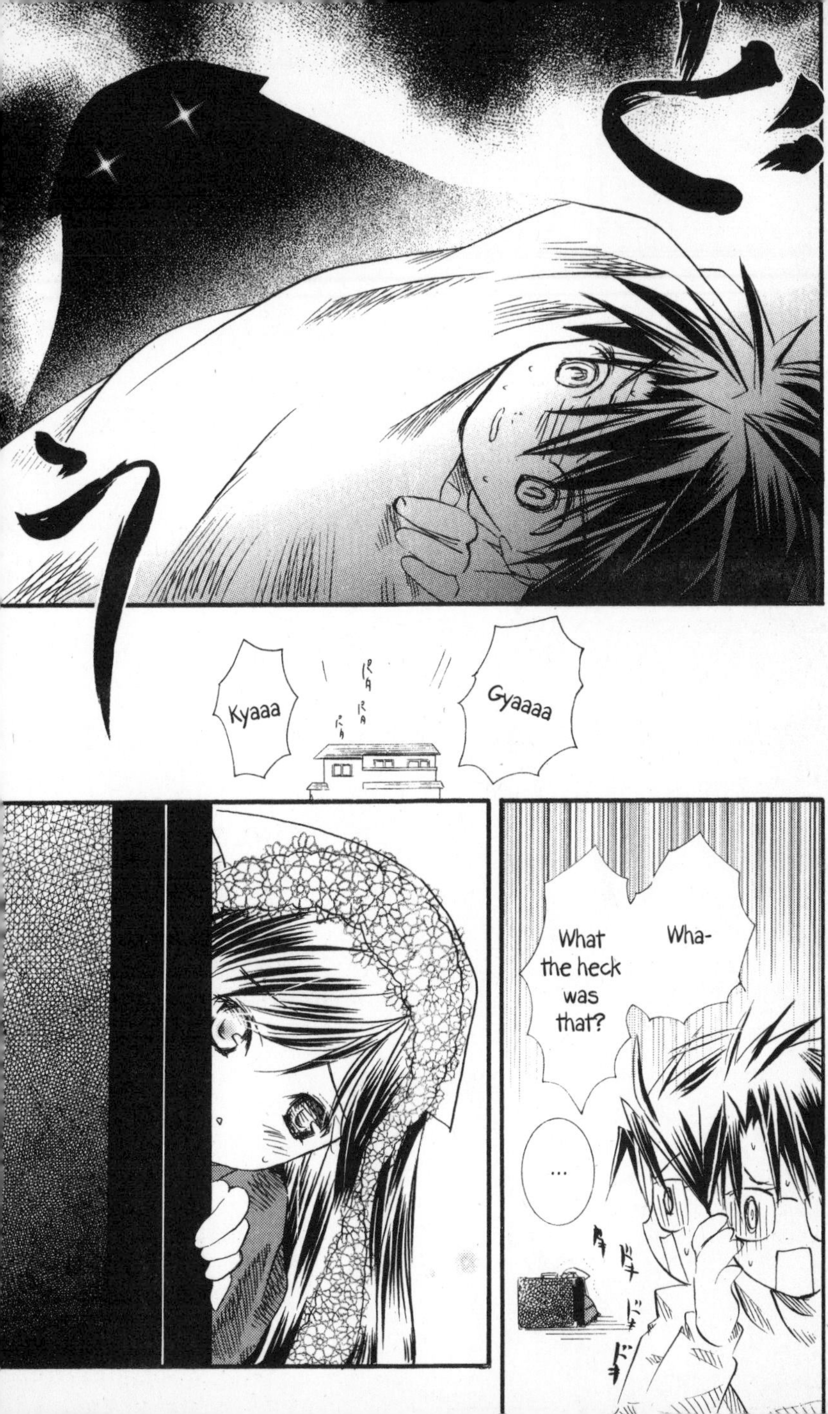
Gyaaaa
Kyaaa
Wha-
What the heck was that?
...

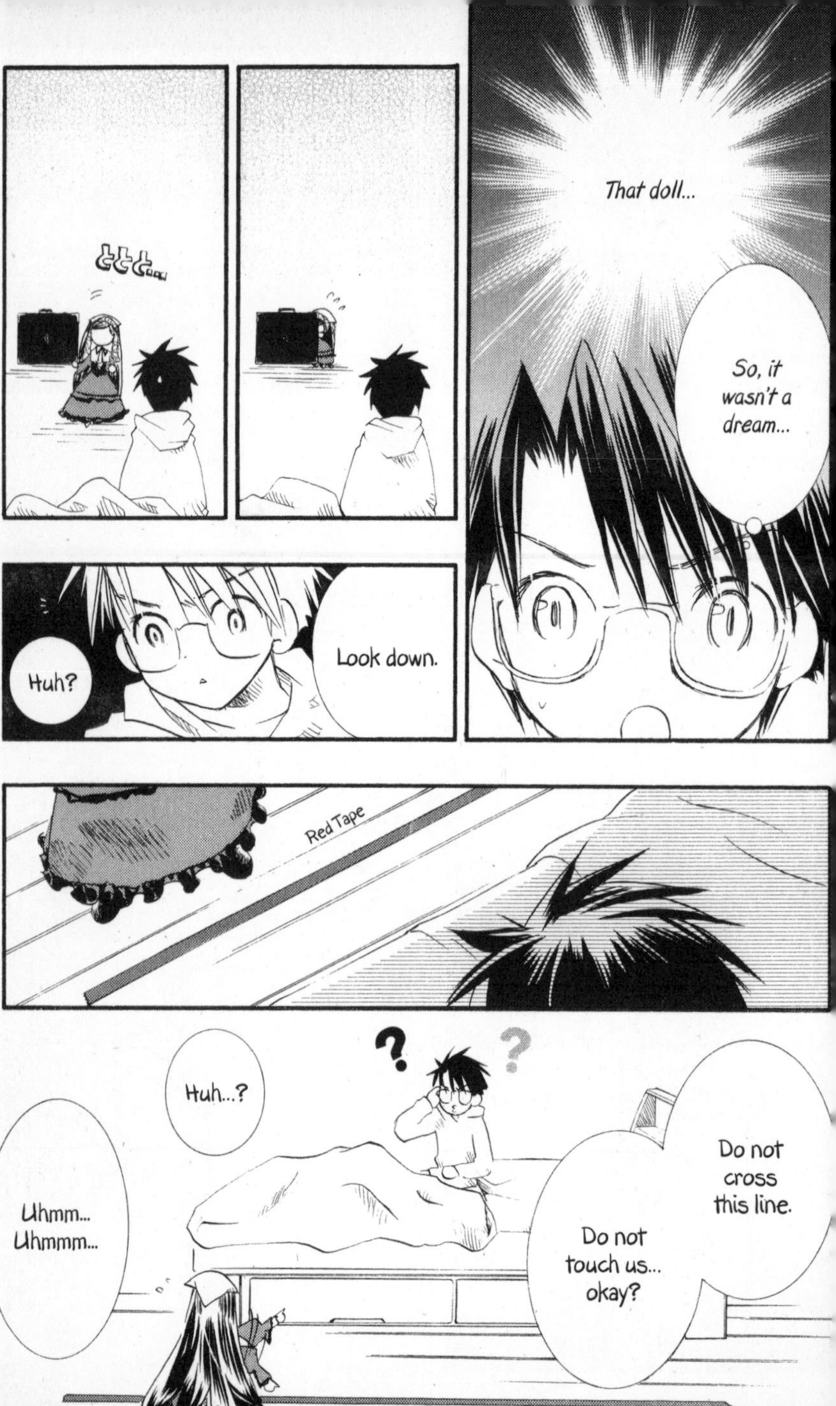
That doll...
So, it wasn't a dream...
ととと...
Look down.
Huh?
Red Tape
Do not cross this line.
Do not touch us... okay?
Huh...?
Uhmm... Uhmmm...

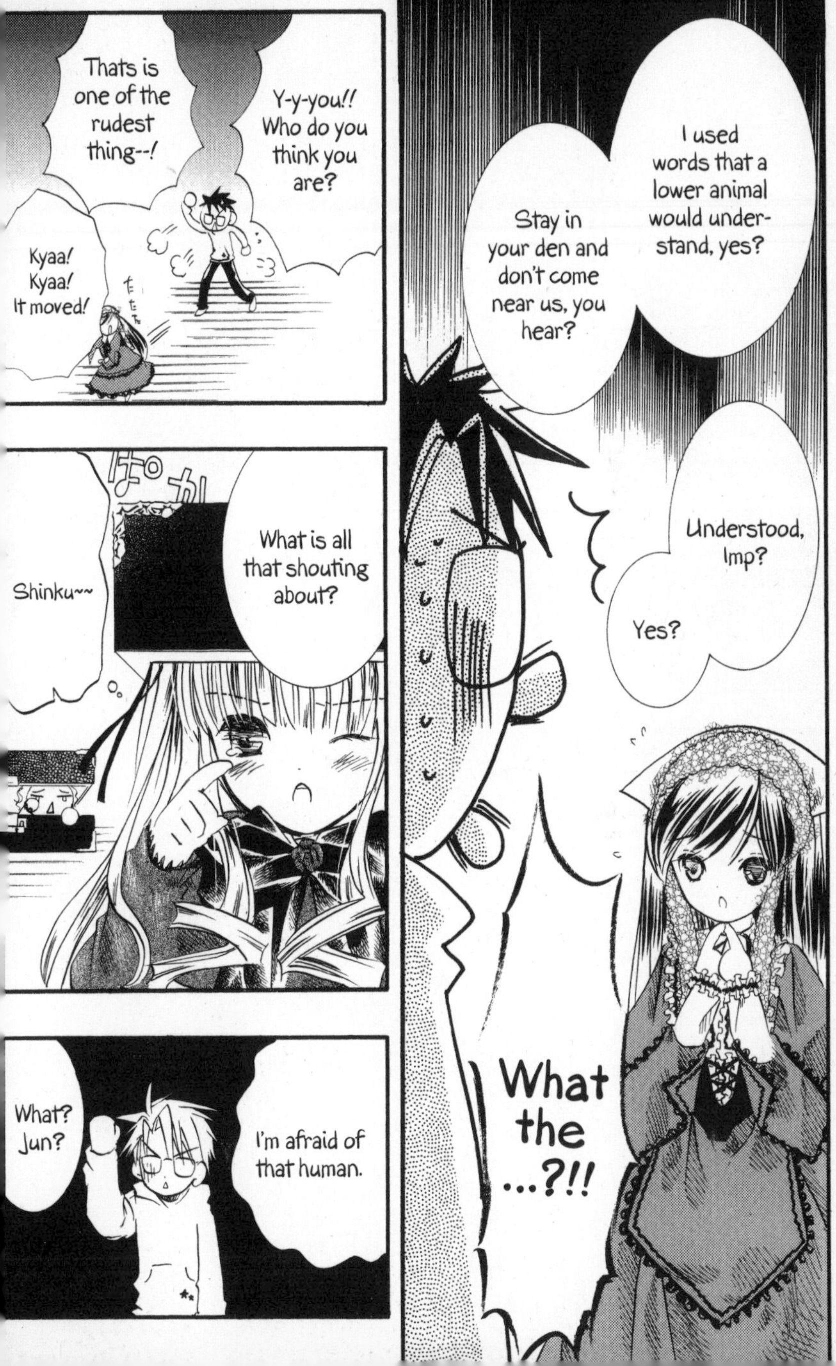

I used words that a lower animal would understand, yes?
Stay in your den and don't come near us, you hear?
Understood, Imp?
Yes?
What the ...?!!
Y-y-you!! Who do you think you are?
Thats is one of the rudest thing--!
Kyaa! Kyaa! It moved!
What is all that shouting about?
Shinku~~
I'm afraid of that human.
What? Jun?

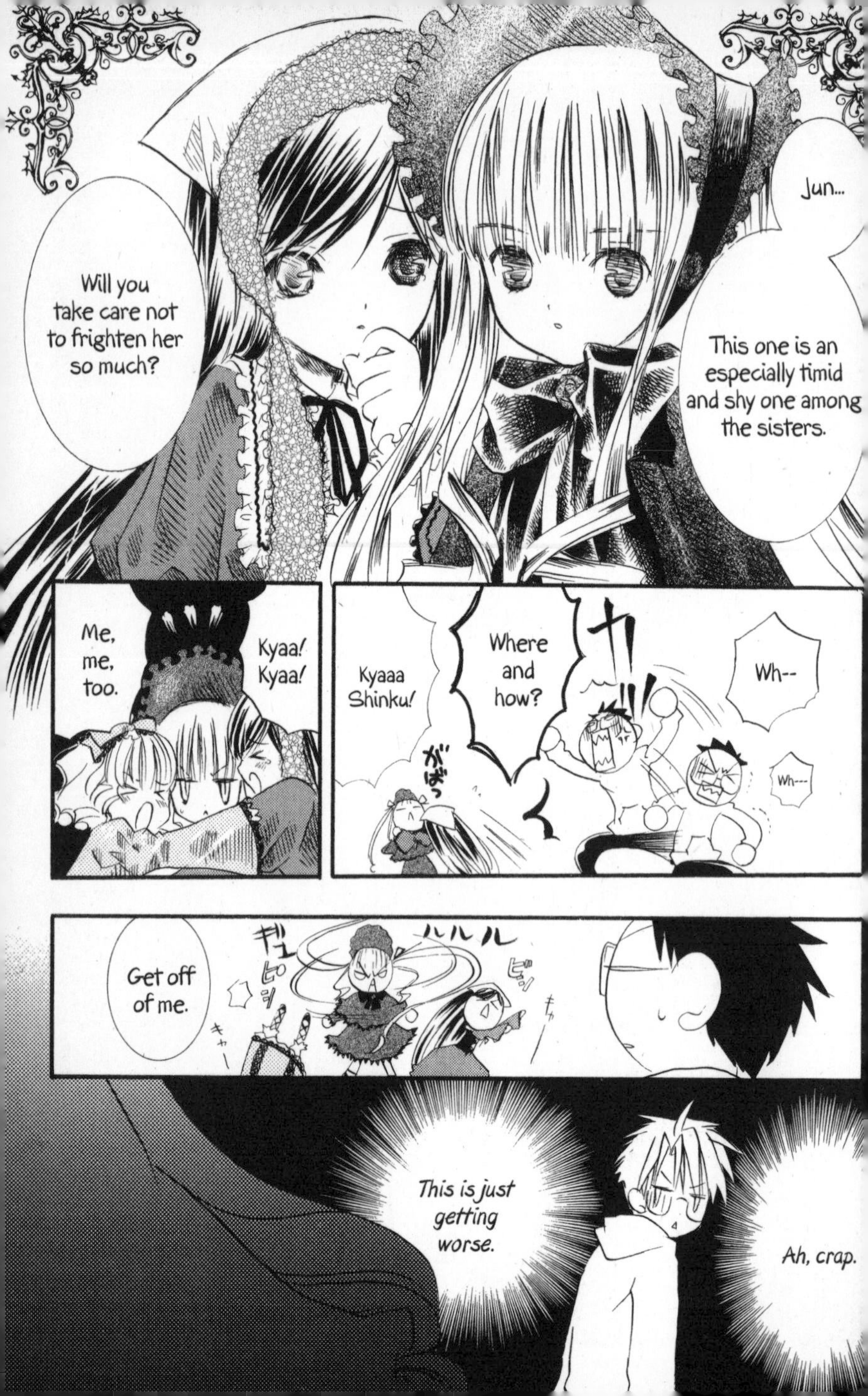

Jun...
This one is an especially timid and shy one among the sisters.
Will you take care not to frighten her so much?
Wh--
Wh---
Where and how?
Kyaaa Shinku!
がばっ
Kyaa! Kyaa!
Me, me, too.
ルルル
Get off of me.
Ah, crap.
This is just getting worse.

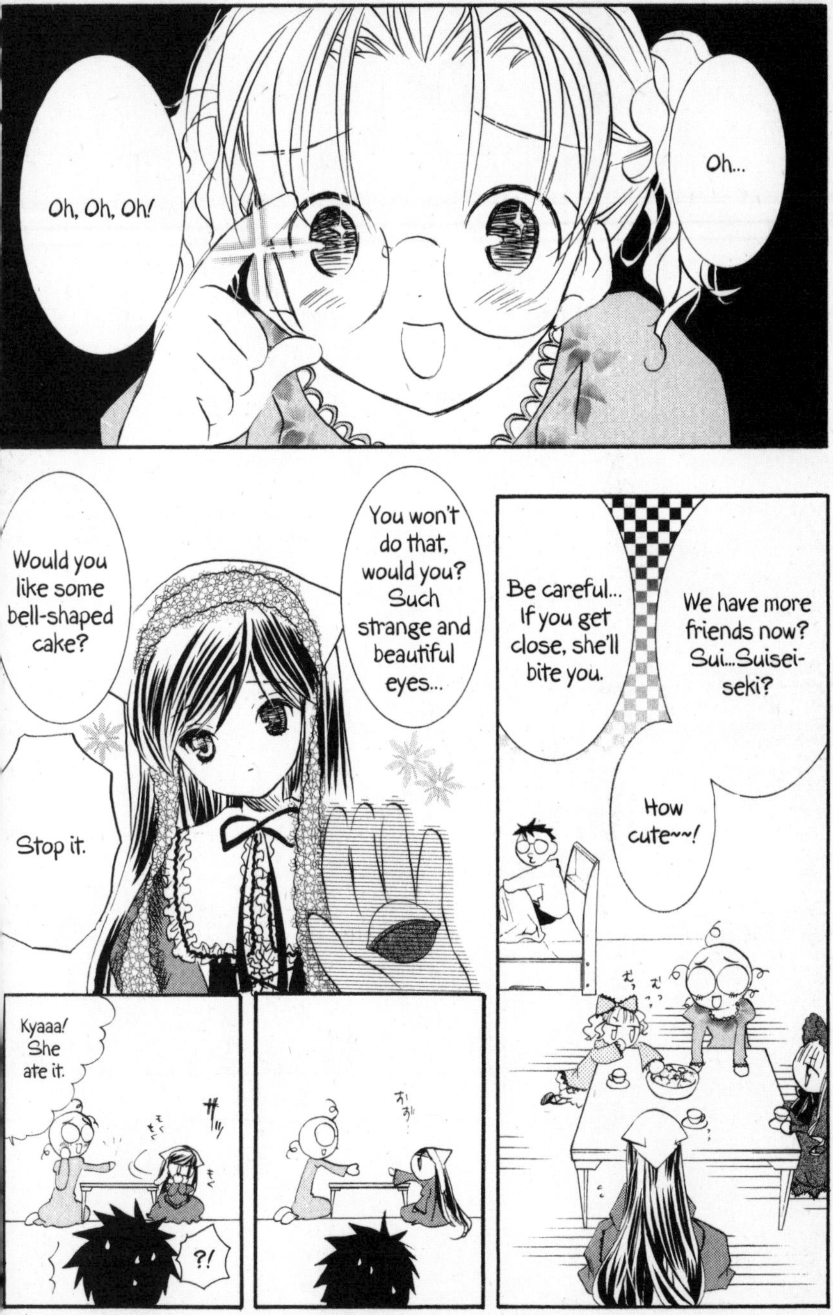
Oh...
Oh, Oh, Oh!
We have more friends now? Sui...Suisei-seki?
Be careful... If you get close, she'll bite you.
How cute~~!
You won't do that, would you? Such strange and beautiful eyes...
Would you like some bell-shaped cake?
Stop it.
Kyaaa! She ate it.
?!

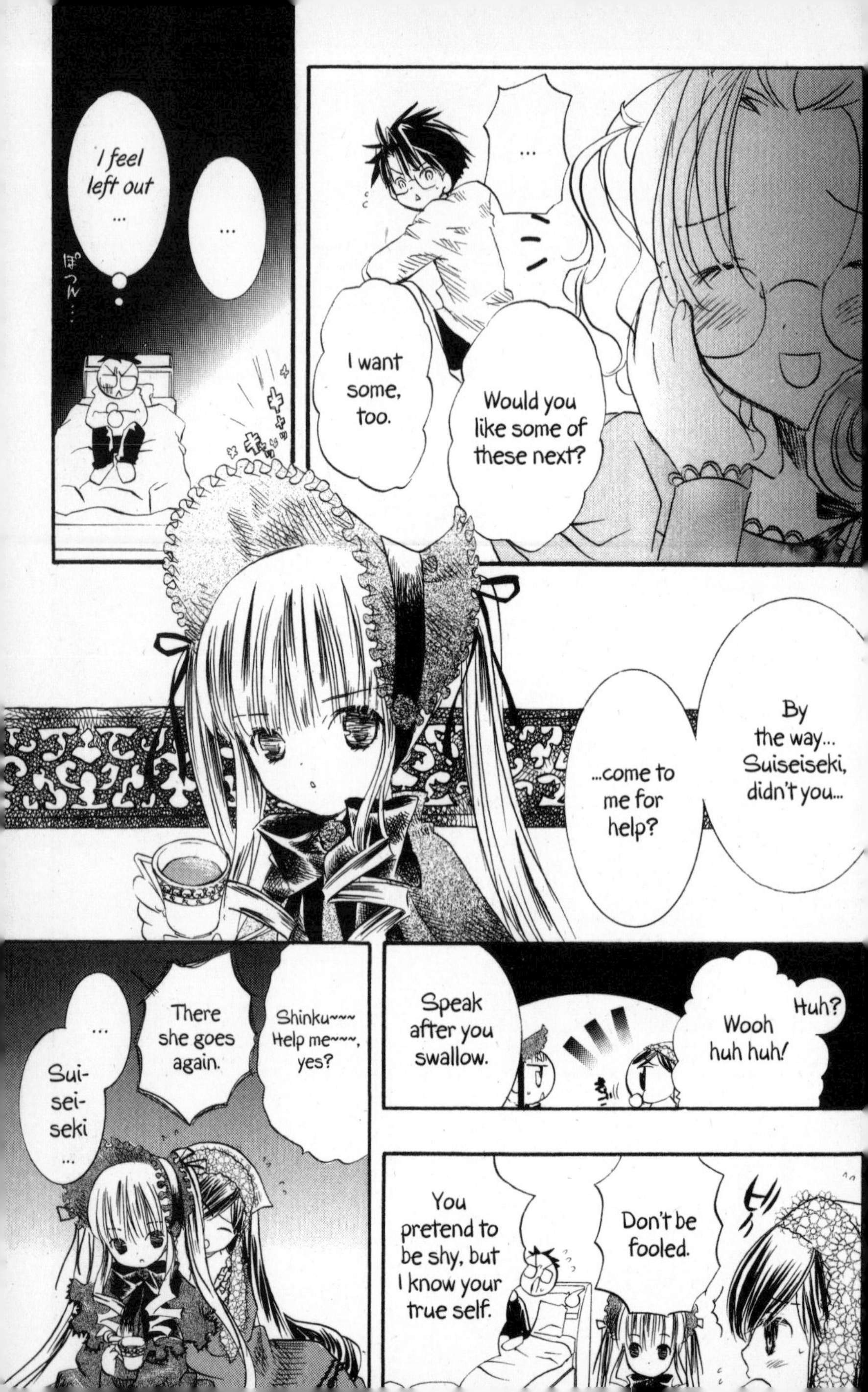

...
Would you like some of these next?
I want some, too.
I feel left out ...
...
ぽつん…
By the way... Suiseiseki, didn't you...
...come to me for help?
Huh?
Wooh huh huh!
Speak after you swallow.
Shinku~~~ Help me~~~, yes?
There she goes again.
... Sui-sei-seki ...
Don't be fooled.
You pretend to be shy, but I know your true self.

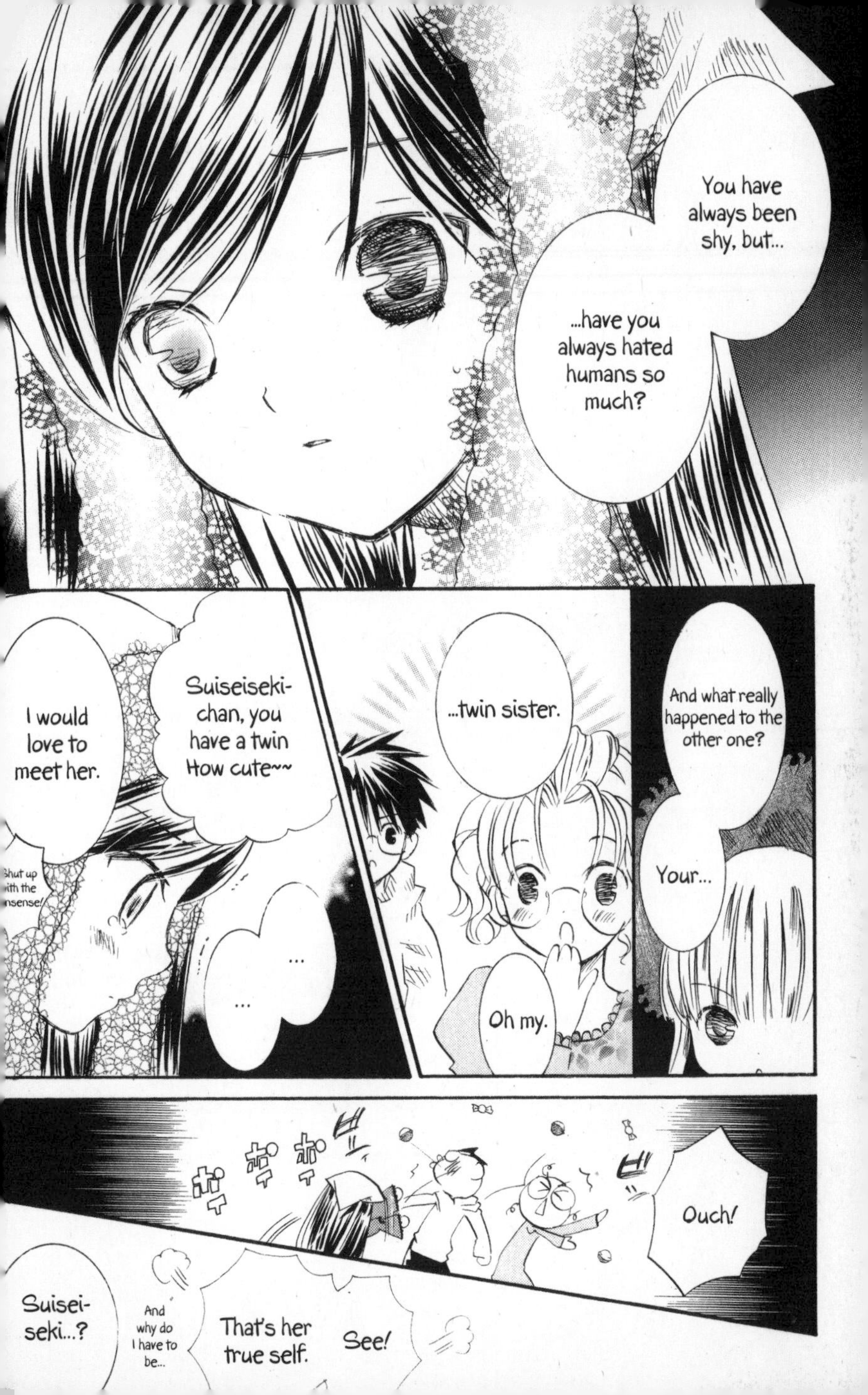
You have always been shy, but...
...have you always hated humans so much?
And what really happened to the other one?
Your...
...twin sister.
Oh my.
Suiseiseki-chan, you have a twin How cute~~
I would love to meet her.
hut up ith the nsense!
...
...
Ouch!
See!
That's her true self.
And why do I have to be...
Suisei-seki...?

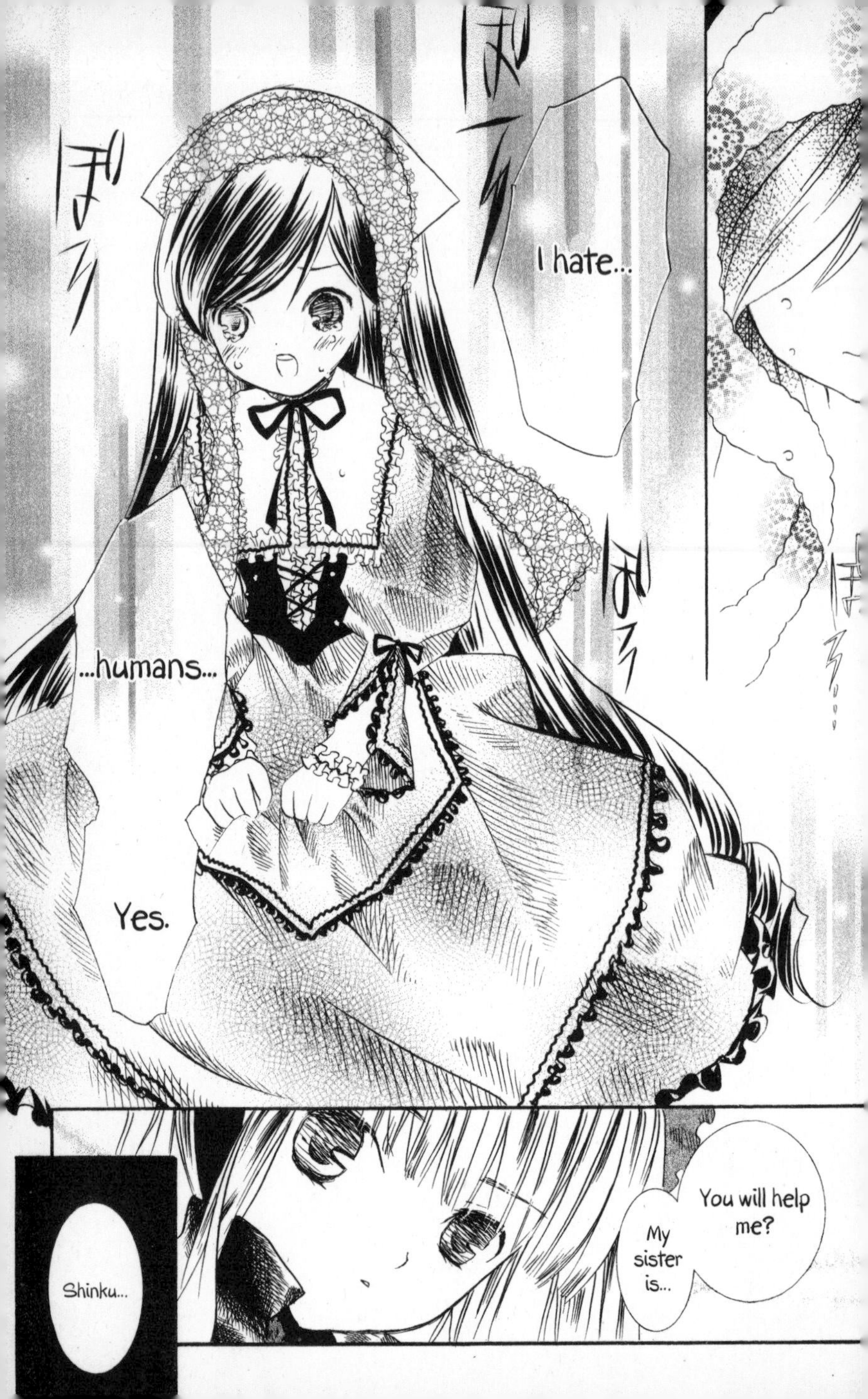
I hate...
...humans...
Yes.
You will help me?
My sister is...
Shinku...

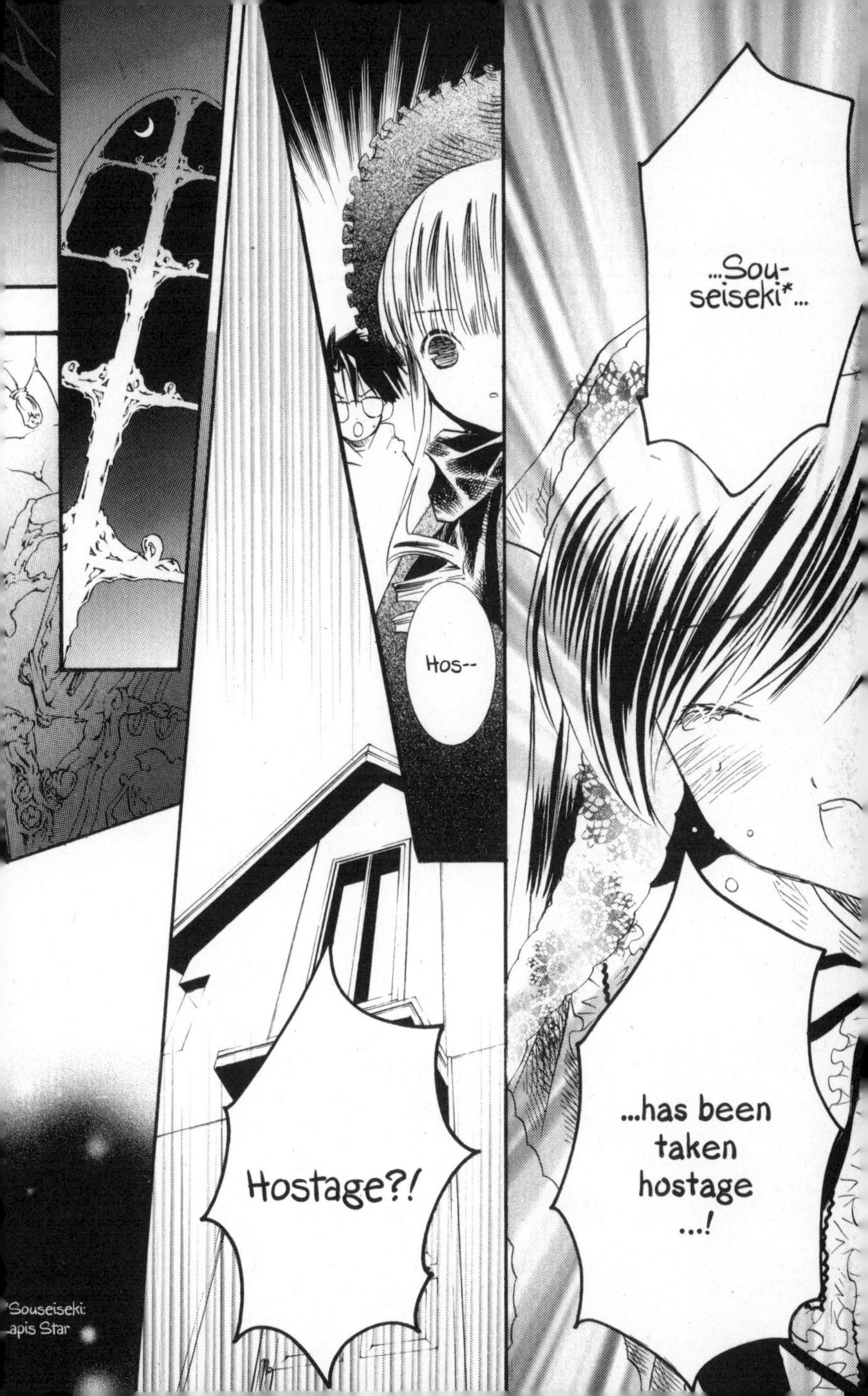
...Sou-seiseki*...
...has been taken hostage ...!
Hos--
Hostage?!
*Souseiseki: Lapis Star

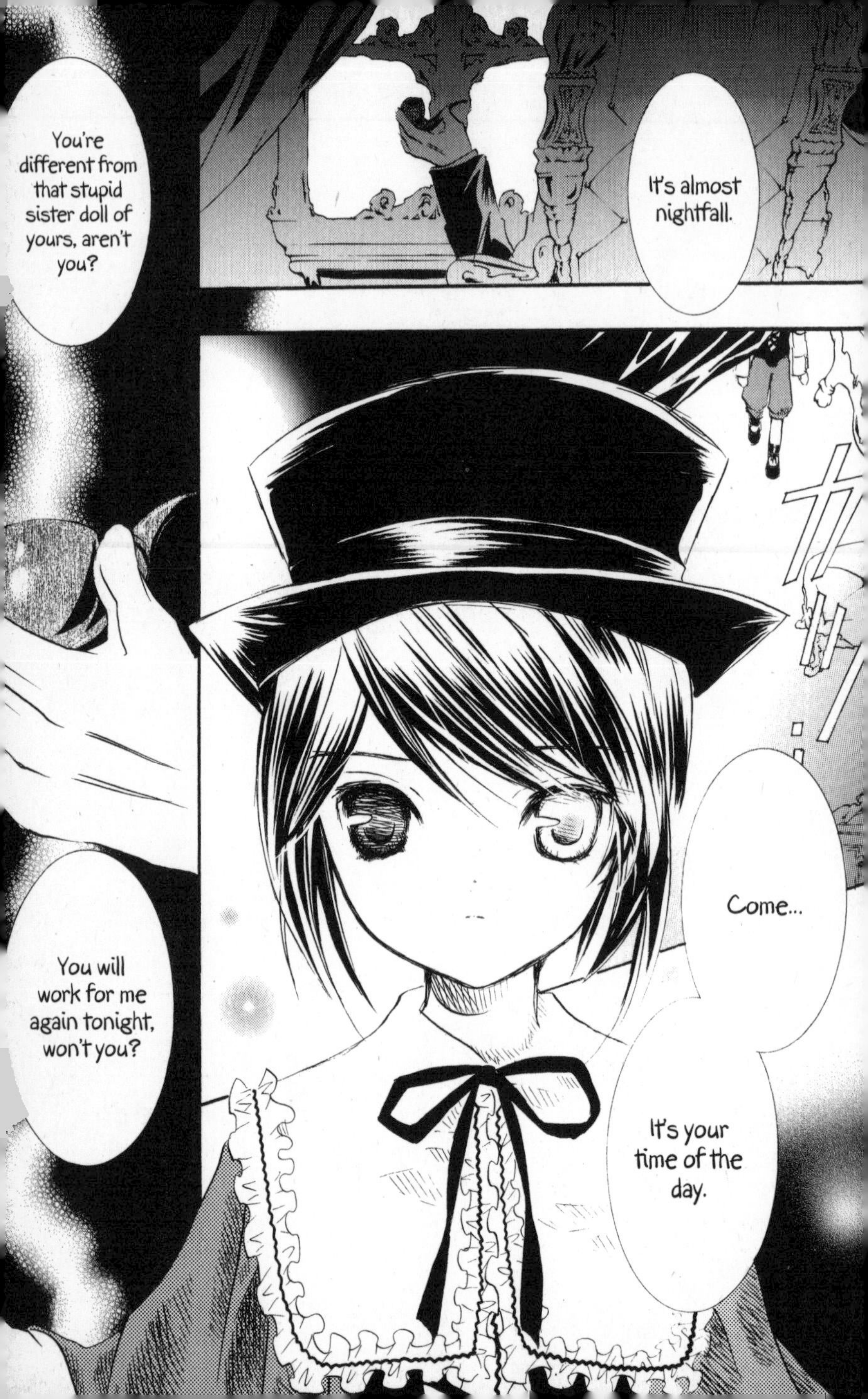
It's almost nightfall.
Come...
It's your time of the day.
You're different from that stupid sister doll of yours, aren't you?
You will work for me again tonight, won't you?

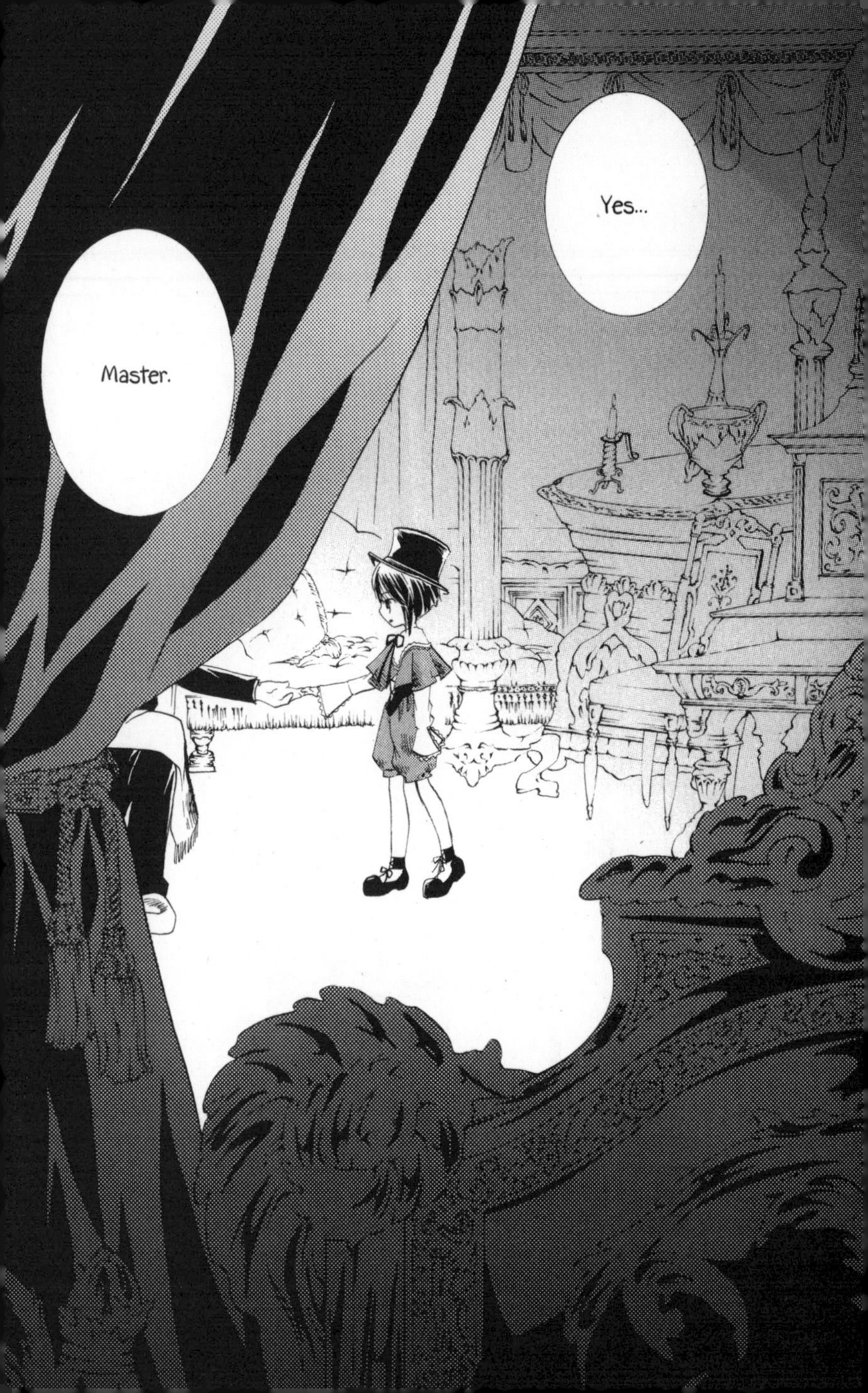
Yes...
Master.

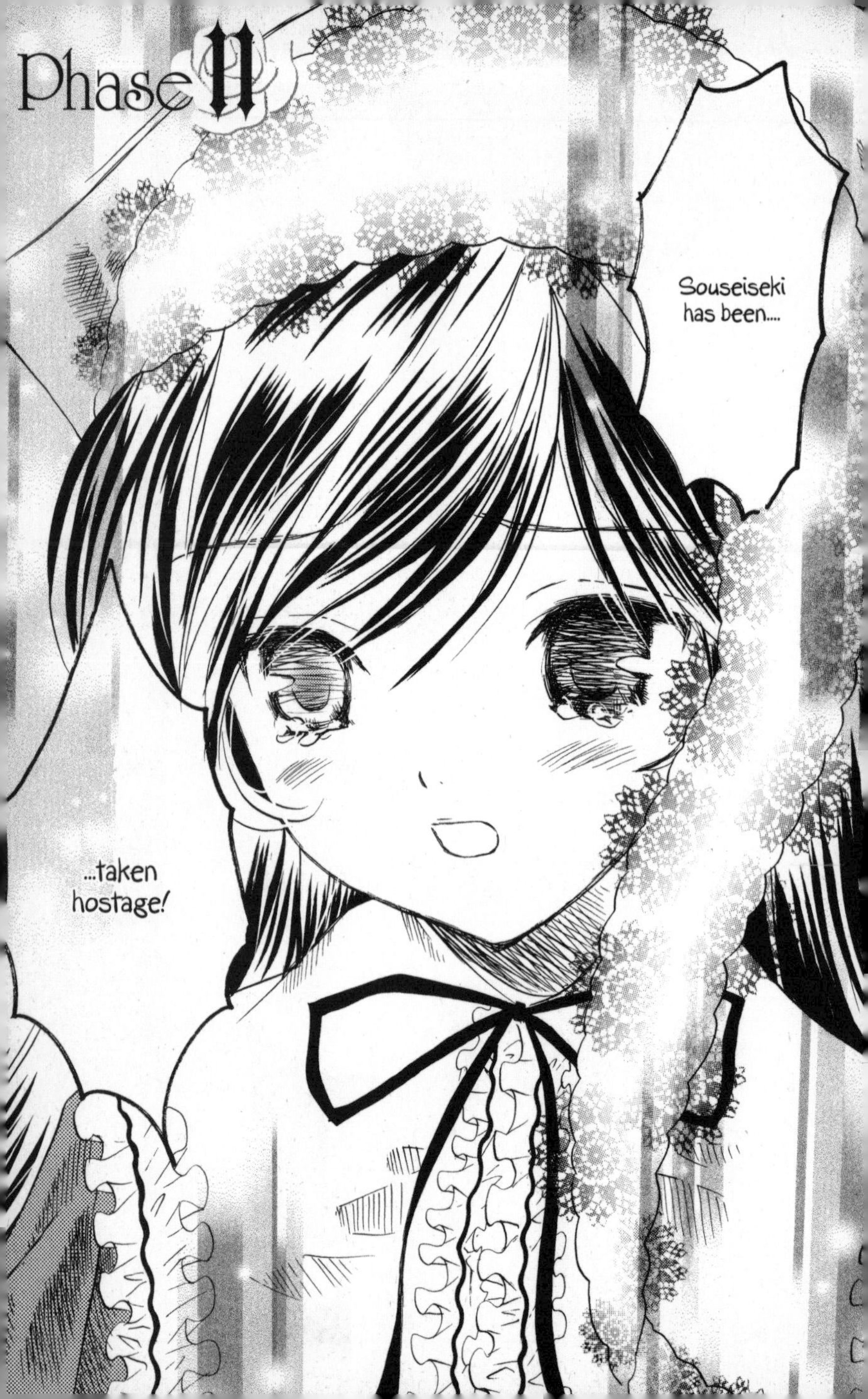
Phase 11
Souseiseki has been....
...taken hostage!

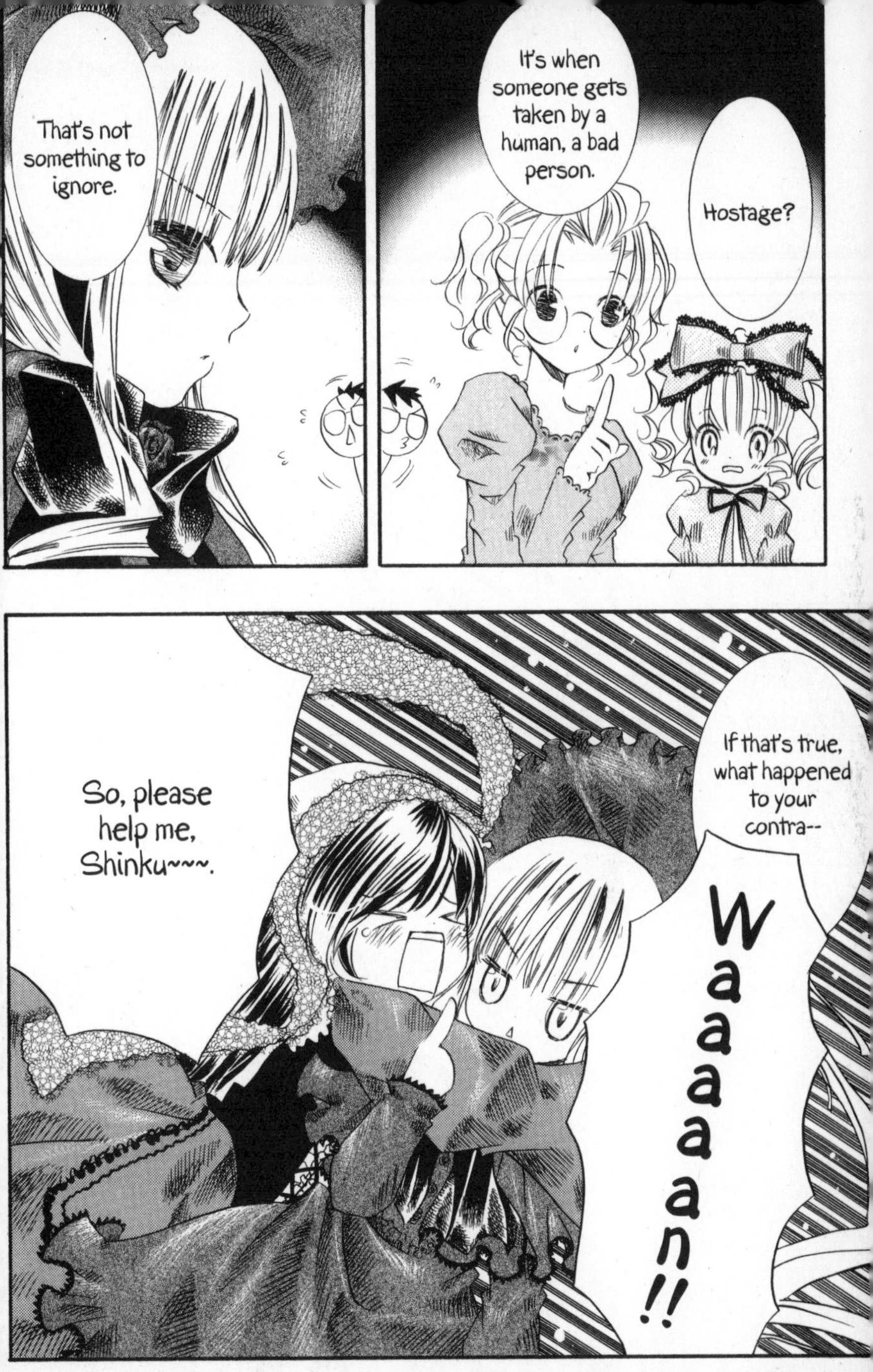
Hostage?
It's when someone gets taken by a human, a bad person.
That's not something to ignore.
If that's true, what happened to your contra--
Waaaaaan!!
So, please help me, Shinku~~~.

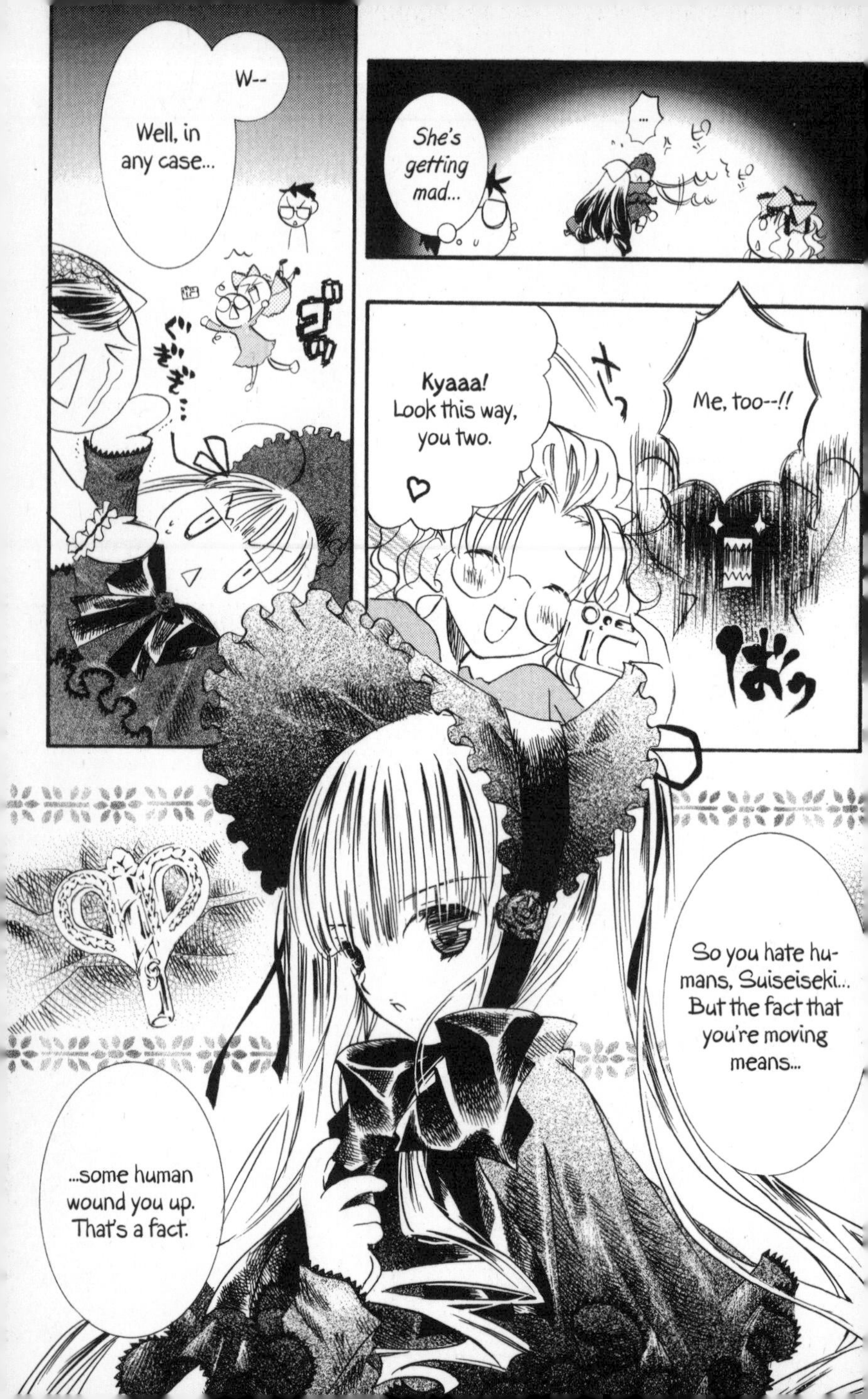
She's getting mad...
...
Me, too--!!
Kyaaa! Look this way, you two. ♥
W--
Well, in any case...
So you hate hu-mans, Suiseiseki... But the fact that you're moving means...
...some human wound you up. That's a fact.

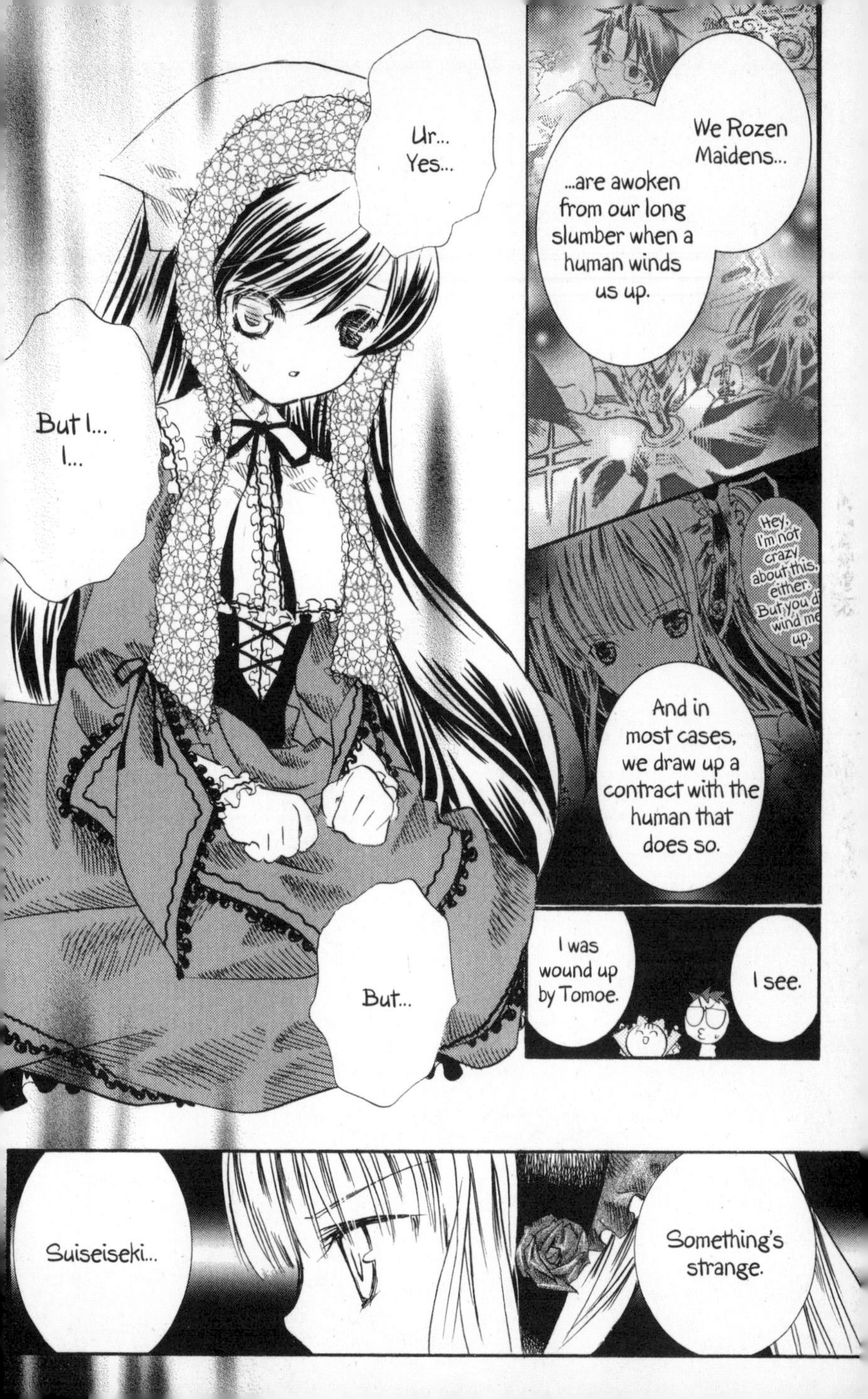
We Rozen Maidens...
...are awoken from our long slumber when a human winds us up.
Hey, I'm not crazy about this, either. But you d wind me up.
And in most cases, we draw up a contract with the human that does so.
I see.
I was wound up by Tomoe.
Ur... Yes...
But I... I...
But...
Something's strange.
Suiseiseki...

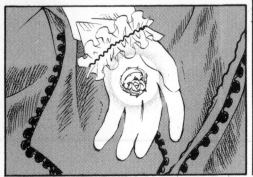

What happened to your ring?

My ring... Suiseiseki's ring...

!!

...be handed to such a human as that!

Will not...

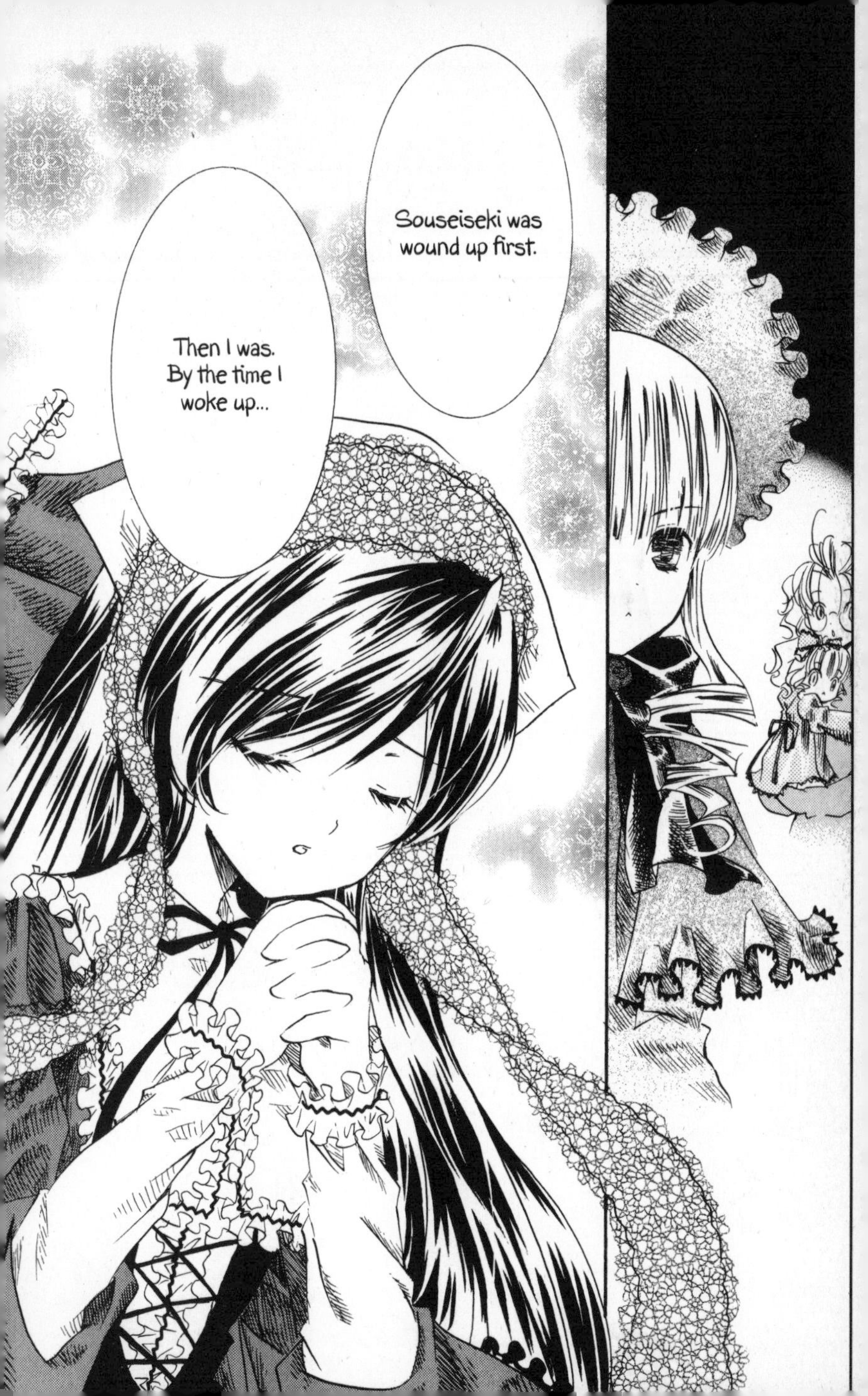
Souseiseki was wound up first.
Then I was. By the time I woke up...

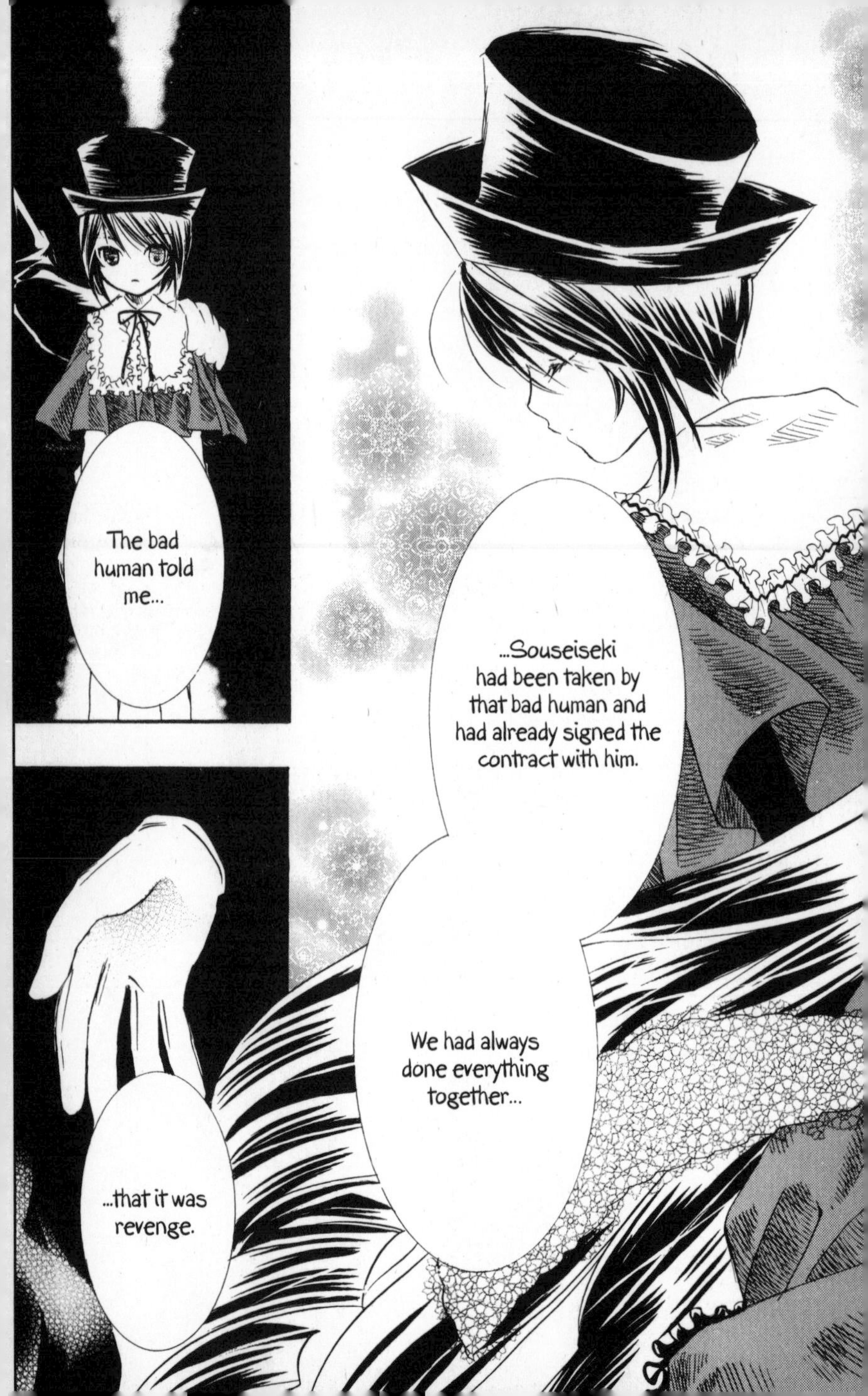
...Souseiseki had been taken by that bad human and had already signed the contract with him.
We had always done everything together...
The bad human told me...
...that it was revenge.

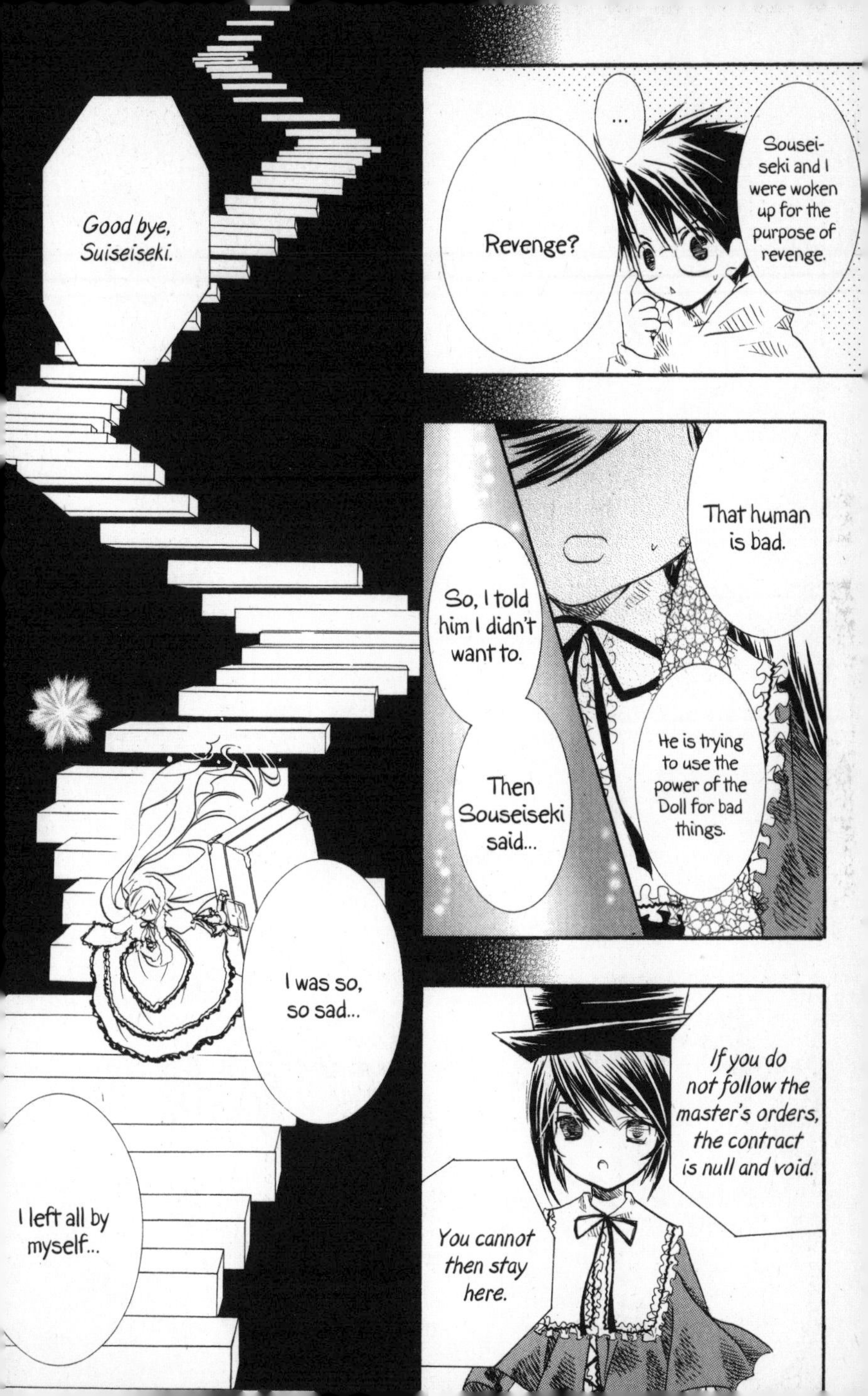

Sousei-seki and I were woken up for the purpose of revenge.
...
Revenge?
That human is bad.
He is trying to use the power of the Doll for bad things.
So, I told him I didn't want to.
Then Souseiseki said...
If you do not follow the master's orders, the contract is null and void.
You cannot then stay here.
Good bye, Suiseiseki.
I was so, so sad...
I left all by myself...

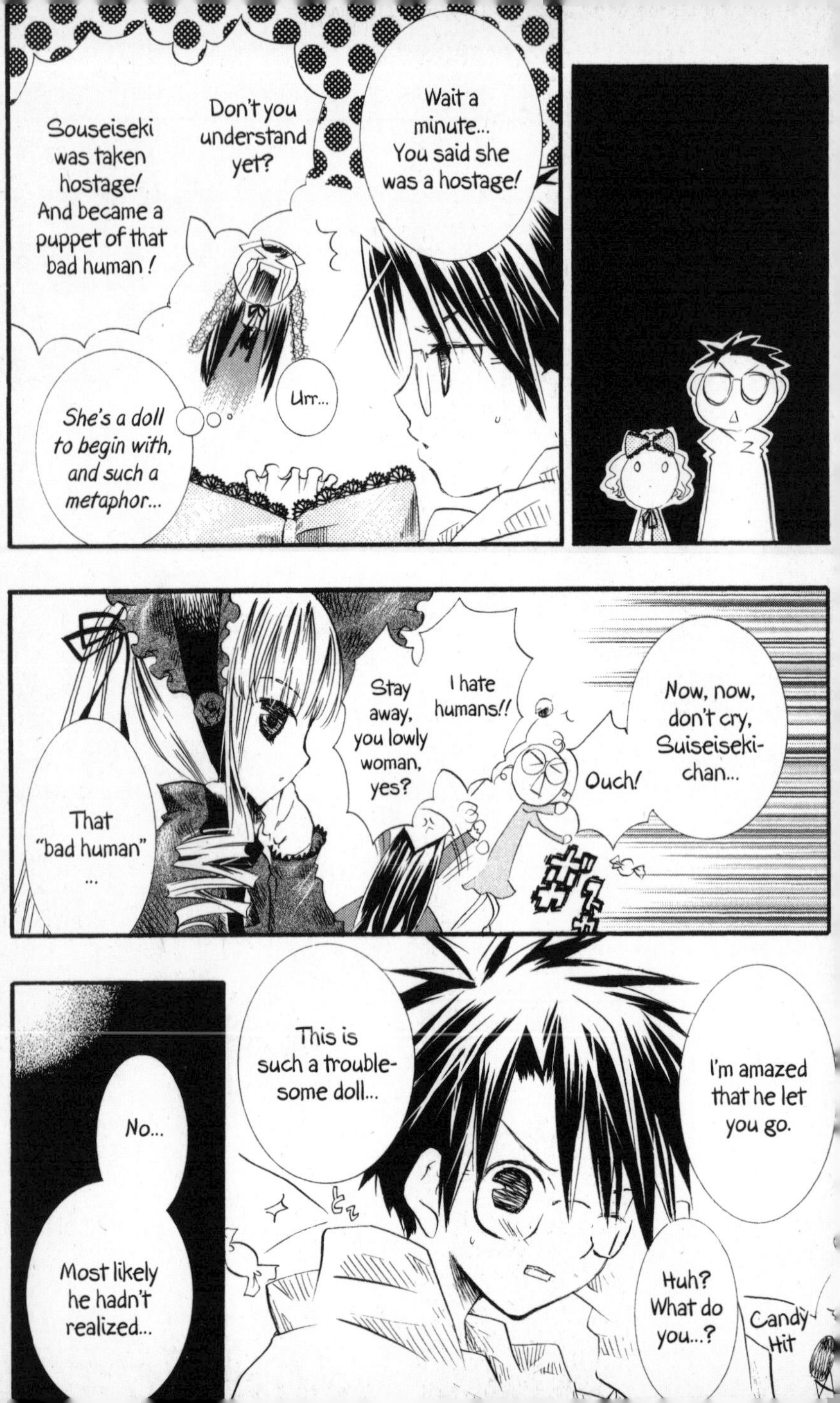
Wait a minute... You said she was a hostage!
Don't you understand yet?
Souseiseki was taken hostage! And became a puppet of that bad human!
Urr...
She's a doll to begin with, and such a metaphor...
Now, now, don't cry, Suiseiseki-chan...
Ouch!
I hate humans!!
Stay away, you lowly woman, yes?
That "bad human" ...
I'm amazed that he let you go.
This is such a trouble-some doll...
Huh? What do you...?
Candy Hit
No...
Most likely he hadn't realized...

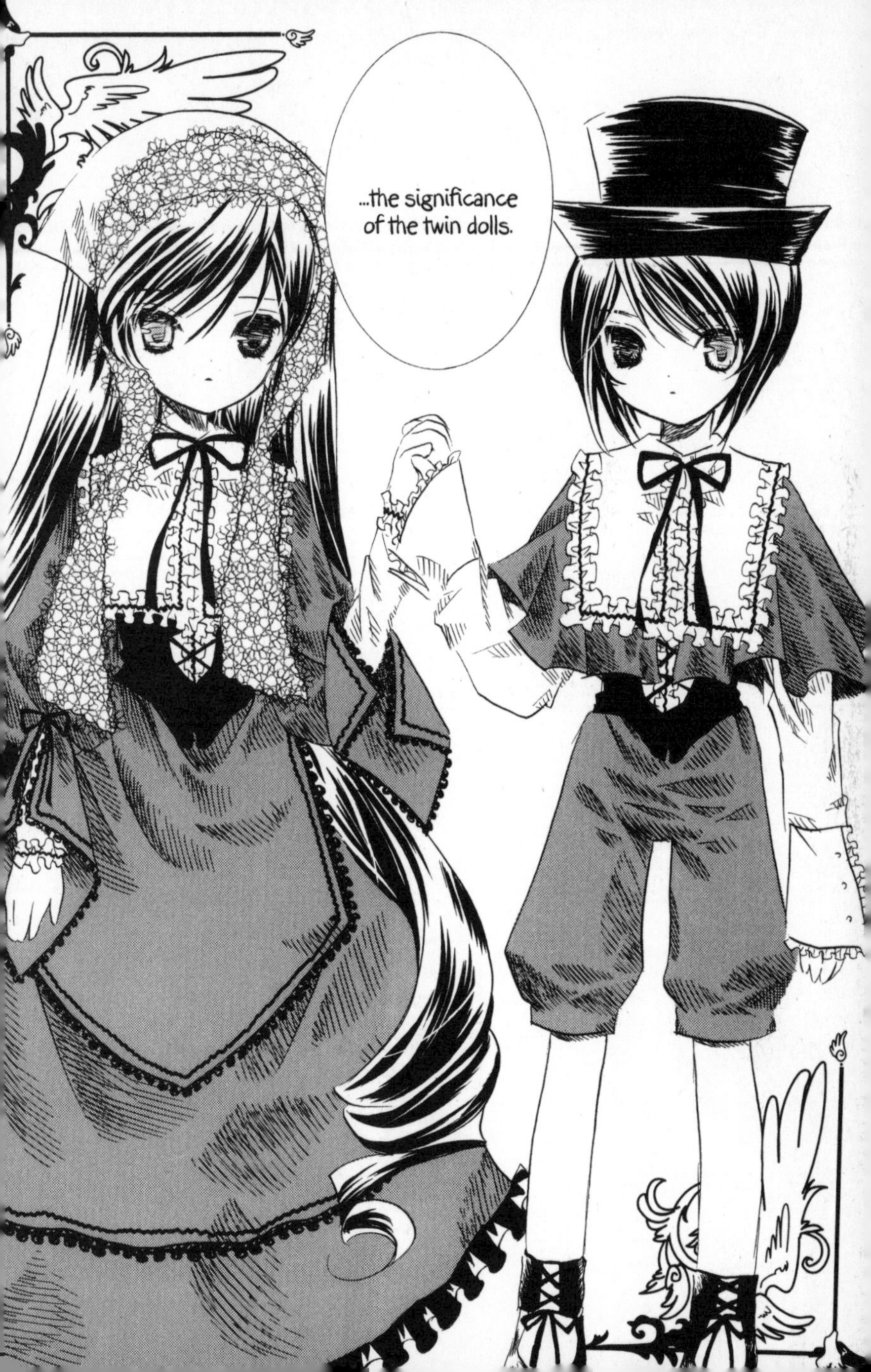
...the significance of the twin dolls.

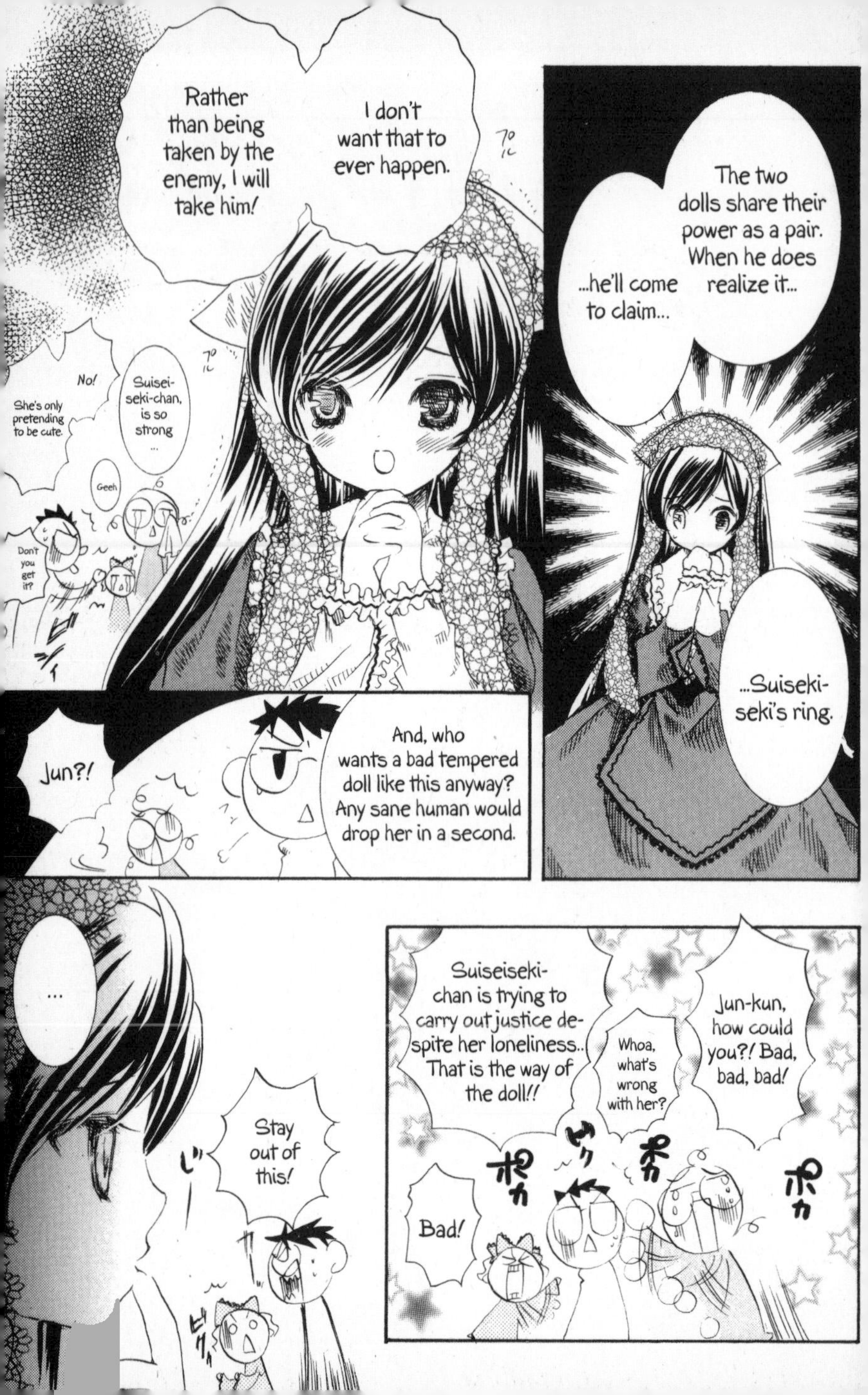
The two dolls share their power as a pair. When he does realize it...
...he'll come to claim...
...Suiseki-seki's ring.
I don't want that to ever happen.
Rather than being taken by the enemy, I will take him!
Suisei-seki-chan, is so strong ...
No!
She's only pretending to be cute.
Geeh
Don't you get it?
And, who wants a bad tempered doll like this anyway? Any sane human would drop her in a second.
Jun?!
Jun-kun, how could you?! Bad, bad, bad!
Whoa, what's wrong with her?
Suiseiseki-chan is trying to carry out justice de-spite her loneliness.. That is the way of the doll!!
Bad!
Stay out of this!
...

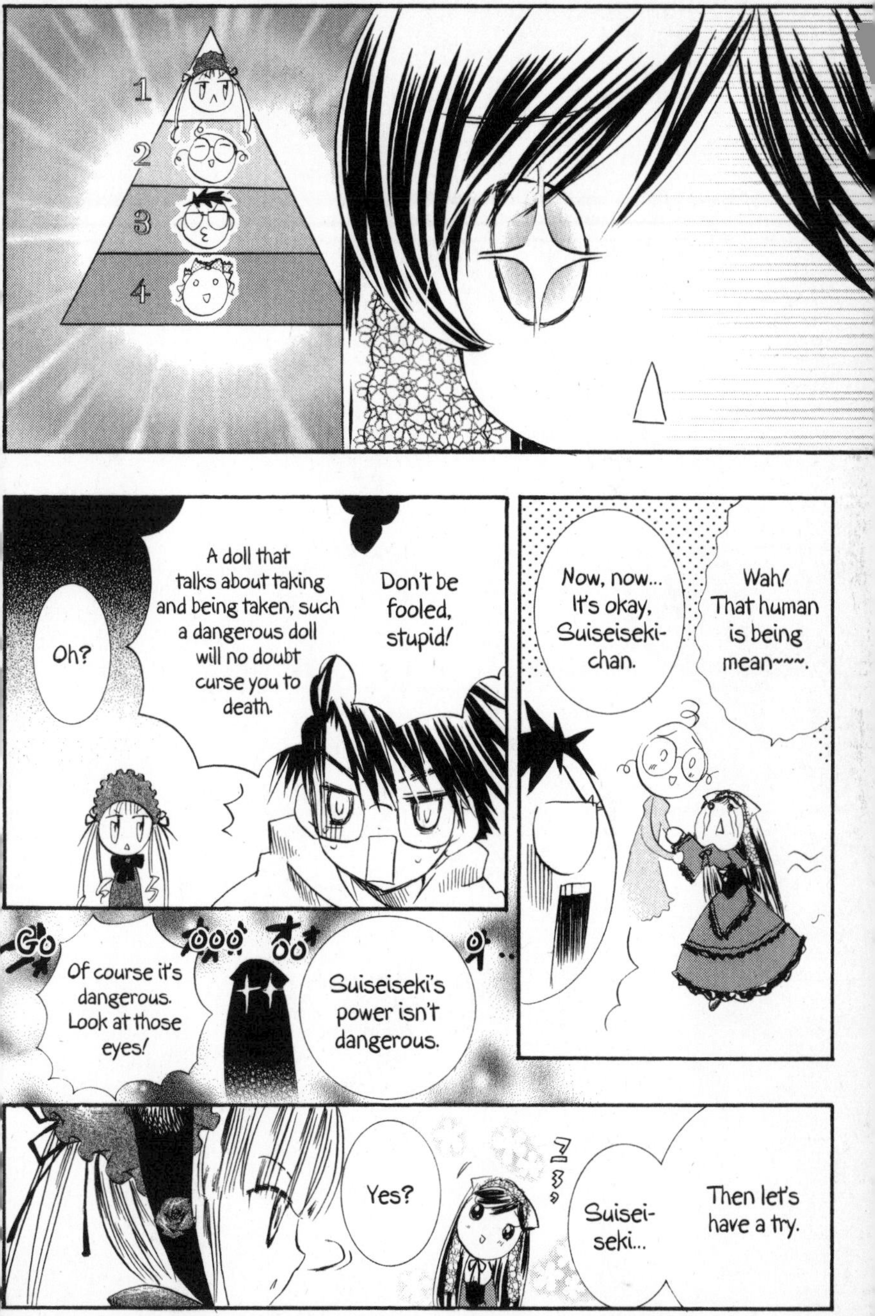
1
2
3
4
Wah! That human is being mean~~~.
Now, now... It's okay, Suiseiseki-chan.
Don't be fooled, stupid!
A doll that talks about taking and being taken, such a dangerous doll will no doubt curse you to death.
Oh?
Suiseiseki's power isn't dangerous.
Of course it's dangerous. Look at those eyes!
Then let's have a try.
Suisei-seki...
Yes?

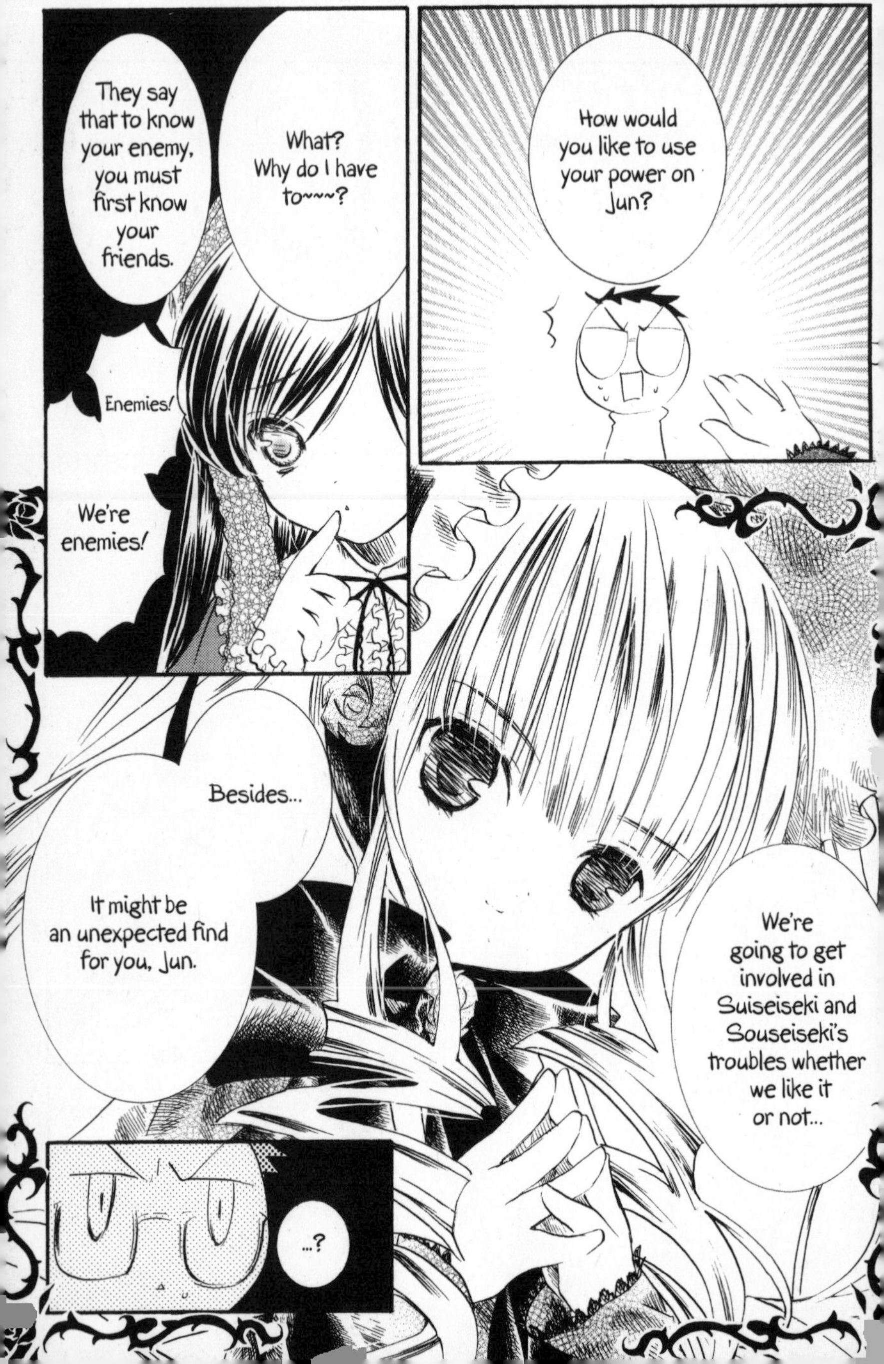
How would you like to use your power on Jun?
What? Why do I have to~~~?
They say that to know your enemy, you must first know your friends.
Enemies!
We're enemies!
We're going to get involved in Suiseiseki and Souseiseki's troubles whether we like it or not...
Besides...
It might be an unexpected find for you, Jun.
...?

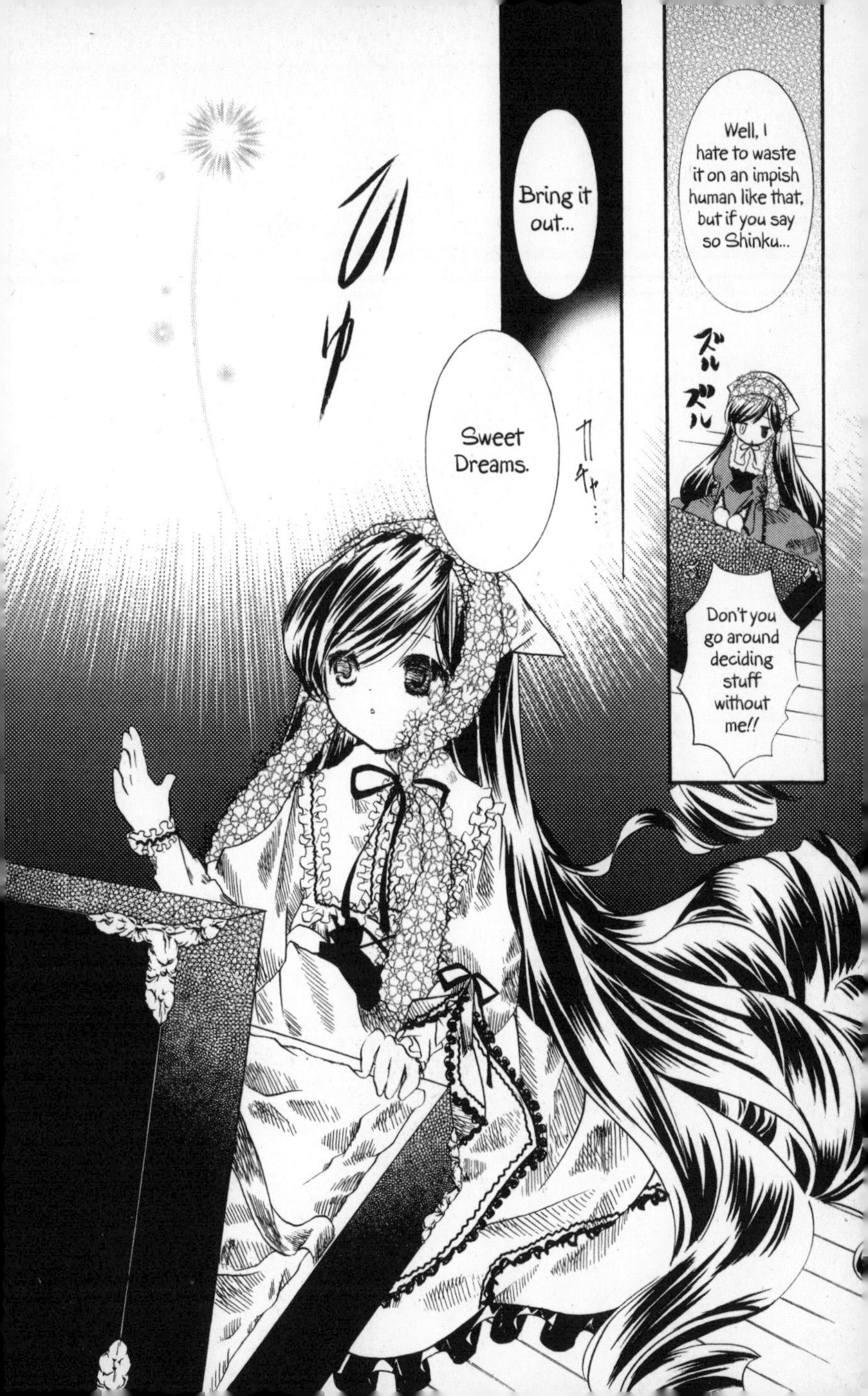
Well, I hate to waste it on an impish human like that, but if you say so Shinku...
ズルズル
Don't you go around deciding stuff without me!!
Bring it out...
Sweet Dreams.
カチャ…

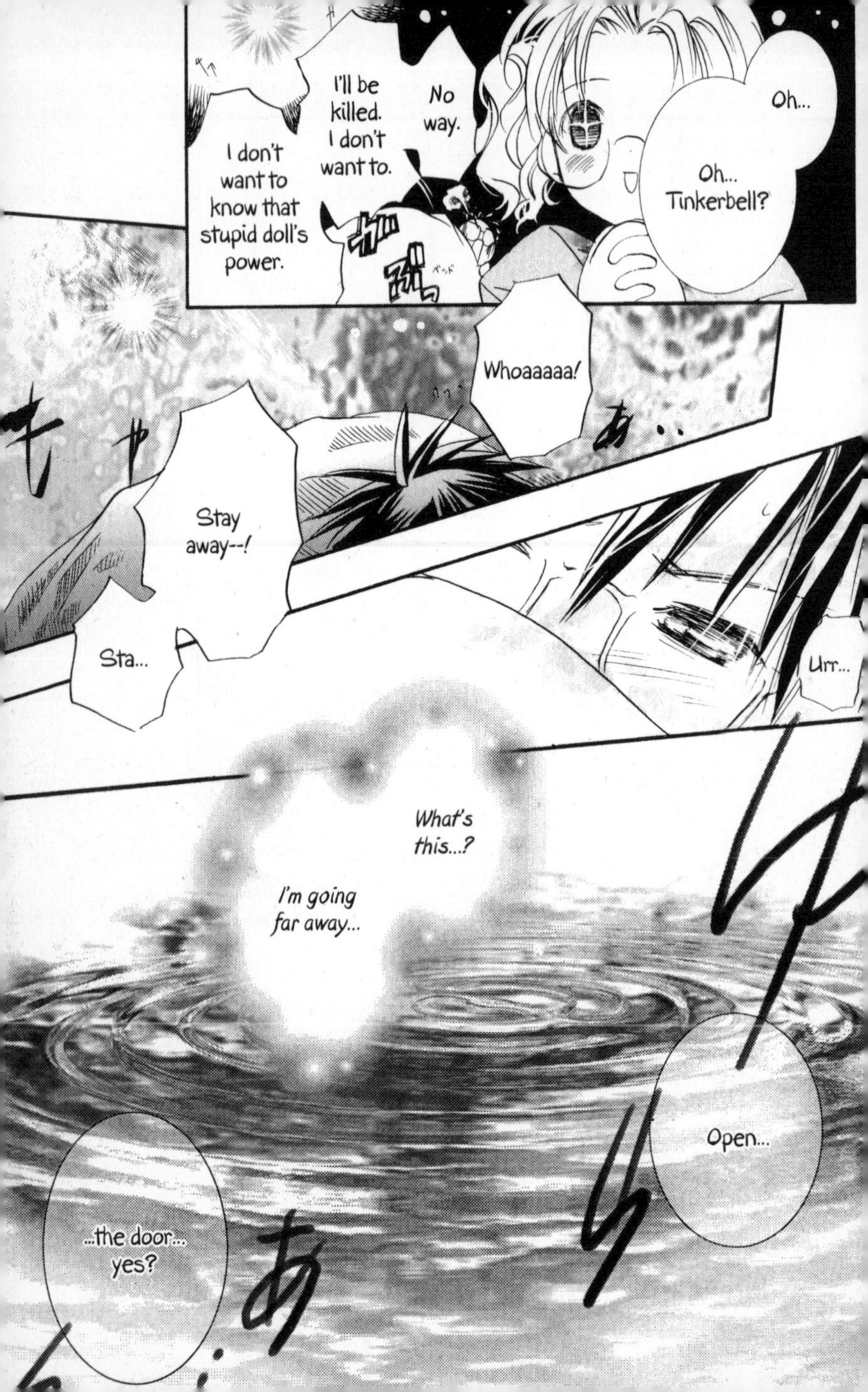
Oh...
Oh... Tinkerbell?
No way.
I'll be killed. I don't want to.
I don't want to know that stupid doll's power.
Whoaaaaa!
Urr...
Stay away--!
Sta...
What's this...?
I'm going far away...
Open...
...the door... yes?

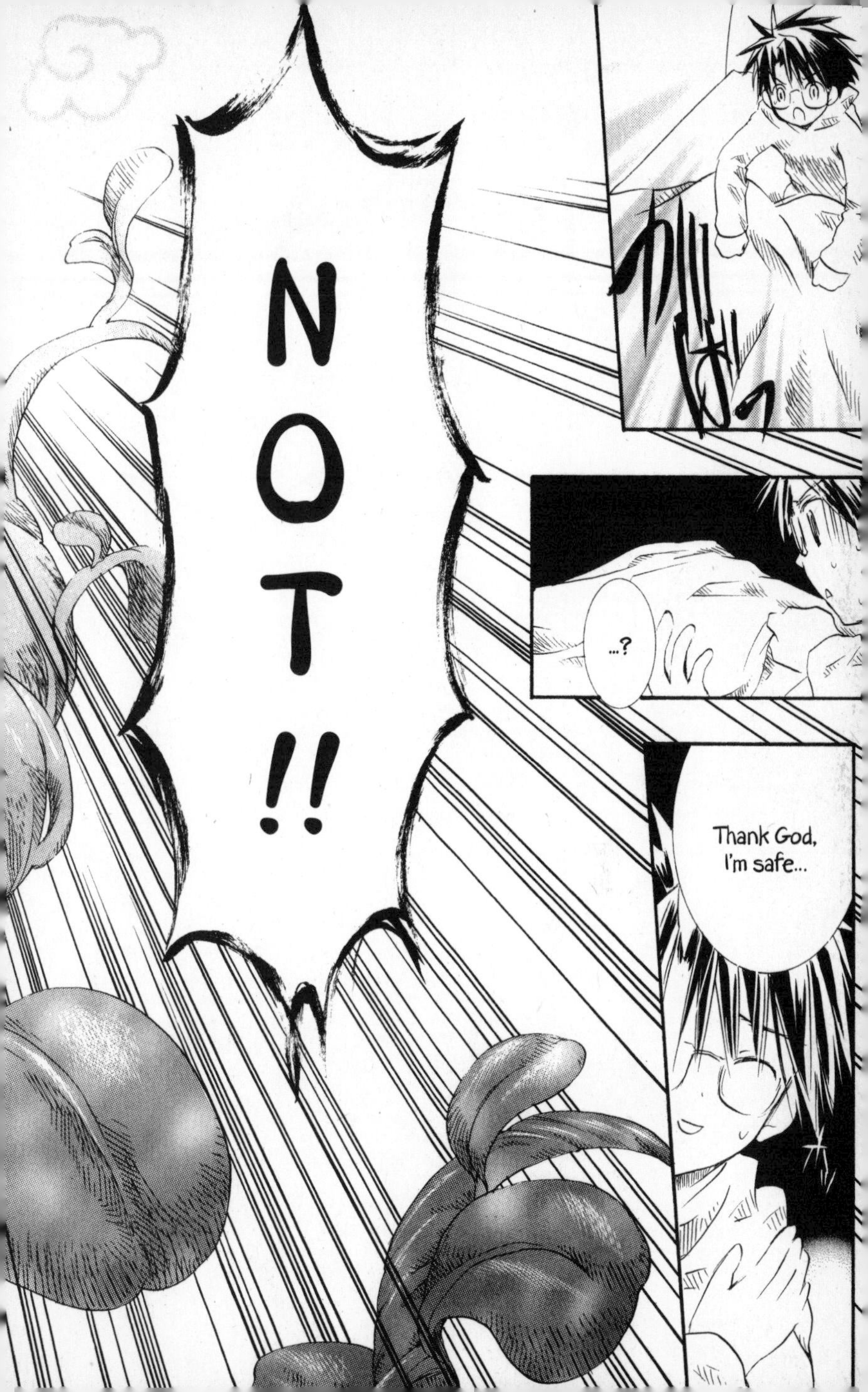
...?
Thank God, I'm safe...
NOT!!

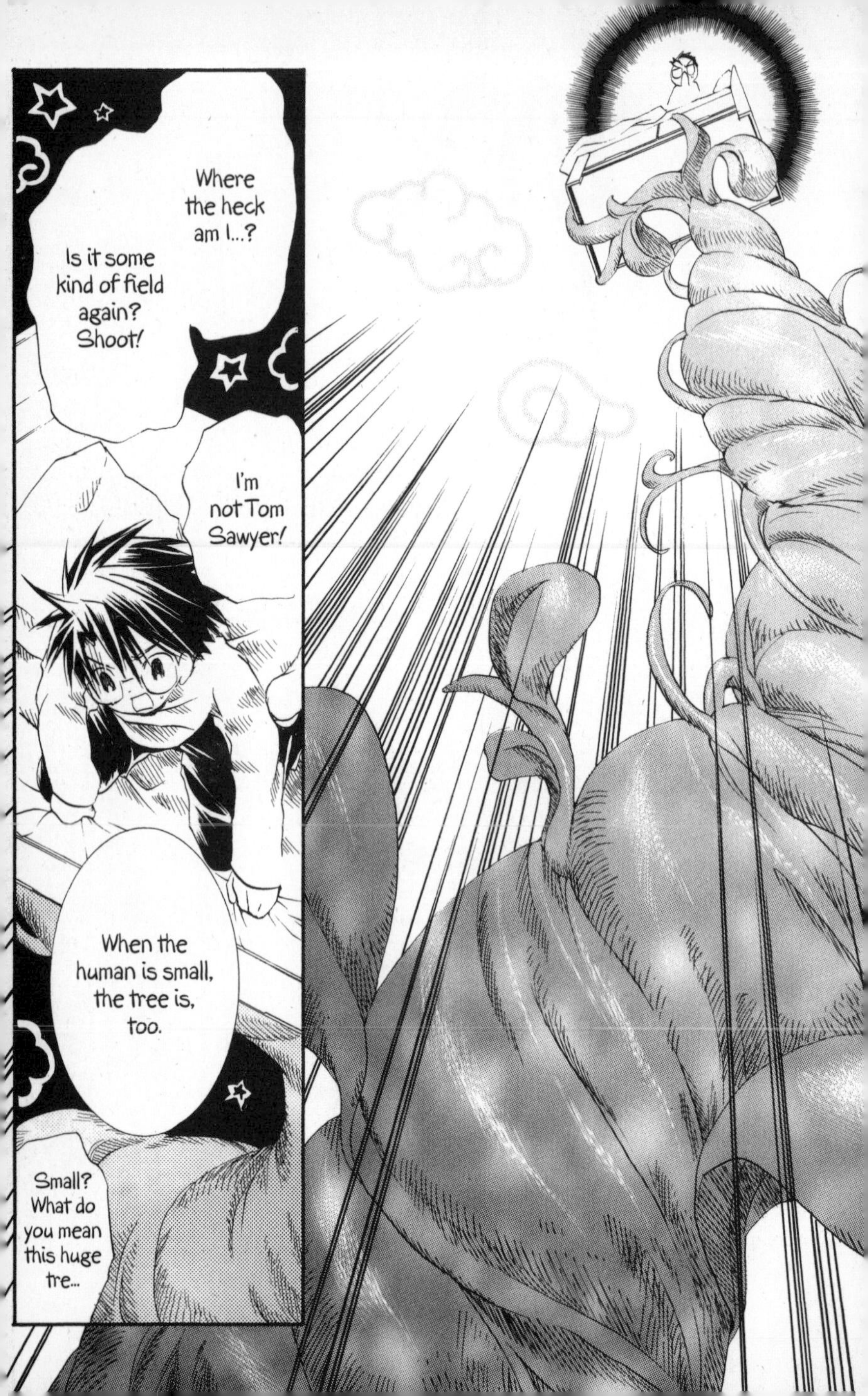
Where the heck am I...?
Is it some kind of field again? Shoot!
I'm not Tom Sawyer!
When the human is small, the tree is, too.
Small? What do you mean this huge tre...

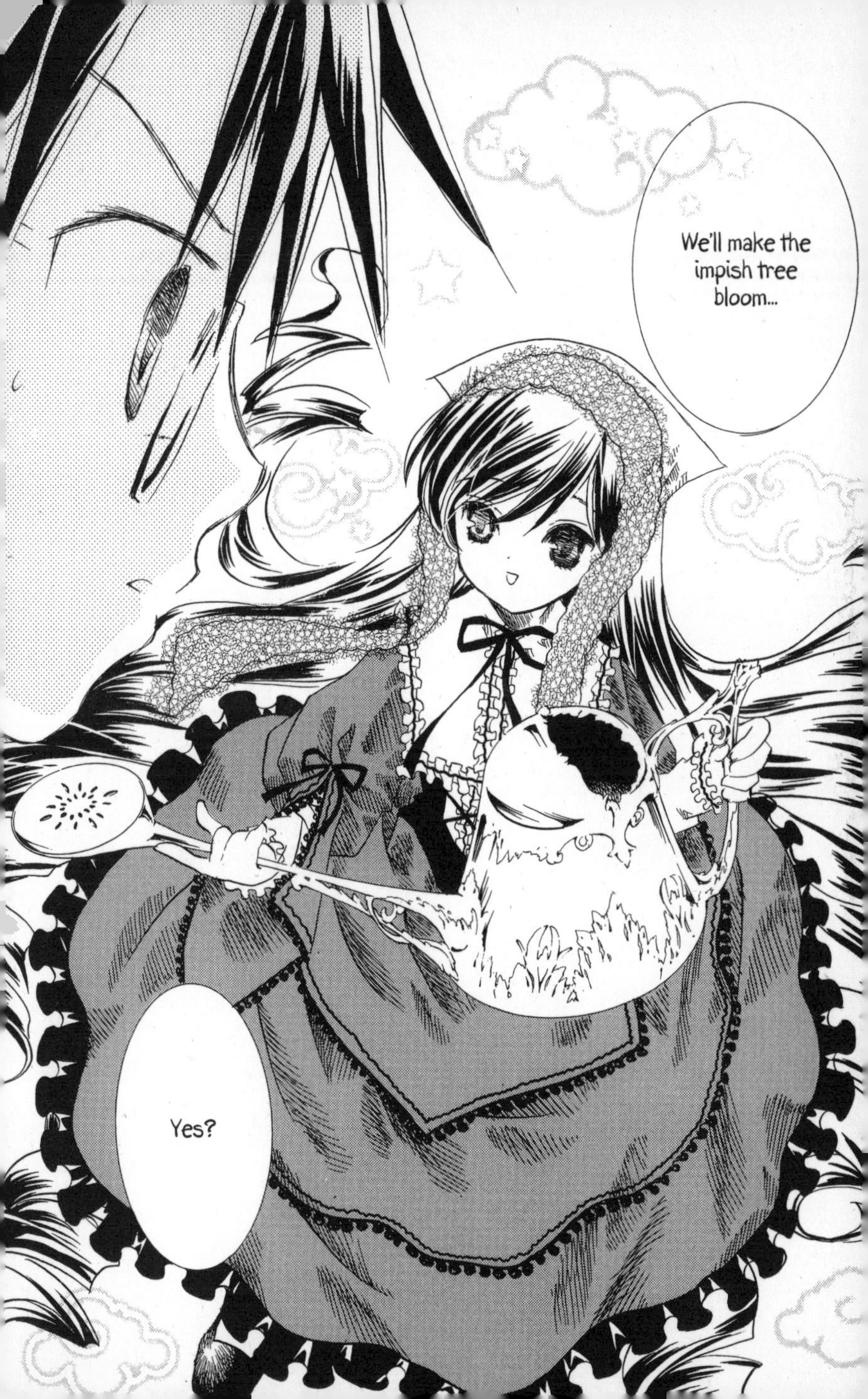
We'll make the impish tree bloom...
Yes?

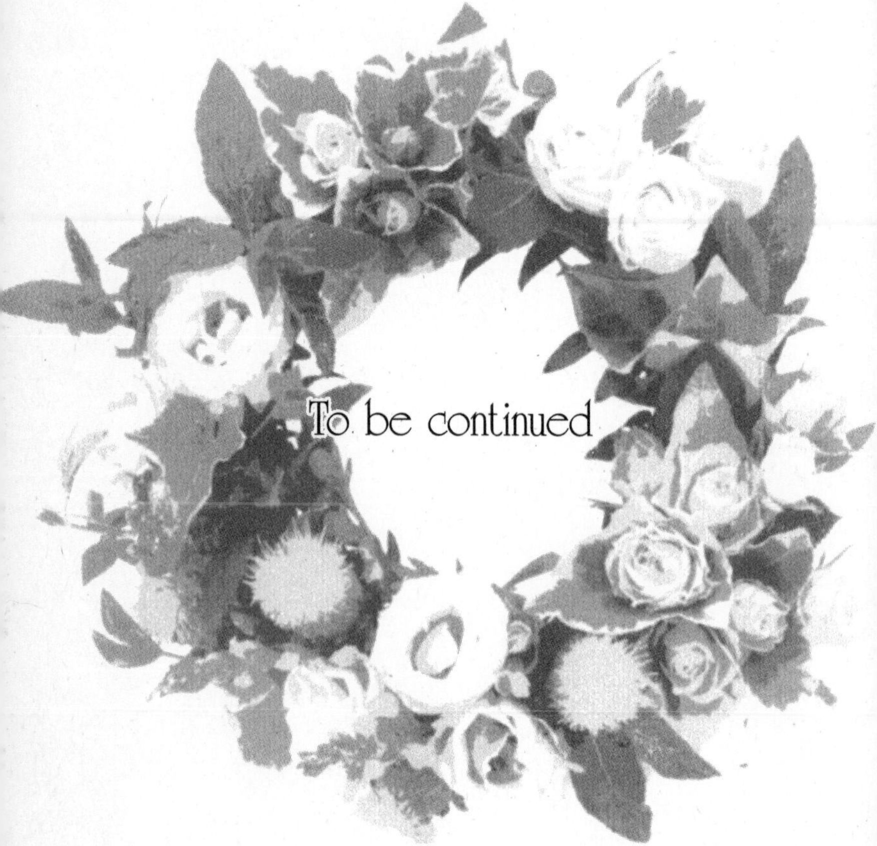
To be continued

all produced by

PEACH·PIt

Shikniko Ebara *** Banri Sendou

MAIN STAFF
Nao

Zaki

Kiniming

Bunbun

Special thanks

T. Oda

Momiji Takako

...and your reading

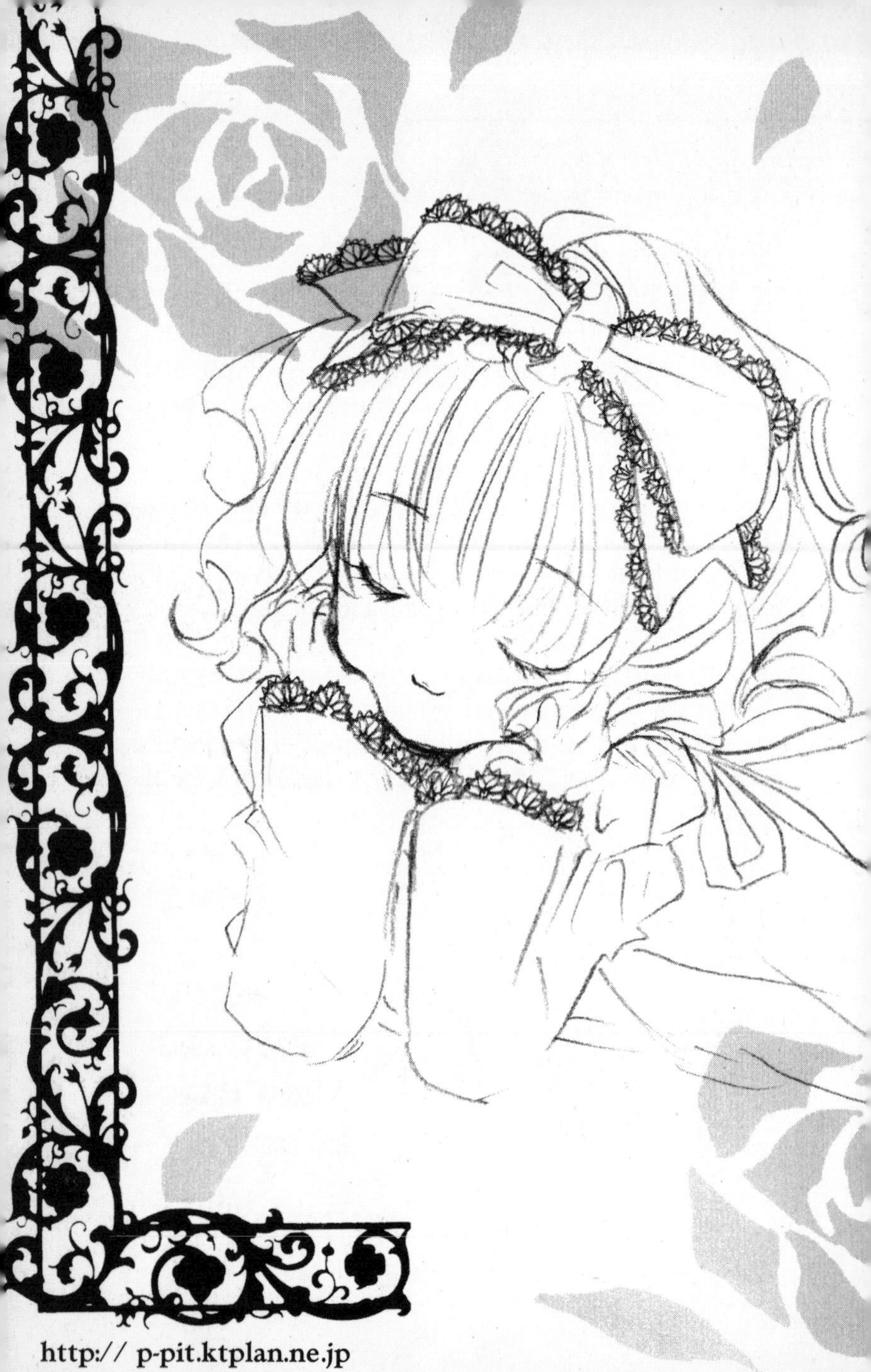

http:// p-pit.ktplan.ne.jp

Next Time in

When Jun and the dolls accompany
Suiseiseki to find her twin, they discover
that Souseiseki is with Suigintoh. After
Suigintoh attacks the group and takes
Shinku's arm, Suiseiseki puts her hatred for
humans aside in order to give Jun her Rosa
Mystica. The doll manages to save everyone
from Suigintouh and they narrowly escape
from the collapsing dream.

After returning home, Shinku is distressed
about losing one of her arms. Jun tries to
console her and decides to recover the doll's
arm from the N-Field with Suiseiseki's help.

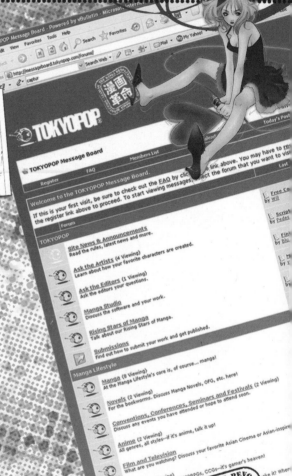

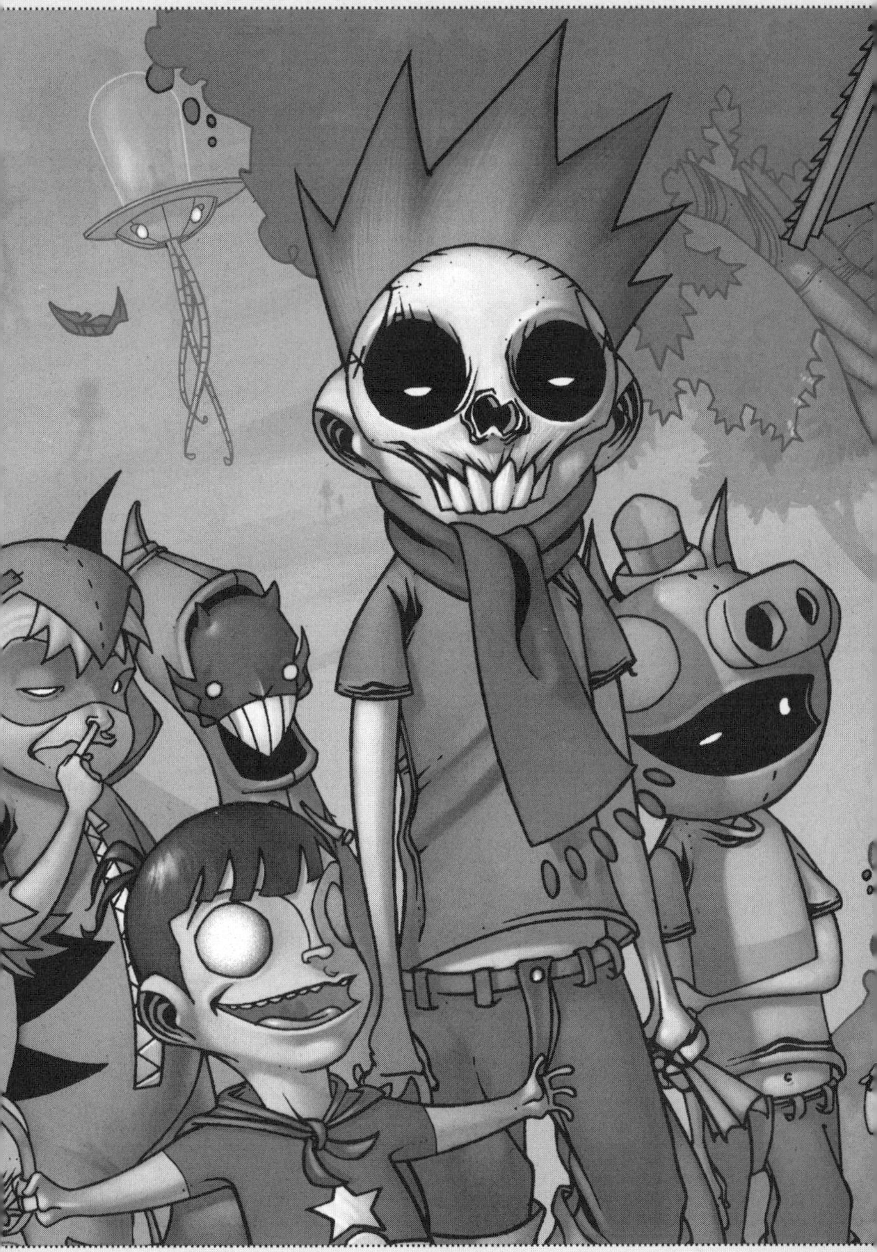